# TROUT FLIES
## FOR RIVERS

# TROUT FLIES
## FOR RIVERS

### PATTERNS FROM THE WEST
### THAT WORK EVERYWHERE

CAROL ANN MORRIS

SKIP MORRIS

STACKPOLE
BOOKS

*Skip and Carol dedicate this book to Carol's parents,*
*Marjorie Marie Pallas and Robert Milton Pallas.*
*They were devoted to family, passionate about life,*
*and committed to helping those in need.*
*They are both deeply missed.*

Copyright © 2009 by Stackpole Books

Published by
STACKPOLE BOOKS
5067 Ritter Road
Mechanicsburg, PA 17055
www.stackpolebooks.com

Printed in China

10 9 8 7 6 5 4 3 2 1

First edition

Text and fly-tying photos by Skip Morris
All other photos by Carol Ann Morris, except as noted
Illustrations by Carol Ann Morris

**Library of Congress Cataloging-in-Publication Data**

Morris, Carol Ann.
　Trout flies for rivers : patterns from the west that work everywhere/ Carol
Ann Morris, Skip Morris. — 1st ed.
　　　p. cm.
　Includes index.
　ISBN 978-0-8117-0476-2
　1. Flies, Artificial—West (U.S.) 2. Fly tying—West (U.S.) 3. Trout
fishing—West (U.S.) I. Morris, Skip. II. Title.
　SH688.U6M667 2009
　688.7'9124—dc22
　　　　　　　　　　　　　　　　　　　　　　2008024419

# Contents

# Preface

I'VE BEEN WORKING out of fly-tying and fly-pattern books—while writing eight myself—for 47 years (I started tying flies at age 10). Based on that experience, here is what I believe we've done right with this book:

1. We included only flies that really work, that is, the good stuff—fly dressings proven by time or trusted by reliable fly-fishing writers, guides, and fly-shop people.
2. For clarity, we listed the materials for each fly in the order in which they are added to the hook.
3. We put tying instructions in the dressing itself, in many cases, or even provided step-by-step instructions with photographs whenever a fly's construction might be baffling.
4. For many of the fly patterns, we provided not just a sample dressing but the whole range of specific imitations—such as the Morris Emerger in a precise green drake version, a pale morning dun version, a blue-winged olive version, and so forth—rather than forcing you to guess at the details of each.
5. We included information to help you fish the flies in the right way at the right place at the right time.
6. We provided not only a solid foundation on the creatures flies imitate (mayflies, stoneflies, caddis...), but also a look at the important hatches (the brown drake, the salmon fly, the October caddis...)
7. We photographed many of the flies from more than one angle—not just a side view, but often a top or underside view or both—to help you tie the fly correctly.
8. We included a DVD demonstrating the tying procedures shown in steps in the book.

Of course, there are all sorts of fly-pattern books out there—books containing strictly bass flies, saltwater flies, even flies for just one state or one fairly small area. And then there are the pattern books that set out to cover all flies for all fishes. But we felt that the subject of flies for trout rivers of the western United States (and western Canada) was just right. It's a big topic, especially since trout rivers are where most fly fishing is practiced, and fly fishers from all over the world come to the North American West to fish its fabled waters. But this is a big book. All in all, everything seemed a proper fit of experience, subject, and scope. We hope you agree.

Regarding scope: I went through the book, fly by fly, to see how many patterns would be solid choices all across North America—from the Pacific coast clear over to the Atlantic. The number? Just about 80 percent! That surprised me—discovering that so many of these flies would be as valuable on Michigan's Au Sable River or Arkansas's White River as on Montana's Madison. And it's a good bet that most of these patterns would move trout in Chile and Sweden and Tasmania. After all, trout are trout, wherever you go. And although mayflies and caddisflies and stoneflies may vary in places, many of the flies in this book are *flexible* imitations: alter their colors and you can match a lot, and you may not need to alter the colors at all.

Carol's name comes first on the cover, as it should. She took most of the photographs, tied many of the flies, and did tons of research; I wrote the text, conducted additional research, and also tied a lot of the flies. All in all, this turned out to be three challenging, frustrating, fascinating, and gratifying years of working together.

—Skip Morris

# Acknowledgments

THANK YOU to all the fly tiers who seriously pitched in on this project and who are listed in the section titled "The Tiers."

But there are others we want to thank.

We thank Judith Schnell, publisher of Stackpole Books, for her patience, keen instincts, experience, and plain good sense. She set this book free to evolve into a better, richer book. (I, Skip, also thank her for wearing proudly—and finally wearing out—that shabby cowboy hat I gave her at a fly-fishing event almost 20 years ago. Yee-haw, Ranger Judith!)

Our thanks to Debra Smith, for performing her job as intermediary between us and Judith so well, and for contributing her own valuable perspective and instincts.

Thanks to our old friend Rick Hafele, professional entomologist and fly-fishing author, for his council on everything that had anything to do with insects.

Thanks to Crystal Lake Resort, of Pine, Colorado, for making possible a full month of firsthand experience with Colorado rivers, fishing, and flies—and especially those tightlipped trout of the South Platte River.

Our thanks to two Montana men—Chuck Stranahan, fly-fishing speaker and owner of Chuck Stranahan's Flies & Guides in Hamilton, and guide David Dedmon, who died only recently, way before his time—for showing us all around the Bitterroot River and its forks, and introducing us to the region's latest flies.

Thanks to Bill Miller, also in Hamilton, Montana, for our stay at his lovely and comfortable Rainbow Point Lodge during one of our Bitterroot adventures.

Thanks also to Patricia Edel of Blue Fly World Class Fishing Adventures in King Salmon for introducing us to those huge, furious Alaska rainbow trout and the flies that take them.

Thanks to our fishing pal, fly-fishing guide Mike Seim of West Yellowstone for all his help in testing Skip's original fly patterns on the Madison, Firehole, and other famous Yellowstone-area rivers.

And our thanks to Lynn Hescock, owner of the Lynn Hescock Guide Service, in Gold Beach, Oregon, for taking us out on Oregon's grand Williamson River, and for helping Skip to hook, land, and release a five-pound rainbow trout on a Morris Minnow.

# Materials

EVEN IF YOU'RE AN EXPERIENCED FLY TIER who knows the materials of our craft well, there may be a few that you don't know. And what if one of them comes up in one of the dressings that follow? Of course, you look here. In addition, you may find some new ideas on familiar materials. If you're fairly new to tying flies, expect to use this chapter often.

## Hooks

Rather than designating a hook brand and model for each fly pattern, we provided specifications, such as "light wire, humped shank (pupa/emerger hook), size 14." You'll be glad we did, because honestly, if you have a box of size 14 Daiichi 1130s, why go out and buy a box of size 14 Tiemco 2487s just because the dressing lists that model? Both hooks are essentially the same size, same shape, and same wire—for tying purposes, the same hook. So whenever you need a hook, just go to the hook chart that follows to select a particular brand and model, or to select an appropriate hook from among the ones you already own. Instead of spending your time buying new hooks and working long hours to pay for them, you can spend it tying flies.

In general, light-wire hooks are for dry flies and for emerger flies that at least partially float, and heavy-wire hooks are for sinking flies: nymphs, streamers, bucktails, wet flies, and tiny fish imitations. Standard-wire hooks are another matter. A standard-wire hook may not keep your dry fly floating quite as long and as high as a light-wire hook would, but if

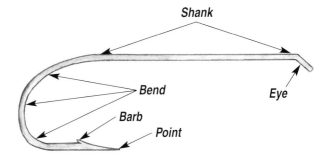

*Parts of a hook*

you hook a big trout, you may be glad of the stronger wire. I've straightened a few light-wire hooks on big trout, usually when I had to steer the fish away from trouble by applying serious pressure. Of course, I've landed big fish on light-wire hooks, too. Usually larger dry flies are tied on a standard-wire hook, but not necessarily. Plenty of seasoned fly fishers prefer standard-wire hooks for all their dry flies, small or large (even heavy wire for big dry flies). But some standard-wire hooks are good for nymphs, too. For example, I use the Daiichi 1260 all the time for many of the large nymphs I tie (and for bigger dry flies, too).

It's not always easy to determine whether a hook has standard wire; in fact, many hook specifications can be difficult to determine. That's because those bad-boy hook companies still haven't gotten together (to the best of my knowledge) and hashed out one set of rules for everyone to follow. So one company's standard-length size 12 hook may be noticeably shorter or longer than another company's standard-length size 12 hook. I had to make some experienced guesses about the specifications of some of the hooks in the accompanying chart, especially when the catalogs failed to list shank length or wire weight. Generally, though, these differences aren't enough to worry about.

Some hook eyes tip down, a "down eye" (the most common); some tip up, an "up-eye"; or the eyes tip neither up nor down, running straight off the shank, a "straight" or "ring eye." And there are slight variations in the curve of a hook's bend, such as a perfect (or sproat) bend. With most fly patterns, the advantages, disadvantages, and applications of eyes and bends are theoretical, which means that a reliable hook is a reliable hook and, therefore, a sound choice, regardless of the angle of its eye or curve of its bend.

Hook models come and go, so some of the ones listed here may be history by the time you read this chapter, and new ones will have emerged. That's life. But the hooks that earn the trust of fly fishers remain in production for decades. Some of the models I fished when I was a kid are still available, and I was a kid in the '50s and '60s!

Finally, don't look for a hidden message in the names of hook models—for instance, CX2041 (a fictitious hook model) means nothing. The names of most hooks are random, although once in a while there'll be a "BL" for "barbless," or something similar.

| Hook Chart | | | | | | |
|---|---|---|---|---|---|---|
| **Hook Type** | **Daiichi** | **Dai-Riki** | **Mustad** | **Partridge** | **Targus** | **Tiemco** |
| **Light Wire** | | | | | | |
| **Short shank** | 1310 | | 539E | K1A | 921 | 102Y |
| | 1330 (UE) | | | | 103 (BL) | 103BL (BL) |
| | 1480 (SE) | | | | 104BL (BL) | 104SP |
| | | | | | | 111 |
| | | | | | | 518 (SE) |
| | | | | | | 921 |
| | | | | | | 2488 (SE) |
| **Standard length** | 1100 | 070 | R30 | | 100 | 100 |
| | 1110(SE) | | 94845 (BL) | TDH | | 100BL (BL) |
| | 1190 (BL) | | | SLD (BL) | | 101 (SE) |
| | | | | SUD (BL) | | 900BL (BL) |
| | | | | YL3A | | 9300 |
| | | | | | | 5210 |
| **·1X long** | | | 80000BR | E1A | 101 (SE) | |
| | | | 94833 | | | |
| | | | 94840 | | | |
| | | | 94842 (UE) | | | |
| **2X long** | 1280 | | 94831 | | 5212 | 5212 |
| | | | | | 5262 | |
| **3X long** | 1770 (BU, SE) | | | | | |
| **Slow-curve shank 2X long** | | | | | 2312 (SE) | 2312 (SE) |
| **Humped shank** | 1130 | | | 15BN (SE) | 2487 | 2487 |
| | 1140 (UE) | | | CZF (SE) | | 2487BL (BL) |
| | 1150 (UE) | | | | | 206BL (UE, BL) |
| | 1153 (UE) | | | | | |
| | 1155 (UE) | | | | | |

BD, bent-down shank; BL, barbless; BU, bent-up shank; SE, straight eye; UE, up eye.

## Hook Chart *continued*

| Hook Type | Daiichi | Dai-Riki | Mustad | Partridge | Targus | Tiemco |
|---|---|---|---|---|---|---|
| **Standard Wire** | | | | | | |
| Short shank | 2170 (SE, BU) | | R48 | | 2091 (UE) | 501 (SE) |
| | 2171 (SE, BU) | | | | | |
| | 2174 (SE, BU) | | | | | |
| Standard length | 1170 | 305 | R50 | YA | | 900BL |
| | 1180 | 310 (SE) | R52S (SE) | YL2A | | |
| | 1182 | | 540 | | | |
| | 1190 (BL) | | 540L | | | |
| | 1220 (BU) | | | | | |
| | 1222 (BU) | | | | | |
| | 1550 | | | | | |
| 1X long | | 300 | | | | |
| | | 320 | | | | |
| 2X long | 1230 (BU) | | R52S (SE) | | | |
| 3X long | 2460 (SE) | 065 | | | 200 (SE) | |
| | 2461 (SE) | | | | | |
| | 2462 (SE) | | | | | |
| Slow-curve shank 2X long | 1260 (SE) | 280 | GRS12ST (SE) | | 2302 | 2302 |
| | | | | YK12ST (SE) | | |
| Slow-curve shank 3X long | 1270 (SE) | 270 (SE) | C53S (SE) | | 200 (SE) | 200R (SE) |
| | 1273 (SE) | | | | | 200RBL (SE, BL) |
| Humped shank | 1250 (UE, BL) | 125 (SE) | C49S (SE) | K14ST (SE) | 2091 (UE) | |
| | 1251 (UE, BL) | | 80250 BR | YK4A | 206BL (UE, BL) | |
| **Heavy Wire** | | | | | | |
| Short shank | 1530 | 075 | | BMN | | 107SP |
| | | | | TWH | | 600SP (SE) |
| | | | | YMMA | | |
| Standard length | 1550 | | R70 | BIN (BL) | 3769 | 760SP |
| | | | R90 | TWH | | 3769 |
| | | | 540 | IN | | 3769SP-BL (BL) |
| | | | | YG3A | | 9300 |
| | | | | YL2A | | |
| 1X long | 1560 | 060 | 39068 | | 3761 | 3761 |
| | | | | | | 3761BL (BL) |
| | | | | | | 3761SP-BL (BL) |
| 2X long | 1710 | 730 | R72 | YH1A | | 5262 |
| | 1740 (UE) | | | | | |

BD, bent-down shank; BL, barbless; BU, bent-up shank; SE, straight eye; UE, up eye.

## Hook Chart *continued*

| Hook Type | Daiichi | Dai-Riki | Mustad | Partridge | Targus | Tiemco |
|---|---|---|---|---|---|---|
| **Heavy Wire** *continued* | | | | | | |
| **3X long** | 1720 | 710 | | D3STF (SE) | 5263 | (SE, 3.5X long) |
| | 1730 (BD) | | | | 777SP | 5263 |
| | | | | | | 5263BL (BL) |
| | | | | | | 947BL (BL, BU) |
| **4X long** | 1750 (SE) | 700B (BD) | R74 | CS17 | 9394 (SE) | 9394 (SE) |
| | 1850 (SE) | 700 | 79580 | D3STF (SE) | 9395 (SE) | 9395 (SE) |
| | 2220 | | | D4AF | | |
| **6X long** | 2340 | | | | 300 | 300 |
| | 2370 (SE, 7X long) | | | | | 765SP (5.5X long) |
| **Slow-curve shank 2X long** | | | | | 7979 (SE) | |
| **Slow-curve shank 3X long** | 1870 (UE) | 285 | | | | |
| **Humped shank** | 1120 | 135 | C068 | CZ (SE) | 3310 (UE) | 2457 |
| | 1150 (UE) | | | K5A | 2457 | 2488H (SE) |
| | | | | SHR (SE, BL) | | |
| **Egg-fly hook** | 1510 | C67S (SE) | | | 105 (SE) | 105 (SE) |
| | 1520 | | | | | 2499SP-BL (SE, BL) |

BD, bent-down shank; BL, barbless; BU, bent-up shank; SE, straight eye; UE, up eye.

## Cements and Glues

**Head cement.** Standard head cements are usually thinner than epoxy and soak into thread easily. Be sure to use good ventilation if they give off an odor or if the manufacturer recommends it.

**Epoxy.** I'm a big fan of two-part epoxy glue as a head cement and all-around tying adhesive. However, many types give off some nasty chemical vapors, so I recommend using a low-odor epoxy, in a well-ventilated area. Be sure to follow all precautions recommended by the manufacturer. You may have to do some hunting to find low-odor epoxy glue. Try fly shops, hobby shops, hardware stores, or online sources. The epoxy I used for years no longer exists, so I did some sniffing around (figuratively and literally) and found one that I could only barely smell: Devcon 2-Ton Crystal Clear Epoxy. It's rated to set up in 30 minutes. I actually prefer "slow-cure" epoxies, the kind that take 30 minutes or longer to cure, because this gives me time to coat lots of fly heads. If applied with care, epoxy glue will give you a smooth, glassy coating that looks great. Try not to get any glue in the hook's eye, because it may take some doing to clear it out.

**Knot Sense.** An odd one is Loon Knot Sense. It comes out like clear honey and then cures quickly in sunlight. It was made for coating leader and leader-to-line knots but has a

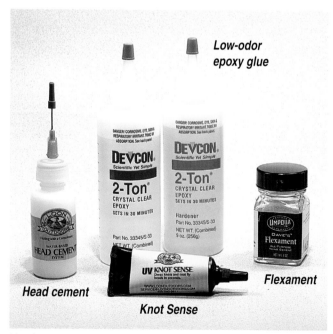

*Head cement and glues*

following among tiers as a head cement and a substitute for epoxy.

**Dave's Flexament.** Dave's Flexament has quite an odor, but it's excellent for toughening feathers and fixing color on foam and all sorts of fly-tying duties. There is a thinner made especially for Dave's Flexament that can save a dried-out bottle or make the consistency just right for coating a turkey quill. An artist's fixative, such as Tuffilm, can also toughen feathers and lock on colors. Use both only in a well-ventilated area.

That should satisfy your need for adhesives. In fact, you can go a long way on just head cement or epoxy. But creative fly tiers are always trying to glue something new to something else, or glue something old to something in a new way, so expect to see fly dressings that call for contact cement, glue for shoe soles—you name it.

## Thread

**Standard threads.** For years I relied on two weights of thread for almost all my tying: 6/0 and 3/0. Then I discovered 8/0, and it soon became my standard. It's great for tying on hooks from size 10 or 8 clear down to 20—even to 24, if thread turns are kept to a minimum. Many, though, still consider 6/0 their standard. Still, for hooks size 20 and smaller, there are real advantages to finer threads such as 10/0, 12/0, and even finer. For large hooks, size 8 and up—especially hooks with long shanks—3/0 offers real strength, and the additional bulk may actually be a plus if the fly is designed to be stout. All this is really a matter of preference—some people tie big flies with 8/0, while others use 3/0 for flies on size 16 hooks.

**Rod thread.** I love size A rod-winding thread for flaring deer hair. Sometimes I'll go up to size D, which is even heavier than A. When I lean on size D, it doesn't break—and I really lean on thread when I flare hair. Size A thread can make good ribs on fly bodies too.

**Other threads.** There are alternatives around with big followings: denier (fine to heavy), flat waxed nylon (very heavy; also functions as floss), and Kevlar (flat, loose, super strong), among others.

**Thread color.** You can go crazy with thread colors—there are dozens—but you needn't. If you have tan and brown (and perhaps black), you can use them for almost everything. Thread color just isn't a big deal to me. Still, a soft-yellow thread head on a Light Cahill dry fly does look rich.

## Wax

Wax can really help you get coarse dubbing, such as hare's mask and goat hair, spun onto thread. With finer furs such as rabbit, wax is optional. The stickiest waxes can leave you, essentially, tarred and feathered. I prefer a wax of low to moderate stickiness.

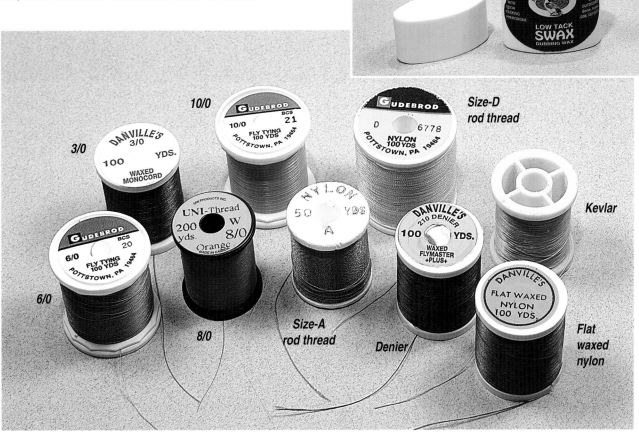

*Threads*

# Beads

Metal beads add lots of weight to nymph and streamer patterns, and they come in gold, brass, black, bright black, and silver, in quite a range of sizes. Tungsten beads are especially heavy and come in various colors and sizes.

Glass beads have caught on with tiers. Many glass beads are translucent, others are opaque, and some are transparent. There are many colors and a wide range of sizes. These beads also provide weight. There are many ways to tie with glass beads, and the best ways (in my opinion) are represented in the dressings in this book. You can visit a bead shop and go crazy with the possibilities, but a fly shop will have the established colors and sizes for tying flies.

Cone heads are used in tying as often as beads are, and are cannonball heavy—reserved only for super-fast-sinking patterns.

# Eyes

Metal barbell eyes suggest real eyes and provide weight. That weight, unlike the weight of a bead or cone, is always concentrated on the top or underside of the hook, which can be a good thing. For example, the weight on the top of a Clouser Minnow flips the fly over in water. Barbell eyes made with lead substitutes are safer for you, your rivers, and the trout than those made of lead. Some barbell eyes are natural metal colors; others are painted, with pupils. New versions of metal barbell eyes come and go.

Realistic dressings may call for realistic eyes, and monofilament eyes are realistic. You can make them by melting the ends of tippet or leader, but most tiers buy them ready-made and precolored black.

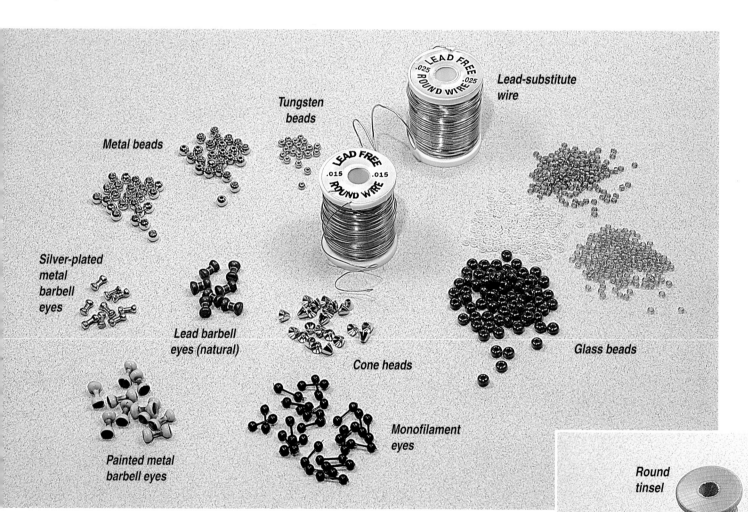

*Beads, eyes, and lead*

*Wire and tinsel*

# Wire

Lead wire comes in various diameters and helps nymphs and other sinking flies sink. Nontoxic substitutes are safer for both you and the rivers you fish.

Copper wire comes in various thicknesses and now in an array of colors. This is good stuff for sinking flies and, in small amounts, in dry flies and emerger patterns.

Gold wire and silver are fine enough and therefore light enough for dry flies, add sparkle and, sometimes, durability. The very finest wires are too fragile, and I prefer wire that is slightly heavier but still fine. Durable gold and silver wires are not difficult to find.

# Synthetic Materials

**Rib and body materials.** Like most synthetic fly materials, the strands we use to make ribs and bodies come in an ever-changing array of thicknesses, colors, configurations, and brand names. Most are flexible and have a gelatinous look. Use whatever suits your eye.

**Leg materials.** Rubber-strand, used primarily for making legs on nymphs and dry flies, now comes in a variety of colors and thicknesses. It even comes with stripes and crosses and metal flakes. Most rubber-strand is even and straight, but Super Floss, Dyna Floss, and Flexi Floss (all quite similar) are wavy, with irregular surfaces, and can be split off into very fine strands; they also come in many colors. All these materials are occasionally used for making ribs or small segmented bodies.

**Sheeting and wing materials.** Synthetic wing and body sheeting is another tying material that keeps shifting form and changing brand names, while growing ever more popular. Some kinds, such as Scud Back and Stretch Flex, are too thick for most wings but are excellent for making shiny, bulging fly bodies and wing cases. Others, such as Zing Wing, are mainly for making wings. Still others, such as Medallion sheeting, can be used for either bodies or wings.

*Synthetic legs, ribs, and sheeting*

# Foam

I tried to find foam in places other than fly shops, but with the exception of whitish clear Ethafoam sheeting, with its pebbly skin, I was nearly always disappointed. Although many foams looked good, they proved too fragile or insufficiently buoyant to pass muster. The most common foam for tying flies is pre-colored foam sheeting, but foam dowels have their uses.

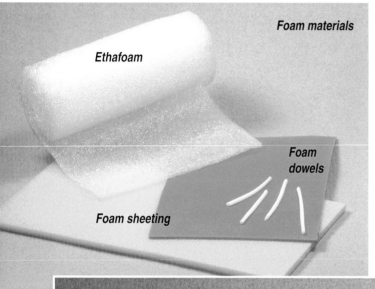

Foam materials

*Ethafoam*

*Foam dowels*

*Foam sheeting*

# Hackles

**Dry-fly hackles.** Just a few decades ago, virtually all dry flies had hackles. The No-Hackle and Compara-dun changed that, but not much—hackles still appear on the great majority of dry-fly designs. Neck hackles come from the skin of the neck and back of a rooster, and are available in a broad size range and can be excellent. Saddle hackles come from the skin of a rooster's rump and can be amazingly long, with fibers of consistent length arranged in dense rows along a fine stem. What more could a fly tier want? Actually, he or she also wants a wide range of sizes, which makes necks preferable. Saddle patches usually come with hackles of only two or maybe three sizes.

Today's dry-fly hackles, necks, and saddles are of much higher quality than the ones I bought as a kid for $3 to $6, but they are also more expensive. A neck designated as a #1 can cost $100! So don't even look at a #1 unless you can afford to buy it—a #1 hackle neck can be very seductive. A good #2 neck or saddle is usually the best deal. A neck or a saddle patch will provide hackles for handfuls of dry flies.

Most of the standard colors for dry-fly hackles are natural, but olive, green, and yellow must be dyed. Barred grizzly hackles are dyed all sorts of handsome colors. Natural hackle colors include the following:

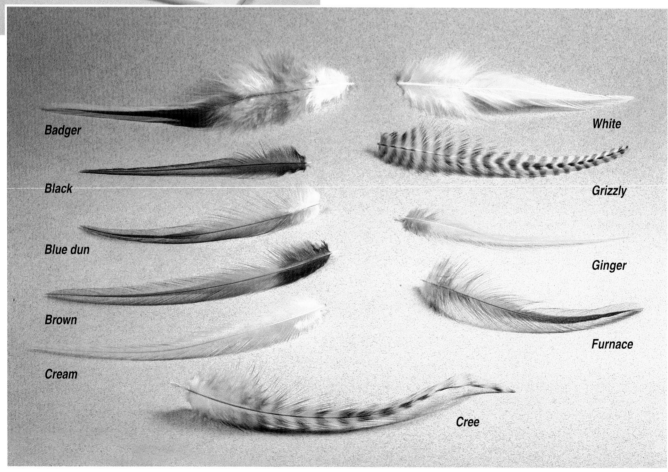

*Badger*

*Black*

*Blue dun*

*Brown*

*Cream*

*White*

*Grizzly*

*Ginger*

*Furnace*

*Cree*

*Hackle colors*

Badger ranges from cream to tan, with a black stripe running up its length.

Black is black.

Blue dun is a bluish gray, ranging from pale to dark.

Brown can vary, but often has a hint of red. The larger hackles may have a black strip up their centers making them essentially furnace hackles.

Cream is cream.

Cree is the oddest of all, like the calico cat of hackle colors: bands of black, cream, and brown across the feather.

Furnace is like badger: with a stripe, but brown overall.

Ginger is a pale to medium golden-tan. Ginger with barring is grizzly ginger.

Grizzly is white with black barring.

White is white.

**Sinking-fly hackles.** Absorbent hen hackles are better and more expensive than they used to be, but not nearly so expensive as dry-fly hackles. Hen-neck hackles, though still supple, have much stiffer fibers than hen-back hackles. You'll find plenty of use for both in the wet flies, nymphs, soft-hackled flies, and flymphs presented in this book.

## Other Feathers

**Pheasant tail.** Pheasant tail fibers are somber beauty—a light brown with black and dark brown markings—and are used in many nymphs and some emergers. The long center feathers have tough, well-marked fibers on both sides of the stem; the other tail feathers have good fibers along one side and fragile, mottled fibers of no value along the other side.

**Quills.** Quill feathers (some are also called "primaries") are broad feathers from the wing or tail of a duck, goose, turkey (the most common), or other bird. Sections cut from these feathers are often used for making wings on dry flies or wing cases on nymphs.

**Breast and flank feathers.** Breast or flank feather from all sorts of birds are commonly used for making nymph tails, nymph legs, dry-fly wings, and the hackle collars on soft-hackled flies. The most common birds that provide such feathers are the partridge, mallard, teal, guinea, and wood duck (although mallard dyed to resemble wood duck is a cheaper and often perfectly satisfactory substitute for real wood duck).

Dry-fly neck (brown)

Saddle and neck hackles

Dry-fly saddle (barred ginger)

Hen neck

Hen hackles

Hen back

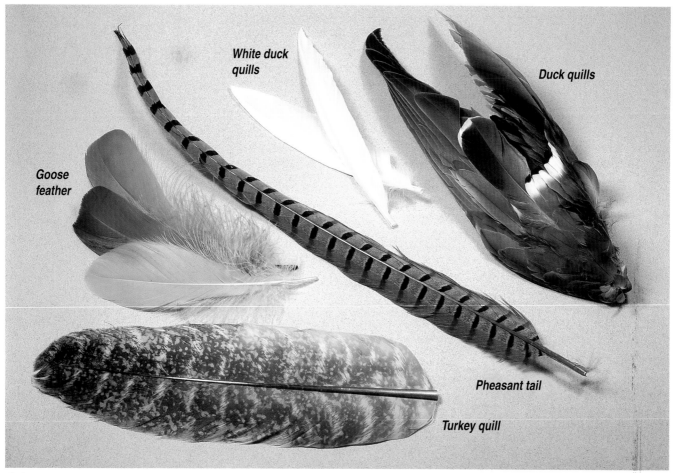

Goose
feather

White duck
quills

Duck quills

Pheasant tail

Turkey quill

*Turkey, goose, duck, and pheasant feathers*

Teal

Bronze
mallard

Guinea

Mallard

Wood duck

Dyed guinea

Partridge

Mallard dyed
wood duck

*Various body feathers*

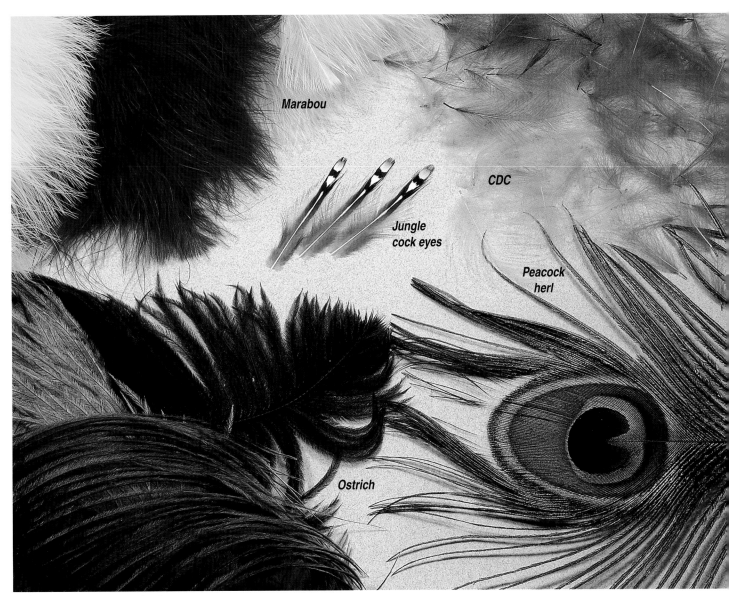

Peacock herls and various feathers

**CDC.** This insignificant, sparse little feather (found encircling the unfortunate location of a duck's rectum) is naturally buoyant and ever more popular for dry flies and emerger patterns.

**Herls.** Peacock herl has been a popular tying material for more than a century owing to its emerald sheen. Ostrich herl is fluffy and longer fibered than peacock, and it comes dyed in many colors.

**Marabou.** No feather I know of is softer or more supple than marabou. Its long, fluffy fibers make streamer wings, nymph legs and gills, and lots of other fly parts that wave and billow with the slightest shift of current. Marabou comes dyed in many colors.

**Jungle cock.** A jungle cock neck is covered with hard, elongated-teardrop-shaped feathers, each with a spot. They don't look like feathers at all, but they do look like eyes. Jungle cock feathers, or "nails" or "eyes," are commonly used to suggest eyes on tiny fish imitations.

# Dubbing

There are two basic types of dubbing—natural and synthetic. Rabbit is now the most popular of the natural dubbings. It is fine, spins easily onto thread, and dyes well to an abundance of colors. Other natural dubbings in common use include muskrat, beaver, badger, otter, and goat. For a spiky dubbing, to create a rough appearance, or suggest legs, hare's mask and squirrel are popular. Unless I have a good reason to do otherwise, I use natural dubbing on flies that sink (or the sinking parts of half-sunken, half-floating emerger flies).

Synthetic dubbings such as poly, Antron, and Super Fine Dry Fly tend not to absorb water and are excellent for dry flies (or the floating half of half-floating emerger flies). I like fine dubbing, such as Super Fine Dry Fly, for slim and small flies, and coarse dubbing, such as poly dubbing and Antron, for dry flies with stout or large bodies.

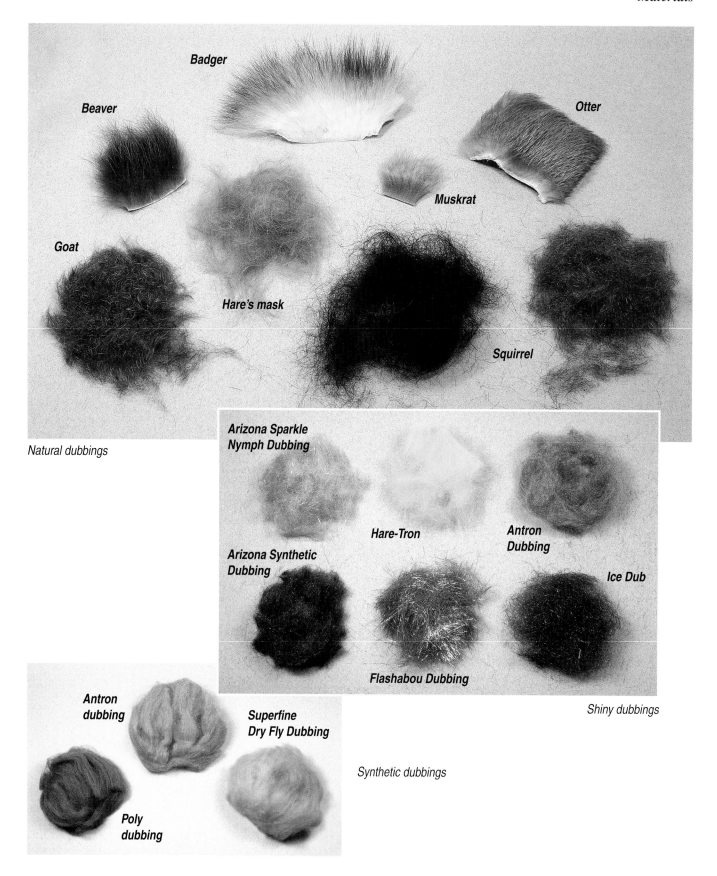

*Natural dubbings*

*Shiny dubbings*

*Synthetic dubbings*

Shiny dubbings—Arizona Sparkle Nymph Dubbing, Hare-Tron, Ice Dub, Arizona Synthetic Dubbing, Antron, and the brilliant Flashabou Dubbing, among others—have a place in nymphs, dry flies, emergers, tiny fish imitations, or any fly that needs some sparkle to make it imitate a bright natural or simply catch a trout's attention.

# Hair

**Deer hair.** Buoyant, pocketed deer hair is the standard for making flared and shaped fly heads and bodies. My favorite is the deer's belly hair, which flares beautifully and cuts cleanly. Deer-body or -belly hair for flaring is often called "spinning," "bass bug," or "Muddler" hair (the last named for the fat-headed Muddler Minnow fly). Other hairs that flare and can be trimmed to shape include antelope (which is excellent, as long as you don't need its broken tips for a hair collar) and softer and finer caribou (good for smaller flies). Elk (see below) is fine for bass bugs but awfully stiff for flaring on most trout flies. Deer hair of other types has other uses. The hair for Compara-dun, Sparkle Dun, and Morris Emerger wings must not flare too much yet still be buoyant; such hair is often marketed as "coastal" or plain "Compara-dun" deer hair. This kind of hair may also be the best choice for deer-hair tails and wings on dry flies.

**Elk hair.** For all bullet heads and the hair hump in such patterns as the Humpies, elk is, in my experience, superior to deer. Elk is the tougher of the two, with the more enduring buoyancy. Many tiers prefer elk for the wings and tails of such patterns as the Wulffs, the Fall Caddis, and the Mikulak Sedge. Elk mane is very long, useful for wings on the biggest stonefly dries and such.

**Moose hair.** Moose body hair is naturally black, much like elk, and is used mostly for dry-fly tails and bullet-heads. Moose mane is coarser and more brittle than moose body hair and is usually a mix of black, cream, and tan or gray hairs; though not so popular nowadays, it is still in use.

**Buck tail.** The long, straight hairs of a buck's tail, though not as spongy as deer-body or -belly hair, are nevertheless buoyant. They often appear as the wings and tails of dry flies. Buck tail, in modest amounts, also fleshes out the wings of many tiny fish imitations (simply called "bucktails").

**Calf tail.** Kinky calf-tail hair is popular for wings and tails of all sorts of dry flies. For small flies, many now prefer calf body hair, which is finer than the tail hair and straight.

**Squirrel tail.** Harder and finer than buck tail, squirrel tail is also used for both dry flies and imitations of tiny fishes.

*Buck tail, squirrel tail, calf tail, and calf body*

*Deer, elk, moose, antelope and carabou hair*

# Chenille

Chenille is a fuzzy cord that comes in several colors, even in variegated colors, and is made of shiny synthetics. Chenille was once the wonder material found in many underwater fly patterns. It may no longer rule the roost, but it is still popular. Vernille and Ultra Chenille are finer, tougher versions of standard chenille. They, too, can make wound fly bodies but are also popular as extended bodies when melted on the end for a taper and toughening.

# Floss

Strands of matte-shiny floss go way back in fly tying and appear on streamers, nymphs, soft-hackled flies, and even some dry-fly dressings. Floss is less popular than it once was but is still a fine material for certain fly patterns. Flat waxed nylon is essentially floss, although it's often used as a heavy thread.

# Yarn

Antron yarn comes in several colors, either as hard, loosely woven strands or as fuzzy, neatly woven rope. Either can make the shuck of an emerger fly, but the two types have very different properties, and you'll probably prefer one or the other for specific tying applications. The subtle sheen of Antron yarn has made it popular. Polypropylene yarn (poly yarn) is shaggy, buoyant, available in various colors, and excellent for dry-fly wings. Wool yarn is flat in color rather than shiny, but it is an old standard for winding thick fly bodies.

# Mylar

**Flashabou.** Flashabou consists of limp, narrow strands of brilliant Mylar, available in many colors. It's used for lively flashing sunken-fly wings, and sometimes for bodies or ribs.

**Krystal Flash.** Essentially, this is Flashabou with a consistent twist, making each strand appear as a row of brilliant pinpoints. Krystal Flash can be used for wings, but when wound, it flattens to look just like wound Flashabou.

**Fine Mylar.** Angel Hair and Lite Brite look like strands of Flashabou cut lengthwise into sixths or eighths—very fine. This material can be blended with dubbing to add sparkle or used as dubbing by itself for a dazzling effect.

**Tinsel.** Flat tinsel comes in strands that are silver on one side and gold on the other, wound onto a spool. Round (or oval) silver or gold tinsel is normally used for ribs or bodies. Both flat and round tinsel comes in various thicknesses. (All tinsel used to be metal, but is now commonly made of Mylar.)

*Chenille, Vernille, floss, Antron, polypropylene, and wool yarn*

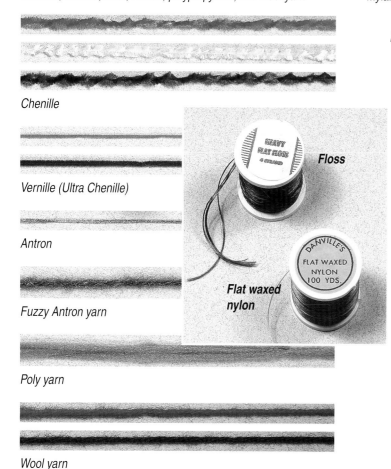

*Chenille*

*Vernille (Ultra Chenille)*

*Antron*

*Fuzzy Antron yarn*

*Poly yarn*

*Wool yarn*

*Floss*

*Flat waxed nylon*

*Mylar*

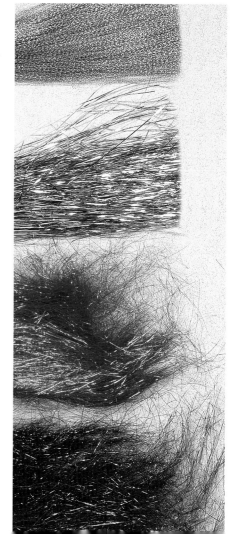

*Krystal Flash*

*Flashabou*

*Lite Brite*

*Angel Hair*

# Fly Proportions and Components

A FLY'S PROPORTIONS—the length of its tail or wing case, or any of its components in relation to the hook and to one another—do matter. Proper proportions make a fly look balanced and elegant to the angler, but more important, they make a fly convincing to the trout. Good proportions make a Gulper Special parachute dry fly truly look like the mayfly dun it is supposed to imitate rather than a tiny tentacled monster. Proportions make a Smurf Stone Black stonefly nymph look like the real nymph instead of an amputee version. And proportions make a Zoo Cougar suggest a real sculpin rather than a yellow veiltail goldfish. So if you get the proportions right, your flies will catch more fish. And of course you won't slam shut your fly boxes whenever your fishing partners wander near.

# Typical Nymph

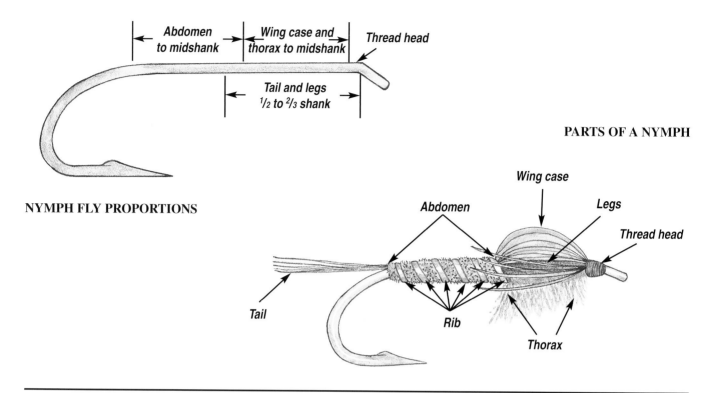

**NYMPH FLY PROPORTIONS**

**PARTS OF A NYMPH**

# Typical Dry Fly

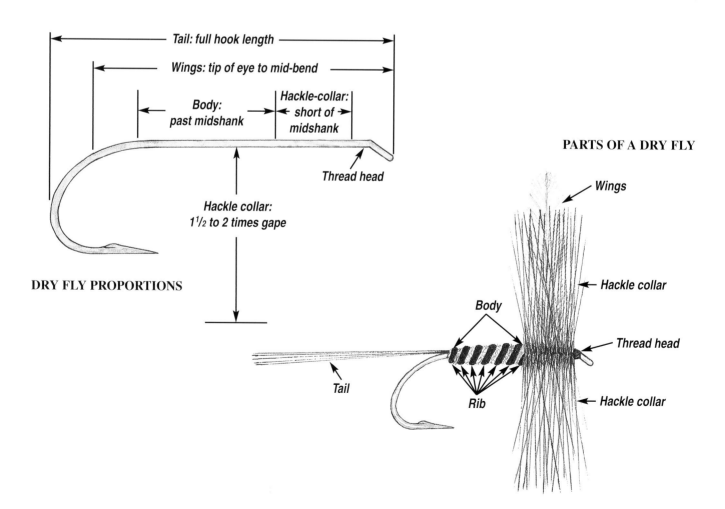

**DRY FLY PROPORTIONS**

**PARTS OF A DRY FLY**

# Typical Stonefly Dry Fly

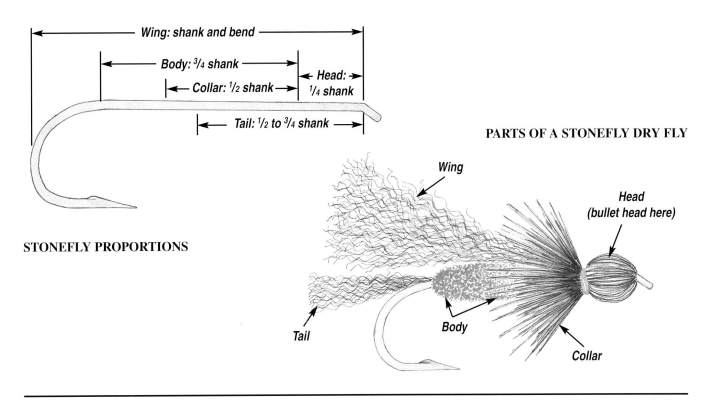

**STONEFLY PROPORTIONS**

Wing: shank and bend

Body: ³/₄ shank

Collar: ¹/₂ shank

Head: ¹/₄ shank

Tail: ¹/₂ to ³/₄ shank

**PARTS OF A STONEFLY DRY FLY**

Wing

Head (bullet head here)

Tail

Body

Collar

# Typical Wet Fly

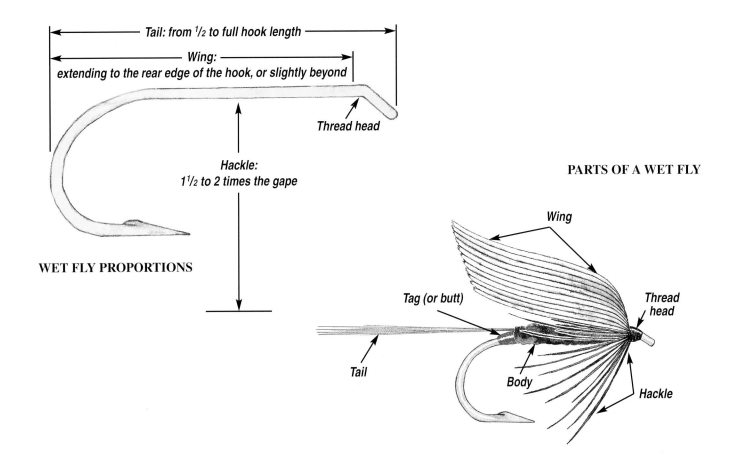

**WET FLY PROPORTIONS**

Tail: from ¹/₂ to full hook length

Wing: extending to the rear edge of the hook, or slightly beyond

Thread head

Hackle: 1¹/₂ to 2 times the gape

**PARTS OF A WET FLY**

Wing

Tag (or butt)

Thread head

Tail

Body

Hackle

# Typical Soft-hackled Fly

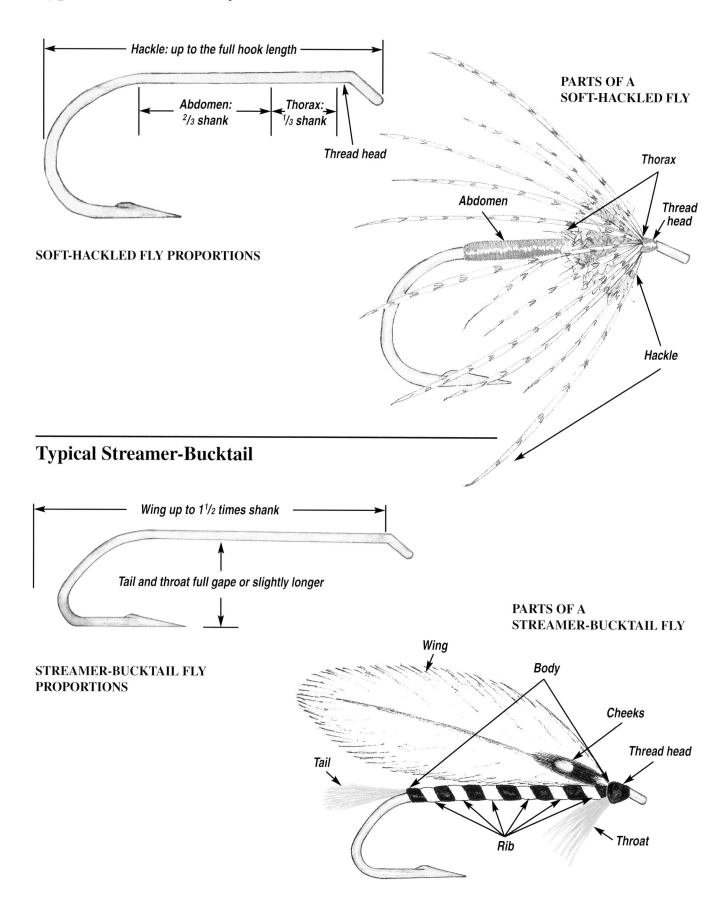

Hackle: up to the full hook length

Abdomen: ²/₃ shank

Thorax: ¹/₃ shank

Thread head

**SOFT-HACKLED FLY PROPORTIONS**

PARTS OF A
SOFT-HACKLED FLY

Thorax

Thread head

Abdomen

Hackle

# Typical Streamer-Bucktail

Wing up to 1¹/₂ times shank

Tail and throat full gape or slightly longer

**STREAMER-BUCKTAIL FLY
PROPORTIONS**

PARTS OF A
STREAMER-BUCKTAIL FLY

Wing

Body

Cheeks

Thread head

Tail

Rib

Throat

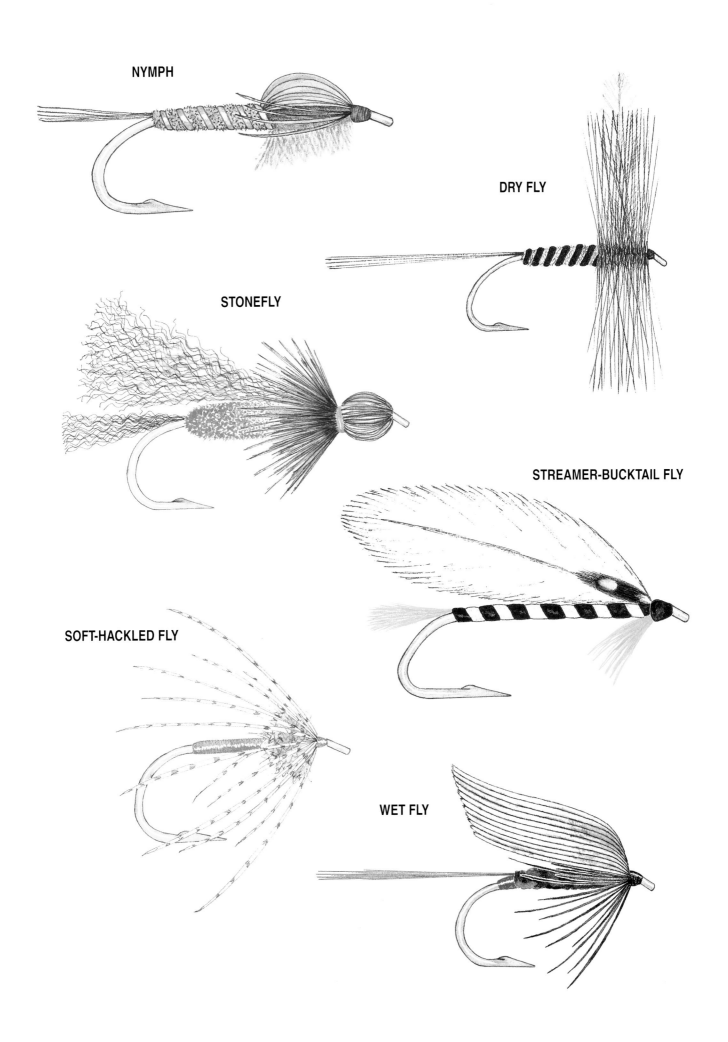

NYMPH

DRY FLY

STONEFLY

STREAMER-BUCKTAIL FLY

SOFT-HACKLED FLY

WET FLY

# Entomology and Fly Patterns

## Understanding Entomology

It's a pretty good bet that the best trout fishermen know their entomology, the study of insects. That's not to say that these efficient and effective fly fishers know a great deal about the caddisflies and midges and other creatures trout eat, but they know what they need to know. They probably know, for example, that most stoneflies hatch not by swimming up in open water but by crawling out onto the shoreline; if so, they also know to toss their dry-fly imitations mostly along the banks rather than out into the middle of the river. They probably know, too, that they'll sometimes do much better with an imitation of the October caddis pupa fished deep than with a dry fly that suggests the adults fluttering around the riverbanks. This is because those adult caddis may not actually be landing on the water, while the pupae are swimming and tumbling down in it where the trout can snap them up. They also probably know when and how the pale morning dun mayfly hatches, so they can come prepared with a proper selection of flies for when the nymphs begin swimming up and sloughing off their underwater skins, to the delight of the trout. If they know all that, they'll know how to fish each of the flies they've brought for the event.

And these are just the aquatic insects, the ones that live in the water. Trout also eat grasshoppers, beetles, ants, and other "terrestrials," as fly fishers call them. And within the river are little fishes called sculpins and crustaceans called scuds, and trout eat these too.

Simply put, the best trout fly fishers know what they need to know not only about flies but also about the creatures their flies imitate. To help you gain that knowledge, the chapters on each of the imitative groups of flies include an introduction to the insects being mimicked.

## Understanding Fly Patterns

Actually, there are many things to know about how a "fly pattern" or "fly dressing"—a listing of the materials for a specific fly design—works. Beginning fly tiers understand few of these aspects, and even many seasoned tiers don't understand all of them. So here is a sample fly pattern, with an explanation of each item in brackets.

It's all pretty logical.

This sample fly pattern includes some alternative materials, and that brings us to what tiers call "substitution"— employing a material different than the one the pattern lists. For example, let's say a nymph pattern calls for a body of Shuggy's Shimmering Boutique Nymph Blend in Burnt Pear. Does your local fly shop or favorite mail-order house carry it? Maybe you can find this material only in sun-ripened kumquat, or perhaps you can't get any of Shuggy's products at all. So if you have to substitute something else, how do you know what color burnt pear is? Is it yellowish brown? Brownish yellow? Green with a touch of cinnamon? Do you have to go out and torch a few Bartletts to find out? And what about

# Sample Fly Pattern

The fly's name.

The designer of the fly—if there is one, and we could find out who it is.

The hook specifications and size range. If we gave you only a specific hook brand and model (for example, the Daiichi 1550), you'd wind up with armloads of hooks. Use the hook chart in chapter 1 to help you select an appropriate hook.

Unless instructed otherwise, wind the wire (usually lead wire) up the hook's shank.

Often a range of thread sizes is listed. Use whichever you like, but generally go with heavier thread for larger hooks, finer for smaller.

In most fly dressings, everything has a purpose. In this case, winding the rib in a different direction than the pheasant toughens the pheasant.

Sometimes listed as "olive partridge," but if you don't know that the natural color of partridge is brown and gray, this way is clearer. The hen back is a substitute, in case you don't have dyed partridge. Whenever there are instructions for making a fly component, the location of those instructions is provided, usually with a page number.

Credit to the person who tied the sample fly in the photo. In this book it's often the person who invented the fly, so you'll see exactly how he or she wanted it to look.

With this fly, the bead is the first material to go on the hook. The dressing presents the materials in the order in which they are used (however, this is an imperfect concept that can be misleading if you follow it blindly.)

Some things don't need explaining—"pheasant tail" naturally refers to the fibers of the tail, not the whole tail.

Alternatives are often presented to make it easier for you to find one that's suitable. Alternatives are especially common when a dressing calls for a particular brand of material, which may be difficult to find.

Anything you need to know or will find particularly interesting about the fly is included here: unusual tying techniques, what it imitates, how or where or when to fish it, why it's constructed the way it is, even some of its history.

## ANATOMICAL *BAETIS* / PMD — *Skip Morris*

*Tied by Skip Morris*

| | |
|---|---|
| **Hook:** | Heavy wire, short to 1X long, sizes 22 to 14. |
| **Head:** | Black metal bead, $5/64$ inch for size 14 hooks, $1/16$ inch for size 16 and smaller. (If you omit the bead, you can add tiny plastic barbell eyes if you like.) |
| **Weight:** | Fine copper wire (optional). |
| **Thread:** | Brown 8/0 or finer. |
| **Tail:** | Pheasant tail (three fibers, split with thread turns if you want, or just two tails). |
| **Rib:** | Fine gold wire, wound opposite the normal direction. |
| **Abdomen:** | Pheasant tail. |
| **Wing case:** | Brown Stretch Flex, Medallion sheeting, or Thin Skin (instructions follow). |
| **Legs:** | Dyed Olive partridge, or hen back (instructions follow). |
| **Thorax:** | Olive-brown rabbit fur. |

**Comments:** Imitates the nymphs of both the PMD and *Baetis* mayflies. You'd have to look at both of the real nymphs—tiny, dark, fine-gilled, and slightly stout, with three tails (though *Baetis* has a short center tail, if any)—side by side to understand why a fairly detailed imitation of one makes a fine imitation of the other.

the dubbing itself—is it coarse, fine, shiny, dull, stunningly bright? There are scads of new tying materials coming and going all the time, and by the time this book is in print, a few new ones will already have appeared while others will have vanished. So in the fly dressings in this book, when we mention a specific material by brand, we usually also provide a general description, a substitute material, or both.

## Finer Points of Substitution

Fly tiers love substitution and often practice it even when it's not necessary. It's their chance to try Antron in place of rabbit dubbing, hackle tips instead of duck primary sections—whatever sparks the imagination. Some of the fly patterns here include logical substitute materials, usually when the material called for in the pattern is uncommon. Most experienced tiers, however, just substitute as they please.

Take the Anatomical/PMD on the previous page. Suppose you want to substitute something else for the legs. Consider the dyed partridge fibers the pattern calls for—they're slender, pliant, and lightly speckled. What about dyed dark-olive calf tail hair? It's slender and pliant, but it probably wouldn't be your best choice; it's kinky, a bit too slender and not nearly as pliant as partridge. Marabou? Too fluffy; it's great for some purposes, but it probably won't look right. Pheasant tail fibers are slightly thicker and slightly stiffer than partridge, but they are a perfectly reasonable substitution and will create convincing legs on this pattern—so go ahead and use them. Actually, the fibers from a lot of feathers will do a good job if they're dyed olive-brown or just brown: guinea, mallard flank, teal, even cul-de-canard (CDC) if you want a little sparkle.

To put this into perspective, we are talking here about one component of a small fly. You could probably use any of the materials just mentioned for the legs of this pattern, and the trout wouldn't care a lick. You could even do something more radical such as building the thorax with a spiky dubbing such as hare's mask or squirrel, teasing some fibers out along the sides to suggest legs—or omit legs altogether. In reality, the importance of the legs of an imitative fly pales in comparison to the size and shape of that fly and how convincingly it suggests the actions of the natural. Still, no real fly tier can throw just anything into a fly and walk away satisfied. It just doesn't go with the temperament. We want our flies to look right, to us. What looks right to the fish, important as that is, comes second.

Sometimes, however, the material really does make a difference in how well the fly fishes. If the wing, body, or tail is a primary part of the fly's effectiveness, the wrong material may result in a dud. Take the Woolly Bugger, an insanely popular broad-purpose streamer fly. It's probably the billowing tail of marabou that accounts for much of the fly's effectiveness, so if you substitute stiff elk hair, your ratio of strikes to casts will likely go down—way down. It would be tough to replace marabou, and why try? Marabou is available in every fly shop, every catalog. Still, if you just can't stick with the original dressing, a rabbit fur Zonker strip might work, or maybe a fine and super-supple synthetic. See what I mean? This substitution business is addictive!

# Mayflies

THE WAY AQUATIC INSECTS TRADE their underwater skins, their "shucks," for wings is perhaps the fly fisher's greatest blessing. Generally, many members of a specific insect—not just a mayfly, but a March brown mayfly, for example—make this metamorphosis all at once in a flurry. This is a boon to trout, with so many edible creatures exposing themselves at one time, and a boon to fly fishers when all those trout gather to feed in earnest. This blessed event is called a hatch. Day after day, if the air and water temperatures are right and the sky is appropriately cloudy or clear, the hatching insects appear as a group at the appointed hour. Or perhaps they don't, since the actions of insects are no more reliable than the actions of fish. Entomologists may understand the logic and motivation behind insect hatches, but most fly fishers attend hatches in happy ignorance, simply grateful that they occur.

The mayfly—with its elegant posture; slender, curving body; and tall, broad, upswept wings—is widely considered the ideal of what a hatching insect in rivers should be. This is partly due to the insect's method of hatching. Mayflies don't creep to shore like stoneflies or shoot away almost instantly

on their new wings like some caddisflies. Instead, mayflies squirm from their shucks at the water's surface and then ride the current sedately for a while out in the open, where everyone can watch and trout can nose down a stomachful of the handsome little creatures.

A mayfly spends the great majority of its life wingless and scurrying underwater among stones (or, in some cases, in vegetation or silt) as a "nymph." When the time is right, this nymph swims up to the surface, where it squirms from its loosened shuck. Fly fishers call it an "emerger" at this vulnerable stage. Once free of its shuck, with its new wings standing atop its back like soft, elongated triangles, it is called a "dun," and it drifts atop currents as it prepares for flight. If no bird or trout takes it, it flies off to rest, mature, and mate. Within a few days or even just a few hours, the fully mature female, now called a "spinner," mates in midair, and then returns to the water to release her eggs. This is her final action—she then lies spent and dying on the surface. (No other insect has a dun or spinner stage.) Each stage in the mayfly's life is important to fly fishers, and each stage inspires lots of fly designs.

23

# Fishing the Stages of the Mayfly

## NYMPH

*Mayfly nymph*

Even if no mayfly nymphs are shimmying up to hatch and no freshly emerged duns are standing atop the currents and drying their new wings, an imitation mayfly nymph is always a reasonable fly choice. It is fished along the bed of a river below a strike indicator—this is standard "indicator fishing" with a nymph—and both the fly and the buoyant indicator drift freely with the current. When a trout takes the nymph, the indicator jerks, and the fly fisher tugs the hook home.

Just before a hatch, when the real nymphs are active but not yet swimming to the surface, a fly pattern that suggests these nymphs, fished deep, can make for fast fishing. Although an emerger or dun imitation is the norm once the adult insects are showing at the surface, a lightly weighted or unweighted nymph suspended a few inches below a dry fly is occasionally more effective than either—sometimes it's the *only* approach that works.

## EMERGER

The emerger stage denotes that brief period when any insect is wriggling from its shuck at the surface of the water—a little like Houdini escaping a straitjacket—and it's a lousy time to be an insect. Struggling to free itself, it can only hope a trout doesn't suck it down before it can rise on its fresh new wings. Trout understand their advantage in this situation, and they use it. Because most mayfly species swim up to emerge from their shucks in the open, they are a big target for trout, fly fishers, and inventive fly tiers. There are scads of fly designs called "emergers," "emerger flies," or "emerger patterns" that imitate mayflies. Since emerging insects are bound up, emerger flies are commonly fished "dead drift," free in the current on slack line and leader, as though they weren't attached to any leader at all.

## DUN

*Mayfly dun*

A just-hatched mayfly, fresh from its shuck with its new wings erect, is called a dun. Traditionally, this stage was the big target for fly tiers and fly fishers. Now it's probably a toss-up between emerger patterns and full-floating dry-fly dun imitations. Dry flies as duns are normally fished dead drift.

## SPINNER

JIM SCHOLLMEYER PHOTO

*Mayfly spinner*

The female spinners are easy pickings for trout. When a number of spinners fly out to drop their eggs, fly fishers call this a "spinner fall." Spinner falls are difficult to spot—the only evidence is the females quietly flitting and then lying low, spent, and almost invisible on the water. Spinner falls normally aren't as concentrated as hatches, and they may occur at night, when there's little if anything fly fishers can do about them. Some occur in daylight, though, and some of these are heavy enough to move trout to serious and single-minded feeding. A spinner imitation is nearly always fished dead drift.

# Specific Hatches

## PRIMARY HATCHES

*Baetis.* The tiny *Baetis* mayfly (commonly called the blue-winged olive, or BWO) can hatch every month of the year. However, it dominates in the off-season—fall through winter—when it's the fly fisher's main game on rivers. *Baetis* prefers foul weather for hatching—heavy, dark clouds or even wind and rain or snow. The nymph is slender and dark brown (although it can be olive or even light olive). The dun has slate-gray wings and an olive underside, and the spinner is reddish brown on its underside, with clear wings. *Baetis* may be the most important mayfly of the West, since its hatches are often heavy, more dependable than most, and can come year round. The *Baetis* nymph likes to "drift," letting the current carry it downstream, around sunrise and sunset. An imitation fished deep can be very effective at these times. Hooks for imitations of all stages run from size 22 to 16.

**March Brown.** The March brown hatches so early in the year that its followers are relatively few. But it can provide real dry-fly action that is well worth braving the chill and rain of late winter. It's a substantial mayfly; the nymph is dark olive to dark brown, and the dun has mottled wings and a tan underside. In fall the March brown reappears. Its hatches tend to be thinner then, but they are usually heavy enough to raise the trout. Imitations of all stages match hooks of size 16 to 10.

**Pale Morning Dun.** All through summer and into fall—the height of the fishing season—trout and fly fishers can count on hatches of pale morning dun (PMD) mayflies on many western rivers. Though small, this mayfly is large enough and plentiful enough to create fine and fairly dependable fishing with dry flies and emerger patterns. The nymph, like most river mayfly nymphs, is dark, usually an olive-brown, although it is sometimes medium or light brown. The dun is angelic—gracefully formed, dainty, and soft yellow all over. The spinner is olive-yellow to brown along its underside, with clear wings. PMD imitations should be tied on hooks of size 18 to 14.

**Green Drake.** The green drake creates a true glory hatch—the stuff of legends—and fly fishers from all over North America gather each late spring into summer on the rivers where it hatches best. The dun is striking: high, gunmetal-gray wings and a stout body of rich green splashed and ribbed with the purest yellow. The nymph is a brown to olive-brown, stout-legged brute. Typically the green drake hatch lasts only three to five weeks and comes off best on cloudy afternoons. Large hooks, size 12 to 8, match all stages.

## LESSER HATCHES

Trout concentrate on each of these "lesser" mayfly families at times. The mahogany dun, *Callibaetis, Tricorythodes,* and the rest are presented here as "lesser hatches" because they're encountered much less frequently than common mayflies such as *Baetis* and the PMD. These lesser hatches, however, can be heavy when you find them.

**Mahogany Dun.** The nymph is dark; the dun is brown-bodied and gray-winged. The mahogany dun hatches in spring and fall but plays hooky in midsummer. Generally, its hatching is sporadic, through midday. Imitations match hook sizes 18 to 12.

**Pale Evening Dun.** The nymph has quite a color range: amber, light olive-brown, dark brown, or some blend of these. The dun varies, too, with a body of cream, tan, or gray. The pale evening dun, as its name implies, hatches from late afternoon through evening, from late spring into fall. Hooks for imitations run from size 16 to 12.

*Tricorythodes.* Tiny as *Tricorythodes* (commonly called the Trico) is, its hatches are often so heavy that big trout rise to them. Both the male and the female spinners return so soon to the water that they commonly mix with the hatching duns. The nymph is a light to dark brown speck. The male dun is blackish brown; the female is this same dark color through the thorax, but green through the abdomen, and both have whitish wings. The female spinner is the same color as the female dun and the male spinner is the same color as the male dun, both with clear wings. Hooks for imitations run from a diminutive size 24 up to 18.

*Flavilinea.* The summer- to fall-hatching *Flavilinea* (commonly called the flav) is a stout, dark nymph and a gray-winged, olive-bodied dun. Flav imitations run from size 16 to 12.

*Callibaetis.* *Callibaetis* (commonly called the speckled spinner) is mainly a lake mayfly, but it does well in a few very slow, weedy rivers. Its nymph is mottled tan-brown; its dun is olive-tan or olive-gray on the underside, with gray wings; and its spinner has clear wings with speckled leading edges and a light gray underside. Middle-size mayfly hooks, 16 to 12, match all stages.

**Brown Drake.** A big mayfly, the brown drake is abundant in a small number of slow-flowing western rivers. The nymph is pale yellow-brown, and the dun runs from yellow-tan to brown underneath splotched by light brown, with light brown wings. Imitations run from hook size 12 to 8.

**Gray Drake.** Though gray drakes are important in only a few western rivers, they may well hatch in abundance in those few. And they are big—size 12 to 8 hooks for imitations. The nymphs are usually light to medium gray, the duns dark gray on top and light gray below, and the spinners deep red to almost black. Since the nymphs creep off to the edges of the slow currents they inhabit before hatching, an artificial nymph is important in the weeks prior to the hatch, and the spinner becomes important once the hatching is well under way. The dun, strangely, is seldom worth imitating.

# Mayfly Nymphs

**Anatomical Nymphs.** I call these my "confidence nymphs." For example, when I'm convinced the trout are focused on real PMD nymphs, I fish my Anatomical *Baetis*/PMD without any doubt in the fly's credibility. In my opinion, the Anatomical Nymphs are just as detailed and realistic as they need to be to convince any trout, but no more so.

**ANATOMICAL *BAETIS*/PMD**          *Skip Morris*

*Top*

*Tied by Skip Morris*

**Hook:**       Heavy wire, short to 1X long, sizes 22 to 14.
**Head:**       Black metal bead, ⁵/₆₄ inch for size 14 hooks, ¹/₁₆ inch for
                size 16 and smaller. (If you omit the bead, you can add tiny
                plastic barbell eyes if you like.)
**Weight:**     Fine copper wire (optional).
**Thread:**     Brown 8/0 or finer.
**Tail:**       Pheasant tail (three fibers, split with thread turns if you want;
                or just two tails).
**Rib:**        Fine gold wire, wound opposite the normal direction.
**Abdomen:**    Pheasant tail.
**Wing case:**  Brown Stretch Flex, Medallion sheeting, or Thin Skin
                (instructions follow).
**Legs:**       Dyed Olive partridge, or hen back.
**Thorax:**     Olive-brown rabbit fur (instructions follow).
**Comments:**   Imitates the nymphs of both the PMD and *Baetis* mayflies.
You'd have to look at both of the real nymphs—tiny, dark, fine-gilled, and
slightly stout, with three tails (though *Baetis* has a short center tail, if
any)—side by side to understand why a fairly detailed imitation of one
makes a fine imitation of the other.

## Making the Wing Case and Legs for an Anatomical Nymph (Anatomical Green Drake)

*(See video instructions on DVD.)*

**1.** Bind a modest bunch of partridge fibers atop the center of the thorax area, tips forward. Trim off and bind the fibers' butts.

**2.** Crease the fibers upright with your thumbnail. Build tight thread turns against the base of the fibers to set them erect.

**3.** Divide the fibers to the sides and then press them down hard with the flat side of your scissors' blades, so the fibers lie down and splay.

**4.** Pull the wing-case material over the top and bind it at the hook's eye. The wing case keeps the leg fibers down and splayed, so a tough wing case wide enough to push down the leg fibers is best.

## ANATOMICAL GREEN DRAKE — *Skip Morris*

*Tied by Skip Morris*

| | |
|---|---|
| **Hook:** | Heavy wire, 1X or 2X long, straight or slow-curve shank, sizes 12, 10, and 8. |
| **Head:** | Black metal bead, $5/64$ inch for size 12, $1/8$ inch for sizes 10 and 8. (If you omit the bead, you can add tiny ready-made plastic barbell eyes if you like.) |
| **Weight:** | Lead wire, 0.015-inch for sizes 12 and 10; 0.020 for size 8. |
| **Thread:** | Brown (or green) 6/0 or 8/0. |
| **Tail:** | Dyed olive (or brown) partridge—a feather tip trimmed close along the stem, leaving a few fibers on either side. |
| **Back:** | Olive or olive-brown Stretch Flex, Scud Back, Medallion sheeting, or Thin Skin, slightly narrower than $1/8$ inch wide. |
| **Rib:** | Fine copper wire (or 4m Uni-mono or 6X tippet). |
| **Abdomen and gills:** | Dyed green and brown ostrich herls. Twist the herls around one side of a dubbing loop and wind the loop up the shank (see instructions on page 97). Trim the underside of the abdomen flat if you wish. |
| **Wing case:** | Same as the back (instructions are on page 26). |
| **Legs:** | Dyed olive (or olive-brown or brown) partridge (instructions are on page 26). |
| **Thorax:** | Arizona Synthetic Dubbing in Peacock, or any dark-olive dubbing. |

**A. P. Nymph.** California fly tier and fly designer Andre Puyans developed the A. P. Nymph series to cover all sorts of mayfly nymphs from pale to dark, small to large.

## Tying the A. P. Nymph (A. P. Muskrat Nymph)

**1.** Bind a modestly thick bunch of tail, leg, and wing-case fibers halfway up the shank. The tips of the fibers create the tail. Trim off some of the fibers so the tail isn't too thick. Bind both the cut and uncut fibers back to the hook's bend.

**2.** Once the abdomen is dubbed and ribbed, dub a full thorax (in front of the fibers' butts, but leave a little bare shank behind the hook's eye.

**3.** Bind the butts of the fibers at the eye to make a wing case. Tug back a few butt fibers and then bind them, angling back along one side. Bind some along the other side.

**4.** Trim off the remaining butts, and then build and complete a thread head (or dub a small head and whip-finish the thread at the eye).

**5.** Trim the side fibers to leg length.

### A. P. MUSKRAT NYMPH                          *Andre Puyans*

*Tied by Carol Ann Morris*

**Hook:**            Heavy wire, standard length or 1X long, sizes 16 to 8.
**Thread:**        Gray 8/0 or 6/0.
**Weight:**       Lead wire (optional).
**Tail, wing case, and legs:** Section of bronze mallard fibers.
**Rib:**              Gold wire.
**Abdomen and Thorax:** Natural darkish muskrat fur (or dyed dark gray rabbit).
**Head:**           Same dubbing as in the abdomen, or just a thread head.
**Comments:**   Instructions for tying all the A. P. Nymphs are above.

### A. P. BLACK BEAVER NYMPH                     *Andre Puyans*

*Tied by Carol Ann Morris*

**Hook:**            Heavy wire, standard length or 1X long, sizes 16 to 8.
**Thread:**        Black 8/0 or 6/0.
**Weight:**       Lead wire (optional).
**Tail, wing case, and legs:** Dark moose body hair.
**Rib:**              Fine copper wire.
**Abdomen and Thorax:** Dyed black beaver fur (or rabbit).
**Head:**           Same dubbing as in the abdomen, or just a thread head.
**Comments:**   The A. P. Nymphs are all tied using the instructions on page 27.

### A. P. OLIVE NYMPH                            *Andre Puyans*

*Tied by Skip Morris*

**Hook:**            Heavy wire, standard length or 1X long, sizes 16 to 8.
**Thread:**        Black 8/0 or 6/0.
**Weight:**       Lead wire (optional).
**Tail, wing case, and legs:** Dyed olive mallard flank.
**Rib:**              Gold wire.
**Abdomen and Thorax:** Dyed olive beaver fur (or dyed olive rabbit).
**Head:**           Same dubbing as in the abdomen, or just a thread head.
**Comments:**   Instructions for tying all the A. P. Nymphs start on page 27.

## A. P. PEACOCK AND PHEASANT NYMPH
*Andre Puyans*

*Tied by Skip Morris*

| | |
|---|---|
| **Hook:** | Heavy wire, standard length or 1X long, sizes 16 to 8. |
| **Thread:** | Black 8/0 or 6/0. |
| **Weight:** | Lead wire (optional). |
| **Tail, wing case, and legs:** | Pheasant tail fibers. |
| **Rib:** | Fine copper wire. |
| **Abdomen and Thorax:** | Peacock herl. |
| **Comments:** | Always make a standard thread head on the A. P. Peacock and Pheasant. Instructions for tying all the A. P. Nymphs are on page 27. |

**Atherton.** The Atherton Dark, Atherton Medium, and Atherton Light are all-purpose mayfly nymph imitations covering a range of shades and sizes. These patterns have been around for decades.

## ATHERTON DARK
*John Atherton*

*Tied by Skip Morris*

| | |
|---|---|
| **Hook:** | Heavy wire, standard length or 1X long, sizes 16 to 10. |
| **Thread:** | Black 8/0 or 6/0. |
| **Weight:** | Lead wire (optional). |
| **Tail:** | Furnace hackle fibers. |
| **Rib:** | Oval gold tinsel. |
| **Abdomen:** | Half-and-half blend of muskrat fur and claret-colored synthetic or natural fur. |
| **Wing case:** | Dyed blue goose quill section. |
| **Thorax:** | Same as the abdomen. |
| **Legs:** | Furnace hackle as a beard or half hackle-collar. |

## ATHERTON LIGHT
*John Atherton*

*Tied by Skip Morris*

| | |
|---|---|
| **Hook:** | Heavy wire, standard length or 1X long, sizes 16 to 10. |
| **Thread:** | Yellow 8/0 or 6/0. |
| **Weight:** | Lead wire (optional). |
| **Tail:** | Barred wood-duck flank fibers. |
| **Rib:** | Oval gold tinsel. |
| **Abdomen:** | Cream fur. |
| **Wing case:** | Dyed gold goose quill section. |
| **Thorax:** | Same as the abdomen. |
| **Legs:** | Gray partridge flank fibers as a beard or splayed in a half circle. |

## ATHERTON MEDIUM
*John Atherton*

*Tied by Skip Morris*

| | |
|---|---|
| **Hook:** | Heavy wire, standard length or 1X long, sizes 16 to 10. |
| **Thread:** | Brown 8/0 or 6/0. |
| **Weight:** | Lead wire (optional). |
| **Tail:** | Natural brown partridge flank fibers. |
| **Rib:** | Oval gold tinsel. |
| **Abdomen:** | Hare's mask fur. |
| **Wing case:** | Dyed blue goose quill section. |
| **Thorax:** | Same as the abdomen. |
| **Legs:** | Brown partridge flank fibers as a beard or splayed in a half circle. |

## BEADED WD40 — *Mark Engler*

*Tied by Skip Morris*

| | |
|---|---|
| **Hook:** | Heavy wire, short shank or standard length (straight shank or humped shank scud-pupa hook), sizes 28 to 16. |
| **Thorax:** | Black metal bead (often tungsten). |
| **Thread:** | Olive-brown 8/0 or 6/0. (Olive-brown was the original color, but brown, olive, black, gray, and dark gray are now common.) |

**Tail and wing case:** Bronze mallard. (Mark prefers bronze mallard, from the shoulder of the bird, which is tougher than mallard flank. Bronze mallard can be light or dark; light was used on the original, but Mark now uses both.)

**Abdomen:** The working thread.

**Comments:** The tying steps are similar to those for my own Ultimate Skip Nymph (instructions are on page 40). Some tiers simply mount the bead of a WD40 ahead of a dubbed thorax rather than working it into the thorax, as here. The original WD40 is usually fished in or near the water's surface as an imitation of a *Baetis* emerger or nymph or an emerging midge, but this fast-sinking version probably suggests a tiny *Baetis* nymph.

## BEADHEAD PALE MORNING DUN NYMPH

*Tied by Rick Hafele*

| | |
|---|---|
| **Hook:** | Heavy wire, humped shank (scud-pupa hook), sizes 18 to 14. |
| **Head:** | Gold metal bead. |
| **Thread:** | Tan 8/0 or 6/0. |
| **Tail:** | Light tan hackle fibers. |
| **Rib:** | Copper wire. |
| **Abdomen:** | Light brown (or brown to dark brown) dubbing, either synthetic or natural. |
| **Thorax:** | Undyed pine squirrel body hair with guard hairs left in. |

**Comments:** Although this is Rick Hafele's dressing, he feels it is too similar to other fly patterns to claim it as his own. (He also grudgingly admits to fathering the son he adores but is quick to give most of the credit to biology and Mother Nature.) He normally fishes it dead drift along the beds of a wide variety of streams—from freestone rivers to tailwaters and spring creeks—that contain PMD mayflies. In slow currents he may swim the fly a little. During a hatch he sometimes fishes it nearer the surface. Cut or tear off the tails, he says, and it becomes an excellent imitation of several varieties of caddis pupae.

**BLM.** Tim Heng's BLMs are strikingly chromelike, which logic tells us should be wrong for an imitation of a mayfly nymph. But near the time of their hatching, real mayfly nymphs bulge with hard, reflective shucks bloated with gas, and sparkle with the gas bubbles that squeeze out and cling to their outsides. So, as it turns out, the brilliance of Tim's patterns has its own logic.

## BLM OLIVE — *Tim Heng*

*Tied by Al Davis*

| | |
|---|---|
| **Hook:** | Heavy wire, standard length (wide gape is optional), sizes 20 to 16. |
| **Thorax:** | Gold metal bead, $5/64$ inch for size 20, $3/32$ inch for sizes 18 and 16. |
| **Thread:** | Olive 8/0. |

**Tail, body, wing case, and legs:** Olive Peacock Angel Hair or Lite Brite.

| | |
|---|---|
| **Rib:** | Fine gold wire. |
| **Comments:** | Instructions for tying the BLM start on page 31. |

## Tying the BLM (BLM Black)

*(See video instructions on DVD.)*

**1.** Slide the bead up the hook, with the small end of the bead's hole facing the hook's eye. Mount the hook in your vise. Start the thread slightly forward (toward the eye) of the center of the shank. Wind the thread tightly back to the hook's bend. Bind a small bunch of fine Mylar—Angel Hair or Lite Brite—atop the bend with just a few tight thread turns. The short ends of the Mylar should extend off the bend as tails. (Wetting the Mylar with tap water makes it easiest to manage.)

**2.** Bind the rib wire on, along the near side of the shank, at the bend.

**3.** Draw back the long, forward ends of the Mylar. Bind the wire slightly past halfway up the shank. Trim off the forward end of the wire. Wind the forward ends of the Mylar stands up to the thread, and bind them atop the shank. (When you first start winding the strands, try to cover the thread turns at the bend with them.)

**4.** Spiral the wire up the Mylar abdomen in a few turns. Spiral the wire opposite the usual direction, "counterwinding" it over the Mylar. Bind the wire slightly past halfway up the shank. Trim off the end of the wire.

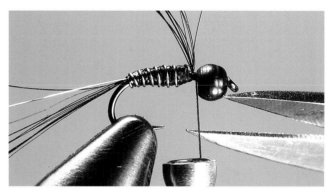

**5.** Draw back the butts of the Mylar and spiral the thread ahead of them. Whip-finish the thread, and then trim it. (Add a little cement to the whip, if you like.)

**6.** Push the bead back over the whip finish. Restart the thread at the front of the bead. Pull the Mylar forward over the bead. Bind the Mylar in front of the bead with a few tight thread turns.

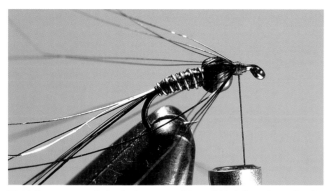

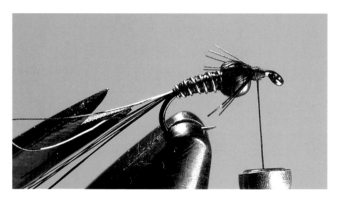

**7.** Pull some strands back along one side and bind them there. Do the same on the other side. Trim any remaining fibers short. Build and complete the usual thread head.

**8.** Trim the side strands to about half the shank's length, for legs. Trim the strands at the bend to this same length, as tails.

## BLM BLACK                                                                       *Tim Heng*

*Tied by Tim Heng*

| | |
|---|---|
| **Hook:** | Heavy wire, standard length (wide gape is optional), sizes 20 to 16. |
| **Thorax:** | Black bead, $5/64$ inch for size 20, $3/32$ inch for sizes 18 and 16. |
| **Thread:** | Black 8/0. |

**Tail, body, wing case, and legs:** Black Angel Hair or Lite Brite.

| | |
|---|---|
| **Rib:** | Fine copper wire. |

## BLM PEACOCK                                                                    *Tim Heng*

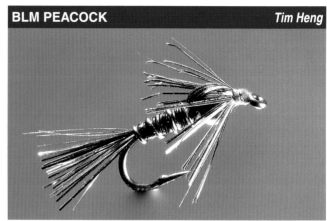

*Tied by Tim Heng*

| | |
|---|---|
| **Hook:** | Heavy wire, standard length (wide gape is optional), sizes 20 to 16. |
| **Thorax:** | Copper metal bead, $5/64$ inch for size 20, $3/32$ inch for sizes 18 and 16. |
| **Thread:** | Olive 8/0. |

**Tail, body, wing case, and legs:** Peacock Angel Hair or Lite Brite.

| | |
|---|---|
| **Rib:** | Fine copper wire. |
| **Comments:** | Instructions for tying the BLM are on page 31. |

## FLASHBACK PHEASANT TAIL

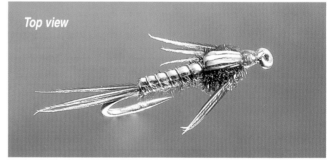

*Top view*

*Tied by Skip Morris*

| | |
|---|---|
| **Hook:** | Heavy wire, standard length or 1X long, sizes 20 to 10. |
| **Thread:** | Brown 8/0 or 6/0. |
| **Tail:** | Pheasant tail fibers. |
| **Rib:** | Fine copper wire. |

**Back and top of wing case:** Pearl Flashabou strands.

| | |
|---|---|
| **Abdomen:** | Pheasant tail fibers. |

**Wing case and legs:** Pheasant tail fibers.

| | |
|---|---|
| **Thorax:** | Peacock herl. |

**Comments:** The Flashabou is pulled forward over the pheasant abdomen and secured at midshank with thread turns; then the wire rib is wound. The Flashabou is doubled back and secured with more thread turns, the wing case and leg fibers are bound on, and the herl is wrapped for the thorax. Complete the wing case and legs as usual, and then pull the Flashabou forward, atop the pheasant wing case, and secure it with thread turns. Complete the legs and head as usual for the standard Troth Pheasant Tail (Instructions are on page 42).

## GIDLOW BOU NYMPH — Arnie Gidlow

*Tied by Arnie Gidlow*

**Hook:**  Heavy wire, humped shank (scud-pupa hook), sizes 20 to 12.

**Thread:**  Olive 8/0 or 6/0.

**Tail, abdomen, thorax, and legs:** Olive marabou. Bind the tips of a section of fibers as tails with only a few tight turns of thread. Bind on the rib wire. Wind the fibers forward as an abdomen; bind them again. Wind the rib, bind it, and trim it. Add the wing-case fibers, and then wind the marabou to the eye to create the thorax. Draw back and bind a few marabou fibers along each side as legs. Trim off the butts of the remaining fibers, complete the wing case and thread head, and then tear off the leg fibers to length.

**Rib:**  Fine gold wire, wound in the opposite direction of the abdomen.

**Wing case:**  Pheasant tail fibers.

**Comments:**  Changing the thread and marabou color to olive-brown, brown, dark brown, or tan-brown would allow the Gidlow Bou Nymph to imitate many different mayfly nymphs and perhaps some small stonefly nymphs.

**Gold-Ribbed Hare's Ear.** This drab, scruffy, elemental mayfly or general-purpose nymph remains popular decade after decade. Occasionally it is even used for imitating small stonefly nymphs. In general, though, at least in my mind, this is a mayfly nymph. Like most fly patterns that just keep showing up, the Gold-Ribbed Hare's Ear is now commonly tied in several colors.

## GOLD-RIBBED HARE'S EAR

*Tied by Skip Morris*

**Hook:**  Heavy wire, standard length or 1X or 2X long, sizes 18 to 8.

**Thread:**  Brown 8/0, 6/0, or, for the largest sizes, 3/0.

**Weight:**  Lead wire (optional).

**Tail:**  Guard hairs from a hare's mask (or substitute partridge or pheasant tail fibers).

**Rib:**  Fine oval gold tinsel.

**Abdomen:**  Hare's mask fur (or squirrel in hare's mask color).

**Wing case:**  Section of turkey quill.

**Thorax:**  Same as the abdomen. Tease out some fur and guard hairs along the sides to suggest legs.

**Comments:**  This is the standard and most common of the Gold-Ribbed Hare's Ear nymphs.

## GOLD-RIBBED HARE'S EAR, BROWN

*Tied by Carol Ann Morris*

**Hook:**  Heavy wire, standard length or 1X or 2X long, sizes 18 to 8.

**Thread:**  Brown 8/0, 6/0, or, for the largest sizes, 3/0.

**Weight:**  Lead wire (optional).

**Tail:**  Guard hairs from a dyed brown hare's mask (or substitute dyed brown partridge or pheasant tail fibers).

**Rib:**  Fine oval gold tinsel.

**Abdomen:**  Dyed brown hare's mask fur (or squirrel).

**Wing case:**  Section of turkey quill.

**Thorax:**  Same as the abdomen. Tease out some fur and guard hairs along the sides to suggest insect legs.

## GOLD-RIBBED HARE'S EAR, OLIVE

*Tied by Carol Ann Morris*

| | |
|---|---|
| **Hook:** | Heavy wire, standard length or 1X or 2X long, sizes 18 to 8. |
| **Thread:** | Olive 8/0, 6/0, or, for the largest sizes, 3/0. |
| **Weight:** | Lead wire (optional). |
| **Tail:** | Guard hairs from a dyed olive hare's mask (or substitute dyed olive partridge or pheasant tail fibers). |
| **Rib:** | Fine oval gold tinsel. |
| **Abdomen:** | Dyed olive hare's mask fur (or squirrel). |
| **Wing case:** | Section of turkey quill. |
| **Thorax:** | Same as the abdomen. Tease out some fur and guard hairs to suggest insect legs. |

## KRYSTAL FLASH BLUE-WINGED OLIVE NYMPH

*Tied by Rick Hafele*

| | |
|---|---|
| **Hook:** | Light to heavy wire, humped shank (pupa-emerger or scud-pupa hook), sizes 20 to 16. |
| **Thread:** | Brown 8/0 or 6/0. |
| **Tail:** | Light tan hackle fibers. |
| **Abdomen:** | Four to six strands of bronze Krystal Flash twisted together. |
| **Wing case:** | Bronze Krystal Flash. |
| **Thorax:** | Undyed pine squirrel with guard hairs. |
| **Comments:** | Rick Hafele (who created the Krystal Flash Blue-Winged Olive Nymph but doesn't consider it original enough to claim as his own) says, "I usually fish this fly in and around riffles in water one to four feet deep. When there is no hatch activity, I like to fish it close to the bottom with a dead-drift presentation. During a hatch, fish this fly just under the surface, or let it sink and then gently lift it toward the surface like a natural swimming up to emerge." |

## MARCH BROWN NYMPH                                    *Bob Jacklin*

*Tied by Bob Jacklin*

| | |
|---|---|
| **Hook:** | Heavy wire, standard length or 1X long, sizes 14 to 10. |
| **Thread:** | Burnt orange 6/0 or 3/0. |
| **Weight:** | Lead wire. |
| **Tail:** | Three pheasant tail fibers, splayed. |
| **Rib:** | Narrow dark brown D-Rib. |
| **Abdomen:** | Natural amber or dyed brown opossum dubbing. |
| **Wing case:** | Brown Scud Back over natural dark turkey tail. |
| **Legs:** | A natural brown partridge feather bound just behind the hook's eye and lying back flat over the thorax, under the wing case. |
| **Thorax:** | Same as the abdomen. |
| **Head:** | Brown Scud Back pulled back over the same dubbing used in the abdomen and bound with a slim thread collar. |
| **Comments:** | Bob developed this fly for the eastern March brown mayfly nymph, but the western March brown isn't much different. He also uses this nymph to imitate a variety of western stonefly nymphs. |

## MICRO MADISON BEADHEAD *BAETIS*
### *Blue Ribbon Flies*

*Tied by Craig Mathews*

| | |
|---|---|
| **Hook:** | Heavy wire, standard length or 1X long, size 18. |
| **Head:** | Copper metal bead, 1.5 mm. |
| **Thread:** | Tan 8/0. |
| **Tail:** | Hungarian partridge. |
| **Rib:** | Small brown Hot Wire. |
| **Abdomen:** | The working thread. |
| **Wing case:** | Strip of pearlescent Mylar sheeting (or substitute a few strands of pearl Flashabou or Krystal Flash). |
| **Thorax:** | Olive Antron dubbing (or another shiny synthetic dubbing). |
| **Comments:** | Craig tells me that both Micro Madison Beadhead nymphs are effective on not only the Madison but also the Yellowstone and Gallatin rivers, Henry's Fork, and other Yellowstone-area streams. As the author and coauthor of several books on Yellowstone flies and fishing, he's to be believed. |

## MICRO MADISON BEADHEAD PMD
*Blue Ribbon Flies*

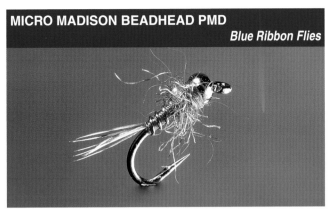

*Tied by Craig Mathews*

| | |
|---|---|
| **Hook:** | Heavy wire, standard length or 1X long, size 16. |
| **Head:** | Copper metal bead, $5/64$ inch. |
| **Thread:** | Brown 8/0 or 6/0. |
| **Tail:** | Hungarian partridge. |
| **Rib:** | Small gold Hot Wire. |
| **Abdomen:** | The working thread. |
| **Wing case:** | Strip of pearlescent Mylar sheeting (or substitute a few strands of pearl Flashabou or Krystal Flash). |
| **Thorax:** | Antron in pheasant tail color (or another shiny synthetic dubbing). |
| **Comments:** | See Micro Madison Beadhead *Baetis* on the previous page. |

**Micro Mayfly Nymph.** Mike Mercer's Micro Mayfly Nymph series imitates, sometimes plausibly and sometimes abstractly, a range of tiny to modest-size mayfly nymphs. As he says in his book *Creative Fly Tying*, the idea for these bright, fast-sinking nymphs came to him while fishing Montana's Madison River, where he found "a bunch of fish in really shallow, fast water" where he "couldn't use a split shot" because it would hang up constantly. He discovered, however, that these patterns worked in all kinds of water: "big, brawling rivers, tiny meadow rivulets, even in lakes with fish chasing *Callibaetis* nymphs."

## MICRO MAYFLY NYMPH, BROWN
*Mike Mercer*

*Tied by Mike Mercer*

| | |
|---|---|
| **Hook:** | Light to heavy wire, short to standard length, sizes 20 to 14. |
| **Head:** | Copper metal bead, extra-small for size 20, small for sizes 18 and 16, medium for size 14. |
| **Thread:** | Camel (or brown) 8/0. |
| **Tail:** | Three pheasant tail fibers, splayed. |
| **Rib:** | Fine silver wire. |
| **Abdomen:** | Stripped peacock herl. |
| **Wing case:** | Golden brown mottled turkey tail with a single strand of pearl Flashabou up its center. Use a rounded coating of clear epoxy glue over the wing case (instructions are on page 38). |
| **Thorax:** | Fine mahogany brown dubbing. |
| **Legs:** | Pheasant tail fibers. |
| **Collar:** | Mahogany brown dubbing. Keep the collar very slim. |

## MICRO MAYFLY NYMPH, CHARTREUSE WIRE
*Mike Mercer*

*Tied by Mike Mercer*

| | |
|---|---|
| **Hook:** | Light to heavy wire, short to standard length, sizes 18 to 14. |
| **Head:** | Copper metal bead, small on size 18 and 16, medium on size 14. |
| **Thread:** | Olive 8/0. |
| **Tail:** | Three dyed yellow pheasant tail fibers, splayed. |
| **Abdomen:** | Small Ultra Wire, chartreuse. |
| **Wing case:** | Golden brown mottled turkey tail with a single strand of pearl Flashabou up its center. Use a rounded coating of clear epoxy glue over the wing case (instructions are on page 38). |
| **Thorax:** | Peacock herl. |
| **Legs:** | Dyed yellow pheasant tail fibers. |
| **Collar:** | Arizona Synthetic Peacock Dubbing, natural. Keep the collar very slim. |

## MICRO MAYFLY NYMPH, ELECTRIC YELLOW
### Mike Mercer

*Tied by Mike Mercer*

| | |
|---|---|
| **Hook:** | Light to heavy wire, short to standard length, sizes 20 to 14. |
| **Head:** | Copper metal bead, extra-small for size 20, small for sizes 18 to 16, medium for size 14. |
| **Thread:** | Yellow 8/0. |
| **Tail:** | Three dyed yellow pheasant tail fibers, splayed. |
| **Rib:** | Small Ultra Wire, amber. |
| **Abdomen:** | Electric Banana Angel Hair. |
| **Wing case:** | Golden brown mottled turkey tail with a single strand of pearl Flashabou up its center. Use a rounded coating of clear epoxy glue over the wing case (instructions are on page 38). |
| **Thorax:** | Mercer's Select Buggy Nymph Dubbing, October caddis (or any amber-orange dubbing). |
| **Legs:** | Dyed yellow pheasant tail fibers. |
| **Collar:** | Same dubbing as in the thorax. Keep the collar very slim. |

## MICRO MAYFLY NYMPH, PHEASANT TAIL
### Mike Mercer

*Tied by Mike Mercer*

| | |
|---|---|
| **Hook:** | Light to heavy wire, short to standard length, sizes 18 to 14. |
| **Head:** | Copper metal bead, small for sizes 18 and 16, medium for size 14. |
| **Thread:** | Camel 8/0. |
| **Tail:** | Three undyed pheasant tail fibers, splayed. |
| **Abdomen:** | Small Ultra Wire, amber. |
| **Wing case:** | Golden brown mottled turkey tail with a single strand of pearl Flashabou up the center. Use a rounded coating of clear epoxy glue over the wing case (instructions are on page 38). |
| **Thorax:** | Peacock herl. |
| **Legs:** | Pheasant tail fibers. |
| **Collar:** | Arizona Synthetic Peacock Dubbing, natural. Keep the collar very slim. |

## MICRO MAYFLY NYMPH, RED WIRE
### Mike Mercer

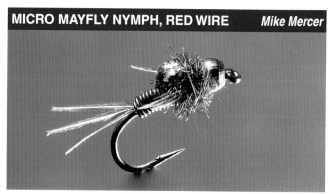

*Tied by Mike Mercer*

| | |
|---|---|
| **Hook:** | Light to heavy wire, short to standard length, sizes 18 to 14. |
| **Head:** | Copper metal bead, small for sizes 18 to 16, medium for size 14. |
| **Thread:** | Camel 8/0. |
| **Tail:** | Three undyed ring-necked pheasant tail fibers, splayed. |
| **Abdomen:** | Small Ultra Wire, red. |
| **Wing case:** | Golden brown mottled turkey tail with a single strand of pearl Flashabou up its center. Use a rounded coating of clear epoxy glue over the wing case (instructions on page 38). |
| **Thorax:** | Peacock herl. |
| **Legs:** | Same as the tail. |
| **Collar:** | Arizona Synthetic Peacock Dubbing, natural. Keep the collar very slim. |

## PHEASANT TAIL
### Frank Sawyer

*Tied by Skip Morris*

| | |
|---|---|
| **Hook:** | Heavy wire, standard length or 1X long, sizes 20 and 18. |
| **Thread:** | None. Use fine copper wire. |
| **Weight:** | Buildup of copper wire at the thorax. |
| **Tail:** | Four pheasant tail fiber tips. |
| **Body:** | Butts of the four pheasant tail fibers spun around the wire and wound to the eye. |
| **Wing case:** | Butts of the four tail and body pheasant tail fibers. |
| **Comments:** | This is the *other* Pheasant Tail nymph. It was developed in England but is an excellent tiny nymph pattern anywhere. It is a natural as a mayfly nymph imitation but also sees a lot of duty as a general sort of searching nymph. After the pheasant and wire are wound up the shank together, separate the wire from the fibers and spiral it back to the rear of the thorax area. Draw back the butts of the pheasant and bind them atop the rear of the thorax. Spiral the wire to the eye, pull the fiber butts forward and down as a wing case, and bind the pheasant with the wire. Trim off the pheasant, half-hitch the wire a few times, and cut it. Add head cement to the half hitches. |

## PHEASANT TAIL, TROTH

See Troth Pheasant Tail on page 42.

## PMD NYMPH — *Blue Ribbon Flies*

*Tied by Craig Mathews*

| | |
|---|---|
| **Hook:** | Light wire, standard length or 1X long, sizes 18 to 14. |
| **Thread:** | Brown 8/0. |
| **Tail:** | Hungarian partridge or wood-duck flank. |
| **Abdomen:** | PMD Z-lon blend (dyed dark brown hare's mask or squirrel mixed with Antron dubbing). |
| **Wing case:** | Strip of black buoyant closed-cell foam sheeting. |
| **Thorax:** | Same dubbing as in the abdomen, picked out at the sides. |

**Comments:** Colors and hook size can be varied to match a number of mayfly nymphs. Craig says that this lightweight nymph, which barely sinks, can be just the thing for large trout that "feel more secure by being able to feed without breaking the surface of the water."

## POXYBACK GREEN DRAKE NYMPH, GOLD BEAD — *Mike Mercer*

*Top view*

*Tied by Mike Mercer*

| | |
|---|---|
| **Hook:** | Standard to heavy wire, 2X long, slow-curve shank (or straight), sizes 12 and 10. |
| **Head:** | Gold metal bead, medium. |
| **Thread:** | Olive 8/0 or 6/0. |
| **Tail:** | Three pheasant tail fibers, splayed. |
| **Rib:** | Fine copper wire. |
| **Back:** | Undyed golden brown mottled turkey tail. |
| **Gills:** | Dyed olive ring-necked pheasant after-shaft feather, atop the abdomen, under the back and ribs. |
| **Abdomen:** | Mercer's Select Buggy Nymph Dubbing, Z-Wing (slightly dark olive). |
| **Wing case:** | Same as the back, but topped with a rounded coating of epoxy glue (instructions on page 38). |
| **Thorax:** | Same as the abdomen. |
| **Legs:** | Golden brown mottled hen saddle fibers. |
| **Collar:** | Same dubbing used in the abdomen, slim. |

**Comments:** This is a shaggy, semirealistic imitation of the green drake nymph. The heavy after-shaft fluff suggests the full gills of the natural.

**POXYBACK *ISONYCHIA***                              *Mike Mercer*

*Top view*

*Tied by Skip Morris*

| | |
|---|---|
| **Hook:** | Heavy to standard wire, slow-curve shank, 2X long, size 10 or 12. |
| **Thread:** | Dark brown 8/0. |
| **Tail:** | Three ostrich herl tips, dyed dark brown or wine color, splayed. |
| **Rib:** | Fine copper wire. |
| **Back:** | Mottled brown turkey tail slip with a single strand of pearl Flashabou up its center, coated with epoxy glue (instructions are on page 38). |
| **Gills:** | After-shaft (filoplume) feather from the underside of a pheasant rump feather, dyed wine or dark brown. |
| **Abdomen:** | Dark brown Buggy Nymph Dubbing, or some kind of dark purple dubbing. |
| **Wing case:** | Same as the back, also with a single strand of Pearl Flashabou up its center and topped with epoxy. (Instructions are on page 38.) |
| **Thorax:** | Same as the abdomen. |
| **Legs:** | Brown speckled partridge feather. |
| **Head:** | Same dubbing as the abdomen. |

**Comments:** *Isonychia,* though considerably less common in the West than in the East, is large enough and plentiful enough in the few western streams it inhabits that trout focus on it from time to time during its long, sporadic hatching period.

# Making an Epoxy-Topped Wing Case (Poxyback PMD)

*(See video instructions on DVD.)*

**1.** Complete the fly as usual, except for adding head cement. Mix some epoxy glue (preferably the sort with minimal vapors) and smear it thinly on top of the wing case. To ensure that the epoxy won't run into the abdomen or legs, don't let it get past the edges of the wing-case material—and perhaps keep it even a little *short* of the edges.

With absorbent natural materials such as turkey, it's best to coat the wing case lightly, turn the fly (as described in step 3) until the epoxy hardens and seals the fibers, and then add a thicker coat the next day (a thick first coat can wick into the thorax and legs). With epoxy-topped flies such as the Copper John (see chapter 12), whose wing case is made of a dense synthetic that epoxy won't penetrate (Thin Skin), one full coating of epoxy should work fine.

**2.** Once the epoxy is largely cured, add another full drop. Tease this epoxy out to the edges of the first epoxy coating.

**3.** The epoxy will smooth out on its own to create a clear dome atop the thorax. Mount the fly in a board that you can turn over frequently, or place it in a motorized wheel until the epoxy is hard. It's most efficient to coat the wing cases of several flies at once. When tying epoxy-topped nymphs with a thread collar at the front of the wing case, such as the Copper John, add head cement (or epoxy glue) to the thread collar and the whip finish only *after* the epoxy atop the wing case is hard. Otherwise, the epoxy is likely to flow heavily onto the collar and bleed back into the thorax.

| POXYBACK PMD | *Mike Mercer* |
| --- | --- |

*Tied by Skip Morris*

**Hook:** Heavy wire, 2X or 3X long, straight or slow-curve shank, sizes 16 to 20.
**Thread:** Orange 8/0 or 6/0.
**Tail:** Three ring-necked pheasant tail fibers.
**Rib:** Single strand of pearl Flashabou.
**Back:** Over the abdomen, a back of turkey tail (or natural dark turkey quill).
**Abdomen:** Blend of several Antron colors to produce rusty orange.
**Gills:** Two clumps of tan marabou emanating from the rear sides of the wing case.
**Wing case:** Dark mottled turkey tail (or natural dark turkey quill), with a drop of epoxy on top. (Instructions begin on previous page.)
**Thorax:** Same as the abdomen.
**Legs:** Golden brown grouse fibers, sparse and divided.
**Head:** Same dubbing as in the abdomen.

**Skip Nymph.** A scruffy and simple nymph pattern—and quick to tie, once you get the hang of it—the Skip Nymph has taken hundreds of mayfly-eating trout for me all over North America and even overseas. It also functions as a general-purpose nymph for searching through promising water, when no hatch is apparent.

| SKIP NYMPH (STANDARD) | *Skip Morris* |
| --- | --- |

*Tied by Skip Morris*

**Hook:** Heavy wire, standard length or 1X long, sizes 20 to 8.
**Thread:** Brown 8/0 or 6/0.
**Weight (optional):** Lead wire or three layers of the copper wire added before the abdomen is formed.
**Rib:** Fine copper wire.
**Abdomen:** Hare's mask, or squirrel in hare's mask color.
**Back, tails, and wing case:** Undyed pheasant tail fibers.
**Thorax:** Same as the abdomen.
**Comments:** Bind on the copper wire, dub the abdomen, and bind on the pheasant tail fibers at the center of the shank. Wind the wire a half turn into the dubbing, and then pull the tips of the fibers down for tails and a back. Take one turn of wire over the fibers and then tug some fiber tips out to both sides (for split tails). Tighten the wire to firm tension (but not tight, which could weaken the tails), and then wind the wire up the fibers as ribs. The butts of the pheasant tail fibers make the wing case, over the dubbed abdomen. Trim out the center pheasant tips, leaving three to five of the tips tugged out to each side as split tails.

## SKIP NYMPH DARK — *Skip Morris*

*Tied by Skip Morris*

**Hook:**           Heavy wire, standard length or 1X long, sizes 20 to 8.
**Thread:**         Brown or black 8/0 or 6/0.
**Weight (optional):** Lead wire or three layers of the copper wire added
                    before the abdomen is formed.
**Rib:**            Fine copper wire.
**Abdomen:**        Dyed dark brown hare's mask or squirrel.
**Back, tails, and wing case:** Dyed dark brown pheasant tail fibers, or dyed
                    black or natural fibers dark side up.
**Thorax:**         Same as the abdomen.
**Comments:**       The tying steps are the same as described for the standard
Skip Nymph on the previous page.

## SKIP NYMPH OLIVE — *Skip Morris*

*Tied by Carol Ann Morris*

**Hook:**           Heavy wire, standard length or 1X long, sizes 20 to 8.
**Thread:**         Olive 8/0 or 6/0.
**Weight (optional):** Lead wire or three layers of copper wire, added before
                    the abdomen is formed.
**Rib:**            Fine copper wire.
**Abdomen:**        Dyed olive hare's mask or squirrel.
**Back, tails, and wing case:** Dyed olive pheasant tail fibers.
**Thorax:**         Same dubbing as in the abdomen.
**Comments:**       Same tying steps as described for the standard Skip Nymph
                    on the previous page.

# Tying the Skip Nymph, Ultimate (Olive)

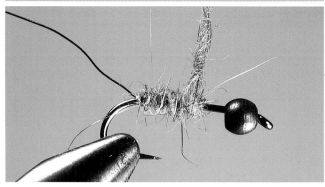

**1.** Mount the bead on the hook with the small end of the bead's hole toward the hook's eye. Start the thread at the center of the shank. Bind copper wire down the shank. Dub slightly past halfway up the shank.

**2.** Bind some pheasant fibers, their tips evened, atop the center of the shank.

**3.** Wind the wire one-half turn forward over the abdomen. Pull down the pheasant and bind it with one light-tension turn of wire. Hold the wire firmly as you tug half the fiber tips out to one side, the other half out to the other side. Tighten the wire to modest tension. Wind the wire tightly up the abdomen in a few ribs.

**4.** Bind and trim the wire. Pull the butts of the pheasant back and bind them. Whip-finish and cut the thread. (Add a little cement to the whip for insurance, if you like.)

**5.** Push the bead firmly back so that it covers the doubled butts of the pheasant. Restart the thread in front of the bead. Dub a short, full, rough collar. (If your bead's hole is too small to fit over the bound butts of the pheasant, keep the bindings over the pheasant particularly short and dub over them a little to conceal them.)

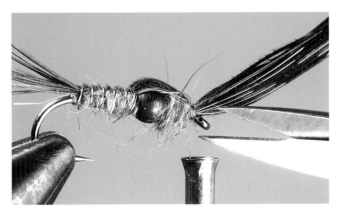

**6.** Draw the pheasant fibers forward over the bead and dubbed collar. Bind the fibers at the eye. Trim the fibers. Complete a thread head.

**7.** Tease out some fibers from the dubbed collar to suggest legs. Trim out the center fiber tips, leaving three to five per side as split tails.

## SKIP NYMPH, ULTIMATE, OLIVE  *Skip Morris*

*Tied by Carol Ann Morris*

**Hook:**        Heavy wire, standard length or 1X long, sizes 18 to 8.
**Bead:**        Black metal.
**Thread:**     Olive 8/0 or 6/0.
**Rib:**          Fine copper wire.
**Abdomen:**  Dyed olive hare's mask or squirrel mixed with fine Mylar (such as Angel Hair or Lite Brite) in silver, olive, and pearl (or use Arizona Sparkle Nymph Dubbing in olive).
**Back, tail, and wing case:** Dyed olive pheasant tail fibers (a couple of strands of green Flashabou or Krystal Flash over the back and wing case are optional).
**Thorax:**     Same as the abdomen.
**Comments:**   The bead really pulls this nymph down, which can be a blessing on both rivers and lakes. Tying instructions begin on previous page.

## SKIP NYMPH, ULTIMATE (STANDARD)     *Skip Morris*

*Tied by Carol Ann Morris*

**Hook:**      Heavy wire, standard length or 1X long, sizes 18 to 8.
**Bead:**      Black metal.
**Thread:**    Brown 8/0 or 6/0.
**Rib:**       Fine copper wire.
**Abdomen:**   Natural hare's mask or squirrel in hare's mask color, mixed
               with fine Mylar (such as Angel Hair or Lite Brite) in silver,
               brown, and pearl (or use Arizona Sparkle Nymph Dubbing in
               Skip's Tannish Brown).
**Back, tails, and wing case:** Undyed pheasant tail fibers ( a couple of
               strands of brown Flashabou or Krystal Flash over the back
               and wing case are optional ).
**Thorax:**    Same as the abdomen.
**Comments:**  The bead really pulls this nymph down, which can be a
blessing on both rivers and lakes. Tying instructions for all the Ultimate Skip
Nymphs begin on page 40.

## SKIP NYMPH, ULTIMATE, DARK     *Skip Morris*

*Tied by Carol Ann Morris*

**Hook:**      Heavy wire, standard length or 1X long, sizes 18 to 8.
**Bead:**      Black metal.
**Thread:**    Dark brown 8/0 or 6/0.
**Rib:**       Fine copper wire.
**Abdomen:**   Dyed dark brown hare's mask or squirrel blended with fine
               Mylar (such as Angel Hair or Lite Brite) in silver, dark brown,
               and pearl (or use Arizona Sparkle Nymph Dubbing in dark
               brown).
**Back, tail, and wing case:** Dyed dark brown pheasant tail fibers ( a couple
               of strands of brown Flashabou or Krystal Flash over the
               back and wing case are optional).
**Thorax:**    Same as the abdomen.
**Comments:**  The bead really pulls this nymph down, which can be a
blessing on both rivers and lakes. Tying instructions are on page 40.

## TROTH PHEASANT TAIL     *Al Troth*

*Top view*

*Tied by Al Troth*

**Hook:**      Heavy wire, standard length or 1X long, sizes 20 to 10.
**Weight (optional):** Fine copper wire over the shank, slightly fuller around
               the thorax. (Lead wire is tricky to build the peacock over.)
**Thread:**    Brown 8/0 or 6/0.
**Tail:**      Pheasant tail fibers.
**Rib:**       Gold wire.
**Abdomen:**   Pheasant tail fibers.
**Wing case:** Pheasant tail fibers.
**Thorax:**    Peacock herl.
**Legs:**      Wing-case pheasant fibertips divided to the sides. Trim off
               the excess fibers, leaving only three to five per side. This is
               the same method described for the A. P. Muskrat Nymph
               (instructions on page 27), except that the fiber legs for the
               Troth Pheasant Tail are *uncut* fiber tips.
**Comments:**  For at least a couple of decades, the Troth Pheasant Tail
shared the Top Mayfly Nymph of the West position (or Most Versatile
Mayfly-like Nymph) with the Gold-Ribbed Hare's Ear, and probably still
does. The Troth Pheasant Tail is often called simply the Pheasant Tail.

# Mayfly Emergers

**Barr Emerger.** There are two basic styles of the Barr Emerger, and the real difference between them is the hook—the "dry" versions have light-wire hooks, and the "wet" versions have heavy wire. But according to Colorado fly designer and guide Tim Heng, it's as common to apply floatant to the wet Barr Emergers and fish them in the surface as it is to drift them deeper. You can fish the wet versions at nearly any depth from the surface to along the riverbed, including a few inches to a foot below a dry fly or indicator. The light-wire dry versions are always fished on top. John Barr designed this pattern to suggest a mayfly nymph ripe for hatching.

## BARR EMERGER, BLUE-WINGED OLIVE (DRY)
### John Barr

*Tied by Skip Morris*

**Hook:** Light to standard wire, short to 1X long, sizes 22 to 16.
**Thread:** Gray 8/0.
**Tail:** Brown dry-fly hackle fibers, tips trimmed to length.
**Abdomen:** Olive-brown synthetic dubbing.
**Wing case and legs:** Blue dun dry-fly hackle fibers, tips trimmed to length.
**Thorax:** Blue dun synthetic dubbing.

## BARR EMERGER, BLUE-WINGED OLIVE (WET)
### John Barr

*Tied by Carol Ann Morris*

**Hook:** Heavy wire, 2X short, humped shank, sizes 22 to 16.
**Thread:** Gray 8/0.
**Tail:** Brown dry-fly hackle fibers, trimmed to length.
**Abdomen:** Olive-brown dubbing.
**Wing case and legs:** Blue dun dry-fly hackle fibers, tips trimmed to length.
**Thorax:** Blue dun dubbing.

## BARR EMERGER, PALE MORNING DUN (DRY)
### John Barr

*Tied by Carol Ann Morris*

**Hook:** Light to standard wire, short to 1X long, sizes 18 to14
**Thread:** Light olive 8/0.
**Tail:** Brown dry-fly hackle fibers, trimmed to length.
**Abdomen:** Olive-brown synthetic dubbing.
**Wing case and legs:** Pale olive dry-fly hackle fibers, tips trimmed to length.
**Thorax:** Pale olive synthetic dubbing.

## BARR EMERGER, PALE MORNING DUN (WET)
### John Barr

*Tied by Carol Ann Morris*

**Hook:** Heavy wire, 2X short, humped shank, sizes 18 to 14.
**Thread:** Light olive 8/0.
**Tail:** Brown dry-fly hackle fibers, trimmed to length.
**Abdomen:** Olive-brown dubbing.
**Wing case and legs:** Pale olive dry-fly hackle fibers, tips trimmed to length.
**Thorax:** Pale olive dubbing.

**Brooks's Sprout.** The Brooks's Sprout series represents a sensible approach to mayfly emerger design—an absorbent shuck and abdomen pushed underwater by a rounded hook shank, with the buoyancy of hackle and foam. The white foam wing provides visibility.

### BROOKS'S SPROUT, *BAETIS*          Bob Brooks

*Tied by Carol Ann Morris*

**Hook:** Light wire, humped shank (pupa-emerger hook), sizes 26 to 16.
**Thread:** Olive 8/0 or 6/0.
**Parachute wing:** Section of white, round, buoyant closed-cell foam, short.
**Parachute hackle:** Medium blue dun.
**Shuck:** Brown Antron.
**Abdomen:** Olive goose biot wound with the fringed side down.
**Thorax:** Dark olive synthetic dubbing.
**Comments:** Tying instructions follow.

## Making the Foam Wing and Parachute Hackle of Brooks's Sprout *(Flavilinea)*

**1.** Trim the butt of the foam cylinder to an angle. Wind some tight thread turns over the front half of the hook's shank (providing something for the foam to grip). Bind the cylinder atop the shank, tipping forward off the hook's eye. Remember, when tying with foam, use *firm* thread turns—*tight* turns can weaken or cut foam.

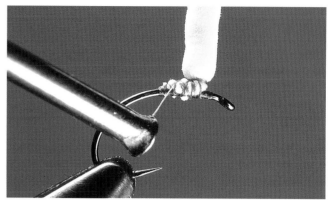

**2.** Take a couple of thread turns around the base of the foam only. Pull the thread back and down the near side of the hook to raise the cylinder to vertical. Keeping the thread taut, wind it around the shank a few times. You'll be winding the thread toward you, over the top of the hook—opposite the normal direction.

**3.** Wind the thread around the base of the cylinder again (wind clockwise, viewed from the top). Pull back on the thread, and then wind it tightly around the shank. You should now be winding the thread in the usual direction. The cylinder is secured upright from both sides, so it will stay centered.

**4.** Mount and, after completing the rest of the fly, complete the parachute hackle, as described for the Little Olive Parachute (instructions on page 63). Trim the cylinder to a short, white spot.

## BROOKS'S SPROUT, *FLAVILINEA* — Bob Brooks

Top view

*Tied by Carol Ann Morris*

**Hook:** Light wire, humped shank (pupa-emerger hook), sizes 16 to 10.
**Thread:** Olive 8/0 or 6/0.
**Parachute wing:** Section of white, round, buoyant closed-cell foam.
**Parachute hackle:** Dyed yellow grizzly.
**Shuck:** Brown Antron over a few mallard-dyed wood-duck fibers.
**Abdomen:** Darkish olive turkey biot (goose biots tend to be too short), with the fringed side out.
**Thorax:** Darkish olive synthetic dubbing.
**Comments:** Tying instructions are on the previous page.

## BROOKS'S SPROUT, MAHOGANY — Bob Brooks

*Tied by Carol Ann Morris*

**Hook:** Light wire, humped shank (pupa-emerger hook), sizes 18 to 12.
**Thread:** Brown 8/0 or 6/0.
**Parachute wing:** Section of white, round, buoyant closed-cell foam.

**Parachute hackle:** Medium blue dun.
**Shuck:** Brown Antron.
**Abdomen:** Mahogany brown turkey biot (goose biots tend to be too short for the larger hook sizes), with the fringed side out.
**Thorax:** Rusty brown fine synthetic dubbing.
**Comments:** Tying instructions are on the previous page.

## BROOKS'S SPROUT, PMD — Bob Brooks

*Tied by Carol Ann Morris*

**Hook:** Light wire, humped shank (pupa-emerger hook), sizes 20 to 14.
**Thread:** Light olive 8/0 or 6/0.
**Parachute wing:** Section of white, round, buoyant closed-cell foam, short.
**Parachute hackle:** Light blue dun.
**Shuck:** Brown Antron.
**Abdomen:** Dyed brown goose biot.
**Thorax:** Light yellowish olive synthetic dubbing.
**Comments:** Tying instructions are on the previous page.

## BROOKS'S SPROUT, TRICO — Bob Brooks

*Tied by Carol Ann Morris*

**Hook:** Light wire, humped shank (pupa-emerger hook), sizes 26 to 18.
**Thread:** Black 8/0 or 6/0.
**Parachute wing:** White, round closed-cell foam, short.
**Parachute hackle:** Black.
**Shuck:** Black Antron.
**Abdomen:** Black goose biot.
**Thorax:** Fine black synthetic dubbing.
**Comments:** Tying instructions are on the previous page.

## CDC SPLIT-WING CRIPPLE, BWO — *Howard Cole*

*Front view*

*Tied by Carol Ann Morris*

**Hook:** Light wire, standard length 1X long, sizes 20 to 14.
**Thread:** Olive dun 8/0.
**Tail:** Wood-duck flank feather fibers over amber Z-lon.
**Abdomen:** Dark olive hackle quill.
**Thorax:** Olive dubbing.
**Wing case:** One dark olive CDC feather.
**Wing:** Black poly yarn.
**Comments:** The wing should be a single length of poly yarn bound just behind and projecting over the hook's eye. To complete the wing and finish the fly, divide the yarn out, up, and back to the sides; then pull the CDC over and down between the wings and bind it behind the eye.

## CDC TRANSITIONAL DUN — *René Harrop*

*Tied by Skip Morris*

**Hook:** Light wire, short shank, size to imitate any mayfly.
**Thread:** 8/0 or 6/0, in a color close to the thorax's color.
**Tail:** Three or four wood-duck fibers, twice the length of the shank. A tuft of hare's mask dubbing projecting back atop the wood-duck fibers.
**Abdomen:** Hare's mask in a color to match that of the natural nymph.
**Thorax:** Any dry-fly dubbing to match the color of the natural dun.
**Wing:** Two CDC feather tips (usually gray, but whatever color matches the natural's wings) set back to back, curving away from each other. The wings should angle up 45 degrees and be somewhat short.
**Legs:** Butts of the CDC feather fibers (cut out the stems), set to the sides and slanting back slightly.
**Comments:** The rear half of the Transitional Dun is a nymph, and the front half is a hatching dun—a half-hatched mayfly. Great idea.

## CDC TUFT EMERGER, TRICO

*Tied by Carol Ann Morris*

**Hook:** Fine wire, humped shank (pupa-emerger hook), sizes 22 to 18.
**Thread:** Brown 8/0 or finer.
**Shuck:** Cream Antron.
**Abdomen:** Fine olive synthetic dubbing.
**Wing:** Dun-color CDC feather, gathered as a short tuft projecting from the top of the thorax.
**Thorax:** Fine dark brown synthetic dubbing.

## EMERGENT CRIPPLE DUN, BROWN — *Shane Stalcup*

*Tied by Al Davis*

| | |
|---|---|
| **Hook:** | Light wire, humped shank (pupa-emerger hook), sizes 22 to 12. |
| **Thread:** | Brown 8/0 or 6/0. |
| **Shuck:** | Tan or medium brown Z-lon yarn or Antron yarn. |
| **Abdomen:** | Small brown D-Rib (or any slim, brown, shiny synthetic body material). |
| **Hackle:** | Brown hen neck or dry-fly hackle, spiraled over the thorax and trimmed on top. |
| **Thorax:** | UV Brown Ice Dub (or some other shiny synthetic dubbing, such as Antron Dubbing, SLF, or Arizona Synthetic Dubbing). |
| **Inner Wing:** | Tuft of the same dubbing used in the thorax. |
| **Wing:** | Brown or mottled brown Medallion sheeting (or another brown synthetic wing sheeting) bound just behind the eye crossways, doubled back along the sides and bound, and trimmed to be rounded on the ends. |
| **Head:** | Same dubbing used in the thorax. |

**Comments:** This brown version of Shane's Emergent Cripple Dun is one of three he presents in his book *Mayflies "Top to Bottom."* The other two are his rust and tan versions.

## FLOATING NYMPH — *René Harrop*

*Tied by Skip Morris*

| | |
|---|---|
| **Hook:** | Light wire, 1X long, sizes 20 to 12. |
| **Thread:** | 8/0 or 6/0 in a color similar to the body color. |
| **Tail:** | Dry-fly hackle fibers, split. |
| **Rib:** | Floss of the natural nymph's color. |
| **Body:** | Antron dubbing of the natural nymph's color. |

| | |
|---|---|
| **Wing case:** | Ball of dark gray poly dubbing spun onto the thread, then slid down in a clump to the hook. The thread is then secured, leaving a ball of poly dubbing to suggest a bulging, splitting wing case. |
| **Legs:** | Dry-fly hackle fibers bound at the sides of the thorax, in the body color. |
| **Head:** | Antron dubbing in the body color. |

**Comments:** Treated with floatant and fished dead drift, René's Floating Nymph suggests a mayfly nymph just beginning to shed its shuck at the surface.

**Foam Emerger.** Craig Mathews says the Blue Ribbon Flies Foam Emergers imitate a range from "emerging dun to stillborn dun to knocked-down semi-awash adult mayfly." He uses them when trout are ignoring intact duns and imitations with distinct wings.

## FOAM *BAETIS* EMERGER — *Blue Ribbon Flies*

*Tied by Craig Mathews*

| | |
|---|---|
| **Hook:** | Light wire, standard length to 1X long, sizes 20 to 16. |
| **Thread:** | Olive 8/0. |
| **Shuck:** | Olive Antron or Z-lon. |
| **Body:** | Olive synthetic dubbing. |
| **Wing case:** | Strip of buoyant gray closed-cell foam sheeting, doubled over the thorax. |
| **Hackle:** | Light blue dun, trimmed flat on the underside about halfway down to the point. |

## FOAM DRAKE MACKEREL EMERGER
### Blue Ribbon Flies

*Front view*

*Tied by Craig Mathews*

| | |
|---|---|
| **Hook:** | Light wire, standard length to 1X long, size 12. |
| **Thread:** | Brown 8/0. |
| **Shuck:** | Amber Z-lon. |
| **Rib:** | Brown single-strand floss, twisted. |
| **Body:** | Tan synthetic dubbing. |
| **Wing case:** | Strip of buoyant gray closed-cell foam sheeting, doubled over the thorax. |
| **Hackle:** | Dyed pale brown grizzly, trimmed flat beneath about halfway down to the point. |
| **Comments:** | "Drake mackerel" is a common name for fall-hatching green drakes. |

## FOAM GREEN DRAKE EMERGER
### Blue Ribbon Flies

*Tied by Craig Mathews*

| | |
|---|---|
| **Hook:** | Light wire, standard length to 1X long, size 12. |
| **Thread:** | Olive 8/0 or 6/0. |
| **Shuck:** | Olive Antron or Z-lon. |
| **Rib:** | Yellow single-strand floss, twisted. |
| **Body:** | Olive synthetic dubbing. |
| **Wing case:** | Strip of black buoyant closed-cell foam, doubled over the thorax. |
| **Hackle:** | Dyed yellow grizzly, trimmed flat underneath about halfway down to the point. |

## FOAM PMD EMERGER
### Blue Ribbon Flies

*Tied by Craig Mathews*

| | |
|---|---|
| **Hook:** | Light wire, standard length to 1X long, sizes 18 to 14. |
| **Thread:** | Yellow 8/0. |
| **Shuck:** | Olive Antron or Z-lon. |
| **Body:** | Light olive-yellow synthetic dubbing. |
| **Wing case:** | Strip of gray buoyant closed-cell foam-sheeting, doubled over the thorax. |
| **Hackle:** | Light blue dun, trimmed flat along the underside about halfway to the point. |

## GREEN DRAKE EMERGER

*Tied by Skip Morris*

| | |
|---|---|
| **Hook:** | Light wire, 2X long, sizes 12 and 10. |
| **Thread:** | Olive or yellow 6/0 or 8/0 . |
| **Tail:** | Moose body. |
| **Rib:** | Heavy yellow thread. |
| **Body:** | Olive dubbing (such as poly dubbing, Super Fine Dry Fly dubbing). |
| **Hackle:** | Grizzly dyed yellowish olive. |
| **Comments:** | Simple, but it works. I've caught some fussy trout on it. |

## HALO EMERGER — *Gary LaFontaine*

*Tied by Skip Morris*

| | |
|---|---|
| **Hook:** | Light wire, standard wire to 1X long, sizes 24 to 8. |
| **Thread:** | 8/0 in a color to match the body color. |
| **Tag:** | Small amount of clear Antron yarn. |
| **Shuck:** | Marabou fibers in a color to match the body. |
| **Thorax:** | Strip of buoyant white closed-cell foam tied atop and across the shank. Trim the foam to short stubs at the sides. |
| **Abdomen:** | Fine poly dubbing in a color to match the natural. Dub around the foam thorax, too. |
| **Wing:** | Elk or deer hair dyed orange. Bind the hair with a thread collar so the tips project forward and the butts project back. Trim the butts straight across over the thorax. |
| **Comments:** | The Halo Emerger suggests a mayfly nymph struggling at the surface to escape its shuck. |

## MINIMAL MAYFLY — *Ralph Headrick*

*Tied by Carol Ann Morris*

| | |
|---|---|
| **Hook:** | Light wire, standard length to 1X long, sizes 22 to 12. |
| **Thread:** | 8/0 or 6/0 in a color to match the body color. |
| **Tail:** | Stiff hackle fibers in a color to match the body. |
| **Body:** | Fine synthetic dubbing in a color to match the natural. |
| **Wing:** | Natural deer body hair, fine texture. |
| **Head:** | Butts of the wing trimmed straight across. |

**Morris Emerger.** If the Compara-dun and the Quigley Cripple hadn't come along first, the Morris Emerger—a hybrid of the two—wouldn't exist. It is a particularly buoyant emerger (especially if you rub floatant into the trimmed hair butts as well as the wing and thorax) that has proven itself on some tough rainbows, cutthroats, and brown trout in several western states. I normally fish the Morris Emergers dead drift during mayfly hatches to rising trout, but you can twitch the fly if that awakens the trout's interest. The flat, tipped wing keeps the fly riding high on a pull of the tippet, just as an upswept bow makes a boat skim the waves. This fly floats stubbornly, catches smart trout, and skims rather than dives on a tug—what more could you want?

## MORRIS EMERGER, *BAETIS* — *Skip Morris*

*Tied by Carol Ann Morris*

| | |
|---|---|
| **Hook:** | Light wire, humped shank (pupa-emerger hook), sizes 22 to 16. |
| **Thread:** | Olive 8/0. |
| **Tail:** | Brown mottled hen saddle, or brown partridge or pheasant tail. |

**Abdomen:**    Dark brown rabbit.
**Thorax:**       Olive synthetic dubbing.
**Wing, legs and burst shuck:** Natural dark coastal deer hair.
**Comments:**   Tying instructions below.

**MORRIS EMERGER, GREEN DRAKE** *Skip Morris*

*Tied by Skip Morris*

**Hook:**        Light wire, humped shank (pupa-emerger hook),
                 sizes 12 to 8.
**Thread:**      Green 8/0 or 6/0.
**Tail:**        Dark olive or brown hen saddle.
**Abdomen:**     Two olive and one brown ostrich herl, twisted in a dubbing
                 loop of thread (Instructions are on page 95). Trim the top
                 and bottom sides if you wish.
**Thorax:**      Buoyant olive synthetic dubbing. (Optional: rib the abdomen
                 with twisted yellow flat-waxed nylon or yellow Super Floss.
                 Or build the olive thorax back to the abdomen; then heavily
                 wax the thread and spin fine yellow dubbing thinly on it, and
                 rib forward over the thorax.)
**Wing, legs, and burst shuck:** Natural dark coastal deer hair.
**Comments:**    Tying instructions below.

## Tying the Morris Emerger (Morris Emerger, PMD)

*(See video instructions on DVD.)*

**1.** Tip the hook down slightly. Bind the tail fibers down the shank. The tails should be about one-half to two-thirds of the total hook length. Bind on the rib wire and then the pheasant tail fibers. Trim off the butts of the tail fibers.

**2.** Spiral the thread to slightly past halfway up the shank. Wind the pheasant up to the thread and then bind and trim it. Wind the wire as ribs up the pheasant, winding opposite the normal direction. Bind the wire at the front of the pheasant abdomen, and trim off the end of the wire.

**3.** Dub a full thorax, but leave plenty of bare hook shank behind the hook's eye, at least $1/16$ inch.

**4.** Angle the hook up to level or tipping slightly up. Wind a couple of tight layers of thread between the thorax and the eye. End with the thread at the front of the thorax.

**5.** Comb the short fibers and fuzz from the butts of some coastal deer hair. Even the hair in a hair-stacking tool. Hold the hair atop the hook, work two turns of thread around the hair at the front of the thorax, and pull the turns tight.

**6.** Add at least a dozen more tight turns of thread as a narrow collar (this collar is the only thing holding the wing). Raise the butts of the hair and trim them straight across, at the rear of the thorax.

**7.** Press the wing firmly upright with your thumbnail; then pull the hair back and make a thread head that pushes back against the hair. This thread head is the only thing holding the wing upright, so make it large and tight. Trim the sides of the hair butts if they flare out too far to the sides. The completed wing, once teased back into place, should angle forward slightly, 45 degrees at most. Add head cement to the thread head (and to the thread collar if you want).

**MORRIS EMERGER, PMD**      *Skip Morris*

Front view

*Tied by Skip Morris*

| | |
|---|---|
| **Hook:** | Light wire, humped shank (pupa-emerger hook), sizes 18 to 14. |
| **Thread:** | Yellow 8/0. |
| **Tail:** | Brown mottled hen back. |
| **Abdomen:** | Pheasant tail (or dark brown rabbit, dubbed). |
| **Thorax:** | Light yellow (or soft yellow with a touch of olive) synthetic dubbing. |

**Wing, legs, and burst shuck:** Bleached (or natural pale) coastal deer hair.

**Comments:** Tying instructions start on previous page.

## NO-HACKLE STILLBORN    *Swisher and Richards*

**Top view**

*Tied by Skip Morris*

**Hook:**       Fine wire, standard length or 1X long, sizes 22 to 12.
**Thread:**     8/0 or 6/0 in a color similar to the thorax color.
**Shuck:**      Hen hackle trimmed to shape (light to dark, depending on the natural). The hackle should be trimmed to slender with a "V" of fibers as shuck tails.
**Abdomen:**    Same dubbing as the thorax.
**Wing:**       Duck quill sections.
**Thorax:**     Synthetic dubbing to match the body color of the natural.
**Comments:**   There are lots of Swisher and Richards stillborn variations—hair shuck, poly-yarn shuck, hackle-tip wings, duck shoulder wings—but this no-hackle version is as established as any. A "stillborn" insect, according to Swisher and Richards, is an adult that failed to fully hatch and lies helplessly trapped in its shuck. For instructions on making the wings, see "Tying the No-Hackle" on page 67.

**Parasol Emerger.** Ted Leeson and Jim Schollmeyer's Parasol series is not so much a new concept as a new angle on a seldom-explored concept—a nymph or emerger hanging from a built-in pontoon. Their puff of yarn on a strand of tippet is quick, simple, and functional. The idea is to suggest a nymph, ripe to hatch, just short of reaching the water's surface.

## PARASOL PHEASANT TAIL
### *Ted Leeson and Jim Schollmeyer*

*Tied by Ted Leeson*

**Hook:**       Light wire, standard length or 1X long, sizes 18 to 14.
**Thread:**     Brown 8/0 or 6/0.
**Parasol:**    Light gray poly yarn tied with a clinch knot to 4X tippet. (Instructions follow.)
**Tail:**       Pheasant tail fibers.
**Rib:**        Fine copper (or gold) wire.
**Abdomen:**    Pheasant tail fibers.
**Thorax:**     Peacock herl.
**Legs:**       Mottled brown hen back hackle fibers or pheasant tail fibers.
**Comments:**   This flexible emerger imitates a number of mayfly nymphs when it's tied in different sizes.

## Making the Parasol of a Parasol Emerger (Parasol PMD/BWO)

*(See video instructions on DVD.)*

**1.** Tie an improved clinch knot tightly around the center of a 2-inch section of poly yarn with a short length of tippet. Trim off the tag end of the tippet.

**2.** Comb out the ends of the yarn to make it fluffy.

**3.** Bind on the tippet about two-thirds up the shank, leaving about ¼ inch or slightly more bare tippet remaining to the yarn. Trim off the butt of the tippet.

**4.** Make the tail and abdomen, pull the yarn and tippet firmly back, and build tight thread turns against the front of the tippet—this should secure the tippet upright.

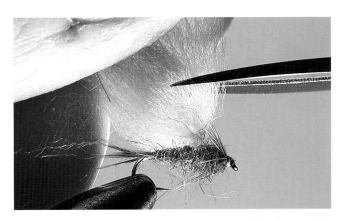

**5.** Gather the ends of the yarn and pull them firmly up. Snip them straight across. The result should be a dense puff of yarn, rounded on top, suspended above the fly by a little bit of tippet.

## PARASOL PMD/BWO    *Ted Leeson and Jim Schollmeyer*

*Tied by Ted Leeson*

**Hook:** Light wire, standard length or 1X long, sizes 20 to 16.
**Thread:** Brown 8/0 or 6/0.
**Parasol:** Two lengths of light gray poly yarn tied with a clinch knot to 4X tippet for hooks size 16 and larger; one section of 5X for hooks size 18 and smaller. (Instructions start on the previous page.)
**Tail:** Mottled brown hen back hackle fibers.
**Rib:** Fine gold (or copper) wire.
**Abdomen:** Arizona Synthetic Golden Peacock Dubbing (or any olive-brown or golden brown dubbing).
**Thorax:** Dark brown dubbing of any kind (rabbit is good).
**Legs:** Mottled brown hen back hackle fibers.
**Comments:** The nymphs of the PMD and BWO mayflies are close in appearance and overlap in their size range, making this an effective imitation of both.

## P. T. EMERGER, PALE MORNING DUN    *Mike Lawson*

*Tied by Al Davis*

**Hook:** Light wire, standard length or 1X long, sizes 22 to 10.
**Thread:** Brown or black 8/0 or 6/0.
**Tail:** Rust-colored Z-lon.
**Back:** Rust-colored Z-lon.
**Rib:** Fine copper wire.
**Abdomen:** Pheasant tail.
**Thorax:** Fine pale yellow synthetic dubbing.
**Wing:** Two CDC feather tips, natural color or dyed dun, over dun-gray Z-lon.
**Legs:** Partridge.
**Head:** Same dubbing as for the thorax.

## PUFF EMERGER, BWO

*Tied by Skip Morris*

| | |
|---|---|
| **Hook:** | Light wire, humped shank (pupa-emerger hook), sizes 22 to 16. |
| **Thread:** | Olive 8/0. |
| **Wing:** | Natural gray CDC fibers, torn from the stem in a bunch, bound crossways atop the hook, then gathered upright as a fluffy tuft. Trim the tuft to a length about equal to the gape's width using a straight, horizontal snip of the scissors. |
| **Shuck:** | A few of the wing fibers bound back along the shank to the bend, trimmed about a gape's width. |
| **Body:** | Fine olive synthetic dubbing. |

**Comments:** This is just one of many possible versions of the Puff Emerger—change colors, change size, and you've got a fly for the PMD or March brown hatch or just about any other mayfly. It hangs from its wing; no floatant required.

**Quigley Cripple.** Since Bob Quigley developed the Quigley Cripple for those contrary trout in California's Fall River way back in the mid-1980s, the fly has been building a legion of followers. It hangs half submerged in the water, the nymph half below the surface and the hatching dun half up in the air.

## QUIGLEY CRIPPLE, GREEN DRAKE  *Bob Quigley*

*Tied by Carol Ann Morris*

| | |
|---|---|
| **Hook:** | Light wire, standard length or 1X long, sizes 14 to 10. |
| **Thread:** | Yellow 8/0 or 6/0. |

| | |
|---|---|
| **Shuck:** | Brown Antron or Z-lon. |
| **Rib:** | Yellow floss twisted with one strand of pearl Flashabou. |
| **Abdomen:** | Olive-brown hare's ear. |
| **Thorax:** | Green deer hair, flared and trimmed, or green synthetic dubbing. |

**Wing and burst wing case:** Natural dark deer hair.

| | |
|---|---|
| **Hackle:** | Grizzly dyed yellow. |

**Comments:** A stacked section of hair is bound, tips forward, with a narrow thread collar, atop the hook in front of the thorax. The butts of the hair are trimmed off at the rear of the thorax, straight across. The hackle is wound mainly over the thread collar, and then a turn or two added in front of the wing.

## QUIGLEY CRIPPLE, MAHOGANY DUN BIOT CRIPPLE  *Bob Quigley*

*Tied by Carol Ann Morris*

| | |
|---|---|
| **Hook:** | Light to standard wire, 2X long, slow-curve shank, sizes 14 and 12. |
| **Thread:** | Dark brown or black 8/0 or 6/0. |
| **Shuck:** | Brown Z-lon or Antron. |
| **Rib:** | Dark brown 3/0 thread. |
| **Abdomen:** | Dark brown goose (or turkey) biot. |
| **Thorax:** | Dark brown synthetic dubbing. |

**Wing and burst wing case:** Dyed black or slate gray deer or elk hair.

| | |
|---|---|
| **Hackle:** | Black or slate gray. |

**Comments:** For tying instructions, see the comments under Quigley Cripple, Green Drake, above.

## QUIGLEY CRIPPLE, OLIVE MARABOU  *Bob Quigley*

*Tied by Skip Morris*

| | |
|---|---|
| **Hook:** | Light wire, standard length or 1X long, sizes 20 to 12. |
| **Thread:** | Light olive 8/0 or 6/0. |
| **Shuck:** | Olive marabou. |
| **Rib:** | Fine gold wire. |

**Abdomen:** Olive marabou.

**Thorax:** Light olive or yellow flared and shaped deer hair or synthetic dubbing.

**Wing and burst wing case:** Natural medium tan-gray deer hair.

**Hackle:** Dyed yellow-olive grizzly or light blue dun.

**Comments:** This is an anomaly: a general-purpose Quigley Cripple for imitating various mayflies with an olive cast. For tying instructions, see the comments under the Quigley Cripple, Green Drake, on the previous page.

### QUIGLEY CRIPPLE, PMD — *Bob Quigley*

*Tied by Skip Morris*

**Hook:** Light wire, standard length or 1X long, sizes 18 to 14.

**Thread:** Olive or yellow 8/0 or 6/0.

**Shuck:** Brown Z-lon or marabou.

**Rib:** Fine copper or red wire.

**Abdomen:** Pheasant tail fibers.

**Thorax:** Pale yellow synthetic dubbing.

**Wing and burst wing case:** Natural or dyed light blue dun elk hair.

**Hackle:** Natural golden ginger or cream.

**Comments:** For tying instructions, see the comments under the Quigley Cripple, Green Drake, on the previous page.

### RS2 — *Rim Chung*

*Tied by Carol Ann Morris*

**Hook:** Light wire, short shank to 1X long, ring-eye, sizes 24 to 12.

**Thread:** Brown 8/0.

**Tail:** Dark dun Microfibetts.

**Body:** Muskrat fur.

**Wing:** Dark dun fluff from the base of saddle hackle, short. The wing should angle upward.

**Comments:** Many tiers prefer CDC for the wing. The RS2 has become a very popular broad-use imitation of an emerging mayfly.

**Smith's CDC Emerger.** Smith's CDC Emergers hang their nymphal abdomens below the surface while being buoyed by their dubbed thoraxes and parachute hackles—the posture of a partially hatched mayfly.

### SMITH'S CDC EMERGER, BWO/FLAV — *Todd Smith*

*Tied by Todd Smith*

**Hook:** Light wire, humped shank (pupa-emerger hook), sizes 22 to 18 for BWOs, sizes 16 and 14 for flavs.

**Thread:** Tan 8/0.

**Tail:** Three lemon wood-duck fibers.

**Shuck:** Brown synthetic dubbing, short (Antron, poly, Super Fine Dry Fly, or similar).

**Abdomen:** Dyed brown goose biot.

**Wing:** Medium or dark dun CDC. (Instructions are on page 70.)

**Thorax:** Olive-gray synthetic dubbing (Super Fine Dry Fly, poly, Antron, or similar).

**Hackle:** Grizzly dyed dun.

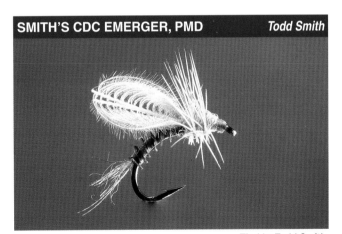

### SMITH'S CDC EMERGER, PMD — *Todd Smith*

*Tied by Todd Smith*

**Hook:** Light wire, humped shank (pupa-emerger hook), sizes 18 and 16.

**Thread:** Yellow 8/0.

**Tail:** Three lemon wood-duck flank fibers.

**Shuck:** Rust synthetic dubbing, short (Antron, poly, Super Fine Dry Fly, or similar).

**Abdomen:** Dyed rust goose biot.

**Wing:** Light dun CDC. (Instructions are on page 70.)

**Thorax:** Pale yellow fine synthetic dubbing with a touch of light olive.

**Hackle:** Light ginger.

**Smith's Freestone Cripple.** Todd Smith's views on mayflies that fail to hatch—what fly fishers call "cripples"—are neat and plausible. First, he believes that because trout recognize cripples as the easiest prey and consequently learn to identify their subtleties among the hatching insects, imitations must be exact. Second, Todd believes that especially in "freestone" rivers, which are formed by runoff and are typically swifter and choppier than spring-fed rivers, buoyant materials must be applied strategically to keep the fly afloat while maintaining the correct posture. It's easy to see how his Smith's Freestone Cripple is a logical result of these views.

## SMITH'S FREESTONE CRIPPLE, PMD    *Todd Smith*

*Tied by Todd Smith*

| | |
|---|---|
| **Hook:** | Light wire, standard length to 1X long, sizes 18 to 14. |
| **Thread:** | Yellow 8/0. |
| **Tail:** | Lemon wood-duck fibers. |
| **Shuck:** | Dyed tan natural dubbing (rabbit, hare's mask, squirrel). |
| **Abdomen:** | Reddish brown goose biot. |
| **Wing:** | Dyed dun yearling elk. |
| **Hackle:** | Light ginger. |
| **Thorax:** | Olive-yellow synthetic dubbing. |
| **Comments:** | For tying instructions, see the comments under Smith's Freestone Cripple, BWO/Flav on this page. |

## SMITH'S FREESTONE CRIPPLE, BWO/FLAV
### *Todd Smith*

*Tied by Todd Smith*

| | |
|---|---|
| **Hook:** | Light wire, standard length to 1X long, sizes 22 to 18 for BWOs, sizes 16 and 14 for Flavs. |
| **Thread:** | Tan 8/0. |
| **Tail:** | Lemon wood-duck fibers. |
| **Shuck:** | Tuft of dyed red-brown natural dubbing (rabbit, hare's mask, squirrel). |
| **Abdomen:** | Brown goose biot. |
| **Wing:** | Dyed dun yearling elk. |
| **Hackle:** | Grizzly dyed dun. |
| **Thorax:** | Fine olive synthetic dubbing. |
| **Comments:** | To make the wing and thorax, trim or part the hackle fibers on top of the thorax, fold the wing forward over the thorax, and bind the wing with a narrow hackle collar. |

## SOUTH PLATTE QUIGLEY    *Scott Fraser*

*Tied by Carol Ann Morris*

| | |
|---|---|
| **Hook:** | Light wire, humped shank (pupa-emerger hook), size 18 or 20. |
| **Thread:** | Olive-brown 6/0 (or 8/0). |
| **Shuck:** | Five or six strands of white Z-lon. |
| **Abdomen:** | The tying thread. |
| **Thorax:** | Synthetic brown-olive dubbing. |
| **Wing:** | Bleached coastal deer or fine, bleached elk trimmed on both ends. |
| **Hackle:** | Light blue dun. |
| **Comments:** | A variation of the Quigley Cripple, designed to imitate *Baetis*. |

# Mayfly Duns

**Bunse Dun.** An especially lightweight foam fly with a Compara-dun wing, the Bunse Dun rides high and fools trout (I've proven this to my own satisfaction). The extended foam body, even with the short-shank hook, makes the fly at least a size larger than its hook size.

### BUNSE GREEN DRAKE DUN — Richard Bunse

*Tied by Skip Morris*

| | |
|---|---|
| **Hook:** | Light wire, short shank, size 12. |
| **Thread:** | Yellow 8/0 or 6/0. |
| **Body:** | Ethafoam sheeting, about $3/32$ inch thick, colored with a green marking pen. |
| **Tail:** | Two mink tail, nutria, or beaver guard hairs. |
| **Wing:** | Natural dark coastal deer hair. |
| **Comments:** | Tying instructions are on page 58. |

### BUNSE LITTLE OLIVE DUN — Richard Bunse

*Tied by Skip Morris*

| | |
|---|---|
| **Hook:** | Light wire, short shank, sizes 20 and 18. |
| **Thread:** | Olive 8/0. |
| **Body:** | Ethafoam sheeting, $3/64$ inch thick, colored olive with a marking pen. |
| **Tail:** | Two mink tail, nutria, or beaver guard hairs. |
| **Wing:** | Natural gray coastal deer hair. |
| **Comments:** | "Little olive" is another common name for the *Baetis* mayfly. Tying instructions are on page 58. |

### BUNSE MARCH BROWN DUN — Richard Bunse

*Tied by Skip Morris*

| | |
|---|---|
| **Hook:** | Light wire, short shank, sizes 18 and 16. |
| **Thread:** | Yellow 8/0 or 6/0. |
| **Body:** | Ethafoam sheeting, $3/64$ inch thick for size 18 and $1/16$ inch thick for size 16, colored ocher (dark yellow) with a marking pen. |
| **Tail:** | Two mink tail, nutria, or beaver guard hairs. |
| **Wing:** | Natural dark (preferably brownish) coastal deer hair. |
| **Comments:** | Tying instructions are on page 58. |

### CLARK'S PALE EVENING DUN — Lee Clark

*Tied by Carol Ann Morris*

| | |
|---|---|
| **Hook:** | Light wire, standard length or 1X long, sizes 16 to 12. |
| **Thread:** | Tan 8/0 or 6/0. |
| **Body:** | One strand each of pale yellow and tan macramé or poly yarn twisted, then doubled, to make a body. The twisted yarn is bound atop the hook about two-thirds up the shank. |
| **Parachute wing:** | The butts of the yarn, set upright and trimmed to wing shape. (Instructions are on page 63.) |
| **Parachute hackle:** | Light blue dun. (Instructions are on page 63.) |

# Tying the Bunse Dun
# (Pale Morning Dun)

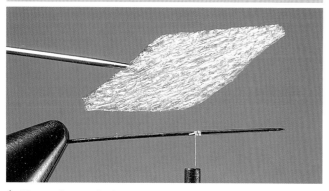

**1.** Mount a fine needle (called a beading needle, which you can buy at a fabric or sewing store) in your vise. Color some whitish, pebbly Ethafoam sheeting (used in packing) with a marking pen. Cut a diamond shape from the foam—the diamond should be three full hook lengths long and slightly over one full hook length wide. Start the thread on the needle and trim off the thread's end.

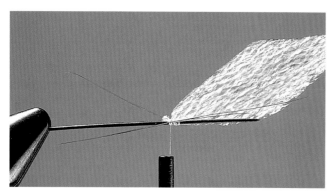

**2.** Bind the tip of the triangle on the far side of the needle. The uncolored surface of the foam should face you. Bind one tail hair along each side of the needle.

**3.** Raise the foam, wind the thread a couple of turns down the needle and hairs, lower the foam, and bind it with a couple of thread turns. Use firm but not tight thread turns over the foam—tight turns will cut or weaken it. Keep building foam sections down the needle in this manner until there are four (including the tip of the foam). Half-hitch the thread and trim it slightly long. Then slide the foam abdomen off the needle.

**4.** Remove the needle from your vise, mount a hook, and start the thread. Make a Compara-dun wing in the center of the shank (see instructions on page 59). Wind the thread to the bend and half-hitch it, but don't cut the thread.

**5.** Remove the hook from the vise. Push the point of the hook down into the center of the last segment of the abdomen. The hook point should come out the center of the last section, opposite the abdomen's seam. Mount the hook back in your vise. Wind two turns of thread over the half-hitched thread on the foam, at the front of the last segment.

**6.** Pull the front of the foam down out of the way. Spiral the thread to the hook's eye, over the butts of the tail fibers. Pull the foam up to the eye and bind it there. Trim off the end of the foam.

**7.** Wind the thread back over the foam; make a turn of thread. Wind the thread back between the rear of the wing and the bend *under* the foam; make a turn or two of thread. Wind the thread forward under the foam again; make another turn between the wing and the hook's eye, over the first turn. Return the thread over the foam to the eye. Whip-finish and trim the thread.

**8.** Cut a slit straight down through the foam on either side of the hair. Pull the hair down into the slits to re-form the Compara-dun wing.

**9.** Tease a little Dave's Flexament (thinned to about three parts thinner to one part Flexament) over the entire body to lock on the color (the liquid will tend to flow out on its own). Add a small drop on the thread head, on the base of the tails, and in the slots along the sides of the thorax holding the wing hair.

---

**BUNSE PALE MORNING DUN**          **Richard Bunse**

*Tied by Skip Morris*

| | |
|---|---|
| **Hook:** | Light wire, short shank, size 18. |
| **Thread:** | Yellow 8/0. |
| **Body:** | Ethafoam sheeting, $3/64$ inch thick, colored pale yellow. |
| **Tail:** | Two mink tail, nutria, or beaver guard hairs. |
| **Wing:** | Bleached coastal deer hair. |
| **Comments:** | Tying instructions begin on previous page. |

**Compara-dun.** Francis Betters's Haystack dry fly of the 1940s inspired the Compara-dun, which emerged in the 1970s as the key fly pattern in Al Caucci and Bob Nastasi's *Hatches.* The Compara-dun may look odd to anglers, but viewed from below—from the trout's perspective—its split tails, slim body, splay of hair legs (the hairs splay after a few casts), and upright wing hair convincingly suggest a mayfly dun. Many fly fishers had doubts about the wing of fanned hair, but the trout settled the matter right away—angler-shy clear-water trout kept falling for Compara-duns, and they still do.

## Tying a Compara-dun Wing (Compara-dun *Flavinea*)

**1.** Start the thread tightly about two-thirds up the shank. Build a tight layer or two of thread as a foundation for the wing. Cut a small bunch of coastal deer hair (a fine, not too soft hair—most deer hair flares too wildly). Hold the hair by its tips and comb out the short fibers and fuzz from the butts. Stack the hair in a hair-stacking tool. Measure the hair against the hook—note the point on the hair, down from its tips, that equals the distance from the tip of the hook's eye to the middle of its bend.

**2.** Bind the hair, by its measured point, atop and about two-thirds up the shank. Add a few tight thread turns, then trim the butts of the hair to taper back and end just before the bend.

**3.** Bind the butts of the hair, and then make split tails (instructions are on page 80). Dub the body up to the rear of the hair wing.

**4.** Push the hair firmly up and back with your thumbnail—really crease the hair at its base.

**5.** Hold the hair firmly back and build lots of tight thread turns against the base of the hair to set it upright.

**6.** Dub a tapered abdomen. Dub back and forth under the wing, then in front of the wing, and complete a standard thread head.

**7.** Front view of a Compara-dun wing.

## COMPARA-DUN, *FLAVILINEA*
### *Al Caucci and Bob Nastasi*

*Tied by Carol Ann Morris*

**Hook:** Light wire, standard length or 1X long, sizes 14 and 12.
**Thread:** Black 8/0 or 6/0.
**Wing/legs:** Natural dark coastal deer hair as a fan.
**Tail:** Dark brown hackle fibers.
**Body:** Dark brownish olive fine synthetic dubbing.
**Comments:** Tying instructions begin on previous page.

## COMPARA-DUN, GREEN DRAKE
### *Al Caucci and Bob Nastasi*

*Tied by Carol Ann Morris*

| | |
|---|---|
| **Hook:** | Light wire, standard length or 1X long, sizes 14 to 10. |
| **Thread:** | Olive 8/0 or 6/0. |
| **Wing:** | Natural dark coastal deer hair. |
| **Tail:** | Dark brown hackle fibers. |
| **Body:** | Brownish olive synthetic dubbing (I prefer medium to light green or olive). |
| **Comments:** | Tying instructions are on page 59. |

## COMPARA-DUN, MARCH BROWN
### *Al Caucci and Bob Nastasi*

*Front view*

*Tied by Skip Morris*

| | |
|---|---|
| **Hook:** | Light wire, standard length or 1X long, sizes 16 to 12. |
| **Thread:** | Tan 8/0 or 6/0. |
| **Wing:** | Natural medium-hue coastal deer hair. |
| **Tail:** | Brown hackle fibers, split. |
| **Body:** | Tan synthetic dubbing. |
| **Comments:** | Based on Caucci and Nastasi's design, this western March brown version seemed to evolve on its own. Tying instructions are on page 59. |

## COMPARA-DUN, PALE MORNING DUN
### *Al Caucci and Bob Nastasi*

*Tied by Carol Ann Morris*

| | |
|---|---|
| **Hook:** | Light wire, standard length or 1X long, sizes 18 to 14. |
| **Thread:** | Olive 8/0 or 6/0. |
| **Wing:** | Natural light (or bleached) coastal deer hair. |
| **Tail:** | Medium blue dun hackle fibers. |
| **Body:** | Fine yellow-olive synthetic dubbing. |
| **Comments:** | Tying instructions are on page 59. |

## FALL RIVER
### *Patrick Butler*

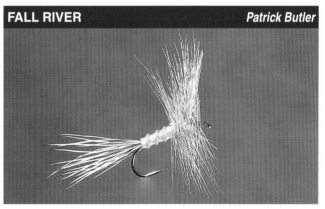

*Front view*

*Tied by Carol Ann Morris*

| | |
|---|---|
| **Hook:** | Light wire, standard length or 1X long, sizes 18 to 12. |
| **Thread:** | Light yellow 8/0 or 6/0. |
| **Wing:** | Barred lemon wood duck, upright and divided. |
| **Tail:** | Natural light tan elk hair. |
| **Rib:** | Yellow (or darkish yellow) thread. |
| **Body:** | Light yellow tying thread or floss. |
| **Hackle:** | Light ginger. |
| **Comments:** | This is an old California standard, developed on the legendary spring creek for which it was named. It sure looks like a PMD mayfly dun, and has probably been used to imitate one more often than not. |

## GULPER SPECIAL                                        *Al Troth*

*Tied by Skip Morris*

**Hook:**      Light wire, standard length to 1X long, sizes 22 to 12.
**Thread:**    8/0 or 6/0 in a color to blend with the body (brown 8/0 for *Tricorythodes*).
**Parachute wing:** Poly yarn in white, orange, yellow, or green (whatever color you can see best. Tying instructions are on page 63.)
**Tail:**      Hackle fibers, same color as the parachute hackle.
**Parachute hackle:** Any reasonable mayfly color (instructions on page 63).
**Body:**      Synthetic dubbing.
**Comments:** I've used Troth's Gulper Special with an olive body and grizzly or blue dun hackle and tail mainly for hatches of tiny *Baetis* mayflies. However, you can pick a mayfly from tiny to large and match it with a Gulper of appropriate size and color.

## ISONYCHIA BICOLOR                              *Polly Rosborough*

*Front view*

*Tied by Al Davis*

**Hook:**      Light wire, standard length or 1X long, size 8.
**Thread:**    Tan 8/0 or 6/0.
**Wing:**      Black hackle tips, upright and divided.
**Tail:**      Dyed brown cock ring-necked pheasant body plumage fibers (often called "church window" feathers).
**Rib:**       Yellow 3/0 tying thread.
**Body:**      Burgundy wine synthetic yarn (or dubbing).
**Hackle:**    One dyed yellow, the other deep purplish dun-gray (or dark blue dun). The yellow hackle trimmed down to 3/16 inch is spiraled in two turns behind and two in front of the wings, so that the main hackle can be wound through it.
**Comments:** Dave Hughes and Rick Hafele say in *Western Mayfly Hatches* that Isonychia bicolor doesn't live in western rivers and believe Polly mistook it for the *Ameletus* mayfly—an easy mistake back in the days when little had been written about western entomology for the fly fisher (though there are other species of *Isonychia* in western rivers). In fact, *Ameletus* lives in shallow water and crawls out to escape its shuck—uncommon for a mayfly—which makes it an elusive hatch for trout. Still, Polly was a sharp fisherman and considered this a mayfly worth imitating. Draw your own conclusions.

## Making a Parachute Wing and Hackle (Little Olive Parachute)

*(See video instructions on DVD.)*

**1.** This method for making a parachute hackle is my own—it's the easiest I know of and achieves the neatest and most durable results. Start the thread and then bind a combed and stacked bunch of hair about three-quarters up the shank. Trim the butts of the hair to a taper and bind them.

**2.** Add the tail. Pull the wing hair firmly up and back, and then crease it upright with your thumbnail.

**3.** Work a few turns of thread—counterclockwise from a top-view—around the base of the wing, and then pull the thread back firmly to secure the wing upright. Maintaining thread tension, lower the thread on the near side of the hook and make a few tight thread turns to lock the thread on. Make these turns opposite the normal direction—that is, toward you over the top of the shank.

**4.** Now the wing is locked upright, but from only one side, and thread tension will tend to pull it to that side. To set the wing from the other side, make a couple of thread turns around the wing—clockwise from the top view this time. Pull the thread back and down the far side of the shank. Maintain thread tension as you wind a few turns of thread around the shank.

**5.** Wind a layer of thread up the base of the wing as far as you plan to wind the hackle, but use only light tension. Wind the thread counterclockwise, viewed from the top. Wind a second layer of thread back down the base of the wing using light but slightly heavier tension.

**6.** Hold the stripped stem of the hackle against the thread layers, and wind another layer up and then down the base of the wing and the stem of the hackle. You should be able to make the thread tension quite firm this time around.

**7.** Draw the hackle's stem back and bind it a little way back along the shank; then trim it off. Dub the body up to just behind the eye.

**8.** Wind the hackle, counterclockwise viewed from the top, down to the body in close turns.

**9.** Drape the hackle's tip, and the hackle pliers, over the far side of the shank behind the eye. Pull the wing firmly back, and wind a few turns of thread over the hackle's tip. Trim off the tip, and complete a thread head.

**10.** Tug and tease the wing and hackle back into position. Add head cement to the thread head. (You may find it easier to add the head cement before pulling the wing and hackle back up.)

**LITTLE OLIVE PARACHUTE**                                              *Dave Hughes*

*Tied by Skip Morris*

**Hook:**       Light wire, standard length or 1X long, sizes 22 to 16.
**Thread:**     Olive 8/0.
**Parachute wing:** White calf tail.
**Tail:**       Blue dun hackle fibers, split.
**Parachute hackle:** Blue dun, parachute style.
**Body:**       Olive dun synthetic dubbing.
**Comments:**   Imitates the blue-winged olive. Tying instructions begin on previous page.

**LOOP WING ADAMS** — *Andre Puyans*

*Front view*

*Tied by Carol Ann Morris*

| | |
|---|---|
| **Hook:** | Light wire, standard length or 1X long, sizes 18 to 12. |
| **Thread:** | Gray or black 8/0 or 6/0. |
| **Tail:** | Grizzly and brown hackle fibers, mixed. |
| **Wing:** | Two slim sections of mallard flank. |
| **Body:** | Muskrat (or gray synthetic dubbing). |
| **Hackle:** | Brown and grizzly, one wound though the other. |

**Comments:** Bind both wing sections projecting back over the body from the center of the thorax area, loop the sections forward, and then bind them both close to where they were first bound on, resulting in two loop wings. Manipulate the sections into two upright parted wings, using thread turns against, between, or even around the wings. This is another variation of the ever-popular Adams dry fly—and a good one.

**Morris May.** For more than a decade the Morris May was my standard mayfly imitation; now I reach for the Morris Emerger more often for mayfly hatches. Still, lots of difficult trout have fallen to Morris Mays, and they're easy flies to tie. Both the light and dark versions in appropriate sizes will match all types of mayflies, but specific imitations may have an edge.

**MORRIS MAY, DARK** — *Skip Morris*

*Tied by Skip Morris*

| | |
|---|---|
| **Hook:** | Light wire, standard length or 1X long, sizes 24 to 10. |
| **Thread:** | Brown 8/0 or 6/0. |
| **Tail:** | Brown hackle fibers, split (or a shuck of brown Antron or Z-lon). |
| **Abdomen:** | Brown poly dubbing (or another synthetic dubbing). |
| **Wing:** | Gray poly yarn in a bunch, trimmed straight across or to a point. |
| **Hackle:** | One brown, spiraled over the thorax and trimmed beneath. |
| **Thorax:** | Same as the abdomen. |

**Comments:** Bind the wing on after completing the abdomen. The yarn should lie back over the abdomen, and the butts of the yarn should be trimmed to a taper and bound over the thorax area. Set the wing upright (or leaning slightly back over the abdomen) in the same way you would set a parachute hackle wing upright, but in reverse, with the wing butts forward (instructions are on page 63).

## MORRIS MAY, GREEN DRAKE — *Skip Morris*

*Tied by Carol Ann Morris*

Hook: Light wire, standard length or 1X long, sizes 12 and 10.
Thread: Olive (or yellow) 8/0 or 6/0.
Tail: Green or grizzly-dyed green hackle fibers, split (or a shuck of brown Antron or Z-lon yarn).
Rib: Stout yellow thread (flat waxed nylon, size A rod thread, or embroidery thread).
Abdomen: Olive poly dubbing (or another synthetic dubbing).
Wing: Black poly yarn in a bunch, trimmed straight across or to a point (a slim section of yellow yarn can be added in front of the black for visibility).
Hackle: One grizzly dyed olive, spiraled over the thorax and then trimmed to a shallow "V" underneath.
Thorax: Same as the abdomen.
Comments: For tying instructions, see the comments under the Morris May Dark on page 65.

## MORRIS MAY, LIGHT — *Skip Morris*

*Tied by Skip Morris*

Hook: Light wire, standard length or 1X long, sizes 24 to 10.
Thread: Tan 8/0 or 6/0.
Tail: Ginger hackle fibers, split (or a shuck of tan Antron or Z-lon).
Abdomen: Tan synthetic dubbing.
Wing: Gray poly yarn in a bunch, trimmed straight across or to a point.
Hackle: One ginger, spiraled over the thorax and trimmed beneath.

Thorax: Same as the abdomen.
Comments: For tying instructions, see the comments under the Morris May Dark on page 65.

## MORRIS MAY MARCH BROWN — *Skip Morris*

*Front view*

*Tied by Carol Ann Morris*

Hook: Light wire, standard length or 1X long, sizes 14 and 12.
Thread: Tan 8/0 or 6/0.
Tail: Brown hackle fibers, split (or a shuck of brown Antron or Z-lon).
Abdomen: Tan synthetic dubbing.
Wing: Tan and brown poly yarn mixed, in a bunch, trimmed straight across or to a point.
Hackle: One brown, spiraled over the thorax and trimmed to a shallow "V" beneath.
Thorax: Same as the abdomen.
Comments: For tying instructions, see the comments under the Morris May Dark on page 65.

**MORRIS MAY, PMD**  *Skip Morris*

*Tied by Carol Ann Morris*

**Hook:** Light wire, standard length or 1X long, sizes 18 to 14.
**Thread:** Yellow 8/0.
**Tail:** Ginger hackle fibers, split (or a shuck of tan Antron or Z-lon).
**Abdomen:** Light yellow (a touch of olive is optional) synthetic dubbing.
**Wing:** Light yellow (or just yellow) poly yarn in a bunch, trimmed straight across or to a point.
**Hackle:** One ginger, spiraled over the thorax and trimmed to a shallow "V" beneath.
**Thorax:** Same as the abdomen.
**Comments:** For tying instructions, see the comments under the Morris May Dark on page 65.

**MORRIS MAY TRICO**  *Skip Morris*

*Tied by Carol Ann Morris*

**Hook:** Light wire, standard length or short, sizes 24 to 20.
**Thread:** Black 8/0.
**Tail:** White hackle fibers, long, split (or a shuck of brown Antron or Z-lon).
**Abdomen:** Blackish brown fine synthetic dubbing.
**Wing:** White poly yarn in a single bunch, trimmed to a point.
**Hackle:** One grizzly, spiraled over the thorax and trimmed to a shallow "V" beneath.
**Thorax:** Same as the abdomen.
**Comments:** For tying instructions, see the comments under the Morris May Dark on page 65.

**No-Hackle.** It's difficult to think of Doug Swisher and Carl Richards's book *Selective Trout* without envisioning their radical dry fly, the No-Hackle. In 1974, when the book was published and the fly came out, the No-Hackle was a drastic departure from the Light Cahill- and Adams-style flies that dominated the scene. The idea was that hackles were just too bushy to suggest insect legs. So they dropped the hackle and avoided altogether anything that would suggest legs. The body and wings, they said, were the important features that trout keyed on with mayfly duns. On difficult trout in clear, slow water—selective trout—the No-Hackle is still in common use today.

## Tying the No-Hackle Fly (Slate/Tan No-Hackle)

**1.** Make split tails (instructions on page 80). Dub a slender, tapered body up about two-thirds of the shank. Snip out a section from each feather in a left-wing–right-wing matching pair of duck primaries. The width of the sections should be about half the shank's length.

**2.** This method for making No-Hackle wings allows most tiers to get good, consistent results. Hold a section up along the near side of the shank as shown, with the section vertical.

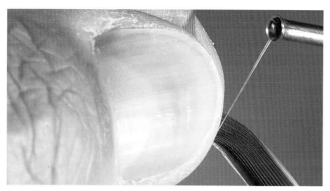

**3.** Wind the thread lightly all the way around the section and the shank until the thread goes down the far side of the shank—do not put any tension on the thread.

**4.** Roll your thumb tip and fingertip forward to enclose the section, thread, and shank. Pull the thread straight down until it is tight. Add a few additional turns over the butt of the section to secure it.

**5.** Hold the other section vertically against the far side of the shank, wind a full turn of thread around it, and pull the thread straight up on the near side of the shank. Use pretty much the same process as described for the far wing, but tighten the thread upward rather than downward. Add a few tight turns over the butt of the section.

**6.** Trim the butts of the sections and bind them up the thorax area. Pull each wing out flat as you work figure-eight turns of thread between the wings and the shank. This sets the wings out from the body a little, producing a good effect. Feel free to work the thread between the wings in whatever manner sets them in a good position.

**7.** You can dub between the wings by applying the dubbing very thinly on the thread, if you like (or not). Dub the thorax. Complete a tapered thread head.

## NO-HACKLE, SLATE/TAN
### Doug Swisher and Carl Richards

*Tied by Todd Smith*

| | |
|---|---|
| **Hook:** | Light wire, 1X long, sizes 16 to 12. |
| **Thread:** | Tan 8/0 or 6/0. |
| **Tail:** | Gray (or medium blue dun) hackle fibers, split. |
| **Body:** | Tan synthetic dubbing. |
| **Wing:** | Natural dark gray duck primary. |
| **Comments:** | Imitates the *Callibaetis* mayfly dun (instructions are on page 67). |

## NO-HACKLE, GRAY/OLIVE
### Doug Swisher and Carl Richards

*Tied by Todd Smith*

| | |
|---|---|
| **Hook:** | Light wire, 1X long, sizes 20 to 16. |
| **Thread:** | Olive 8/0. |
| **Tail:** | Gray (or medium blue dun) hackle fibers, split. |
| **Body:** | Olive synthetic dubbing. |
| **Wing:** | Natural gray duck primary. |
| **Comments:** | Imitates the *Baetis* mayfly dun. Tying instructions begin on page 67. |

## NO-HACKLE, GRAY/YELLOW
### Doug Swisher and Carl Richards

*Tied by Todd Smith*

| | |
|---|---|
| **Hook:** | Light wire, 1X long, sizes 18 to 14 |
| **Thread:** | Yellow 8/0 or 6/0. |
| **Tail:** | Gray (or medium blue dun) hackle fibers, split. |
| **Body:** | Yellow synthetic dubbing. |
| **Wing:** | Natural gray duck primary. |
| **Comments:** | Imitates the pale morning dun mayfly dun (instructions are on page 67). |

## NO-HACKLE, SLATE/OLIVE
### Doug Swisher and Carl Richards

*Tied by Todd Smith*

| | |
|---|---|
| **Hook:** | Light wire, 1X long, sizes 16 to 12. |
| **Thread:** | Olive 8/0 or 6/0. |
| **Tail:** | Gray (or medium blue dun) hackle fibers, split. |
| **Body:** | Olive synthetic dubbing. |
| **Wing:** | Natural dark gray duck primary. |
| **Comments:** | Imitates the *Flavilinea* mayfly dun (instructions are on page 67). |

**Paradrake.** The original Paradrakes came from Doug Swisher and Carl Richards, coauthors of the groundbreaking book *Selective Trout.* Mike Lawson's version—with the body hair drawn back from the hook's eye like a bullet head—makes a lot of sense. The extended hair abdomen becomes flexible once wet, allowing the hook to do its work without the complication of a stiff lever.

Here's how to tie a Paradrake: After setting the wing and binding up its base, bind on the tails at the bend; then bind on the hair around the eye, as for a bullet head (instructions are on page 146). Pull the hair back and make a couple of firm thread turns around the hair in front of the wing. Spiral the thread down the hair and shank, off the end of the shank and around the hair only, add a few tight turns, and then spiral the thread back up to just in front of the wing to create a series of thread crosses along the body. Trim the ends of the hair carefully to leave three or four moose hairs as tails. Bind on a hackle, then wind it down the base of the wing (instructions are on page 63).

## PARADRAKE, BROWN DRAKE — *Mike Lawson*

*Tied by Skip Morris*

**Hook:**             Light wire, standard length or 1X long, sizes 12 to 10.
**Thread:**          Black 8/0, 6/0, or 3/0.
**Parachute wing:** Natural tan elk hair (instructions are on page 63).
**Tail:**               Natural dark moose body.
**Body:**             Natural tan-brown elk hair (a core of monofilament is optional).
**Parachute hackle:** Grizzly dyed yellow (because this is an unusual hackle, you can substitute a regular grizzly or light brown hackle) one size larger than normal (for example, a size 12 hook takes a size 10 hackle). Instructions for making a parachute hackle are on page 63.
**Comments:**     Written instructions for tying the Paradrakes are in the introduction on previous page.

## PARADRAKE, GREEN DRAKE — *Mike Lawson*

*Tied by Skip Morris*

**Hook:**             Light wire, 1X long (standard dry-fly hook), sizes 12 and 10.
**Thread:**          Yellow 8/0, 6/0, or 3/0.
**Parachute wing:** Dyed dark gray elk hair (instructions are on page 63).
**Tail:**               Natural dark moose body hair.
**Body:**             Dyed olive elk hair.
**Parachute hackle:** Grizzly dyed yellow-olive (instructions are on page 63).
**Comments:**     Written instructions for tying the Paradrakes are in the introduction on previous page.

**Smith's CDC Parachute.** Todd Smith is a true spring-creek authority, having logged a lifetime's experience on Silver Creek and Henry's Fork of the Snake River—two legendary spring-fed rivers. And for years he was a commercial fly tier. So the Smith's CDC Parachutes do just what Todd designed them to do: float stubbornly and high with a naturally translucent wing, and mimic the posture of a mayfly dun.

## Making Reverse-Fiber Wings and a CDC Parachute Hackle (Smith's CDC Parachute, BWO/Flav)

*(See video instructions on DVD.)*

**1.** Microfibetts are more expensive than hackle fibers, so rather than using my method for making split tails (instructions are on page 80), bind on the fibers together and then divide them with crisscrossed turns of thread. Bind a goose biot by its tip at the bend, advance the thread, wind the biot just past halfway up the hook, and bind and trim the butt of the biot.

**2.** Hold two feathers (CDC or partridge for Smith's CDC Parachutes) back to back, tips evened; then stroke the fibers down toward their butts and hold them there firmly.

**3.** Bind the feathers atop the shank about three-quarters up the shank. Trim and bind the butts, and then set the wings upright as you would for a single parachute wing (instructions are on page 63). Trim off the tips of the wings. (Getting these wings right may take some practice.)

**6.** Dub the thorax area, moving the thread loop out of the way as you dub. Keep the thread loop against the base of the wings.

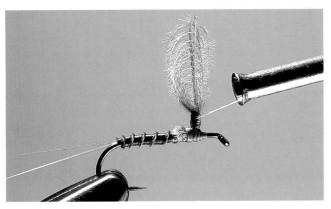

**4.** Wind the thread up and then down the wings, increasing thread tension with each layer, until you've added four layers to stiffen the base of the wings.

**7.** Hold the thread loop toward you under light tension. Separate the sides of the loop a little. Strip all the longer fibers from a CDC feather, in four bunches. Pick up each bunch of fibers and slide it between the sides of the thread loop. Add the first bunch with its stripped butts to your right, the next with the butts to the left, then right again, then left. Push the bunches toward the fly, so the fibers are close together and close to the fly.

**5.** Lightly wax a few inches of the thread (heavy wax may gum up the CDC fibers), double the thread in front of the wing, and then wind the thread back over itself to secure a thread loop, often called a "dubbing loop" (instructions are on page 95).

**8.** Hang a dubbing whirl in the end of the thread loop, hang the tool and the loop over your finger, and give the whirl a spin. With a dubbing twister, just insert the tool and twist it. The fibers and thread should form a sort of long-fibered, fluffy chenille.

**9.** Clamp English hackle pliers on the end of the twisted thread loop and remove the tool. Stroke all the CDC fibers to one side of the thread. Wind the twisted thread loop up the thread-covered base of the wings until the CDC fibers meet the wings. Now wind the twisted loop and fibers down the base of the wing in close turns. When you reach the thorax, bind the end of the thread loop just behind the eye. Trim the end of the loop, and build and complete a tapered thread head.

**10.** Stroke the CDC fibers down and trim them all straight across in one snip. This should result in a collar of fibers of about equal length surrounding the wing—a CDC parachute hackle collar.

**11.** If any of the fibers missed the trimming, or if the ends are a little uneven, trim the fibers to a neat circle. Here's a top view of the CDC hackle.

### SMITH'S CDC PARACHUTE, BWO/FLAV    *Todd Smith*

*Tied by Todd Smith*

**Hook:**　　　Light wire, standard length or 1X long, sizes 20 to 12.
**Thread:**　　Gray (or olive or brown) 8/0.
**Tail:**　　　Two dark dun (grayish-brown) Microfibetts, split.
**Abdomen:**　Darkish olive goose biot.
**Parachute wing:** Two medium or dark dun CDC feathers, their fibers stroked down, tips trimmed off (instructions begin on page 70).
**Parachute hackle:** Dyed olive CDC (instructions begin on page 70).
**Thorax:**　　Fine natural or synthetic darkish olive dubbing.
**Comments:**　Because BWO and *Flavilinea* duns are similar in form and have overlapping color ranges, Todd was able to concoct a dressing that, in different sizes, imitates both mayflies.

## SMITH'S CDC PARACHUTE, *CALLIBAETIS*
### Todd Smith

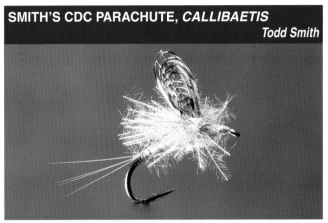

*Tied by Todd Smith*

**Hook:** Light wire, standard length or 1X long, sizes 16 to 12.
**Thread:** Tan 8/0.
**Tail:** Two medium or dark dun (grayish-brown) Microfibetts, split.
**Abdomen:** Tan or tan-olive goose biot.
**Parachute wing:** Two natural brown partridge feathers, the fibers stroked down the stem and the tips trimmed off (instructions are on page 70).
**Parachute hackle:** Natural brown CDC (instructions are on page 70).
**Thorax:** Fine tan or olive-tan synthetic or natural dubbing.

## SMITH'S CDC PARACHUTE, PMD          Todd Smith

*Tied by Todd Smith*

**Hook:** Light wire, standard length or 1X long, sizes 18 to 14.
**Thread:** Yellow 8/0.
**Tail:** Two light dun Microfibetts, split.
**Abdomen:** Pale yellow or pale olive-yellow goose biot.
**Parachute wing:** Two light dun (grayish-brown) CDC feathers, the fibers stroked down and the tips trimmed off (instructions are on page 70).
**Parachute hackle:** Dyed pale yellow CDC (instructions are on page 70).
**Thorax:** Fine pale yellow or pale yellow-olive synthetic or natural dubbing.

**Sparkle Dun.** The Sparkle Dun is clearly the offspring of the Compara-dun —a Compara-dun with a shuck rather than the original split tails. Both flies float well on their dubbed bodies and deer-hair wings. With its shuck, the Sparkle Dun seems to be trying to be an emerger pattern. But it just floats too high, I decided, to miss the dry-fly category. For over two decades the Sparkle Dun has proven itself everywhere there are trout.

## SPARKLE DUN, BWO          Blue Ribbon Flies

*Tied by Craig Mathews*

**Hook:** Light wire, standard length or 1X long, sizes 24 to 16.
**Thread:** Olive 8/0.
**Shuck:** Gray or olive Z-lon or Antron yarn.
**Wing:** Natural dark coastal deer hair (instructions are on page 59).
**Body:** Olive Super Fine Dry Fly dubbing or another fine synthetic dubbing.
**Comments:** For imitating *Baetis* mayfly duns.

## SPARKLE DUN, *CALLIBAETIS*
### Blue Ribbon Flies

*Tied by Craig Mathews*

**Hook:** Light wire, standard length or 1X long, sizes 16 and 14.
**Thread:** Tan 8/0.
**Shuck:** Gray or olive Z-lon or Antron yarn.
**Wing:** Natural medium-hue coastal deer hair (instructions are on page 59).
**Body:** Tan Super Fine Dry Fly dubbing or another fine synthetic dubbing.

## SPARKLE DUN, DRAKE MACKEREL
*Blue Ribbon Flies*

*Tied by Craig Mathews*

| | |
|---|---|
| **Hook:** | Light wire, standard length or 1X long, size 12. |
| **Thread:** | Tan 8/0. |
| **Shuck:** | Brown Z-lon or Antron yarn. |
| **Wing:** | Natural medium-dark coastal deer hair (instructions are on page 59). |
| **Rib:** | Twisted loop of brown Pearsall's Marabou Silk Floss or a single strand of brown 3/0 tying thread. After the body is dubbed, run the rib clear up to the eye of the hook. |
| **Body:** | Tan (or light brown) synthetic dubbing (Super Fine Dry Fly, Antron . . .). |

**Comments:** For imitating green drake mayfly duns. Drake mackerels are green drakes that hatch in the fall.

## SPARKLE DUN, FLAV/SMALL WESTERN GREEN DRAKE
*Blue Ribbon Flies*

*Tied by Craig Mathews*

| | |
|---|---|
| **Hook:** | Light wire, standard length or 1X long, sizes 16 and 14. |
| **Thread:** | Olive 8/0. |
| **Shuck:** | Olive Z-lon or Antron yarn. |
| **Wing:** | Natural medium-hue coastal deer hair (instructions are on page 59). |
| **Body:** | Olive-brown Super Fine Dry Fly dubbing or another fine synthetic dubbing. |

**Comments:** For imitating both the lesser green drake and *Flavilinea* mayfly duns.

## SPARKLE DUN, GRAY DRAKE
*Blue Ribbon Flies*

*Tied by Craig Mathews*

| | |
|---|---|
| **Hook:** | Light wire, standard length or 1X long, sizes 14 to 10. |
| **Thread:** | Gray 8/0. |
| **Shuck:** | Gray Z-lon or Antron yarn. |
| **Wing:** | Natural medium-hue coastal deer hair (instructions are on page 59). |
| **Rib:** | Black single-strand floss, flat waxed nylon, or heavy thread. After the body is dubbed, run the rib clear up to the hook's eye. |
| **Body:** | Gray Super Fine Dry Fly dubbing or another fine synthetic dubbing. |

## SPARKLE DUN, GREEN DRAKE
*Blue Ribbon Flies*

*Tied by Craig Mathews*

| | |
|---|---|
| **Hook:** | Light wire, standard length or 1X long, sizes 14 to 10. |
| **Thread:** | Olive or green 8/0. |
| **Shuck:** | Olive Z-lon or Antron yarn. |
| **Wing:** | Natural dark coastal deer hair (instructions are on page 59). |
| **Rib:** | Yellow single-strand floss, flat waxed nylon, or heavy thread. After the body is dubbed, run the rib clear up to the hook's eye. |
| **Body:** | Olive or green Super Fine Dry Fly dubbing or another fine synthetic dubbing. |

## SPARKLE DUN, IMPROVED PMD
### Blue Ribbon Flies

*Tied by Craig Mathews*

| | |
|---|---|
| **Hook:** | Light wire, standard length or 1X long, sizes 18 to 14. |
| **Thread:** | Pale yellow 8/0. |
| **Shuck:** | Brown Z-lon or Antron yarn topped with cream CDC or marabou (the topping is optional). |
| **Wing:** | Natural pale coastal deer hair (instructions are on page 59). Run the butts of the shuck up the back of the wing and then trim them to the wing's length. |
| **Abdomen:** | The pale yellow working thread (over the butts of the shuck material). |
| **Thorax:** | Pale yellow Super Fine Dry Fly dubbing or another fine synthetic dubbing. |

**Comments:** You can modify any of the Sparkle Duns to make them Improved Sparkle Duns—this PMD version serves as an example. It may be confusing for fly tiers when an originator alters his or her dressings, but improving on one's creations is a natural tendency for those who design fly patterns.

## SPARKLE DUN, MAHOGANY DUN
### Blue Ribbon Flies

*Tied by Craig Mathews*

| | |
|---|---|
| **Hook:** | Light wire, standard length or 1X long (standard dry-fly hook), size 16. |
| **Thread:** | Brown 8/0. |
| **Shuck:** | Brown Z-lon or Antron yarn. |
| **Wing:** | Natural medium-hue coastal deer hair (instructions are on page 59). |
| **Body:** | Mahogany brown Super Fine Dry Fly dubbing or another fine synthetic dubbing. |

## SPARKLE DUN, WHITE WING BLACKS
### Blue Ribbon Flies

*Tied by Craig Mathews*

| | |
|---|---|
| **Hook:** | Light wire, standard length or 1X long, sizes 24 to 18. |
| **Thread:** | Black 8/0. |
| **Shuck:** | Brown Z-lon or Antron yarn. |
| **Wing:** | White coastal deer hair (instructions are on page 59). |
| **Body:** | Black Super Fine Dry Fly dubbing or another fine synthetic dubbing. |

**Comments:** For imitating *Tricorythodes* mayfly duns.

## THORAX DUN
### Vince Marinaro

*Tied by Skip Morris*

| | |
|---|---|
| **Hook:** | Light wire, standard length or 1X long, whatever size matches the natural. |
| **Thread:** | 8/0 or 6/0 in the thorax color. |
| **Wing:** | Two upright breast feathers or webby hackles trimmed (or burned) to wing shape. |
| **Tail:** | Hackle fibers, split (instructions are on page 80). |
| **Hackles:** | After the thorax is dubbed as a ball, one hackle is wound angling back on top, forward underneath. The second hackle is wound angling the other way. The hackles aren't so much wound around the shank but rather behind and in front of the wings and around the thorax. No other fly we know of has hackle wound in this manner. |

**Abdomen and Thorax:** Synthetic dubbing matching the color of the natural.

**Comments:** Use whatever colors and hook size match the natural. Few fly fishers tie or fish this peculiar design by Marinaro, author of the ground-breaking *A Modern Dry-Fly Code*. The design is supposed to show the trout a clean wing outline, a bit of the thorax but no abdomen, and split tails. The more conventional version of the Thorax Dun follows.

## THORAX DUN

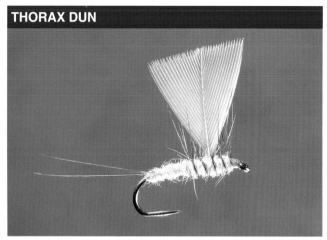

*Tied by Skip Morris*

**Hook:** Light wire, standard length or 1X long, sizes 18 to 12.
**Thread:** 8/0 or 6/0 in a color similar to the body color.
**Wing:** Medium gray turkey flats or duck shoulder, parted. (Many tiers make a single wing of poly yarn, bunched turkey flat fibers, or such.)
**Tail:** Medium gray hackle fibers, split. Use whatever color matches the particular mayfly you're imitating. (Instructions are on page 80).
**Body:** Buoyant synthetic dubbing (poly, Super Fine Dry Fly, Antron . . .). The body color should match that of the natural.
**Hackle:** One, wound over the front half of the body, both behind and in front of the wing, in only four to eight turns. Trim the underside of the hackle flat or in a shallow "V".
**Comments:** This contemporary version of Marinaro's original Thorax Dun can be tied in various sizes and colors to suggest a variety of mayflies. The pale morning dun version in the photo is only one possibility.

## USUAL                                   *Fran Betters*

*Tied by Todd Smith*

**Hook:** Light wire, standard length or 1X long, sizes 22 to 12.
**Thread:** Gray 8/0 or 6/0 (Betters sometimes uses hot orange or chartreuse).
**Wing:** Guard hairs from the pad of a snowshoe hare's foot. (Don't make any special effort to fan out the fibers, like a Compara-dun wing.)
**Tail:** Guard hairs from the pad of a snowshoe hare's foot.

**Body:** Underfur from a hare's foot (the fur combed out when preparing the wing). Betters uses dyed Australian opossum to match mayflies of various colors, but the original pattern uses creamy undyed hare's foot.
**Comments:** The Usual evolved from Betters's Haystack, which in turn was the forerunner of the Compara-dun and Sparkle Dun. Tie the Usual in whatever size and color best match the particular mayflies you wish to imitate. The rough design of the Usual is based on the natural buoyancy of the fur from the snowshoe hare's foot. This fly has lots of fans.

## YARN WING DUN                          *Gary Borger*

*Tied by Skip Morris*

**Hook:** Light wire, standard length or 1X long, sizes 16 to 6.
**Thread:** Color to blend with the body color, 8/0 or 6/0.
**Tail:** Hackle fibers fanned around a bump of thread turns (instructions are on page 80, but don't trim out the center fibers).
**Body:** Synthetic dubbing in a color to match the natural's color.
**Hackle:** One hackle spiraled forward from midshank, spiraled back, and then forward again to splay the fibers. Trim the fibers away beneath the body. Hackle color should match wing color.
**Wing:** Poly yarn bound on just behind the eye and trimmed in front (for a small head) and to wing length behind.
**Comments:** Use whatever colors and hook size match the natural.

# Mayfly Spinners

## CDC BIOT SPINNER, BLUE-WINGED OLIVE
### René Harrop

*Tied by Al Davis*

**Hook:** Light wire, standard length or 1X long, sizes 20 to 16.
**Thread:** Olive 8/0 or 6/0.
**Wing:** Two light blue dun (grayish-brown) CDC feathers set straight out to the sides with crisscrossed turns of thread. Atop the wings, light blue dun Z-lon or Antron yarn.
**Tail:** Light blue dun Betts' Tailing Fibers or hackle fibers, split or flared (instructions are on page 80).
**Abdomen:** Dyed olive goose or turkey biot.
**Thorax:** Medium olive or olive-brown Super Fine Dry Fly dubbing or other synthetic dubbing.

## CDC BIOT SPINNER, *CALLIBAETIS*   René Harrop

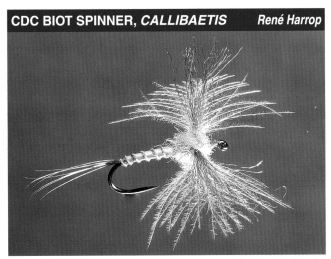

*Tied by Skip Morris*

**Hook:** Light wire, standard length or 1X long, sizes 16 to 12.
**Thread:** Tan 8/0 or 6/0.
**Wing:** Two light blue dun CDC feathers set straight out to the sides with crisscrossed turns of thread. Atop the wings, brown Z-lon or Antron yarn.
**Tail:** Light blue dun (grayish-brown) Betts' Tailing Fibers or hackle fibers, split or flared (instructions are on page 80).
**Abdomen:** Dyed tan goose or turkey biot.
**Thorax:** Tan Super Fine Dry Fly dubbing or other synthetic dubbing.

## CDC BIOT SPINNER, PALE MORNING DUN
### René Harrop

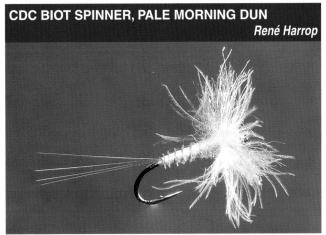

*Tied by Al Davis*

**Hook:** Light wire, standard length or 1X long, sizes 20 to 16.
**Thread:** Yellow 8/0 or 6/0.
**Wing:** Two light blue dun CDC feathers set straight out to the sides with crisscrossed turns of thread. Atop the wings, light blue dun Z-lon or Antron yarn.
**Tail:** Light blue dun (grayish-brown) Betts' Tailing Fibers or hackle fibers, split or flared (instructions are on page 80).
**Abdomen:** Dyed olive-yellow goose or turkey biot.
**Thorax:** Olive-yellow Super Fine Dry Fly dubbing or other fine synthetic dubbing.

## CDC BIOT SPINNER, RUSTY   René Harrop

*Tied by Al Davis*

**Hook:** Light wire, standard length or 1X long, sizes 20 to 14.
**Thread:** Brown 8/0 or 6/0.
**Wing:** Two light blue dun CDC feathers set straight out to the sides with crisscrossed turns of thread. Atop the wings, light blue dun Z-lon or Antron yarn.
**Tail:** Light blue dun (grayish-brown) Betts' Tailing Fibers or hackle fibers, split or flared (instructions are on page 80).
**Abdomen:** Dyed rust goose or turkey biot.
**Thorax:** Rust Super Fine Dry Fly dubbing or other synthetic dubbing.
**Comments:** The Rusty CDC Biot Spinner imitates the spinners of several mayflies—many spinners have brownish or rust-colored bodies. When western fly fishers are unsure which mayfly spinner is falling, many reach for some sort of rusty spinner fly out of reflex. The results usually justify the strategy.

## CDC BIOT SPINNER, TRICO — *René Harrop*

*Tied by Al Davis*

| | |
|---|---|
| **Hook:** | Light wire, standard length or 1X long, sizes 20 and 22. |
| **Thread:** | Black 8/0. |
| **Wing:** | Two white CDC feathers set straight out to the sides with crisscrossed turns of thread. Atop the wings, light blue dun Z-lon or Antron yarn. |
| **Tail:** | Light blue dun (grayish-brown) Betts' Tailing Fibers or hackle fibers, split or flared (instructions are on page 80). |
| **Abdomen:** | Dyed black goose or turkey biot. |
| **Thorax:** | Black Super Fine Dry Fly dubbing or other synthetic dubbing. |

## CDC TRICO SPENT SPINNER

*Tied by Carol Ann Morris*

| | |
|---|---|
| **Hook:** | Light wire, short shank to 1X long (standard dry-fly hook), sizes 26 to 18. |
| **Thread:** | Black 8/0. |
| **Tail:** | White or blue dun Microfibetts, split. |
| **Body:** | Black thread, may be coated with head cement. |
| **Wing:** | White or blue dun CDC barbs, with one strand of pearlescent Krystal Flash on top. |

**Comments:** The wing is a bunch of CDC fibers stripped from the stem, bound crossways and topped with a strand of Krystal Flash, with the ends trimmed straight across.

## GIDLOW *CALLIBAETIS* — *Arnie Gidlow*

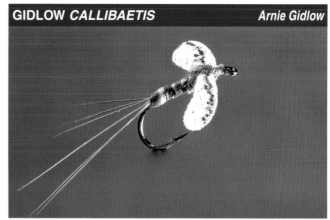

*Tied by Arnie Gidlow*

| | |
|---|---|
| **Hook:** | Light wire, standard length (or 1X long), size 14. |
| **Thread:** | Gray 6/0 (or 8/0). |
| **Tail:** | Split medium dun (grayish-brown) Microfibetts or hackle fibers (instructions are on page 80). |
| **Abdomen:** | Slender strip of Razor Foam (a very thin, buoyant closed-cell foam sheeting) marked with a permanent brown marking pen along one edge, and wound up the shank. |
| **Wing:** | Nature's Wing (or another pale synthetic wing sheeting). The sheeting is cut in the shape of two opposing wings with a narrow waist between them. Speckle the leading edge of the wings with a fine-tip permanent black marking pen. Bind the wings at their waist atop the shank. |
| **Thorax:** | Gray buoyant synthetic dubbing. |

## HACKLE SPINNER, GRAY DRAKE — *Blue Ribbon Flies*

*Tied by Craig Mathews*

| | |
|---|---|
| **Hook:** | Light wire, standard length or 1X long, size 12. |
| **Thread:** | Light tan 8/0 or 6/0. |
| **Tail:** | Blue dun hackle fibers. |
| **Rib:** | Brown single-strand floss or 3/0 tying thread. |
| **Abdomen:** | Fine synthetic light tan dubbing. |
| **Top of thorax:** | Slim strip of gray buoyant synthetic foam sheeting. Draw a slim line down the center with a black permanent marking pen. |
| **Wing:** | Light tan or light ginger hackle wound heavily over the shank through the thorax area. Part the fibers on top and then flatten them to the sides with the foam strip; trim the fibers away beneath. |

## HACKLE SPINNER, PMD — *Blue Ribbon Flies*

*Tied by Craig Mathews*

**Hook:** Light wire, standard length or 1X long, size 16.
**Thread:** Light olive 8/0.
**Tail:** Blue dun hackle fibers.
**Abdomen:** Light olive fine synthetic dubbing.
**Top of thorax:** Slim strip of gray buoyant closed-cell foam sheeting.
**Wing:** Blue dun hackle wound heavily over the shank through the thorax area. Part the fibers on top and then flatten them to the sides with the foam strip; trim the fibers away beneath.

## KRYSTAL WING BWO SPINNER — *Scott Sanchez*

*Tied by Scott Sanchez*

**Hook:** Light wire, 1X long, sizes 20 to 14.
**Thread:** Rust-brown 8/0.
**Wing:** 10 to 12 strands of pearl Krystal Flash, trimmed to length on the ends.
**Tail:** Split clear Microfibetts or pale gray hackle fibers (instructions are on page 80).
**Rib:** Loop of the working thread, twisted.
**Body:** Fine olive-gray synthetic dubbing (Super Fine Dry Fly, Antron . . .).

**Comments:** Scott likes to bind on the wings first. The wings, which came from a George Harvey dressing, pick up the light and glow to help the angler see the fly, but from the trout's view, they are clear like the real insect's wings.

## PARA-SPIN, RUSTY SPINNER — *Bob Jacklin*

*Top view*

*Tied by Bob Jacklin*

**Hook:** Light wire, standard length or 1X long, sizes 18 to 12.
**Thread:** Rust (orange-brown) 8/0 or 6/0.
**Parachute wing:** White poly yarn or Antron yarn. Trim the wing short. You can press it down after winding the hackle so that it splays and add a little head cement to keep it splayed if you like (instructions are on page 63).
**Parachute hackle:** Grizzly, two or three sizes larger than the hook size (instructions are on page 63).
**Tail:** Natural brown buck tail.
**Butt:** Black dubbing, any kind.
**Abdomen:** Dyed rust (orange-brown) goose or turkey biot.
**Thorax:** Dyed rust (orange-brown) beaver (or rust synthetic dubbing).

**Comments:** The hackle of the Para-Spin implies not the legs but the wings of a mayfly spinner. When western fly fishers are unsure which mayfly spinner is falling, many reach for some sort of rusty spinner, since many spinners have brownish or rust-colored bodies. The results usually justify the strategy.

## PARA-SPIN, TRICO — *Bob Jacklin*

*Tied by Bob Jacklin*

**Hook:** Light wire, standard length or 1X long, sizes 20 and 18.

**Thread:** Black 8/0.

**Parachute wing:** White poly yarn or Antron yarn. Trim the wing short (instructions are on page 63).

**Parachute hackle:** Grizzly, two or three sizes larger than the hook size (instructions are on page 63).

**Tail:** Two long white Microfibetts, split.

**Abdomen:** Black dyed beaver (or fine synthetic dubbing, such as Super Fine Dry Fly or Antron).

**Thorax:** Same dubbing as for the abdomen.

**Comments:** The hackle of the Para-Spin implies not the legs but the wings of a mayfly spinner.

## POLY-FOAM SPINNER — *Bill Blackstone*

*Tied by Skip Morris*

**Hook:** Light wire, short shank, sizes 22 to 12.

**Thread:** 8/0 or 6/0 in the color of the thorax.

**Tail:** Three bristles from a Simmons white sable paintbrush or three Microfibetts, splayed.

**Abdomen:** Strip of poly 2D foam trimmed to a point and colored with a permanent marking pen to match the natural spinner. The abdomen is tied on a needle and then slid free when complete. (According to Bill, 2D foam is available in electronics stores.)

**Rib:** Working thread, spiraled up the needle-supported foam abdomen.

**Thorax:** Synthetic dubbing to match the color of the real spinner's thorax.

**Wing:** Clear 6mm vinyl sheeting from a plastic bag, trimmed to the shape of two wings. Score veins in the sheeting with a needle or bodkin before binding the wing on.

**Comments:** This unusual fly is unusually realistic. Like many mayfly imitations, the Poly-Foam Spinner can be varied in size and color to imitate just about any natural spinner.

## Making Split Hackle-fiber Tails (Poly-Wing Spinner)

*(See video instructions on DVD.)*

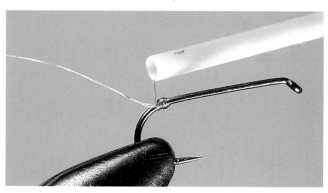

**1.** There are many ways to make split tails on a dry fly. This is my method, which is efficient and easy to execute and produces good results. Start the thread at the bend. Wind the thread over itself until you've created a tight little thread ball. (It may help to work the thread forward and backward over the same spot, so that it crisscrosses rather than just piles up on itself.)

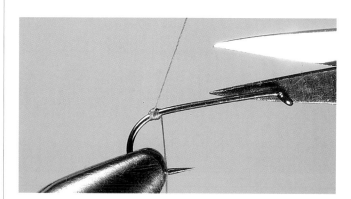

**2.** Pull the tag end of the thread forward and make a few tight thread turns over it. Trim off the tag end of the thread.

**3.** Spiral the thread forward. Even the tips of some hackle fibers, and then strip them from the stem. Bind them on about halfway up the shank. Hold the fibers back and slightly elevated under firm tension. Spiral the thread tightly back to within a few turns of the thread ball.

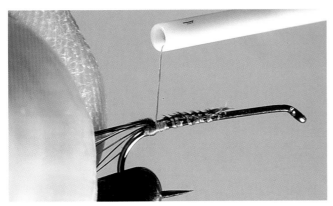

**4.** Pull the fibers firmly down, so they angle toward the floor and some slip down the sides of the thread ball. Wind the thread the rest of the way back to the thread ball in tight turns. Keep the thread tight when you reach the ball, and then wind the thread tightly forward a few turns.

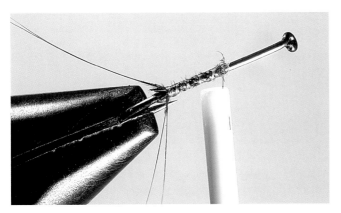

**5.** When you release the fibers, they should splay out in a fan. Trim off any side fibers that angle below the line of the shank. Trim out the center fibers, leaving two to four fibers on each side.

**6.** The completed split tails (I reversed the hook in the vise so the tails would show up).

## POLY-WING SPINNER

*Tied by Skip Morris*

| | |
|---|---|
| **Hook:** | Fine wire, standard length or 1X long, sizes 24 to 10. |
| **Thread:** | 8/0 or 6/0 in a color to match the body color. |
| **Tail:** | Split hackle fibers in the body color (instructions begin on previous page). |
| **Wing:** | Gray poly yarn (white for Tricos). |
| **Body:** | Buoyant synthetic dubbing, any mayfly color. |

**Comments:** A basic and reliable spinner imitation that I've used successfully for decades. By varying the hook size and body color, you can make the Poly-Wing Spinner imitate the spinner of the PMD, BWO, *Callibaetis*, and so forth.

## POLY-WING SPINNER, TRICO

*Tied by Skip Morris*

| | |
|---|---|
| **Hook:** | Light wire, short to standard length, sizes 26 to 20. |
| **Thread:** | Brown 8/0. |
| **Tail:** | White or ginger hackle fibers, split (instructions are on page 80). |
| **Abdomen:** | Fine olive synthetic dubbing. |
| **Wing:** | White poly yarn. |
| **Thorax:** | Fine brown synthetic dubbing. |

**Comments:** A well-established version of the versatile Poly-Wing Spinner.

**Profile Spinner.** Mike Mercer grew frustrated when his middle-aged eyes couldn't find mayfly spinner patterns lying flush on the water like the naturals. Thus he developed his Profile Spinner series, with bright and highly visible upright wings. In his book *Creative Fly Tying,* he says his Profile Spinner "is quickly becoming my 'go-to' pattern when searching broken water for random risers."

**PROFILE SPINNER, GREEN DRAKE**    *Mike Mercer*

*Top view*

*Tied by Mike Mercer*

| | |
|---|---|
| **Hook:** | Light wire, standard length or 1X long, sizes 12 and 10. |
| **Thread:** | Olive 8/0. |
| **Tail:** | Blue dun hackles. |
| **Abdomen:** | Dyed olive turkey biot. |
| **Parachute wing:** | Orange and yellow macramé yarn (or Antron or poly yarn) mixed (instructions are on page 63). |
| **Parachute hackle:** | Dyed olive grizzly (instructions are on page 63). |
| **Spent wing:** | Dun Z-lon (or Antron yarn). |
| **Thorax:** | Mercer's Select Buggy Nymph Dubbing in Micro Mayfly (or another light olive synthetic dubbing, such as poly or Super Fine Dry Fly). |

**PROFILE SPINNER, GREEN DRAKE FOAM BODY**
*Mike Mercer*

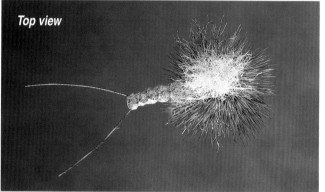

*Top view*

*Tied by Mike Mercer*

| | |
|---|---|
| **Hook:** | Heavy wire, short shank, straight eye (Mike prefers the Tiemco 2499SP), sizes 12 and 10. |
| **Thread:** | Olive 8/0. |
| **Tail:** | Two stripped dyed olive grizzly hackle stems. |
| **Extended abdomen:** | Buoyant yellow closed-cell foam sheeting cut to a tapered strip and bound up a beading needle in sections, then removed from the needle (instructions are on page 58). Color the top olive and the underside tan with waterproof permanent marking pens. |
| **Parachute wing:** | Orange and yellow macramé yarn (or Antron or poly yarn) mixed. (Instructions are on page 63.) |
| **Parachute hackle:** | Dyed olive grizzly (instructions are on page 63). |
| **Spent wing:** | Dun Z-lon (or Antron yarn). |
| **Thorax:** | Mercer's Select Buggy Nymph Dubbing in Micro Mayfly (or another light olive synthetic dubbing, such as poly or Super Fine Dry Fly). |
| **Comments:** | Mike's buoyant and intriguing imitation of a green drake mayfly spinner. |

## PROFILE SPINNER, PMD — *Mike Mercer*

*Top view*

*Tied by Mike Mercer*

**Hook:** Light wire, standard length or 1X long, sizes 18 and 16.
**Thread:** Camel (light brown) 8/0.
**Tail:** Blue dun hackles.
**Abdomen:** Dyed rust (orange-brown) turkey biot.
**Parachute wing:** Orange and yellow macramé yarn (or Antron or poly yarn) mixed (instructions are on page 63).
**Parachute hackle:** Blue dun (instructions are on page 63).
**Spent wing:** Dun Z-lon (or Antron yarn).
**Thorax:** Rusty Brown Super Fine Dry Fly dubbing (or another rust-brown synthetic dubbing, such as poly dubbing).

## PROFILE SPINNER, TRICO — *Mike Mercer*

*Tied by Mike Mercer*

**Hook:** Light wire, standard length 1X long, sizes 24 to 18.
**Thread:** Camel (light brown) 8/0.
**Tail:** Blue dun hackles.
**Abdomen:** Turkey biot dyed chocolate brown.
**Parachute wing:** Orange macramé yarn (or Antron or poly yarn) mixed (instructions are on page 63).
**Parachute hackle:** Blue dun (instructions are on page 63).
**Spent wing:** Dun Z-lon (or Antron yarn).
**Thorax:** Mahogany Brown Super Fine Dry Fly dubbing (or another fine, dark brown synthetic dubbing).

## SMITH'S SPINNER, BROWN DRAKE — *Todd Smith*

*Tied by Todd Smith*

**Hook:** Standard or light wire, 2X long, slow-curve shank, size 10.
**Thread:** Tan 8/0.
**Tail:** Four dark dun (grayish-brown) Microfibetts, split into two groups.
**Rib:** Brown 6/0.
**Back:** Strip of fine brown buoyant closed-cell foam sheeting. The sheeting should be ribbed up the abdomen and then form a sort of wing case over the wings and thorax.
**Abdomen:** Tan buoyant natural (or synthetic) dubbing.
**Wing:** Two natural gray partridge flank feathers.
**Thorax:** Same dubbing as for the abdomen.
**Comments:** This imitation of the brown drake mayfly spinner is made more buoyant by the strip of closed-cell foam up its top.

## SUNDOWN SPINNER, BROWN — Jan Weido

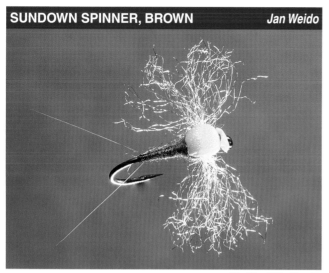

*Tied by Skip Morris*

| | |
|---|---|
| **Hook:** | Light wire, standard length or 1X long, sizes 18 to 14. |
| **Thread:** | Brown 8/0 or 6/0. |
| **Tail:** | Medium blue dun Microfibetts, split. |
| **Abdomen:** | Rusty brown synthetic dubbing. |
| **Back:** | Short strip of yellow or white buoyant closed-cell foam sheeting, atop the thorax. |
| **Wing:** | White crinkled Z-lon. |
| **Thorax:** | Rusty brown dubbing. |

**Comments:** The foam back makes this fly more visible and more buoyant. The Sundown Spinner could certainly be tied in colors other than brown.

## TRIPLE WING SPINNER, *BAETIS* — David R. Ellis

*Tied by Carol Ann Morris*

| | |
|---|---|
| **Hook:** | Light wire, standard length or 1X long, sizes 20 to 14. |
| **Thread:** | Rusty brown 8/0. |
| **Tail:** | Dun (grayish-brown) Microfibetts, split. |
| **Body:** | Rusty olive-brown fine synthetic dubbing. |
| **Wing:** | Hi-Vis wing material no. 16 (or substitute light gray Antron or poly yarn) bound on in three close bunches. |

## TRIPLE WING SPINNER, TRICO MALE, BLACK/WHITE — David R. Ellis

*Tied by Carol Ann Morris*

| | |
|---|---|
| **Hook:** | Light wire, short to 1X long, sizes 22 to 18. |
| **Thread:** | White 8/0. |
| **Tail:** | Dun (grayish-brown) Microfibetts, split. |
| **Abdomen:** | The working thread. |
| **Wing:** | Hi-Vis wing material no. 16 (or substitute light gray Antron or poly yarn) bound on in three close buches. |
| **Thorax:** | Black Superfine Dry Fly dubbing (or another fine synthetic dubbing). |

# Caddisflies

THE EMERGENCE OF a typical mayfly is all elegance—the slipping from a glassy shuck to drift high on the currents with glistening new wings. Compared with that, the hatching of a caddisfly seems like a mad scramble. And it really is a scramble—the pupa flails the water with its elongated legs, trying to reach the surface, and when it does, it pops from its shuck into erratic flight. There are variations, but that is the standard pandemonium of a hatching caddisfly.

Still, the caddisfly in all its varieties and stages has its appeal. The reclusive *Rhyocophila* caddis larva, for example, is often a stunning green, as though illuminated. The adult *Hydropsyche* flits in swarms of mating adults like flickering sunlit clouds along the edges of rivers. It all makes a fascinating show. Elegance isn't everything.

A caddisfly spends most of its life as a "larva," a fat little worm with legs. Some types hide or scuttle about the under-sides of stones or waterlogged bark, others climb about openly within a protective case, and others hide behind an underwater web. A month or two before hatch time, the larva constructs a shelter in which it matures into a "pupa," complete with antennae, wing pads, and long stroking legs. At hatch time the pupa emerges from its shelter and then swims for the surface (a few varieties swim to the shoreline). At the surface, the pupa throws off its shuck. This process may take a little while with some kinds of caddisflies, while others just squirt from their shucks as soon as they touch the surface and then flutter nervously away. The adult caddis gets thirsty and returns to the water occasionally for a drink. Once the female's eggs are fertilized, she returns to the water to either drop or actually swim down to deposit her eggs. There are lots of opportunities here for trout to feed on the various stages of a caddisfly.

# Fishing the Stages of the Caddisfly

### LARVA

*Caddisfly larva*

Like any underwater insect, caddis larvae can be swept to trout by a misstep or a surge of current. Wherever there is an abundance of any small aquatic life in a river, caddis larvae included, trout will be lying in wait, and the wise fly fisher will be open to drifting imitations below a strike indicator along the riverbed. Rivers with a heavy population of a particular caddis always hold promise with a larval imitation fished dead drift.

### PUPA

*Caddisfly pupa*

After spending from a few months up to three years as a larva, the caddis matures to a pupa, with legs, antennae, and the wing pads that contain its future wings. When the time is right, the pupa swims vigorously to the surface, where it throws off its shuck and rises on its new wings (although the October caddis swims to shore and crawls out of the water to shed its shuck). Trout often prefer imitations of the pupa during a hatch. These fly patterns can be fished dead drift, but the most common tactics are to work the fly weakly just under the water's surface or use a method called the "Leisenring lift," allowing the fly to sink along with the current until it's deep, then stopping the rod so the fly swings upward like the ascending pupa.

### EMERGER

Even though caddis tend to pop quickly from their shucks at the water's surface and take right to wing, in an almost instant emergence, caddis emerger flies *are* effective. This may be because some individual caddisflies naturally take longer than others to escape their shucks, or because some run into serious problems with the operation. The trout seek these slower-hatching caddis, which require less effort to catch than the fast-hatching ones. In any case, fish most caddis emerger patterns dead drift, or perhaps with a light, occasional tug to suggest the insect's struggle.

### ADULT

*Caddisfly adult*

The adults of most caddis varieties waste little time in exercising their new wings. This means that the trout have more opportunities to catch pupae and emergers than adults during a hatch. Still, there are some caddis that hatch sedately and take the time to stretch their wings before using them, in which case a high-floating dry fly can be excellent (as can an emerger). Another opportunity for the dry fly is when the adult caddis flies to the water to drink or when the female returns to drop her eggs—she drifts and skitters atop the current, as should your dry-fly imitation. Some caddis swim underwater to lay their eggs, and a wet fly can be twitched a few inches to a foot or so down to imitate them.

# Specific Hatches

*Hydropsyche.* The larva of the *Hydropsyche* caddisfly (sometimes called the spotted sedge) is tan to bright green. It spins and weaves a net that it then patrols, leaving the shelter it constructs when enough food has collected to make the effort worthwhile. When too many larvae crowd the same stone, some drift freely to another rock, provided the trout don't catch them. The pupa, like the larva, is tan to green. It hatches in open water. The adult's underside runs from tan to dark green. The female adult swims underwater in the evening to deposit her eggs. Hooks for imitations of all stages run from sizes 16 to 10.

*Rhyacophila.* The green—sometimes vivid green—larva of *Rhyacophila* (also known as the green rock worm) lives among rocks in lively currents. The pupa is typically darker, more of an olive, and hatches out in open water. The adult runs tan to green on its underside. The female adult swims down to deposit her eggs. Imitations of all three stages run from sizes 14 to 8.

**Mother's Day Caddis.** This small, dark caddis (*Brachycentrus*, also known as the American Grannom) hatches in spring and again in fall. The larva constructs a case of plant fibers to live in, which it attaches to a stone in the current. The pupa is a strong swimmer and heads for the surface in the open. Escape from the shuck at the surface is slow and mayfly-like, so emerger flies and adult imitations fished dead drift are effective. The adult female returns to the water in the afternoon or evening to lie flat on the surface and release her eggs, or in some cases she swims down and deposits the eggs on the streambed.

The colors of the three stages of the Mother's Day caddis vary greatly. Only the black head and legs and a little of the cream to green body of the larva are exposed beyond the larval case, which itself varies considerably in color. The pupa is green, usually with dark markings along the back. The adult's wings are dark—dark brown, dark gray, or even black—and the body is dark olive. Hooks sizes 18 to 14 are appropriate for all imitations.

**October Caddis, *Dicosmoecus*.** The giant of western river caddisflies, the October caddis appears from September well into October, mainly in the coastal states but also in western Idaho and Montana. The larva spends its life in a case it constructs of gravel and sand, which it carries around as it climbs laboriously over the streambed. The larva cements the case to a stone, pupates within the case for several weeks, and then leaves the case to stroke fast and furiously along the streambed to shore, where it climbs out of the water and struggles from its shuck. The adult female returns to drop her eggs from late in the afternoon until dark. The larva appears mostly as a darkish, variegated capsule with a little pale body showing behind the blackish head and legs. Trout will eat the larva, case and all. The pupa is amber-orange through the abdomen, medium to dark brown through the thorax and legs. The adult has brown wings and a yellow to darkish orange body. Imitations are huge, like all stages of the natural—matched by hook sizes 10 to 6, 2X or 3X long.

*There are other varieties of caddis that may be worthy of imitation regionally or briefly, but the ones described above are common in the West.*

# Caddis Larvae

**BEAD HEAD NET BUILDER**                                          *John Barr*

*Tied by Carol Ann Morris*

| | |
|---|---|
| **Hook:** | Heavy wire, humped shank (scud-pupa hook), sizes 14 to 10. |
| **Head:** | Gold metal bead. |
| **Thread:** | Black 8/0 or 6/0. |
| **Tail:** | Z-lon or Antron, ginger with a cream or amber body, or olive with an olive body, short. |
| **Rib:** | Clear 3X monofilament tippet. |
| **Back:** | Slim strip of orange mottled Thin Skin (or substitute orange latex or other sheeting). Make marks up the back with a brown permanent marking pen once the fly is completed. |
| **Abdomen:** | Slightly shiny synthetic dubbing or synthetic-natural blend in green, cream, or amber. |
| **Thorax:** | Natural dark ostrich herl wound over the same dubbing used for the abdomen. |

**Comments:** The standard Net Builder dressings without the bead are described later in this chapter. To convert them to bead head versions, simply add a bead, as described here.

**BEADHEAD GREEN ROCK WORM**

*Tied by Rick Hafele*

| | |
|---|---|
| **Hook:** | Heavy wire, standard length or 1X long, humped shape is optional, sizes 16 to 12. |
| **Head:** | Gold metal bead. |
| **Weight:** | 8 to 10 wraps of lead wire. |
| **Body:** | Six strands of bright green Krystal Flash twisted together. |
| **Thorax:** | Pine squirrel body hair with guard hairs left in. |

**Comments:** Rick Hafele (who is reluctant to claim this design as his own because it's too similar to other fly patterns) calls the Beadhead Green Rock Worm his favorite caddis larva imitation. He says, "In bright green . . .

it is an excellent imitation of green rock worm larvae (*Rhyacophila* sp.). But many species of net-spinning caddis larvae (*Hydropsyche* sp. and *Cheumatopsyche* sp.) are also bright green, which dramatically increases the appeal of this fly to trout. You can also use a different color of Krystal Flash for the body to imitate other species of net-spinning caddis that are not bright green."

## DESCHUTES CASED CADDIS — *John Hazel*

*Tied by Skip Morris*

**Hook:** Heavy wire, 2X to 4X long, sizes 10 to 6.
**Thread:** Black 3/0.
**Weight:** Lead wire.
**Rib:** Fine copper wire.
**Abdomen:** Peacock herl and one brown rooster hackle over dubbed dark green rabbit.
**Thorax:** White rabbit dubbing.
**Head:** Black goat fur (or substitute black hare's mask or squirrel body).
**Comments:** Lead wraps cover the rear two-thirds of the hook's shank, peacock herls and wire are bound on at the bend, and the lead is covered with dubbing and tapered with it at both ends. The herl is wound up the abdomen area, bound, and trimmed. The hackle is bound at the *front* of the abdomen area. The white rabbit thorax is dubbed. The hackle is then spiraled back over the peacock to the bend. The wire is spiraled forward through the hackle and up the dubbed thorax as three or four ribs, then bound and trimmed. The head is dubbed and picked out, and the hackle is trimmed short. The Deschutes Cased Caddis imitates the great cased larva of the October caddis. Trout eat the larva, case and all, digest the good parts, and expel the rest.

## GREEN ROCK WORM — *Polly Rosborough*

*Tied by Skip Morris*

**Hook:** Heavy wire, 1X long, size 8.
**Thread:** Black 8/0 or 6/0.
**Weight:** Lead (optional).
**Body:** Insect green synthetic yarn (or substitute dubbing, natural or synthetic).
**Legs:** Speckled guinea hen dyed green.
**Head:** Black ostrich herl.
**Comments:** Polly's time-tested imitation of the *Rhyacophila* caddis.

## KILLER CADDIS (OLIVE) — *Dennis Brown*

*Tied by Skip Morris*

**Hook:** Heavy wire, humped shank (scud-pupa hook), sizes 18 to 12.
**Body:** Three to five small or "midge" olive glass beads, depending on hook size.
**Thread:** Chartreuse for the butt, wine color after, 8/0 or 6/0.
**Butt:** Olive Antron dubbing.
**Head:** Black (or brown) rabbit or other natural dubbing.
**Comments:** Slide on the beads. Start the thread at the bend, dub, whip-finish the thread (add head cement if you like), and trim the thread. Then slide back the beads, restart the thread in front of the beads, and complete the fly. The Killer Caddis can be tied in any caddis larva color—brown, dark green, amber, tan, whatever. This may be the most popular of all the new glass-bead flies.

## LIGHT CADDIS — *Polly Rosborough*

*Tied by Carol Ann Morris*

**Hook:** Heavy wire, standard length or 1X long, size 8.
**Thread:** Black 8/0, 6/0, or 3/0.
**Body:** Dubbed cream fox or badger fur.
**Legs:** Barred lemon wood-duck fibers tied in at the throat.
**Head:** Black ostrich, spun around the thread.
**Comments:** A simple all-around caddis larva imitation that Polly used for his "light caddis" hatch (whatever that is). There's no reason the size and color can't be varied to imitate several caddisflies.

## LITTLE GREEN ROCK WORM — *Bob Jacklin*

*Tied by Bob Jacklin*

**Hook:** Heavy wire, humped shank (scud-pupa hook), sizes 18 to 12.
**Head:** Black tungsten bead.
**Thread:** Black 6/0.
**Rib:** Green Span Flex (a flexible strand with a soft shine; you can substitute fine rubber-strand, flat waxed nylon, or heavy thread).
**Abdomen:** Chartreuse dubbing—rabbit or a fine synthetic dubbing.
**Collar:** Peacock herl, spun around the working thread for durability. Keep the collar slim.
**Comments:** Bob has had great success with his Little Green Rock Worm on such Yellowstone-area rivers as the renowned Madison.

## NET BUILDER, AMBER — *John Barr*

*Tied by Carol Ann Morris*

**Hook:** Heavy wire, humped shank (scud-pupa hook), sizes 14 to 8.
**Thread:** Black 8/0 or 6/0.
**Tail:** Ginger Z-lon.
**Back:** Orange mottled oak Thin Skin (or some other synthetic sheeting). Make marks along the back with a brown permanent marking pen once the fly is completed.
**Rib:** Clear 3X monofilament tippet.
**Abdomen:** Any slightly shiny amber synthetic dubbing.
**Thorax:** Undyed natural gray ostrich herl wound over the same dubbing used for the abdomen.
**Head:** The front of the Thin Skin doubled back on top and bound.
**Comments:** In *Nymph-Fishing Rivers and Streams*, entomologist Rick Hafele says the net-spinning family *Hydropsychidae* includes "more than 140 species." You shouldn't have trouble finding use for John Barr's three color-schemes for his Net Builder.

## NET BUILDER, CREAM — *John Barr*

*Tied by Carol Ann Morris*

**Hook:** Heavy wire, humped shank (scud-pupa hook), sizes 14 to 8.
**Thread:** Black 8/0 or 6/0.
**Tail:** Ginger Z-lon.
**Back:** Orange mottled oak Thin Skin (or some other synthetic sheeting). Make marks up the back with a brown permanent marking pen after the fly is completed.
**Rib:** Clear 3X monofilament tippet.
**Abdomen:** Cream Sow-Scud (or any dubbing with a light tan sheen).
**Thorax:** Undyed natural dark ostrich herl wound over the same dubbing used for the abdomen.
**Head:** The front of the Thin Skin doubled back on top and bound.
**Comments:** In *Nymph-Fishing Rivers and Streams*, entomologist Rick Hafele says the net-spinning family *Hydropsychidae* includes "more than 140 species." You shouldn't have trouble finding use for John Barr's three color-schemes for his Net Builder.

**NET BUILDER, OLIVE**                                    *John Barr*

*Tied by Carol Ann Morris*

**Hook:**       Heavy wire, humped shank (pupa-scud hook), sizes 14 to 8.
**Thread:**     Black 8/0 or 6/0.
**Tail:**       Light olive Z-lon.
**Back:**       Strip of orange mottled oak Thin Skin (or another synthetic sheeting). Make marks along the back with a permanent brown marking pen after the fly is completed.
**Rib:**        Clear 3X monofilament tippet.
**Abdomen:**    Green Net Builder Scintilla (or another dubbing with a light green sheen).
**Thorax:**     Undyed natural dark ostrich herl wound over the same dubbing used for the abdomen.
**Head:**       The front of the Thin Skin doubled back on top and bound.
**Comments:**   In *Nymph-Fishing Rivers and Streams*, entomologist Rick Hafele says the net-spinning family *Hydropsychidae* includes "more than 140 species." You shouldn't have trouble finding use for John Barr's three color-schemes for his Net Builder.

## Making the Abdomen of Oswald's BH Rock Roller

*(See video instructions on DVD.)*

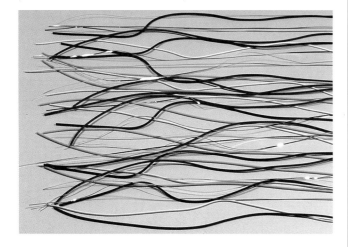

**1.** Duncan sent instructions, and I experimented with them and came up with what follows, which is fairly close to his approach. Randomly lay out four to seven 8-inch sections of each of the colors of rubber-strand, along with six to ten lengths each of gold and silver Mylar strand.

**2.** With the bead on the hook and the hook in your vise, wind lead up most of the shank right up to the bead. Bind the lead and then spiral the thread to the bend. Pick up all the rubber-strand and Mylar, and try to even them on one end. Trim the end straight across. Hold the end of the bundle down around the shank at the bend. Hold the bulk of the bundle off the bend, with the trimmed end of the bundle toward the eye. Wind two light-tension turns of thread over the end of the bundle, and then pull the thread tight. Add two or three more tight thread turns.

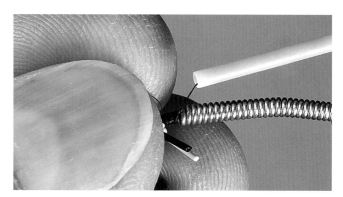

**3.** Stroke back the ends of the bundle, pull the thread forward, and add a few tight turns of thread in front of the bundle.

**4.** Trim off the bundle about ½ inch behind where it is bound. This should leave short ends of rubber-strand and Mylar on either side of the thread securing them. While holding the bundle in your right hand (assuming you're right-handed), stroke back the bound ends of the rubber-strand and Mylar with your left hand to get them out of the way. Push the end of the bundle down around the shank, reach around with your left hand, and work the bobbin to add two turns of thread around the bundle. Pull the thread tight, as before.

**5.** Trim off the front of the bundle.

**6.** Keep binding the end of the strand bundle and cutting it off, continuing up most of the lead-wrapped shank in this manner. Dub the remaining short distance to the bead, whip-finish and trim the thread, and add head cement to the whip finish.

**7.** Trim the rubber-strand and Mylar down to a full, elongated taper—to suggest the case of a caddis larva. Trim closely enough underneath to clear the gape and provide the hook with plenty of bite.

## OSWALD'S BH ROCK ROLLER — *Duncan Oswald*

*Tied by Duncan Oswald*

| | |
|---|---|
| **Hook:** | Heavy wire, 3X long (a hook with a sharp downward bend in the shank is preferred), sizes 16 to 6. |
| **Head:** | Black metal bead. |
| **Weight:** | Lead wire. |
| **Thread:** | Heavy, black. Duncan uses Nymo, but size A rod thread and even 3/0 will work. |
| **Abdomen:** | Black, brown, tan, and white round rubber-strand mixed with gold and silver High Voltage (an especially bright Mylar; you could substitute Flashabou or Krystal Flash). Bind on the rubber-strand and Mylar much as you'd bind on and flare deer hair; then trim. (Try brown, black, and gray for a quieter effect.) |
| **Thorax:** | Black rabbit blended with a small amount of Antron (marketed as "Wabbit" dubbing; or use a shiny synthetic or plain dyed rabbit). |

**Comments:** A truly original fly design is a rarity in my experience, and Oswald's BH Rock Roller is truly original. It also caught on fast. It imitates the cased larva of the hulking October caddis. Trout don't mind eating the works and letting their innards digest the food and eliminate the rest.

## PEEKING CADDIS — *George Anderson*

*Tied by Skip Morris*

| | |
|---|---|
| **Hook:** | Heavy wire, 1X or 2X long, sizes 22 to 18. |
| **Weight (optional):** | Lead wire under the abdomen. |
| **Thread:** | Black 8/0, 6/0, or 3/0 (up the abdomen only). |
| **Rib:** | Fine gold wire. |
| **Abdomen:** | Hare's mask, dubbed. |
| **Thorax:** | Pale yellow or olive fur, dubbed. |
| **Legs:** | Brown partridge flank fibers. |
| **Head:** | Black ostrich. |

**Comments:** The Peeking Caddis can be tied weighted or unweighted. It imitates a cased caddis larva.

## RAL'S CADDIS LARVA — *Raleigh Boaze Jr.*

*Tied by Skip Morris*

**Hook:**        Heavy wire, 1X long (humped or straight shank), sizes 16 to 8.

**Thread:**       Black 8/0 or 6/0.

**Weight (optional):** Lead wire.

**Foundation:**   Yarn (or dubbing) in a color similar to the abdomen color.

**Abdomen:**      Originally, a strip of latex sheeting cut from a dental dam, colored with a waterproof permanent marking pen and wound up most of the yarn-wrapped shank, with the turns of latex overlapping to suggest segmentation. Today, precolored latex strips, such as Scud Back and Stretch Flex, are a standard choice.

**Thorax:**       Peacock herl, spun around the thread for durability.

**Comments:**     Ral's Caddis Larva is among the first latex-bodied flies. Latex easily makes a translucent body with crisp segmentation, like the body of a real caddis larva. In the original pattern, which, I believe, first appeared in the book *The Fly Tyer's Almanac,* the latex was uncolored and the thorax was dubbed. The version presented here has become the standard, and colored latex makes it more versatile than the original. Peacock herl, with its elegant sparkle and reputation for attracting trout, was bound to work its way into the thorax.

## RICK'S CADDIS (*RHYACOPHILA*) — *Rick Hafele*

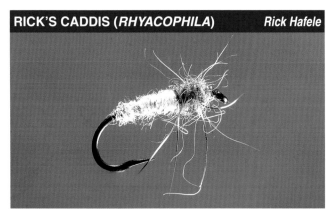

*Tied by Skip Morris*

**Hook:**        Heavy wire, 1X or 2X long, sizes 16 to 10.

**Thread:**       Brown 8/0 or 6/0.

**Weight (optional):** Lead wire.

**Abdomen:**      Bright green natural or synthetic fur.

**Thorax:**       Natural tan-brown hare's mask or a similar color of squirrel, or any natural or synthetic fur.

**Comments:**     Other colors can be used in the abdomen to imitate other caddis species.

## RICK'S KRYSTAL CADDIS — *Rick Hafele*

*Tied by Skip Morris*

**Hook:**        Heavy wire, 1X or 2X long, sizes 16 to 12.

**Thread:**       Brown 8/0 or 6/0.

**Weight (optional):** Lead wire.

**Abdomen:**      Several strands of bright green flashy Mylar such as Krystal Flash or Krystal Hair, twisted together and wound up the lead.

**Thorax:**       Natural hare's mask fur, dubbed.

**Comments:**     Lead is optional. The brilliant abdomen of this fly suggests the almost glowing green of the ubiquitous *Rhyacophila* larva.

## Tying the Rip Caddis

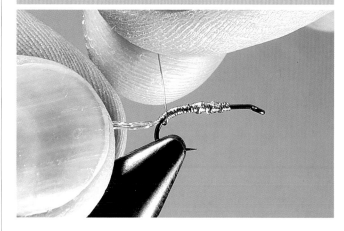

**1.** Start the copper wire about two-thirds up the shank, as you would start thread (you'll need quite a few tight windings down the shank, toward the bend, to lock the smooth wire onto the smooth shank). Double some strands of Krystal Flash over the wire, and then bind the Krystal Flash down the shank and partway down the bend. Unlike thread, wire holds its shape and remains in place on the shank without the weight of a bobbin.

**2.** Add a couple of tight turns of wire. Divide the strands of Krystal Flash into two equal groups. Stroke dubbing wax along one group of strands, and then dub along the strands themselves. Push the dubbing on the strands right down to the hook.

**3.** Cut the wire from the spool if you haven't already done so; cut it a bit long, so you have enough wire to tie the rest of the fly. Spin the two groups of Krystal Flash—the dubbed and bare groups—together with the wire (not too tightly, or the wire may break). Once they are spun, clamp English hackle pliers (the all-metal kind, with the coil) onto the ends of the Krystal Flash and wire. Wind the spun strands and wire about two-thirds to three-quarters up the shank. (Option: wind the wire two-thirds up the shank; then spin together and wind only the strands of Krystal Flash for the abdomen—without the wire. The abdomen will be slightly slimmer. If you don't like the look of the wire mixed into the abdomen, this is the solution. The abdomen will be plenty tough without the wire.)

**4.** Separate out the strands of Krystal Flash and wire, and wind a few tight turns of the wire over the ends of the strands. Trim off the ends of the strands.

**5.** Wax the wire, and spin fur fairly heavily onto it. Dub the thorax. Half-hitch the wire at the eye a few times (or whip-finish the wire, if you prefer). Cut the wire and add head cement to the half hitches. Pick out the fur at the sides of the thorax for legs (or let a few casts of the fly do it later).

## RIP CADDIS — *Rick Hafele and Skip Morris*

*Tied by Skip Morris*

| | |
|---|---|
| **Hook:** | Heavy wire, 1X, 2X, or 3X long (humped or slow-curve shank optional), sizes 14 to 8. |
| **Thread:** | Fine copper wire (switch to brown thread for making the thorax if you wish). |
| **Abdomen:** | Three to five strands of pearl Krystal Flash (or another Mylar strand) and small copper wire spun with rabbit fur of any caddis color. (Note that the lighter you dub, the brighter the fly becomes, because more of the Krystal Flash shows through.) |
| **Thorax:** | Natural tan-brown hare's mask fur or a similar color of squirrel, dubbed (or dyed dark brown hare's mask or squirrel if that matches the natural). |

**Comments:** Using copper wire in place of thread adds weight without bulk. It's really quite manageable, although you'll find a few half hitches easier than a whip finish with wire. The Krystal Flash may not look very shiny, camouflaged by the fuzz of rabbit dubbing, but in water it sparkles through like the bubbles clinging to the reflective shuck of a real caddis larva—hold a Rip Caddis in a glass of water and see for yourself. I usually use light green rabbit for *Rhyacophila* and tan for *Hydropsyche*, but you can use any caddis color—cream, brown, tannish yellow—for imitating any of the caseless larvae. Adjust the hook size to suit. A tan version is illustrated below.

## TAN CADDIS LARVA

*Tied by Skip Morris*

| | |
|---|---|
| **Hook:** | Heavy wire, humped shank (scud-pupa hook), sizes 16 to 8. |
| **Weight:** | Lead wire. |
| **Thread:** | Brown 8/0 or 6/0. |
| **Abdomen:** | Tan fur (rabbit is good) or a shiny synthetic dubbing. |
| **Legs:** | Natural brown partridge, as a beard on the underside. |
| **Thorax:** | Undyed tan-brown hare's mask or squirrel in hare's mask color. |

**Comments:** I got this one from Dave Hughes's original *Western Stream-side Guide*. It's a simple and effective imitation of the *Hydropsyche* larva.

# Caddis Pupae

## ALL-ROUNDER CADDIS PUPA — John Barr

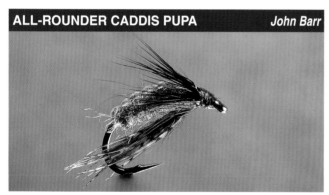

*Tied by Carol Ann Morris*

| | |
|---|---|
| **Hook:** | Heavy wire, humped shank (scud-pupa hook), sizes 16 to 12. |
| **Thread:** | Olive 8/0 or 6/0. |
| **Back:** | Strip of clear plastic cut from a freezer bag (or clear latex such as Stretch Flex or Scud Back). |
| **Rib:** | 4X monofilament tippet. |
| **Body:** | Brown-olive Scintilla (or another slightly shiny synthetic dubbing). |
| **Legs and antennae:** | Natural brown partridge fibers bound so they sweep back along the underside. |
| **Wing pads:** | Black rabbit fur, pushed straight over the hook's eye, bound as a collar. |

**Comments:** In *Tying Flies with Jack Dennis and Friends,* John says his All-Rounder Caddis Pupa is "durable and adapts well to a variety of hatch situations."

## BRICK BACK OCTOBER CADDIS — Skip Morris

With bead

With eyes

*Tied by Skip Morris*

| | |
|---|---|
| **Hook:** | Heavy wire, 2X long, slow-curve shank, sizes 10 to 6. |
| **Head (optional):** | Black metal bead, 1/8 inch (5/32 inch is an option on the largest hooks). |
| **Weight:** | Lead wire. |
| **Thread:** | Brown 3/0, 8/0, or 6/0. |
| **Butt:** | Short, full ball of the same dubbing used for the abdomen. |
| **Abdomen:** | Amber and orange rabbit fur mixed with fine, chopped silver, pearl, and yellow Mylar strands, such as Angel Hair or Lite Brite (or just buy Arizona Flyfishing's Sparkle Nymph Dubbing in the color Skip's October caddis). The bars are made with brown poly yarn. (Substitutes for the poly yarn include Stretch Flex or Scud Back, Antron yarn, and—if you want a truly brilliant fly—Krystal Flash or Flashabou.) |
| **Hackle:** | One dyed brown grizzly or brown hen saddle or hen neck hackle, longish (my favorite is Whiting's Soft Hackle). Any big, soft brown hackle will work, even the base of a dry-fly neck hackle. |
| **Eyes:** | Extra-small black plastic barbell eyes. (Eyes are optional without a bead, but never use them with a bead.) |
| **Thorax:** | Brown or dark brown rabbit mixed with fine, chopped silver, pearl, and brown Mylar, or just dark brown rabbit (or Arizona Flyfishing's Sparkle Nymph Dubbing in brown or dark brown). |

**Comments:** The tying of the Brick Back October Caddis is unique and therefore requires a little instruction. With the lead windings and bead on the shank (if you choose to use a bead), wind a ball of dubbing on the shank behind the lead. Bind a length of poly yarn atop and over the rear third of the lead. Wax a long stretch of thread and spin dubbing moderately thickly onto 8 to 10 inches of it. Make a long dubbing loop (instructions follow) and twist it. (At this point, I like to whip-finish the thread near the eye and cut the thread.) Wind some of the dubbing loop onto the shank to make a short section of the body. Pull the yarn forward and down, and then wind on one or two turns of the dubbing loop to secure the yarn and create a rib. Pull the yarn back and build another short section of the abdomen; then wind another turn or two of the dubbing loop around the shank and over the yarn for another rib and another little bar of brown. Continue in this manner until you've created five to seven bars up the back of a full and sparkling abdomen (real October caddis pupae have this pattern of brown bars up the backs of their abdomens and have sparkling bodies due to the gases within their shucks and the clinging bubbles without). The abdomen should cover about two-thirds of the shank. Bind the ends of the dubbing loop and yarn (by restarting the thread, if you cut it), and then trim them both closely. Bind on a webby hackle at the front of the abdomen and wind on a turn or two. Dub a thorax, and then complete the fly with a whip finish and head cement against the rear of the bead. If you omitted the bead, add a set of barbell eyes, a dubbed head, and a whip finish with a little head cement.

This has been a deadly fly for me in the fall on rivers with heavy hatches of the hulking late-season October caddis—particularly on Oregon's Deschutes River. You can let the Brick Back October Caddis sink and then swing it up and into the bank, mimicking the quick swim of the real pupa. But because some October caddis pupae emerge faulty and tumble along the riverbed (and many others do this while they're awakening their swimming legs after lying near dormant for so long in their cases), I usually fish my Brick Back October Caddis dead drift. The free-drifting pupae are the easiest to catch and probably the ones the trout prefer.

## Making a Dubbing Loop

**1.** The thread should come off the shank about ¼ inch up from where the dubbing loop will start. Wax the thread and then spin dubbing along it. The length of the thread you dub depends on how much shank you'll be dubbing (with the Brick Back October Caddis, you'll need to dub about 8 to 10 inches).

**2.** Run bare thread back to the hook, about ¼ inch up from where you want the loop to start. Wind the thread tightly back over its two ends to the rear of the area you want to dub. You now have a dubbing-loop locked in place.

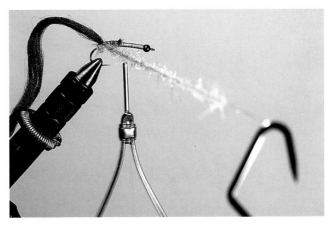

**3.** Spin the loop with a dubbing whirl or twister.

**4.** Clamp the end of the loop in the jaws of English hackle pliers. You needn't pull the loop tight any longer, because its twist will hold everything together. Wind the dubbing loop up the shank to build a tough, dubbed body or thorax.

Dubbing one side of a dubbing loop is common, but there are other approaches: the dubbing can be slipped *in between* the sides of the loop for a shaggy effect; even materials for legs can be slipped into the loop.

## COPPER BEAD Z-WING CADDIS, AMBER
### Mike Mercer

*Tied by Mike Mercer*

| | |
|---|---|
| **Hook:** | Heavy wire, humped shank (scud-pupa hook), sizes 16 to12. |
| **Head:** | Copper bead, small on size 16, medium on sizes 14 and 12. |
| **Thread:** | Camel (light brown) 8/0 or 6/0. |
| **Rib:** | Medium copper wire. |
| **Back:** | Golden brown turkey tail. |
| **Body:** | Mercer's Select Buggy Nymph Dubbing in amber caddis (or any coarse amber dubbing). |
| **Wing pads:** | Ginger Z-lon or Antron yarn. |
| **Wing:** | Single strand of pearl Flashabou, extending back over the top of the body. |
| **Collar:** | Rear half, same dubbing as for the body; front half, peacock herl. |
| **Comments:** | Imitates the *Hydropsyche* caddis pupa. |

## COPPER BEAD Z-WING CADDIS, CHARTREUSE
### Mike Mercer

*Tied by Mike Mercer*

| | |
|---|---|
| **Hook:** | Heavy wire, humped shank (scud-pupa hook), sizes 18 to 14. |
| **Head:** | Copper bead, small on sizes 18 and 16, medium on size 14. |
| **Thread:** | Olive 8/0 or 6/0. |
| **Rib:** | Chartreuse 3/0 Monocord (or a similar heavy thread). |
| **Back:** | Golden brown turkey tail. |
| **Body:** | Mercer's Select Buggy Nymph Dubbing in caddis green (or another coarse green dubbing). |
| **Wing pads:** | Light olive Z-lon or Antron yarn. |
| **Wing:** | Single strand of Pearl Flashabou, extending back over the top of the body. |
| **Collar:** | Rear half, same dubbing as for the body; front half, peacock herl. |
| **Comments:** | Mike tells me that he uses this pattern to imitate the Mother's Day caddis, but that it can suggest other caddis pupae. |

**Deep Sparkle Pupa.** The research for his book *Caddisflies* (published in 1981) lead Gary LaFontaine to conclude that the reflective veil of Antron around the abdomen of his Sparkle Pupa looks like the real thing. The veil suggests the shiny gases inside and outside the clinging shuck of a real caddis pupa ripe for hatching. He developed the Emergent Sparkle Pupa to be fished near the water's surface, and the Deep Sparkle Pupa that follows, to drift along the riverbed, just as the real pupae do after first squirming free of their pupal shelters.

In *Caddisflies,* Gary calls the four specific dressings for his Deep Sparkle Pupa that follow his "primary" color and size variations, which cover about 70 percent of caddis hatches. They are essentially the same variations he lists for his Emergent Sparkle Pupa (described later in this chapter).

To tie the Deep Sparkle Pupa, divide the yarn that is bound down the shank into four sections. Pull each section forward to cover all four sides of the body—near side, far side, top, and bottom—and bind the yarn lightly at the front of the body. Push the tip of a bodkin or needle in between the yarn and the body, and pull out the yarn. Do this all the way around the body until the yarn surrounds the body like a bubble. Then complete the tying of the fly.

## DEEP SPARKLE PUPA, BROWN AND BRIGHT GREEN
### Gary LaFontaine

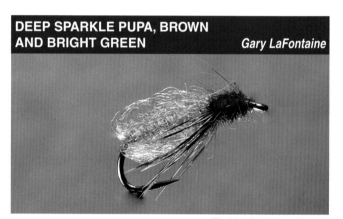

*Tied by Carol Ann Morris*

| | |
|---|---|
| **Hook:** | Light wire (to heavy wire), standard length to 1X long, sizes 18 to 12. |
| **Thread:** | Green or olive 8/0 or 6/0. |
| **Weight:** | One layer of lead wire. |
| **Veil:** | Medium olive Antron or Z-lon yarn, combed, tied in at the bend, and drawn forward around the body in a bubble (instructions are above). |
| **Body:** | One-third olive Antron dubbing and two-thirds bright green Antron dubbing, blended. |
| **Legs:** | Bunch of natural dark grouse fibers on each side of the body. |
| **Head:** | Dyed brown marabou strands spun around the thread (or dubbing). |
| **Comments:** | This fly can represent various common caddisflies. |

## DEEP SPARKLE PUPA, BROWN AND YELLOW
*Gary LaFontaine*

*Tied by Carol Ann Morris*

| | |
|---|---|
| **Hook:** | Light wire (to heavy wire), standard length to 1X long, sizes 18 to 12. |
| **Thread:** | Yellow, gold, or tan 8/0 or 6/0. |
| **Weight:** | One layer of lead wire. |
| **Veil:** | Russet (yellowish olive) or gold Antron or Z-lon yarn, combed, tied in at the bend, and drawn forward around the body in a bubble (instructions are on page 96). |
| **Body:** | One-half russet or gold Antron dubbing and one-half brown Antron dubbing, blended. |
| **Legs:** | Bunch of grouse fibers on each side of the body. |
| **Head:** | Dyed brown marabou strands spun around the thread (or dubbing). |
| **Comments:** | Represents various common caddisflies. |

## DEEP SPARKLE PUPA, GINGER
*Gary LaFontaine*

*Tied by Carol Ann Morris*

| | |
|---|---|
| **Hook:** | Light wire (to heavy wire), standard length to 1X long, sizes 18 to 12. |
| **Thread:** | Amber or light brown 8/0 or 6/0. |
| **Weight:** | One layer of lead wire. |
| **Veil:** | Amber Antron or Z-lon yarn, combed, tied in at the bend, and drawn forward around the body in a bubble (instructions are on page 96). |
| **Body:** | One-half cream Antron dubbing and one-half amber Antron dubbing, blended. |
| **Legs:** | Bunch of grouse fibers on each side of the body. |
| **Head:** | Dyed cream marabou strands spun around the thread (or dubbing). |
| **Comments:** | Represents various common caddisflies. |

## DEEP SPARKLE PUPA, DARK GRAY
*Gary LaFontaine*

*Tied by Carol Ann Morris*

| | |
|---|---|
| **Hook:** | Light wire (to heavy wire), standard length to 1X long, sizes 18 to 12. |
| **Thread:** | Gray or brown 8/0 or 6/0. |
| **Weight:** | One layer of lead wire. |
| **Veil:** | Gray Antron or Z-lon yarn, combed, tied in at the bend, and drawn forward around the body in a bubble (instructions are on page 96). |
| **Body:** | One-half gray Antron dubbing and one-half dark brown Antron dubbing, blended. |
| **Legs:** | Bunch of grouse fibers on each side of the body. |
| **Head:** | Dyed dark gray marabou strands spun around the thread (or dubbing). |
| **Comments:** | Represents various common caddisflies. |

## GIDLOW FUZZY CADDIS PUPA, OLIVE   *Arnie Gidlow*

*Tied by Arnie Gidlow*

| | |
|---|---|
| **Hook:** | Heavy wire, humped shank (scud-pupa hook), sizes 18 to 12. |
| **Thread:** | Olive 6/0. |
| **Head:** | One opaque green glass bead. |
| **Abdomen:** | Three to five clear glass beads, threaded up the shank. Over the beads and between them, olive Ice Dubbing, picked out to look shaggy. (For instructions, see Pettis's Gold Bead Pulsating Caddis Pupa on page 98.) |
| **Wing pads:** | Dyed brown goose quills, one per side angling down, trimmed blunt. |
| **Legs:** | Natural brown partridge flank fibers. |
| **Thorax:** | Dyed olive ostrich herl. |
| **Antennae:** | Two pheasant tail fibers. |
| **Comments:** | You can tie the Gidlow Fuzzy Caddis Pupa in whatever colors match the hatch. This is a quick-sinking pattern with lots of translucence. |

## GLASSTAIL CADDIS PUPA, EMERALD    *Mike Mercer*

*Top view*

*Tied by Mike Mercer*

**Hook:**          Heavy wire, humped shank (scud-pupa hook),
                   sizes 16 to 12.
**Head:**          One gunmetal-colored glass bead, slipped up the shank.
**Thorax:**        Two emerald green glass beads, slipped up the shank.
**Thread:**        Olive 8/0 or 6/0.
**Extended-body core:** Fine pale Kevlar thread.
**Extended abdomen:** Three emerald green beads (same as used for the
                   thorax). The Kevlar thread goes around the end bead and
                   through the two others.
**Thorax dubbing:** Olive Buggy Nymph Dubbing or any coarse dubbing.
                   Spin the dubbing in a thread loop (dubbing loop) and build it
                   between two beads, then forward under a bead; build it
                   between the next two beads, and so on. (For instructions,
                   see Pettis's Gold Bead Pulsating Caddis Pupa on pages 98
                   and 99.)
**Antennae:**      Lemon-barred wood-duck flank fibers.
**Legs:**          Brown partridge or speckled brown hen saddle, wound
                   ahead of the thorax beads.
**Wing case:**     Strip of brown or black Thin Skin over the herl only.
**Upper thorax:**  Peacock herl, short.
**Comments:**      This design has plenty of shine and weight. Mike believes
the translucence and crisp segmentation of the beads are what make the
Glasstail Caddis Pupa so effective.

## OCTOBER CADDIS NYMPH    *Paul Wolflick*

*Tied by Skip Morris*

**Hook:**          Heavy wire, 3X long (Paul prefers a slow curve shank),
                   size 8.
**Thread:**        Black 8/0, 6/0, or 3/0.
**Weight:**        Lead wire.
**Rib:**           Narrow pale orange gelatinous rib material, such as D-Rib,
                   V-Rib, Larva Lace.
**Abdomen:**       Rusty orange rabbit dubbing.
**Hackle:**        One furnace hen hackle.
**Head:**          Peacock herl.
**Comments:**      Paul designs his flies to suit the trout waters around his
home in central Oregon.


**Pettis's Pulsating Caddis Pupa.** One clever way to use glass beads is to create a segmented abdomen with a soft glow and the weight to pull the fly down. Glass beads have an ever-increasing following among fly tiers.

## PETTIS'S GOLD BEAD PULSATING CADDIS PUPA (*BRACHYCENTRUS*)    *Jim Pettis*

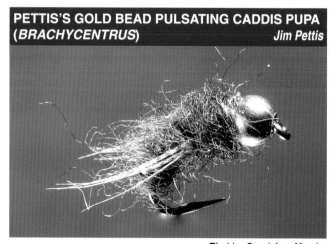

*Tied by Carol Ann Morris*

**Hook:**          Heavy wire, humped shank (scud-pupa hook),
                   sizes 16 and 14.
**Thread:**        Olive 8/0 or 6/0.
**Head:**          Gold metal bead.

**Body:** Three to four small deep-green glass beads. Olive-brown Buggy Nymph Dubbing (or other coarse dubbing) dubbed between the beads. Wind a turn or two of dubbing behind the last bead, wind the dubbing forward under the bead, wind a turn or two of dubbing between the beads, wind the dubbing forward under the next bead, and so on.

**Legs:** Wood-duck flank fibers.

**Thorax:** Dark brown Buggy Nymph Dubbing (or other coarse dubbing).

## PETTIS'S GOLD BEAD PULSATING CADDIS PUPA (*HYDROPSYCHE*)
*Jim Pettis*

*Tied by Skip Morris*

**Hook:** Heavy wire, humped shank (scud-pupa hook), sizes 16 to 12.

**Thread:** Olive 8/0 or 6/0.

**Head:** Gold metal bead.

**Body:** Three to five small light-orange glass beads. Lava brown Buggy Nymph Dubbing (or some other coarse dubbing) dubbed between the beads. (For tying instructions, see Pettis's Gold Bead Pulsating Caddis Pupa *Brachycentrus* on page 98.)

**Legs:** Wood-duck flank fibers.

**Thorax:** Dark brown Buggy Nymph Dubbing (or some other coarse dubbing).

## PETTIS'S PULSATING CADDIS PUPA (*BRACHYCENTRUS*)
*Jim Pettis*

*Tied by Carol Ann Morris*

**Hook:** Heavy wire, humped shank (scud-pupa hook), sizes 16 and 14.

**Thread:** Olive 8/0 or 6/0.

**Body:** Four to five small deep-green glass beads. Olive-brown Buggy Nymph Dubbing (or some other coarse dubbing) dubbed between the beads. (For tying instructions, see Pettis's Gold Bead Pulsating Caddis Pupa *Brachycentrus* on page 98.)

**Legs:** Wood-duck flank fibers.

**Head:** Dark brown Buggy Nymph Dubbing (or some other coarse dubbing).

## PETTIS'S PULSATING CADDIS PUPA (*HYDROPSYCHE*)
*Jim Pettis*

*Tied by Skip Morris*

**Hook:** Heavy wire, humped shank, (scud-pupa hook), sizes 16 to 12.

**Thread:** Olive 8/0 or 6/0.

**Body:** Four to six small orange glass beads, threaded up the hook's shank. Lava brown Buggy Nymph Dubbing (or other coarse dark brown dubbing) dubbed up and between the beads. (For tying instructions, see Pettis's Gold Bead Pulsating Caddis Pupa *Brachycentrus* on page 98.)

**Legs:** Wood-duck flank fibers.

**Head:** Dark brown Buggy Nymph Dubbing.

## SOLOMON'S CADDIS PUPA — *Larry Solomon*

*Tied by Skip Morris*

**Hook:** Heavy wire 1X or 2X long, sizes 18 to 12.

**Thread:** Dark 8/0 or 6/0.

**Weight (optional):** Lead wire.

**Rib:** Dark 3/0 tying thread (I usually use dark brown or, if the body is dark, black).

**Body:** Dubbing, usually olive green, although any appropriate color can be used.

**Wing pads:** Dark sections from the tip of a duck quill.

**Antennae and legs:** Brown partridge (hen saddle is a good substitute).

**Head:** Peacock or ostrich herl.

**Comments:** Larry's fairly detailed caddis pupa can imitate most varieties by varying size and color.

## STRAWMAN — *Paul Young*

*Tied by Skip Morris*

**Hook:** Heavy wire, 2X long, sizes 14 to 10.

**Thread:** Brown 8/0 or 6/0.

**Tail:** Mallard flank fibers.

**Rib:** Pale yellow thread or floss through the spun hair.

**Body:** Natural gray-brown deer hair, spun and shaped, not too dense (instructions are on page 268).

**Hackle:** Partridge or grizzly hen.

**Comments:** An early imitation of a cased caddis, the Strawman still sees action.

## TUNGSTEN OCTOBER CADDIS PUPA — *Mike Mercer*

*Tied by Mike Mercer*

**Hook:** Heavy wire, 2X long, slow-curve shank, sizes 8 and 6.

**Head:** Black tungsten bead, medium.

**Thread:** Camel 8/0 or 6/0.

**Rib:** One strand of pearl Flashabou.

**Back:** Dyed brown marabou strands.

**Abdomen:** Mercer's Select Buggy Nymph Dubbing in October caddis (or some other pale orange dubbing).

**Wing pads:** Dyed brown marabou, one clump on each side extending just past the end of a strip of Shimazaki Air Thru Fly Wing (or another pale gray or clear synthetic sheeting).

**Antennae:** Two undyed pheasant tail fibers.

**Hackle:** Natural golden brown hen back feather or natural brown grouse.

**Collar:** Rear half is the same dubbing as in the abdomen; front half is dyed brown ostrich herl or marabou, spun around the thread and wound.

**Comments:** Fish the Tungsten October Caddis Pupa dead drift or cast it upstream, let it sink, and then swing it slowly up and in.

# Caddis Emergers

## CDC CADDIS EMERGER, OLIVE — *René Harrop*

*Tied by Skip Morris*

**Hook:** Light wire, standard length to 1X long, sizes 20 to 14.

**Thread:** Olive 8/0 or 6/0.

**Rib:** Fine gold wire.

**Abdomen:** Dubbing blend of chopped olive angora goat and olive rabbit or mohair.

**Collar:** Partridge or speckled hen fibers, sparse.

**Wing:**     Two olive CDC feather tips.
**Antennae:**     Two wood-duck fibers (or mallard dyed wood-duck color).
**Thorax:**     Same dubbing as the abdomen, but a charcoal gray color.
**Comments:**     The CDC Caddis Emerger hangs by its buoyant wings. Fish it dead drift during caddis hatches to rising or bulging trout. Olive is only one possible color scheme—brown, gray, and tan are also common.

**Emergent Sparkle Pupa.** Gary LaFontaine's Emergent Sparkle Pupa is fished at the surface, a true caddis emerger pattern (the *Deep* Sparkle Pupa was described earlier). This pattern can be tied in a wide range of hook sizes and colors, but according to Gary, the four that follow "cover approximately 70 percent of the situations an angler will encounter involving emerging caddisflies." The peculiar puffy veil around the abdomen is the result of Gary's extensive study of caddis pupae underwater; he considered it the best solution to imitating the sparkling, bloated shuck around the body of a real hatching caddisfly.

To tie the Emergent Sparkle Pupa, divide the veil-yarn that is bound down the shank into four sections. Pull each section forward to cover all four sides of the body—near side, far side, top, and bottom—and bind the yarn lightly at the front of the body. Push the tip of a bodkin or needle in between the yarn and the body, and pull out the yarn. Do this all the way around the body until the yarn surrounds the body like a bubble. Tease a tiny amount of the yarn free to trail the fly as a shuck, and trim the shuck to length. Then complete the tying of the fly.

### EMERGENT SPARKLE PUPA, BROWN AND BRIGHT GREEN — *Gary LaFontaine*

*Tied by Carol Ann Morris*

**Hook:**     Light wire, standard length or 1X long, sizes 18 to 12.
**Thread:**     Green or olive 8/0 or 6/0.
**Shuck and body veil:** Medium olive Antron or Z-lon yarn (instructions are in the introduction to the Emergent Sparkle Pupa, on this page).
**Body:**     One-third olive and two-thirds bright green Antron dubbing, blended.
**Wing:**     Natural dark brown deer hair.
**Head:**     Dyed brown marabou fibers spun around the thread and wound, or brown dubbing.

### EMERGENT SPARKLE PUPA, BROWN AND YELLOW — *Gary LaFontaine*

*Tied by Carol Ann Morris*

**Hook:**     Light wire, standard length or 1X long, sizes 18 to 12.
**Thread:**     Yellow, gold, or tan 8/0 or 6/0.
**Shuck and body veil:** Russet (yellowish brown) or gold Antron or Z-lon yarn (instructions are in the introduction to the Emergent Sparkle Pupa, on this page).
**Body:**     One-half russet or gold and one-half brown Antron dubbing, blended.
**Wing:**     Natural light deer hair.
**Head:**     Dyed brown marabou strands spun around the thread and wound, or brown dubbing.

### EMERGENT SPARKLE PUPA, DARK GRAY — *Gary LaFontaine*

*Tied by Carol Ann Morris*

**Hook:**     Light wire, standard length or 1X long, sizes 18 to 12.
**Thread:**     Gray or brown 8/0 or 6/0.
**Shuck and body veil:** Gray Antron or Z-lon yarn (instructions are in the introduction to the Emergent Sparkle Pupa, on this page).
**Body:**     One-half gray and one-half dark brown Antron dubbing, blended.
**Wing:**     Undyed dark gray deer hair.
**Head:**     Dark gray marabou strands spun around the thread and wound, or dark gray dubbing.

## EMERGENT SPARKLE PUPA, GINGER
### Gary LaFontaine

*Tied by Carol Ann Morris*

**Hook:** Light wire, standard length or 1X long, sizes 18 to 12.

**Thread:** Amber or light brown 8/0 or 6/0.

**Shuck and body veil:** Amber Antron or Z-lon yarn (instructions are in the introduction to the Emergent Sparkle Pupa, on page 101).

**Body:** One-half cream and one-half amber Antron dubbing.

**Wing:** Natural light deer hair.

**Head:** Dyed cream marabou strands spun around the thread and wound, or cream dubbing.

**Iris Caddis.** The Iris Caddises cover two very common river caddisflies of the West. Craig Mathews dresses the Irises all over with floatant and fishes them dead drift to trout feeding on a caddis hatch. The loop of yarn suggests the partly free wings slipping from the shuck.

## IRIS CADDIS, AMBER
### Blue Ribbon Flies

**Front view**

*Tied by Craig Mathews*

**Hook:** Light wire, short to standard length, straight or humped shank (just about any light-wire, shortish hook), size 14.

**Thread:** Amber (or tan or yellow) 8/0 or 6/0.

**Shuck:** Gold or amber Z-lon or Antron yarn, short.

**Body:** Amber Z-lon or Antron dubbing.

**Wing:** Loop of white (or blue dun) Z-lon or Antron yarn, over the abdomen and extending to about the bend.

**Head:** Tan buoyant synthetic (or natural) dubbing (poly, Antron) picked out a bit to appear rough.

**Comments:** This version imitates most emerging *Hydropsyche* caddisflies. The tan version imitates smaller *Hydropsyche*.

## IRIS CADDIS, OLIVE
### Blue Ribbon Flies

*Tied by Craig Mathews*

**Hook:** Light wire, short to standard length, straight or humped shank (just about any light-wire, shortish hook), size 16.

**Thread:** Olive 8/0.

**Shuck:** Gold or amber Z-lon or Antron yarn, short.

**Body:** Olive Z-lon or Antron dubbing.

**Wing:** Loop of white (or blue dun) Z-lon or Antron yarn, over the abdomen and extending to about the bend.

**Head:** Tan buoyant synthetic (or natural) dubbing (poly, Antron) picked out a bit to appear rough.

**Comments:** This version imitates an emerging *Brachycentrus* caddis.

## IRIS CADDIS, TAN
### Blue Ribbon Flies

*Tied by Craig Mathews*

**Hook:** Light wire, short to standard length, humped or straight shank (just about any light-wire, shortish hook), size 16.

**Thread:** Tan 8/0 or 6/0.

**Shuck:** Gold or amber Z-lon or Antron yarn.

**Body:** Tan Z-lon or Antron dubbing.

**Wing:** Loop of white (or blue dun) Z-lon or Antron yarn, over the abdomen and extending to about the bend.

**Head:** Tan buoyant synthetic (or natural) dubbing (poly, Antron) picked out a bit to appear rough.

**Comments:** The amber version imitates larger *Hydropsyche* caddis, and this version imitates smaller ones.

## MICRO DEVIL BUG
### *Roger Hill's variation of the standard Devil Bug*

*Tied by Carol Ann Morris*

| | |
|---|---|
| **Hook:** | Light wire, standard length or 1X long, size 20 or 18. |
| **Thread:** | Tan or black 8/0. |
| **Body:** | Hare's ear or Antron dubbing in any caddis color. |
| **Trailing shuck:** | Tan and a little orange Sparkle Yarn (or Antron yarn), mixed. |
| **Hump:** | Tan Sparkle Yarn (or Antron yarn). After the yarn is bound lightly at the hook's eye, pull it up a little to form a loose hump; then add tight thread turns. |
| **Head:** | The butts of the yarn, trimmed to a stub. |
| **Comments:** | One of the few tiny caddis emergers. |

## PARTRIDGE CADDIS EMERGER, OLIVE
### *Mike Lawson*

*Tied by Skip Morris*

| | |
|---|---|
| **Hook:** | Light wire, standard length or 1X long, sizes 20 to 12. |
| **Thread:** | Olive 8/0. |
| **Shuck:** | Fine kinky olive Z-lon for larger hooks, Antron yarn for smaller. |
| **Rib:** | Fine copper wire. |
| **Abdomen:** | Olive Antron dubbing. |
| **Wing:** | Two brown partridge feathers over a little olive Z-lon (Antron for smaller hooks). |
| **Thorax:** | Arizona Peacock Dubbing (originally, peacock herl). |
| **Comments:** | Mike normally fishes his Partridge Caddis Emergers half sunken, with floatant on the wing only. |

## PARTRIDGE CADDIS EMERGER, TAN
### *Mike Lawson*

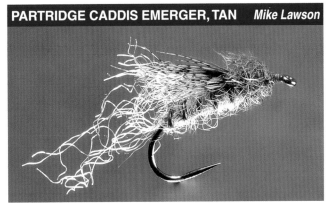

*Tied by Skip Morris*

| | |
|---|---|
| **Hook:** | Light wire, standard length or 1X long, sizes 20 to 12. |
| **Thread:** | Tan 8/0. |
| **Shuck:** | Fine kinky tan Z-lon for larger hooks, Antron yarn for smaller. |
| **Rib:** | Fine copper wire. |
| **Abdomen:** | Tan Antron dubbing. |
| **Wing:** | Two brown partridge feathers over a little tan Z-lon (Antron for smaller hooks). |
| **Thorax:** | Arizona Bronze Peacock Dubbing (originally, peacock herl). |
| **Comments:** | Mike normally fishes his Partridge Caddis Emergers half sunken, with floatant on the wing only. |

## PETTIS'S PULSATING CADDIS EMERGER (*BRACHYCENTRUS*)
### *Jim Pettis*

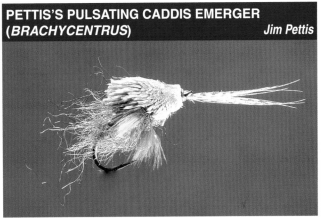

*Tied by Carol Ann Morris*

| | |
|---|---|
| **Hook:** | Light to standard wire, 2X long, slow-curve shank, size 16. |
| **Thread:** | Olive 8/0 or 6/0. |
| **Abdomen:** | Three small deep-green glass beads. Dub olive-brown Buggy Nymph Dubbing (or another coarse dubbing) up and between the beads. For instructions, see Pettis's Gold Bead Pulsating Caddis Pupa (*Brachycentrus*) on page 98. |
| **Wing pads:** | Dark olive-brown marabou. |
| **Thorax:** | Light hare's ear Buggy Nymph Dubbing (or another coarse dubbing). |
| **Legs:** | Wood-duck fibers, projecting forward under the hook's eye. |
| **Wings and head:** | Medium to dark gray undyed deer hair, trimmed to shape. For instructions, see page 268. |

## PETTIS'S PULSATING CADDIS EMERGER (*HYDROPSYCHE*)
*Jim Pettis*

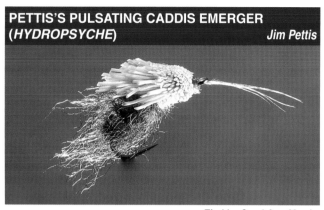

*Tied by Carol Ann Morris*

**Hook:** Light to standard wire, 2X long, slow-curve shank, size 16.
**Thread:** Olive 8/0 or 6/0.
**Abdomen:** Three small light-orange glass beads. Dub lava brown Buggy Nymph Dubbing (or another coarse dubbing) up and between the beads. (For tying instructions, see Pettis's Gold Bead Pulsating Caddis Pupa *Brachycentrus* on page 98.)
**Wing pads:** Dark olive-brown marabou.
**Thorax:** Pale olive-yellow Scintilla Multipurpose Dubbing (or another coarse, light-sheen dubbing).
**Legs:** Wood-duck fibers.
**Wings and head:** Light tan elk hair, trimmed to shape (instructions are on page 268).

## POP-TOP CADDIS EMERGER
*Andy Burk*

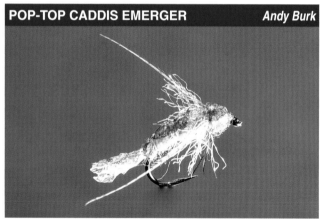

*Tied by Carol Ann Morris*

**Hook:** Light wire, humped shank (pupa-emerger hook), sizes 18 to 14.
**Thread:** Tan 8/0 or 6/0.
**Body:** Tan dubbing under a taper-cut strip of tan closed-cell foam, colored on top with a brown waterproof marking pen. The foam is called Ethafoam—a whitish foam sheeting with a pebbly surface, usually used as a packing material. Bind the foam atop the front of the dubbed abdomen. Spiral the working thread back over the foam and body to the bend, and then spiral the thread back up to the front of the abdomen. The pointed tip of the foam should extend back, as a shuck.
**Legs:** Grouse fibers.
**Wing:** Dun Z-lon.

**Antennae:** Mallard flank fibers.
**Head:** Tan dubbing, with the front of the foam strip over the top and bound at the hook's eye.
**Comments:** The buoyant foam tends to hold only the back of the fly to the surface of the water. Coat the colored foam with thinned Dave's Flexament if you want the color to endure.

## SLF CADDIS
*Davy Wotton*

*Tied by Carol Ann Morris*

**Hook:** Light wire, humped shank (pupa-emerger hook), sizes 14 to 8.
**Thread:** Pale yellow 8/0 or 6/0.
**Abdomen:** Olive (#11) SLF dubbing (or another coarse, shiny synthetic dubbing).
**Sheath:** Zing Wing.
**Legs:** Brown dry-fly hackle.
**Thorax:** Rust brown (#37) SLF dubbing.
**Antennae:** Wood-duck flank fibers, bound on at the eye, projecting forward, then doubled back and bound.
**Comments:** The sheath is trimmed to a rounded tip and bound on around the body like a clear, nearly encircling wing—but it's a sheath. So this really is an emerging caddis pupa, not a winged adult.

**X Caddis.** The X Caddis variations cover the common western river caddisflies and can be modified to imitate others. This fly pattern is designed to suggest a caddis that failed partway through its hatching—what fly fishers call a "cripple." Craig Mathews dresses the X Caddises with floatant and fishes them dead drift to rising trout during a caddis hatch. He believes that trout recognize the easy opportunity cripples offer and tend to seek them.

## X CADDIS, CADDIS GREEN — *Blue Ribbon Flies*

*Tied by Craig Mathews*

**Hook:** Light wire, standard length or 1X long, size 16.
**Thread:** Olive 8/0.
**Shuck:** Gold or amber Z-lon or Antron yarn, short.
**Body:** Caddis green Z-lon or Antron dubbing.
**Wing and head:** Deer hair, bound at the hook's eye atop the shank. Trim the butts to make the head.
**Comments:** This version imitates the *Rhyacophila* caddis.

## X CADDIS, LITTLE BLACK — *Blue Ribbon Flies*

*Tied by Craig Mathews*

**Hook:** Light wire, standard length or 1X long, size 20.
**Thread:** Black 8/0.
**Shuck:** Gold or amber Z-lon, short.
**Body:** Black Z-lon or Antron dubbing.
**Wing and head:** Dark caribou hair, bound at the hook's eye atop the shank. Trim the butts to make the head.
**Comments:** This version imitates the *Glossosoma* caddis.

# Caddis Adults

## BUNDLED CDC MICROCADDIS

*Tied by Carol Ann Morris*

**Hook:** Light wire, short shank to 1X long, sizes 22 to 18.
**Thread:** 8/0 in a color to match the body of the natural.
**Body:** The working thread.
**Wing:** Three or four bunches of CDC fibers the same color as the wing, bound atop the hook at intervals and trimmed to shape (see the instructions on page 111).
**Hackle:** CDC barbs spun in a dubbing loop, wound up the shank, and trimmed to length (see the instructions on page 70), or a couple of turns of dry-fly hackle. Either kind of hackle should be trimmed off underneath. Making a CDC hackle collar on the shank is essentially the same as making a CDC parachute hackle on a wing.
**Comments:** This is a miniature version of a western caddisfly pattern—the Mikulak Sedge—whose wing is composed of three or more bunches of deer hair. A deer-hair wing is impractical on tiny hooks, but one made of CDC is quite workable.

**DELTA WING CADDIS** *Larry Solomon*

*Top view*

*Tied by Skip Morris*

**Hook:** Light wire, standard length or 1X long, sizes 22 to 10.

**Thread:** Olive 8/0 or 6/0 (or whatever color matches the abdomen color).

**Abdomen:** Light olive dubbing (other colors can be used).

**Wing:** Gray hen neck hackles tied spent and slanting slightly back.

**Hackle:** Brown, fibers trimmed away underneath (any caddis colors can be used).

**Thorax:** Light olive synthetic dubbing (any caddis color can be used).

**Comments:** Larry says that the Delta Wing Caddis suggests "an adult caddis that cannot quite extricate itself from its pupal overcoat, or a partially crippled insect of that species." This makes the fly pattern almost an emerger . . . almost.

**Elk Hair Caddis.** The Elk Hair Caddis is a high floater, and an excellent dry fly for skittering (which can be deadly with an adult caddis imitation). And it may still be the most popular western caddis dry fly, even after all these years. If you substitute synthetic dubbing for the original hare's mask, you can make any color variation you like. The wing can be any shade of natural or dyed elk.

**ELK HAIR CADDIS** *Al Troth*

*Tied by Al Troth*

**Hook:** Light wire, standard length or 1X long, sizes 18 to 8.

**Thread:** Tan 3/0 (some tiers prefer 6/0 or 8/0, especially for the smaller sizes, but 3/0 allows tight turns that really secure the wing).

**Rib:** Fine gold wire.

**Body:** Hare's mask fur.

**Hackle:** One brown, bound on at the front of the body, spiraled back to the bend, and then secured with a couple of turns of the wire rib. The rib is then spiraled forward through the hackle to the front of the body, secured with tight thread windings, and trimmed off.

**Wing:** Bleached (or natural light) elk hair.

**Head:** Butts of the wing hair.

**Comments:** This is the original and standard dressing for the Elk Hair Caddis.

## ELK HAIR CADDIS, BLACK
### Variation of Al Troth's pattern

*Tied by Skip Morris*

| | |
|---|---|
| **Hook:** | Light wire, standard length or 1X long, sizes 18 to 8. |
| **Thread:** | Black 8/0, 6/0, or 3/0. |
| **Rib:** | Fine gold wire. |
| **Body:** | Black synthetic dubbing. |
| **Hackle:** | One black, bound on at the front of the body, spiraled back to the bend, and then secured with a couple of turns of the wire rib. The rib is then spiraled forward through the hackle to the front of the body, secured with tight thread windings, and trimmed off. |
| **Wing:** | Dyed black elk hair. (To make the fly easier to spot, you can bind yellow or orange poly yarn atop the hair and then trim the yarn to the end of the wing and head.) |
| **Head:** | Butts of the wing hair. |
| **Comments:** | A popular variation. |

## ELK HAIR CADDIS, OLIVE
### Variation of Al Troth's pattern

*Tied by Skip Morris*

| | |
|---|---|
| **Hook:** | Light wire, standard length or 1X long, sizes 18 to 8. |
| **Thread:** | Olive 8/0, 6/0, or 3/0. |

| | |
|---|---|
| **Rib:** | Fine gold wire. |
| **Body:** | Olive synthetic dubbing. |
| **Hackle:** | One olive (or barred dyed olive or brown), bound on at the front of the body, spiraled back to the bend, and then secured with a couple of turns of the wire rib. The rib is then spiraled forward through the hackle to the front of the body, secured with tight thread windings, and trimmed off. |
| **Wing:** | Bleached (or natural light) elk hair. |
| **Head:** | Butts of the wing hair. |
| **Comments:** | A popular variation. |

## FALL CADDIS

*Tied by Skip Morris*

| | |
|---|---|
| **Hook:** | Light wire, 2X or 3X long, sizes 10 to 6. |
| **Thread:** | Black 8/0, 6/0, or 3/0. |
| **Rib:** | One brown hackle, slightly small, spiraled up the body. |
| **Body:** | Orange synthetic dubbing. |
| **Wing:** | Natural brown deer hair. |
| **Hackle:** | Brown, heavy. |
| **Comments:** | We found this pattern in Dave Hughes's *The Western Streamside Guide*. Dave uses the Fall Caddis to imitate the great October caddis. |

## FLAT WING CADDIS

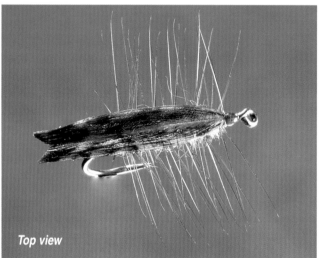

*Top view*

*Tied by Skip Morris*

| | |
|---|---|
| **Hook:** | Light wire, standard length or 1X long, sizes 22 to 12. |
| **Thread:** | Brown 8/0 or 6/0. |
| **Rib:** | One brown hackle spiraled up the body, trimmed top and bottom (other colors can be used). |
| **Abdomen:** | Gray synthetic dubbing (other colors can be used). |
| **Wing:** | Partridge feather coated with head cement or epoxy, then drawn between a horizontal toothpick and a flat surface (such as a flat plastic lid or a magazine) to draw out most of the cement and narrow the feather. When the cement is fully set, cut a notch in the tip of the feather. |
| **Comments:** | This style produces a durable wing with a precise silhouette. |

## GIDLOW EB CADDIS                     *Arnie Gidlow*

*Tied by Arnie Gidlow*

| | |
|---|---|
| **Hook:** | Light to 1X heavy, humped shank (scud-pupa or pupa-emerger hook), sizes 18 to 10. |
| **Thread:** | Tan 8/0 or 6/0. |
| **Body:** | Ultra Chenille (also known as Vernille) burned on the tip and bound on well up the shank. Mark small dots up the underside with a brown permanent marking pen. |
| **Underwing:** | Tan EP Fibers (fine, translucent synthetic fibers). |
| **Wing:** | Tan Swiss straw, one length with a notch trimmed in its tip. Wrap the wing partway down the sides of the body. |
| **Hackle:** | Tan Henry's Fork Hackle, trimmed long on the sides and close on top and below. (Henry's Fork Hackle is CDC fibers fixed to a thread core. You can substitute CDC fibers locked crossways in a dubbing loop as described on pages 70 and 71.) |
| **Comments:** | The Ultra Chenille extended body is an interesting and unusual touch. |

## GIDLOW FOAM CADDIS — *Arnie Gidlow*

*Front view*

*Top view*

*Tied by Arnie Gidlow*

**Hook:** Light wire, standard length, sizes 18 to 10.

**Thread:** Gray 8/0 or 6/0.

**Body:** Strip of very thin gray buoyant closed-cell foam sheeting (Arnie uses Razor Foam), one edge darkened with a brown permanent marking pen. Bind the strip up the shank, and then wrap the strip up the shank in abutting turns.

**Wing:** Same foam used for the body, cut to a single, notched wing shape.

**Hackle:** Light dun Henry's Fork Hackle (CDC fibers fixed to a thread core). It can be wound as hackle, then trimmed to length. An alternative would be CDC fibers locked crossways in a dubbing loop (see pages 70 and 71). Making a CDC hackle collar is essentially the same process as making a CDC parachute hackle. Trim off the fibers on the top and underside.

**Comments:** Other colors can be substituted to match different real caddisflies.

## GIDLOW SPRING CREEK CADDIS — *Arnie Gidlow*

*Front view*

*Top view*

*Tied by Arnie Gidlow*

**Hook:** Light wire, standard length, sizes 18 to 10.

**Thread:** Brown 8/0 or 6/0.

**Body:** Strip of very thin tan buoyant closed-cell foam sheeting, darkened along one edge with a black permanent marking pen. Bind the strip up the shank; then wrap the strip up the shank in abutting turns.

**Wing:** Nature's Wing, cut to a single, notched wing shape. (Nature's Wing is a synthetic sparkling foam sheeting with crosshatching. You can substitute another synthetic sheeting.)

**Hackle:** Brown Henry's Fork Hackle (CDC fibers fixed to a thread core), trimmed top and bottom, with the remaining fibers trimmed longish. A substitute would be CDC fibers locked crossways in a dubbing loop (see pages 70 and 71). Making a CDC hackle collar is essentially the same process as making a CDC parachute hackle.

## GODDARD CADDIS
*John Goddard*

*Tied by Skip Morris*

**Hook:** Light wire, standard length or 1X long, sizes 16 to 8.

**Thread:** Brown 8/0 or 6/0. (Skip prefers gray size A rod-winding thread for flaring the deer hair.)

**Wing and body:** Natural gray deer hair, flared, packed, and trimmed to shape (instructions are on page 268).

**Hackle:** Brown.

**Antennae (optional):** Brown hackle stems stripped of fibers.

**Comments:** The Goddard Caddis is a well-established pattern that floats a long time owing to its compressed deer-hair body.

## HEMINGWAY CADDIS

*Tied by Skip Morris*

**Hook:** Light wire, standard length or 1X long, sizes 18 to 12.

**Thread:** Olive 8/0 or 6/0.

**Rib:** Medium blue dun hackle spiraled up the body.

**Body:** Olive synthetic dubbing.

**Underwing:** Wood-duck fibers.

**Wing:** Section of natural gray duck quill trimmed to a rounded tip and rolled around the top half of the body.

**Thorax:** Peacock herl.

**Hackle:** One medium blue dun, spiraled up the thorax.

**Comments:** A trusty old-timer that remains viable.

## HENRYVILLE SPECIAL
*Hiram Brobst*

*Tied by Skip Morris*

**Hook:** Light wire, standard length or 1X long, sizes 20 to 12.

**Thread:** Brown 8/0 or 6/0.

**Rib:** One grizzly (one size smaller than usual), spiraled up the body.

**Body:** Olive floss or synthetic dubbing.

**Wing:** Natural gray duck quill over wood duck or mallard dyed wood-duck color.

**Hackle:** Brown.

**Comments:** Another old-timer that's too good to fade.

## KING'S RIVER CADDIS
*Wayne "Buz" Buszek*

*Tied by Skip Morris*

**Hook:** Light wire, standard length to 1X long, sizes 16 to 10.

**Thread:** Brown 8/0 or 6/0.

**Body:** Raccoon fur or brown synthetic dubbing.

**Wing:** Section of mottled brown turkey quill with a notch cut in the tip.

**Hackle:** Brown.

**Comments:** An older, proven adult caddis imitation named for the California river on which it was developed. Spraying the turkey feather with an artist's fixative or coating it with thinned Dave's Flexament before cutting out the section toughens the wing significantly.

## Tying the Mikulak Sedge

*(See video instructions on DVD.)*

**1.** Run the thread tightly up and back down the shank—creating a foundation to hold the wing sections. Stack a gape- to a gape-and-a-half-long bunch of hair, and bind it in front of the bend as a tail (which is really part of the wing). Keep the bound butts of the hair short, covering only about one-quarter of the shank. Dub over the butts of the hair.

**2.** Stack and bind on another bunch of hair—the length of the last bunch, or a little longer. Keep the bound butts short again, and dub over them.

**3.** Continue making wing and dubbing sections until about a fifth of the shank remains. Do not cut the butts of the last bunch of elk; instead, bind them forward to barely short of the eye. Trim the butts straight across as a head, now or after the hackle is added.

**4.** Bind a hackle at the rear of the bindings over the last bunch of wing hair. Wind the hackle forward in close turns, bind and trim off its tip, and whip-finish and trim the thread. You can whip finish the thread behind the hair-butt head or on the shank in front of the head and behind the hook's eye. Add head cement to the whip finish. Trimming the hackle fibers off underneath to flat across or to form a shallow "V" is optional.

| **MIKULAK SEDGE** | *Art Mikulak* |
| --- | --- |

*Tied by Skip Morris*

**Hook:** Light or standard wire, 1X to 2X long, sizes 10 to 6.
**Thread:** 8/0, 6/0, or 3/0 in the hackle color.
**Tail:** Natural tan-gray elk hair (or deer).
**Body and wing:** Two to four natural tan-gray elk-hair (or deer-hair) wings, each divided by a short section of dubbed abdomen. Use any buoyant dubbing (I prefer synthetics such as poly or Antron dubbing) in any color—tan, orange, brown, gray.
**Head:** Butts of the last wing, trimmed short.
**Hackle:** One brown (or any color).
**Comments:** From what I understand, Art Mikulak designed this pattern to imitate caddisfly adults on trout lakes. It has become a standard pattern on British Columbia's famous Kamloops Lakes for imitating the huge traveler sedge. However, I've been proving for the past few years that it's a fine fly for rivers, too. I generally use it in orange, to imitate the October caddis.

**PARACHUTE CADDIS** *Ed Schroeder*

*Top view*

*Tied by Skip Morris*

**Hook:** Light wire, standard length or 1X long, sizes 18 to 10.
**Thread:** Cream 8/0 or 6/0.
**Parachute wing:** White calf tail (instructions are on page 63).
**Parachute hackle:** Grizzly, parachute (instructions are on page 63).
**Abdomen:** Hare's mask fur (or synthetic dubbing).
**Wing:** Mottled turkey quill section, notched in the end.
**Thorax:** Hare's mask fur (or synthetic dubbing).
**Comments:** The white upright wing provides visibility and a base for the parachute hackle. Colors can be altered to match a variety of caddis adults. The wing will be much more durable if the turkey feather is sprayed with artist's fixative or coated with thinned Dave's Flexament before the wing section is cut from it. The Parachute Caddis developed a considerable following soon after it surfaced and has proven itself.

**Skaddis.** The Skaddis is about as simple as a caddis imitation can be. It creates a convincing silhouette for the trout and floats very well for a sparse dressing. I tie it mostly in the brown and tan versions below—one or the other is always close enough to the natural to work—but you can tie the Skaddis in whatever colors match a specific caddis.

**SKADDIS DARK** *Skip Morris*

*Tied by Skip Morris*

**Hook:** Light wire, standard length or 1X long, sizes 22 to 8.
**Thread:** Brown 8/0 or 6/0.
**Abdomen:** Brown poly dubbing (or another synthetic dubbing).
**Wing:** Brown poly yarn, with a little yellow poly yarn atop the wing, trimmed to match the wing's length, as a strike indicator. Two to four strands of pearl Krystal Flash under the wing, trimmed to the wing's length, is optional.
**Hackle:** Brown, spiraled up the thorax (trimming the fibers on the underside to a "V" is optional).
**Thorax:** Same as the abdomen.

## SKADDIS LIGHT — *Skip Morris*

*Tied by Skip Morris*

| | |
|---|---|
| **Hook:** | Light wire, standard length or 1X long, sizes 22 to 8. |
| **Thread:** | Tan 8/0 or 6/0. |
| **Abdomen:** | Tan poly dubbing (or another synthetic dubbing). |
| **Wing:** | Tan poly yarn. Two to four strands of pearl Krystal Flash under the wing, trimmed to the wing's length, is optional. |
| **Hackle:** | Ginger, spiraled up the thorax (trimming the fibers on the underside to a "V" is optional). |
| **Thorax:** | Same as the abdomen. |

## ST. VRAIN CADDIS, OLIVE — *A. K. Best*

*Tied by Carol Ann Morris*

| | |
|---|---|
| **Hook:** | Light wire, standard length or 1X long, sizes 20 to 12. (A. K. prefers an up-eye hook for sizes 18 and 20.) |
| **Thread:** | Olive 8/0 or 6/0. |
| **Body:** | Dyed golden-olive beaver or rabbit fur (or a synthetic dubbing such as Super Fine Dry Fly or Antron). A. K. makes the body slimmer in front than at the rear, so the wing lies down. |
| **Wing:** | Natural dark brown elk hair. Keep the wing on the sparse side. |
| **Hackle:** | Brown, full. |
| **Comments:** | A. K. Best has written several fly-tying books, including *A. K.'s Fly Box,* which includes this pattern. He says that his St. Vrain Caddis is easy to spot during heavy caddis hatches, when most adult caddis imitations are camouflaged among the naturals. It's also a good fly for skating, which can pay off with caddis dry flies. |

## ST. VRAIN CADDIS, YELLOW — *A. K. Best*

*Tied by Carol Ann Morris*

| | |
|---|---|
| **Hook:** | Light wire, standard length or 1X long, sizes 20 to 12. (A. K. prefers an up-eye hook for sizes 18 and 20.) |
| **Thread:** | Yellow 8/0 or 6/0. |
| **Body:** | Dyed pale yellow beaver or rabbit fur (or a synthetic dubbing such as Super Fine Dry Fly or Antron). A. K. makes the body slimmer in front than at the rear, so the wing lies down. |
| **Wing:** | Natural light elk hair or bleached deer hair. Keep the wing on the sparse side. |
| **Hackle:** | Light ginger, full. |
| **Comments:** | According to A. K., this yellow version, though primarily for caddis hatches, is a fine pattern for the little yellow stoneflies (yellow sallies), as long as the wing isn't too thick. |

## WOOLLY WING

This very effective and buoyant imitation of a caddis adult can also suggest a stonefly adult. (See chapter 6.)

# Stoneflies

ALTHOUGH STONEFLY hatches hardly compare with the bread-and-butter hatches of the ubiquitous and long-winded midge or the pale morning dun mayfly, they are nevertheless a big deal in the West—their numbers may be great and the individuals are enormous. The giant salmonfly is legendary, measuring as long as two joints of a man's finger. The equally important golden stonefly is only a shade smaller. But there are also modest-size and even little stoneflies in the West that deserve fly fishers' attention, and most of these are active when the great, ostentatious stoneflies are not, in the winter and midsummer.

The flattened, stout-legged stonefly nymph lives beneath rocks in swift currents. At hatch time it creeps to the shallows and climbs out of the water to split and slough its shuck. The now-winged adult stays among the brush and trees along the river's edge, flitting, crawling, and mating. Female stoneflies return to the water from late afternoon into the evening to release their eggs.

# Fishing the Stages of the Stonefly

## NYMPH

*Stonefly nymph*

The standard approach to fishing an imitation stonefly nymph is below a strike indicator, dead drift. Because the real nymphs live in quick currents, a heavily weighted imitation is needed to get the fly down to the fish before it is swept to the end of its drift. Additional weight on the leader may be required. In rivers with lots of huge salmonfly or golden stonefly nymphs, patterns that mimic those nymphs are a sound choice throughout the season. But just prior to the hatch, when the nymphs are migrating to shore, the fishing can be red hot.

## ADULT

*Stonefly adult*

Since stonefly nymphs crawl to the shallows to hatch, there is no mayfly-like open-water emergence to bring the trout up to feed in the middle of a riffle. Instead, the adults gather in streamside brush, grasses, and tree limbs, where they scurry and mate and tumble accidentally to the water. When the females later return to the river to release their eggs, some wind up trapped on the water. So, during a stonefly hatch, a dry fly should be drifted or twitched wherever the adults are showing, which is usually near or even right up against the banks. To imitate small stoneflies, some fly fishers successfully fish adult caddis imitations.

# Specific Hatches

**Salmonfly.** This insect is a monster—up to 2 inches long through the body—and its hatching is legendary. The nymph is stout, resembling a flattened black armadillo, but elongated and with a large head. The adult is blackish with an orange underside and dark brown wings. The salmonfly hatches for a two- to three-week period in late spring or summer in only a modest number of rivers, which become remarkably popular about then. Imitations of both nymphs and adults run from sizes 8 to 2, on long-shank hooks.

**Golden Stone.** About the time the salmonflies are finishing up, the golden stones appear. The golden stone hatch is actually a bit more common than the salmonfly hatch. Golden stones are only a shade smaller and every bit as important. The nymph is mottled brown on its back and light tan to pale gold beneath. The adult is darkish gold all over its body, with light brown wings. Imitations of both nymphs and adults run from sizes 8 to 4, on long-shank hooks.

*Skwala.* An anomaly, *Skwala* typically climbs out on exposed midstream boulders to hatch, then scrambles across the water's surface to shore—an excellent opportunity for trout. The trout also get a fine shot at the females when they either fly out and drop to the water or skitter out from shore across the currents to release their eggs. This large, dark stonefly hatches from late winter into spring. The nymph is yellowish, the adult yellow-tan to darkish brown. Hook sizes for imitations of both run from 10 to 6, 2X long. This size seems huge, until you consider the salmonfly...

**Yellow Sally.** "Yellow sally" is a loose term for small summer stoneflies whose adults have yellow or olive-yellow undersides. Some call these insects little yellow stoneflies. They hatch mostly through midsummer. The females often return to the water in the middle of the day to drop their eggs and fire up the trout. Hook sizes for both nymphs and adults run from 16 to 10.

**Little Green Stonefly.** There are actually quite a few small stoneflies grouped under this name, and they all hatch from late spring through summer. The nymph is brown or green; the adult is usually bright green. Because its hatching is normally sporadic rather than concentrated, imitating the nymph is only occasionally rewarding. But the adult females drop to the water to release their eggs in the afternoon and evening, which can be enough to move the trout. Imitations of both nymphs and adults run from sizes 16 to 12.

**Little Brown and Little Black Stoneflies.** There are four major families and a heap of genera and species, but all the little brown and little black stoneflies typically hatch in the cold months of winter and early spring. The color of both nymphs and adults varies from light brown to nearly black. There are good small stonefly imitations for both nymphs and adults, but standard mayfly nymphs and caddis dry flies can serve as well. Hooks for imitations range from sizes 18 to 12.

*There are other stoneflies, but the ones described here are the most common and reliable.*

# Stonefly Nymphs

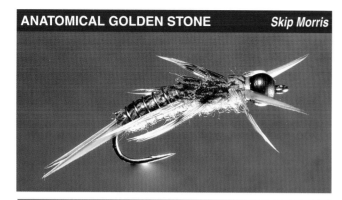

**ANATOMICAL GOLDEN STONE**     *Skip Morris*

*Top view*

*Tied by Skip Morris*

**Hook:** Heavy or standard wire, 2X or 3X long (slow-curve shank and straight eye preferred), sizes 8 and 6.

**Head:** Black or gold metal bead.

**Weight:** Lead wire, 0.025-inch diameter. A length is bound up each side of the shank to help re-create the flattened body of a real stonefly nymph. Push the ends of the lead right up into the hole in the rear of the bead or against the rear of the bead. (It's not a bad idea to secure the lead with low-odor epoxy glue or head cement, and let the glue or cement harden before tying the rest of the fly. It's most efficient to do a bunch of these at one time.)

**Thread:** Tan, gold, or yellow 8/0, 6/0, or 3/0.

**Tail:** Dyed light brown or tan goose or turkey biots (or tan or brown rubber-strand), longish.

**Rib:** Medium- or fine-diameter copper wire, or gold or amber copper wire.

**Abdomen:** Antique gold natural or synthetic dubbing (I usually use Antron dubbing).

**Back of the abdomen:** Strip of Thin Skin in mottled oak golden stone (or a pheasant or hen back feather toughened with Dave's Flexament, or some other mottled golden synthetic sheeting). Bind on the strip at the front of the abdomen, pull the strip down, and secure it with the rib.

**Legs:** Sections cut from a mottled golden brown or mottled brown hen back hackle. Snip the stem into short sections with leg-thick fibers. Bind the largest set at the front of the abdomen, with the fibers angling back. Bind over the short, cut stem. Dub, and then add a wing case at the front of the short dubbed section. The first two sets of legs sweep back; the legs of the final section with the shortest fibers should angle forward.

**Thorax:** Same as the abdomen.

**Wing cases:** Fairly wide strip of Thin Skin in mottled oak golden stone, trimmed to two wing cases, and then each is bound by its point (or a pheasant or hen back feather toughened with Dave's Flexament, or some other mottled brown-gold synthetic sheeting). The frontmost third wing case is slimmer and bound at both ends like a typical nymph wing case.

**Antennae:** Dyed light brown or tan goose or turkey biots (or fine tan or brown rubber-strand), somewhat short.

**Comments:** The soft legs give this intricate fly pattern movement and life in the water. It's a real handful at the vise and too complicated to provide tying instructions here. But if you look closely at the photograph and dressing and experiment a bit, you'll get it. If you believe that realism in fly patterns provides anglers with an edge, this is the fly for you. And it sure looks sharp in a fly box!

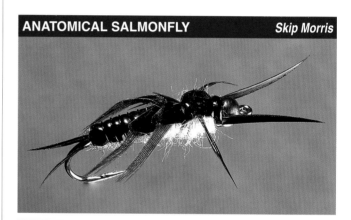

**ANATOMICAL SALMONFLY**     *Skip Morris*

*Top view*

*Tied by Skip Morris*

**Hook:** Heavy to standard wire, 2X or 3X long (slow-curve shank and straight eye preferred), sizes 8 to 4.

**Head:** Black metal bead.

**Thread:** Black 8/0, 6/0, or 3/0.

**Weight:** Lead wire, 0.025-inch diameter. A length is bound up each side of the shank to help re-create the flattened body of a real stonefly nymph. Push the ends of the lead right up into the hole in the rear of the bead or against the rear of the bead. (It's not a bad idea to secure the lead with low-odor epoxy glue or head cement, and let the glue or cement harden before tying the rest of the fly. It's most efficient to do a bunch of these at one time.)

**Tail:** Dyed black goose or turkey biots, short (or brown or black rubber-strand).

**Rib:** Black medium- or fine-diameter copper wire (Ultra Wire) or medium-diameter natural copper wire.

**Abdomen:** Light brown natural or synthetic dubbing (I usually use Antron dubbing).

**Back of the abdomen:** Strip of black Thin Skin (or a pheasant or hen back feather colored with a black permanent marking pen and toughened with Dave's Flexament, or some other black synthetic sheeting). Bind on the strip at the front of the abdomen, pull the strip down, and secure it with the rib.

**Legs:** Sections cut from a dyed or natural black hen back hackle. Snip the stem into short sections with leg-thick fibers. Bind the largest set at the front of the abdomen, with the fibers angling back. Bind over the short, cut stem. Dub, and then add a wing case at the front of the short dubbed section. The first two sets of legs sweep back; the legs of the final section with the shortest fibers should angle forward.

**Thorax:** Light tan natural or synthetic dubbing, picked out to slightly shaggy (I prefer Arizona Sparkle Nymph Dubbing).

**Wing cases:** Fairly wide strip of black Thin Skin, trimmed to two wing cases, and then each is bound by its point (or a pheasant or hen back feather colored with a permanent black marking pen and toughened with Dave's Flexament, or some other black synthetic sheeting). The frontmost third wing case is slimmer and bound at both ends like a typical nymph wing case.

**Antennae:** Dyed black goose or turkey biots (or fine brown or black rubber-strand), longish.

**Comments:** The soft legs give this intricate fly pattern movement and life in the water. It's a real handful at the vise, but if you believe that realism in fly patterns provides anglers with an edge, give it a try.

## BARR GOLDEN STONE                                                    *John Barr*

*Tied by Carol Ann Morris*

**Hook:** Heavy wire, 3X long, sizes 10 to 6.

**Weight (optional):** Lead wire.

**Thread:** Tan 3/0. (Switch to brown thread for the head. Or do as John does: color the head with a permanent marking pen before adding head cement.)

**Tail:** Dyed ginger goose biots.

**Rib:** Fine monofilament (tippet).

**Back:** Strip cut from a heavy freezer bag (or substitute clear latex strips, such as Stretch Flex or Scud Back).

**Body:** Cream coarse synthetic dubbing (Buggy Nymph Dubbing, Fly Rite).

**Legs:** Ginger hen hackle or a large, soft ginger hackle from a dry-fly neck.

**Comments:** Dub heavily to just past the center of the shank, bind on the hackle, and then dub a little more heavily to barely short of the hook's eye. Spiral the hackle to the eye and bind it there, pull the plastic strip over the body and bind it at the eye, and then wind the mono rib forward to the eye in ever-widening spirals. Try to avoid winding the rib over the hackle fibers; preferably, keep it between the turns of hackle. This is a plausible shiny-backed imitation of the underrated golden stone nymph.

## BIRD'S STONEFLY NYMPH — *Cal Bird*

*Tied by Skip Morris*

| | |
|---|---|
| **Hook:** | Heavy wire, 3X long, sizes 10 to 4. |
| **Thread:** | Orange 8/0, 6/0, or 3/0. |
| **Weight:** | Lead wire. |
| **Tail:** | Dyed brown goose biots. |
| **Rib:** | Orange floss or heavy thread. |
| **Abdomen:** | Brown muskrat fur or dyed brown rabbit fur. |
| **Wing case:** | Dark mottled turkey primary or dyed brown teal. |
| **Legs:** | Furnace or brown saddle hackle. |
| **Thorax:** | Peacock herl. |

**Comments:** Bird's Stonefly Nymph has become a classic imitation of the salmonfly nymph.

## BITCH CREEK

*Tied by Skip Morris*

| | |
|---|---|
| **Hook:** | Heavy wire, 3X long, sizes 10 to 4. |
| **Thread:** | Black 8/0, 6/0, 3/0. |
| **Weight (optional):** | Lead wire. |
| **Tail:** | White rubber-strand. |
| **Abdomen:** | Black and orange chenille woven to put the black on top and orange beneath (instructions are on page 130). |
| **Hackle:** | Brown, spiraled over the thorax. |
| **Thorax:** | Black chenille. |
| **Antennae:** | White rubber-strand. |

**Comments:** An old and proven imitation of the salmonfly nymph. Why the white antennae and tails? We don't know. You can certainly use black or brown rubber-strand instead.

## BLACK RUBBER LEGS

*Tied by Skip Morris*

| | |
|---|---|
| **Hook:** | Heavy wire, 3X long, sizes 8 to 4. |
| **Thread:** | Black 6/0 or 3/0. |
| **Antennae (optional):** | Black rubber-strand. |
| **Tail:** | Black rubber-strand. |
| **Legs:** | Black rubber-strand, three lengths bound crossways on the shank to create six legs in all. |
| **Weight:** | Lead wire. Bind on the legs, then wind the lead up the shank and around each strand, where it is bound on with an open spiral of the lead wire. |
| **Abdomen:** | Black chenille. |

**Comments:** There was considerable confusion over which dressing should be called the Rubber Legs and which should be called the Girdle Bug—the only difference in the two patterns is the use of white or black rubber-strand. The matter worked itself out: the Girdle Bug has white strands, and the Rubber Legs has become the Black Rubber Legs, with black rubber-strands for tails, antennae, and legs. With the black strands the fly resembles a salmonfly nymph, and lots of fly fishers treat is as such. To make it even more like a salmonfly nymph, you can move all the legs up into the thorax area. This can also serve as an attractor nymph.

## BOX CANYON STONE — *Mims Barker*

*Tied by Skip Morris*

| | |
|---|---|
| **Hook:** | Heavy wire, 2X to 4X long, sizes 10 to 8. |
| **Thread:** | Black 8/0, 6/0, or 3/0. |
| **Weight:** | Lead wire. |
| **Tail:** | Dark brown goose biots. |
| **Abdomen:** | Black yarn twisted for a segmented look. |
| **Wing case:** | Mottled tan-brown turkey quill section. |
| **Hackle:** | Furnace hen hackle spiraled over the thorax (dark brown and black are good substitutes). |
| **Thorax:** | Black dubbing (rabbit, squirrel). |

**Comments:** A reliable, time-tested salmonfly nymph imitation.

## BROOKS STONE (OR MONTANA STONE NYMPH)
### Charles Brooks

*Tied by Skip Morris*

**Hook:** Heavy wire, 4X long, size 4.
**Thread:** Black 6/0 or 3/0.
**Weight:** Lead wire.
**Tail:** Originally, six fibers of black raven or crow primary split. Most tiers now use two dyed black goose biots.
**Rib:** Fine copper wire.
**Abdomen:** Black wool yarn or dubbed black rabbit.
**Gills:** Gray or white ostrich herl wound along the base of the hackles. (To make the herl tough, spin it with 3/0 thread before winding it.)
**Hackle:** One grizzly and one grizzly dyed brown (or substitute standard brown) spiraled together in two or three turns over the thorax. Hackles can be saddles or large, soft, dry-fly neck hackles.
**Thorax:** Black fuzzy yarn (or rabbit).
**Head:** Black fuzzy yarn (or rabbit).
**Comments:** Charles Brooks was the author of several books, including *Nymph Fishing for Larger Trout*. He designed his stonefly nymph so that at whatever angle a trout views it, the hackle legs appear in the outline. Brooks believed this made the nymph more effective. He, his books, and his theories had a substantial following, and they still do.

## CHICKABOU STONE NYMPH, BROWN
### Henry Hoffman

*Tied by Carol Ann Morris*

**Hook:** Heavy wire, 3X long, sizes 8 to 4.
**Thread:** Brown 6/0 or 3/0.
**Weight:** Lead wire.
**Tail:** Brown-dyed barred Chickabou tips.
**Rib:** Fine gold wire, counterwound.
**Abdomen:** One or two barred brown Chickabou feathers, bound by the tips and wound up the shank.
**Wing case:** Section of turkey quill, or one or two Chickabou plumes, pulled forward over the thorax.
**Legs:** One dyed brown grizzly soft hackle, spiraled up the thorax. (Here, "soft hackle" means a broad, soft-fibered rooster hackle, but hen saddle or a big, soft, dry-fly hackle makes a good substitute.)
**Thorax:** One brown-dyed barred Chickabou, bound by the tips and wound up the shank.
**Comments:** All the soft materials make for lots of movement in the water. The Chickabou Stone Nymph is a reasonable concept taken to its reasonable limit.

## COPPER BACK YELLOW SALLIE — *Tom Larimer*

*Top view*

*Tied by Al Davis*

**Hook:** Heavy (or standard) wire, 2X long, slow-curve shank, sizes 16 and 14.
**Thread:** Yellow or tan 8/0 or 6/0.
**Antennae:** Tannish yellow goose biots.
**Tail:** Brown goose biots, separated by a little ball of dubbing—a blend of two-thirds Tri-lobal golden yellow dubbing and one-third Haretron dubbing in golden stone (or any gold, shiny synthetic dubbing).
**Abdomen:** Small copper wire.
**Wing case:** Section of turkey tail topped with one strand of pearl Krystal Flash over its center. Add a bulge of epoxy glue atop the wing case (instructions are on page 38).
**Thorax:** Same dubbing as that separating the tails.
**Legs:** Mottled brown hen back (hen saddle), a short section of the tip bound at the eye and laid flat over the abdomen, covered by the wing case.
**Collar:** Same dubbing as that separating the tails.
**Comments:** Obviously inspired by the Copper John, the Copper Back Yellow Sallie imitates the yellow sally stonefly, despite the disparity in spelling.

## DARK STONE — *Polly Rosborough*

*Tied by Carol Ann Morris*

**Hook:** Heavy wire, 3X long, sizes 6 to 2.
**Thread:** Tan 6/0 or 3/0.
**Tail:** Two fibers of dyed dark brown pheasant tail, split.
**Body:** Dubbed cream badger fur, guard hairs removed. Polly painted the body with a dark brown enamel down the back and halfway down the sides. Today, we would use a permanent marking pen.
**Legs:** Dyed dark brown pheasant tail fibers tied in as a beard or splayed as a half collar across the underside.
**Wing case:** Bunch of natural dark (or dyed dark brownish black) ostrich herls. You can either bind on the herls so their tips extend one-third back over the body or just tear them off at that length.
**Comments:** After several decades on the scene, Polly's flies continue to catch trout. His Dark Stone is an imitation of the salmonfly nymph.

## EARLY BLACK STONEFLY NYMPH

*Tied by Skip Morris*

**Hook:** Heavy wire, 1X or 2X long, sizes 16 to 10.
**Thread:** Black 8/0 or 6/0.
**Weight:** Lead wire.
**Tail:** Two natural dark gray goose biots.
**Abdomen:** Very dark gray rabbit (or another dubbing).
**Wing cases:** Two folded sections of dyed black goose quill (or another quill feather section, such as turkey or duck). Bind on a quill section, double it forward over a needle held crossways, and then bind the top of the section down. If you pull the needle back firmly against the doubled section, it will crease and appear folded.
**Thorax:** Same as the abdomen.

**Legs:** Very dark gray hen saddle or neck, as a beard splayed in a half circle.

**Comments:** Although this is an eastern pattern, it imitates a small blackish stonefly nymph and is therefore a natural for the winter *Capnia* or any of the little dark stone nymphs. A rib of copper wire; black or even clear fine rib material, such as V-Rib or Larva Lace; or just tippet would be a logical addition.

## EARLY BROWN STONEFLY NYMPH

*Tied by Skip Morris*

**Hook:** Heavy wire, 1X or 2X long, sizes 16 to 10.
**Thread:** Tan 8/0 or 6/0.
**Weight:** Lead wire.
**Tail:** Dyed tan turkey (or goose) biots.
**Abdomen:** Medium brown rabbit (or some other dubbing).
**Wing cases:** Two folded sections of natural dark mottled turkey quill.
**Thorax:** Same as the abdomen.
**Legs:** Natural or dyed brown hen saddle or neck hackle, as a beard splayed in a half circle.

**Comments:** Although this is an eastern pattern, it fits the western little brown stoneflies just fine. See the Early Black Stonefly Nymph on page 120 for additional comments and tying instructions.

## GIRDLE BUG

*Tied by Skip Morris*

**Hook:** Heavy wire, 3X long, sizes 8 to 4.
**Thread:** Black 6/0 or 3/0.
**Antennae (optional):** White rubber-strand.
**Tail:** White rubber-strand.
**Legs:** White rubber-strand.
**Weight:** Lead wire. Bind on the legs, then wind the lead up the shank and around each strand where it is bound on with an open spiral of the lead wire.

**Abdomen:** Black chenille.

**Comments:** This is certainly an odd imitation of a big stonefly nymph—how many of the naturals have white legs and antennae? (answer: none)—but it works. It can also serve as an attractor nymph.

## GOLDEN STONE — *Al Troth*

*Tied by Skip Morris*

**Hook:** Heavy wire, 3X long, sizes 10 and 8.
**Thread:** Yellow 8/0, 6/0, or 3/0.
**Weight (optional):** Lead wire.
**Tail:** Goose or turkey biots dyed gold.
**Rib:** Stripes drawn across the back with a black marking pen.
**Body:** Blend of amber, yellow, and gold angora goat and tan fox, dubbed.
**Legs:** Dyed gold partridge flank fibers, as a beard splayed in a half-circle (or substitute mallard dyed wood duck).
**Wing case:** Gold-dyed teal or mallard flank fibers extending from behind the dubbed head back over one-third of the body.
**Head:** Same dubbing as in the body.
**Comments:** If Al likes it, it's got to be good. It's as simple as that.

## GOLDEN STONE NYMPH — Polly Rosborough

*Tied by Skip Morris*

**Hook:** Heavy wire, 3X long, sizes 6 to 4.
**Thread:** Gold 6/0 or 3/0.
**Tail:** Two small bunches of barred teal fibers dyed dark gold, split into two short tails.
**Rib:** Heavy antique gold thread (size A rod thread or such).
**Back:** Barred teal feather dyed dark gold.
**Body:** Gold synthetic yarn.
**Legs:** Barred teal fibers dyed dark gold, tied in at the throat.
**Wing case:** Barred teal dyed dark gold. Bind the fibers just back from the eye, and trim them off straight across about one-third down the body. Instead of a bundle of fibers, you can bind the tip of the feather flat atop the hook and trim it.
**Comments:** You can substitute mallard dyed wood duck for the teal. Another time-tested Rosborough pattern.

## GROVE'S STONE

*Tied by Skip Morris*

**Hook:** Heavy wire, 4X long (humped or bent with pliers), sizes 10 to 2.
**Thread:** Brown 8/0, 6/0, 3/0.
**Weight:** Lead wire.
**Tail:** Monofilament dyed brown or colored with a marking pen.
**Abdomen:** Olive-brown (or brown) wool yarn with tan wool yarn underneath, secured with the rib.
**Rib:** Originally, dyed brown flat monofilament. V-Rib, D-Rib, or the like is a good choice.
**Wing case:** Loop of olive-brown (or brown) wool yarn.
**Legs:** Breast or flank feather, flat, divided into three sections per side, and each section cemented at its tip.
**Thorax:** Tan (or brown) wool yarn.
**Antennae:** Monofilament dyed brown or colored with a marking pen.

**Comments:** Here's one for those who believe in realistic nymphs. It's time tested, and the time it takes to tie one may test your patience. Mainly an imitation of the salmonfly nymph but can serve for the golden stone too.

## HAIR LEG STONEFLY NYMPH — Gary Borger

*Tied by Skip Morris*

**Hook:** Heavy wire, 3X long, sizes 10 to 2.
**Thread:** Black 3/0.
**Weight:** Lead wire.
**Tail:** Black goose biots.
**Rib:** Originally, flat monofilament, but now black or clear ribbing such as V-Rib or Larva Lace.
**Abdomen:** Black dubbing or yarn, picked out for a fuzzy effect.
**Wing cases:** Two turkey tail sections doubled and creased lengthwise and coated with head cement or epoxy glue.
**Thorax and legs:** Black dubbing and black calf tail spun together in a dubbing loop.
**Comments:** Imitates the salmonfly nymph.

**Jacklin's Stonefly nymphs.** Bob Jacklin is a real authority on tying flies and western river fly fishing, so you can trust his stonefly nymph patterns that follow.

## JACKLIN'S BRIGHT GREEN STONEFLY NYMPH — Bob Jacklin

*Tied by Bob Jacklin*

**Hook:** Standard to heavy wire, 2X or 3X long (slow-curve shank preferred), sizes 16 and 14.
**Thread:** Fluorescent green 8/0 or 6/0.
**Weight:** Lead wire. (Bob binds D-Rib along both sides of the lead windings to broaden the body of the fly.)

**Tail:** Dyed green goose biots or two dyed green pheasant tail fibers.

**Rib:** Fine chartreuse D-Rib.

**Abdomen:** Tan opossum dubbing.

**Wing case:** Green Scud Back over natural light mottled turkey quill.

**Legs:** Natural gray partridge flank feather lying flat atop the thorax, under the wing case.

**Thorax:** Same as the abdomen.

**Head:** Green Scud Back doubled back over the same dubbing used for the abdomen and bound with a narrow thread collar.

**Comments:** This Jacklin design imitates similarly colored nymphs of the little green stonefly complex.

## JACKLIN'S EARLY BLACK STONEFLY NYMPH
*Bob Jacklin*

*Tied by Bob Jacklin*

**Hook:** Standard to heavy wire, 2X or 3X long (slow-curve shank preferred), sizes 14 and 12.

**Thread:** Black 8/0 or 6/0.

**Weight:** Lead wire. (Bob binds D-Rib along both sides of the lead windings to broaden the body of the fly.)

**Tail:** Dyed black goose biots.

**Rib:** Narrow black D-Rib. Keep the ribs close together.

**Abdomen:** Tan opossum dubbing.

**Wing case:** Black Scud Back over natural dark turkey tail.

**Legs:** Dyed black partridge or hen back, the feather lying flat atop the thorax under the wing case.

**Thorax:** Same as the abdomen.

**Head:** Black Scud Back doubled back over the same dubbing used for the abdomen and bound with a narrow thread collar.

**Comments:** Imitates *Capnia,* the little winter stonefly.

## JACKLIN'S GIANT SALMONFLY NYMPH
*Bob Jacklin*

*Tied by Bob Jacklin*

**Hook:** Standard (or heavy) wire, 2X or 3X long (slow-curve shank preferred), sizes 6 to 2.

**Thread:** Black 3/0.

**Weight:** Lead wire. (Bob binds D-Rib along each side of the wire windings to broaden the body of the fly.)

**Tail:** Dyed black goose biots.

**Abdomen:** Strip cut from a bicycle tire inner tube.

**Wing cases:** Two notched, and a third pulled forward and bound in front, each cut from a bicycle tire inner tube.

**Legs:** Slim knotted strips cut from a bicycle tire inner tube.

**Thorax:** Tan opossum fur, dubbed.

**Head:** Strip cut from a bicycle tire inner tube, pulled back over some of the thorax's dubbing and bound with a thread collar.

**Antennae (optional):** Dyed black pheasant tail fibers.

**Comments:** The Giant Salmonfly Nymph is unusually realistic compared with most imitations of this insect. Using an inner tube for the abdomen, legs, and wing cases is clever. Bob tested and retested this fly, perfecting it, for more than 30 years. That's good enough for me.

## JACKLIN'S GOLDEN STONEFLY NYMPH
*Bob Jacklin*

*Tied by Bob Jacklin*

**Hook:** Standard to heavy wire, 2X or 3X long, sizes 8 and 6.
**Thread:** Black 3/0.
**Weight:** Lead wire. (Bob binds some D-Rib along each side of the lead windings to broaden the body of the fly.)
**Tail:** Dyed tan or brown goose biots.
**Rib:** Narrow brown D-Rib (or some other premade ribbing).
**Abdomen:** Opossum dubbing in golden stone (or rabbit in a darkish or antique gold).
**Wing case:** Brown Scud Back over mottled turkey quill.
**Legs:** Brown partridge or a pheasant body feather lying flat atop the thorax.
**Thorax:** Same as the abdomen.
**Head:** Brown scud back doubled back over the same dubbing used for the abdomen and bound with a narrow thread collar.

## JACKLIN'S LITTLE OLIVE STONEFLY NYMPH
*Bob Jacklin*

*Tied by Bob Jacklin*

**Hook:** Standard or heavy wire, 2X or 3X long (slow-curve shank preferred), sizes 12 and 10.
**Thread:** Olive 6/0 or 3/0.
**Weight:** Lead wire. (Bob binds D-Rib along both sides of the lead windings to broaden the body of the fly.)
**Tail:** Dyed olive goose biots.
**Rib:** Narrow olive D-Rib (or another rib material).
**Abdomen:** Olive opossum.
**Wing case:** Olive Scud Back over natural light mottled turkey quill.

**Legs:** Natural gray partridge flank feather lying flat over the thorax, under the wing case.
**Thorax:** Same as the abdomen.
**Head:** Olive Scud Back pulled back over the same dubbing used for the abdomen, bound with a narrow thread collar.
**Comments:** Imitates similarly colored nymphs of the little green stonefly complex.

## JACKLIN'S WESTERN YELLOW STONE NYMPH
*Bob Jacklin*

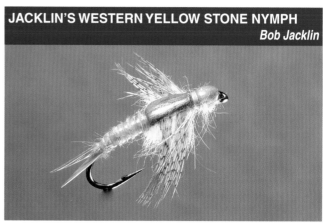

*Tied by Bob Jacklin*

**Hook:** Standard to heavy wire, 2X long, slow-curve shank, sizes 12 to 8.
**Thread:** Yellow 6/0 or 3/0.
**Weight:** Lead wire. (Bob binds a length of D-Rib along each side of the lead windings to broaden the body of the fly.)
**Tail:** Dyed yellow goose biots.
**Rib:** Fine yellow D-Rib (or another shiny rib material).
**Abdomen:** Dyed yellow opossum dubbing.
**Wing case:** Natural light turkey quill under yellow Scud Back (translucent rubbery sheeting).
**Legs:** Natural light partridge flank feather flat atop the thorax, under the wing case.
**Thorax:** Same as the abdomen.
**Head:** Same dubbing as for the abdomen, with yellow Scud Back doubled back over the dubbing and bound with a thread collar.
**Comments:** Imitates *Isoperla*, one of the yellow sally stoneflies.

## KAUFMANN BLACK STONE — *Randall Kaufmann*

*Tied by Carol Ann Morris*

| | |
|---|---|
| **Hook:** | Heavy wire, 4X to 6X long, sizes 6 to 2. |
| **Thread:** | Black 6/0 or 3/0. |
| **Weight:** | Lead wire. (Randall likes to flatten the lead windings with flat-nose pliers.) |
| **Antennae:** | Dark brown or black goose (or turkey) biots. |
| **Tail:** | Dark brown or black goose (or turkey) biots. |
| **Rib:** | Fairly thick, black premade rib material, such as V-Rib or Larva Lace. |
| **Abdomen:** | Mixture of 60 percent black, purple, claret, red, amber, fiery brown, blue, and hot orange angora goat and 40 percent black Hare-Tron (or Antron or rabbit). |
| **Thorax:** | Same as the abdomen. |
| **Wing cases:** | Three separate sections of turkey tail, a notch cut into the edge of each, coated with Flexament. |
| **Head:** | Same dubbing as for the abdomen, short. |
| **Comments:** | The original salmonfly version of the Kaufmann Stone. |

## KAUFMANN BLACK STONE, BEAD HEAD RUBBER LEGS — *Randall Kaufmann*

*Tied by Carol Ann Morris*

| | |
|---|---|
| **Hook:** | Heavy wire, 4X to 6X long, sizes 6 to 2. |
| **Head:** | One gold, brass, or black metal bead. |
| **Weight:** | Lead wire. (Randall likes to flatten the lead windings with flat-nose pliers.) |
| **Thread:** | Black 6/0 or 3/0. |
| **Antennae:** | Dark brown or black goose (or turkey) biots. |
| **Tail:** | Dark brown or black goose (or turkey) biots. |
| **Rib:** | Fairly thick, black premade rib material, such as V-Rib or Larva Lace. |
| **Abdomen:** | Mixture of 60 percent black, purple, claret, red, amber, fiery brown, blue, and hot orange angora goat and 40 percent black Hare-Tron (or Antron or rabbit). |
| **Thorax:** | Same as the abdomen. |
| **Wing cases:** | Three separate sections of turkey tail, a notch cut into the end of each, coated with Flexament. |
| **Legs:** | Black round rubber, two pair, bound on between the first and second wing cases. |
| **Collar:** | Same dubbing as for the abdomen, short. |
| **Comments:** | This variation of the original Kaufmann Stone is a reliable imitation of the salmonfly. If you replace the bead and collar with a head of the same dubbing as in the abdomen, you have the Kaufmann Black Stone, Rubber Legs. Or you can drop the legs and keep the bead. |

## KAUFMANN GOLDEN STONE — *Randall Kaufmann*

*Tied by Carol Ann Morris*

| | |
|---|---|
| **Hook:** | Heavy wire, 4X to 6X long, sizes 12 to 8. |
| **Thread:** | Brown 6/0 or 3/0. |
| **Weight:** | Lead wire. (Randall likes to flatten the lead windings with flat-nose pliers.) |
| **Antennae:** | Dyed golden brown goose (or turkey) biots. |
| **Tail:** | Dyed golden brown goose (or turkey) biots. |
| **Rib:** | Fairly thick, amber, premade rib material, such as V-Rib or Larva Lace. |
| **Abdomen:** | Mixture of 60 percent gold, amber, rust, blue, and orange angora goat and 40 percent dyed golden brown rabbit or Hare-Tron. |
| **Thorax:** | Same dubbing as for the abdomen. |
| **Wing cases:** | Three separate sections of turkey tail, a notch cut into the end of each, coated with Flexament. |
| **Head:** | Same dubbing as for the abdomen, short. |
| **Comments:** | The original golden stonefly version of the Kaufmann Stone. |

## KAUFMANN GOLDEN STONE, BEAD HEAD RUBBER LEGS
*Randall Kaufmann*

*Tied by Carol Ann Morris*

| | |
|---|---|
| Hook: | Heavy wire, 4X to 6X long, sizes 12 to 8. |
| Head: | Gold metal bead. |
| Weight: | Lead wire. (Randall likes to flatten the lead windings with flat-nose pliers.) |
| Thread: | Brown 6/0 or 3/0. |
| Antennae: | Dyed golden brown goose (or turkey) biots. |
| Tail: | Dyed golden brown goose (or turkey) biots. |
| Rib: | Fairly thick, amber premade rib material, such as V-Rib or Larva Lace. |
| Abdomen: | Mixture of 60 percent gold, amber, rust, blue, and orange angora goat and 40 percent dyed golden brown rabbit or Hare-Tron. |
| Thorax: | Same as the abdomen. |
| Wing cases: | Three separate sections of turkey tail, a notch cut into the end of each, coated with Flexament. |
| Legs: | Tan, white, black, or brown rubber-strand, one pair per side, bound on between the first and second wing cases. |
| Collar: | Same dubbing as for the abdomen, short. |
| Comments: | If you replace the bead and collar with a head of the same dubbing as in the abdomen, you have the Kaufmann Golden Stone, Rubber Legs. Or you can drop the legs and keep the bead. |

## LITTLE YELLOW STONE
*Polly Rosborough*

*Tied by Al Davis*

| | |
|---|---|
| Hook: | Heavy wire, 3X long, size 10. |
| Thread: | Chartreuse or light yellow 8/0 or 6/0. |
| Tail: | Dyed chartreuse barred mallard fibers, short. |
| Body: | Dyed chartreuse rabbit fur. |

| | |
|---|---|
| Legs: | Same fibers as the tail, as a beard. |
| Wing case: | Same fibers as the tail, trimmed about one-third back over the body. |
| Comments: | Polly suggested a coating of greenish brown enamel over the back of the body as an option but didn't seem to think it was important. Today, a marking pen would be used to add color to a nymph body. The Little Yellow Stone is an imitation of the larger specimens of the little yellow stonefly complex. Polly's fly patterns have been around for decades, and the verdict was rendered long ago: they are effective beyond a reasonable doubt. |

## MONTANA STONE

*Tied by Skip Morris*

| | |
|---|---|
| Hook: | Heavy wire, 3X long, sizes 10 to 6. |
| Weight: | Lead wire. |
| Thread: | Black 8/0, 6/0, or 3/0. |
| Tail: | Black hackle fibers. |
| Abdomen: | Black chenille. |
| Wing case: | Black chenille, doubled. |
| Legs: | Black saddle hackle, spiraled over the thorax. |
| Thorax: | Yellow chenille. |
| Comments: | An old-time Montana pattern that's still popular here and perhaps even more popular in Europe. |

**Morristone.** I've caught many, many trout on this simple and easy-to-tie (once you get the hang of it) pattern. I think the yarn helps get the hook into the fish—the teeth catch in the weave, giving you more time to set the hook before the trout can blow out the fly. Anything that gives you an edge in nymph fishing is a blessing. You can add a black or gold bead as the head of any of the Morristone or Quiverstone variations.

# Tying the Morristone

**1.** Trim off the tip of a hen back feather, trim back the sides of the tip's stem a little, and then trim out the center of the tip, leaving a few fibers on either side as tails. On the left is an uncut hen back feather, on the right is a feather cut for tails. Save the lower section of the feather to make the legs.

**2.** Wind lead wire well short of the bend and eye (and a short second layer of finer wire over the thorax area). Trim and bind the lead wire. Bind the tail by its trimmed stem. Against the rear of the lead, bind some yarn; then, slightly ahead of the yarn, bind on the rib material.

**3.** Bind a section (or two sections, one atop the other) of pheasant tail fibers atop the center of the shank. Stroke the fibers back from the cut end of the hen back feather you used to make the tails—only the fibers on about the last ¹/₈ inch of the feather should still angle forward. Bind the cut hen feather by this last ¹/₈ inch of stem (with the "V" of fibers projecting forward atop the pheasant, the curve of the hen feather facing up). Trim off the ends of the hen fibers.

**4.** Wind the thread to the eye, pull the pheasant and hen forward, and bind them lightly. Wind the yarn forward to the rear of the pheasant. (If you take the first turn of yarn behind the rib material, you'll find the rib easier to wind later.) Back off the thread turns holding the pheasant and hen, wind the yarn to a bit short of the eye, bind the end of the yarn, and trim it off.

**5.** Wind the rib just as you did the yarn, with plenty of ribs over the abdomen and only three or four over the thorax area.

**6.** Pull the hen feather forward and bind it a little short of the eye. Trim four slots in the fibers to create six legs.

**7.** Pull the pheasant down on top of the hen for a wing case. Bind and trim off the ends of both the pheasant and the hen. Dub a head, whip-finish the thread, and add head cement to the whip finish.

## MORRISTONE (STANDARD) — *Skip Morris*

*Tied by Skip Morris*

| | |
|---|---|
| **Hook:** | Heavy wire, 3X or 4X long (a slow-curve shank is optional), sizes 10 to 4. |
| **Thread:** | Brown 8/0, 6/0 or 3/0. |
| **Weight:** | Lead wire. (I like to add a short second layer of finer lead wire in the thorax area.) |
| **Tail:** | Mottled brown hen back tip with the center trimmed out. |
| **Rib:** | Dark brown or brown medium-diameter premade rib material, such as V-Rib or Larva Lace. |
| **Body:** | Dark gray or dark brown woven yarn (usually wool or fuzzy Antron). Chenille or Vernille is a good substitute. |
| **Wing case:** | Pheasant tail fibers, dark side showing. |
| **Legs:** | Body of the hen back hackle used for the tail. Trimming slots in the fibers to leave six legs is optional. |
| **Head:** | Dark brown dubbing (dyed rabbit is good). |

**Comments:** A versatile imitation of both the salmonfly nymph and darker golden stonefly nymphs. It's easy to tie once you get used to its unconventional construction.

## MORRISTONE, GOLDEN STONE — *Skip Morris*

*Tied by Skip Morris*

| | |
|---|---|
| **Hook:** | Heavy wire, 3X to 4X long (a slow-curve shank is optional), sizes 10 to 6. |
| **Thread:** | Brown 8/0, 6/0, or 3/0. |
| **Weight:** | Lead wire, with a second layer of finer lead wire over the thorax area. |
| **Tail:** | Mottled brown hen back hackle tip, with the center trimmed out. |
| **Rib:** | Small or medium copper wire. |
| **Underbody (optional):** | Dyed gold rabbit dubbed on a loop of thread, pulled up under the body and bound at the front of the body, secured with the rib. (It looks neat but isn't critical.) |
| **Body:** | Brown woven yarn (usually wool or fuzzy Antron). Chenille or Vernille is a good substitute. |
| **Wing case:** | Natural pheasant tail fibers, light side showing. |
| **Legs:** | Body of the hen back hackle used for the tail. Trimming slots in the fibers to leave six legs is optional. |
| **Head:** | Dark brown dubbing (dyed rabbit is good). |

## MORRISTONE, SALMONFLY — *Skip Morris*

*Tied by Al Davis*

| | |
|---|---|
| **Hook:** | Heavy wire, 3X or 4X long (a slow-curve shank is optional), sizes 8 to 4. |
| **Thread:** | Dark brown or black 6/0 or 3/0. |
| **Weight:** | Lead wire, with a short layer of finer lead wire over the thorax area. |
| **Tail:** | Tip of a dyed black hen back hackle, with its center trimmed out. |
| **Rib:** | Dark brown or brown medium-diameter premade rib material, such as V-Rib or Larva Lace. |
| **Underbody (optional):** | Light tan rabbit dubbed on a loop of thread, pulled up under the body and bound at the front of the body, secured with the rib. (It looks neat but isn't critical.) |

**Body:**    Blackish brown or chocolate or black woven yarn (usually wool or fuzzy Antron). Chenille or Vernille is a good substitute.
**Wing case:**    Dyed very dark or black pheasant tail fibers.
**Legs:**    Body of the hen back hackle used for the tail. Trimming slots in the fibers to leave six legs is optional.
**Head:**    Black or very dark brown dubbing (rabbit is good).

## PEBBLE BEAD STONEFLY, BROWN — Joe Warren

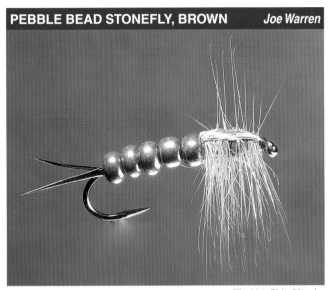

*Tied by Skip Morris*

**Hook:**    Heavy wire, 3X long (slow-curve or bent shank, or straight shank), sizes 10 to 2.
**Thread:**    Brown 6/0.
**Abdomen:**    Five brown glass beads.
**Tail:**    Dyed brown goose biots.
**Weight (optional):** Lead wire through the thorax area.
**Wing case:**    Mottled brown-tan turkey quill section.
**Legs:**    One brown hackle spiraled up the thorax.
**Thorax:**    Brown dubbing (any kind).
**Antennae (optional):** Brown rubber-strand.
**Comments:**    The beads provide weight and the hard, shiny look of the nymph's exoskeleton—a sensible design. The Pebble Bead Stonefly (Brown) normally imitates the salmonfly, but in smaller sizes it could suggest *Skwala*.

## POXYBACK BIOT GOLDEN STONE — Mike Mercer

*Top view*

*Tied by Mike Mercer*

**Hook:**    Heavy (or standard) wire, 2X long, slow-curve shank, sizes 18 to 6.
**Thread:**    Tan 8/0 or 6/0.
**Antennae:**    Sulfur orange turkey biots, mottled with a brown permanent marking pen.
**Head:**    Gold metal bead, large for hook sizes 8 and 6, medium for 12 and 10, small for 14 and 16, extra-small for 18.
**Weight:**    A length of lead wire bound along each side of the shank.
**Tail:**    Sulfur orange turkey biots, mottled with a brown permanent marking pen.
**Abdomen:**    Sulfur orange turkey biots, wrapped up the lead and mottled on top with a brown permanent marking pen.
**Legs:**    Golden brown mottled hen saddle hackle, mounted flat over the thorax.
**Wing case:**    Natural golden brown turkey tail, topped with a dome of epoxy glue (instructions are on page 38).
**Thorax:**    Mercer's Select Buggy Nymph Dubbing in golden stone (or another rough yellow-orange or gold dubbing).
**Comments:**    Bind the antennae on first, with minimal thread turns; whip-finish the thread down the shank, cut the thread, and then slide the bead up to the eye. Then restart the thread and complete the fly. It's easy to concentrate on full-grown stonefly nymphs and forget that smaller individuals of various ages are also down there with the trout. Judging by the hook range for the Poxyback Biot Golden Stone, it seems Mike hasn't forgotten.

**QUIVERSTONE**                                          *Skip Morris*

*Tied by Skip Morris*

**Hook:**      Heavy wire, 3X to 4X long (a slow-curve shank is optional), sizes 10 to 4.
**Thread:**    Brown 8/0, 6/0 or 3/0.
**Weight:**    Lead wire, with a short second layer of finer lead wire in the thorax area.
**Tail:**      Fine brown (or black) rubber-strand or the tip of a mottled brown hen back feather with the center cut out, leaving three to five fibers on each side.
**Rib:**       Medium-diameter dark brown or brown premade rib material, such as V-Rib or Larva Lace.
**Body:**      Dark gray woven yarn (usually wool or fuzzy Antron). Chenille or Vernille is a good substitute.
**Wing case:** Pheasant tail fibers, dark side showing.
**Legs:**      Medium-diameter brown (or black) rubber-strand. Mount the legs as follows: Loop a length of rubber-strand around the yarn at about the center of the thorax area. Wind on half a turn of yarn to secure the rubber-strand to the near side of the hook, loop another rubber-strand around the yarn on the far side of the hook, and wind the yarn another half-turn to secure that strand. Pull the ends of the strands back toward the tail, and then wind a full turn of yarn against the front of the strands to set all the legs angling out from the thorax. Wind the yarn the rest of the way forward, and bind and trim it. Trim the legs to length.
**Head:**      Dark brown dubbing (dyed rabbit is good).
**Comments:**  Vary the colors to imitate the salmonfly, golden stone, or other stonefly nymphs. Sometimes these rubber-strand legs seem more effective than the original hen back fiber legs. I suspect they work best in the fastest water, but I have no definitive evidence.

# Weaving a Fly Body (Rubber Legs Brown Stone)

**1.** After winding on, trimming, and binding the lead wire (leaving some space behind it), double and bind a length of rubber-strand behind the lead to form the tails. Bind tan yarn along the far side of the shank. Bind a strand of brown yarn on the near side of the shank. Spiral the thread up the shank and lead to just short of the eye, whip-finish, and trim off the thread (it will just get in your way if you don't). You shouldn't have to release either end of the yarn throughout the whole weaving process.

**2.** Turn the vise so the fly is pointing directly away from you. Hold the tan yarn out to the left (in your left hand) and the brown yarn out to your right (in your right hand). Keep constant tension on both lengths of yarn throughout the weaving process.

**3.** Swing the tan yarn to your right *underneath* the hook.

**4.** Raise the tan yarn and hold it stationary. Swing the brown yarn towards the hook eye (around the tan yarn), over the *top* of the hook and to your left. You just made the first lock of the weave on the right side of the fly.

**5.** Swing the tan yarn towards the hook eye and under the hook to your left. Raise the tan yarn in front of the brown yarn. Now swing the brown yarn towards the hook eye and over the hook to the right to complete another lock. Just keep weaving in this manner until you've woven a little past halfway up the shank.

**6.** With the weaving completed, hold both ends of the yarn firmly down. Turn the vise to face to the right, as usual. Pick up the bobbin and restart the thread over the ends of the yarn (you can hold the ends of the yarn down and hold the end of the thread in your left hand as you restart the thread with your right). Bind the ends of the yarn thoroughly by repeatedly passing the bobbin over the hook, letting the bobbin hang, and then regrasping it for the next turn. Raise and trim off the ends of the yarn and thread.

If you are tying the Rubber Legs Brown Stone (and not some other woven fly), trim the tails to length, and complete the thorax with rubber-strand legs and dubbing.

**RUBBER LEGS BROWN STONE**     *George Anderson*

*Tied by Skip Morris*

| | |
|---|---|
| **Hook:** | Heavy wire, 3X long, sizes 12 to 6. |
| **Thread:** | Brown 8/0, 6/0, or 3/0. |
| **Weight:** | Lead wire. |
| **Tail:** | White rubber-strand. |
| **Abdomen:** | Chocolate brown and tan yarn woven—brown on top, tan below. Any kind of yarn that suits you is fine (wool, Antron, and the like). |
| **Legs:** | Two sets of white rubber-strands projecting from the thorax. |
| **Thorax:** | Hare's mask fur, dubbed. |

**66 Sick Stones.** Damien Nurre developed his stonefly nymphs for the mighty Lower Deschutes River—these nymphs go down fast.

**66 SICK STONE NYMPH, BLACK**     *Damien Nurre*

*Tied by Damien Nurre*

| | |
|---|---|
| **Hook:** | Heavy wire, 3X or 4X long (bent shank preferred), sizes 8 to 4. |
| **Cone head:** | Black metal. |
| **Weight:** | A few turns of 0.025- or 0.035-inch lead wire under the thorax area. |
| **Thread:** | Black Flymaster size A (or 3/0). |
| **Tail:** | Dyed black goose biots. |
| **Back:** | Black V-Stretch or Thin Skin or Medallion sheeting. |
| **Rib:** | Extra-small black V-Rib (or any fine rib material). |
| **Body:** | Ice Dub (or any fine, sparkling dubbing), a mix of black, peacock, and blue or purple. |
| **Legs:** | Black round rubber-strand, a section bound and doubled to make two legs along each side. |
| **Wing case:** | End of the back material, doubled back and notched. |
| **Comments:** | Imitates the salmonfly nymph. |

## 66 SICK STONE NYMPH, GOLDEN — *Damien Nurre*

*Tied by Damien Nurre*

| | |
|---|---|
| **Hook:** | Heavy wire, 3X or 4X long (bent shank preferred), sizes 8 and 6. |
| **Cone head:** | Gold metal. |
| **Weight:** | A few turns of 0.025- or 0.035-inch lead wire under the thorax area. |
| **Thread:** | Dark rust or brown Flymaster size A (or 3/0). |
| **Tail:** | Dyed brown goose biots. |
| **Back:** | Brown V-Stretch or Thin Skin or Medallion sheeting. |
| **Rib:** | Extra-small brown V-Rib (or any fine rib material). |
| **Body:** | Golden Ice Dub, or any golden shiny dubbing. |
| **Legs:** | Black-barred brown rubber-strand, a section bound and doubled to make two legs along each side. |
| **Wing case:** | End of the back material, doubled back and notched. |
| **Comments:** | Imitates the golden stonefly nymph. |

**Smurf Stone.** John Smeraglio owns the Deschutes Canyon Fly Shop along the Lower Deschutes River. The Deschutes is justly famous for its heavy salmonfly and golden stonefly hatches, making it an ideal laboratory for John to develop, test, and retest his Smurf Stones. These nymphs are simple in form and easy to tie, but they present a plausible semblance of a big stonefly nymph.

Here's how to tie a Smurf Stone: Wind on and bind the lead wire. Bind on the biot antennae, spiral the thread to the bend, and bind on the biot tails. Bind the yarn and V-Rib from just behind the hook's eye back to its bend—underneath the hook's shank. Wind the yarn halfway up the shank and bind it. Wind the V-Rib up the yarn in five or six open spirals. Bind the V-Rib at midshank and trim off the end. Bind on the hackle at the front of the abdomen you just created. (John prefers to bind on the hackle by the tip, but you can bind it on by the butt if you prefer.) Wind the thread to the eye, wind the yarn to the eye and bind it there, and then spiral the hackle up the yarn in three or four turns. Bind the hackle at the eye and trim off the end of the hackle. Press the thorax firmly between your thumb and finger to set the hackle fibers out to the sides. Complete the usual thread head.

## SMURF STONE BLACK — *John Smeraglio*

*Tied by John Smeraglio*

| | |
|---|---|
| **Hook:** | Standard or heavy wire, 2X or 3X long (slow-curve shank preferred), sizes 8 and 6. |
| **Thread:** | Black 6/0 or 3/0. |
| **Weight:** | Lead wire. |
| **Antennae:** | Dyed black goose biots. |
| **Tail:** | Dyed black goose biots. |
| **Rib:** | Narrow black V-Rib (or another rib material such as Larva Lace or Body Lace). |
| **Abdomen and thorax:** | Black yarn. John uses a blend of mohair, wool, and nylon that he buys at a fabric store, but any fuzzy woven yarn (Antron, wool) will do. |
| **Legs:** | Dyed black hackle—saddle, hen neck, or whatever has long and supple fibers. |
| **Comments:** | See the introduction to the Smurf Stones on this page for tying instructions. Imitates the salmonfly nymph. |

## SMURF STONE GOLDEN — *John Smeraglio*

*Tied by John Smeraglio*

**Hook:** Standard to heavy wire, 2X or 3X long (slow-curve shank preferred), sizes 8 and 6.
**Thread:** Gold (or yellow) 6/0 or 3/0.
**Weight:** Lead wire.
**Antennae:** Dyed gold goose biots.
**Tail:** Dyed gold goose biots.
**Rib:** Narrow gold V-Rib.
**Abdomen and thorax:** Gold yarn. John uses a blend of wool, mohair, and nylon, but any woven fuzzy yarn (Antron, wool) will do.
**Legs:** Dyed gold saddle or hen back—any hackle with long, supple fibers.
**Comments:** See the introduction to the Smurf Stones on page 132 for tying instructions. Imitates the golden stonefly nymph.

## SMURF STONE PURPLE — *John Smeraglio*

*Tied by John Smeraglio*

**Hook:** Standard or heavy wire, 2X or 3X long (slow-curve shank preferred), sizes 8 and 6.
**Thread:** Black or purple 6/0 or 3/0.
**Weight:** Lead wire.
**Antennae:** Dyed purple goose biots.
**Tail:** Dyed purple goose biots.
**Rib:** Narrow purple V-Rib (or other rib material such as Larva Lace or D-Rib).

**Abdomen and thorax:** Purple yarn. John uses a blend of wool, mohair, and nylon, but any fuzzy woven yarn (Antron, wool . . .) will do.
**Legs:** Dyed purple hackle—saddle, hen neck, or any hackle with long, pliant fibers.
**Comments:** See the introduction tot he Smurf Stones on page 132 for tying instructions. John has found that in low light or when his other Smurf Stone colors fail, purple usually works. It makes no sense, but trout behavior frequently makes no sense.

## TED'S STONE — *Ted Trueblood*

*Tied by Skip Morris*

**Hook:** Heavy wire, 3X long, sizes 10 to 6.
**Thread:** Black 8/0, 6/0, or 3/0.
**Weight (optional):** Lead wire.
**Tail:** Brown or reddish brown goose biots.
**Abdomen:** Brown chenille.
**Wing case:** Doubled brown chenille.
**Hackle:** Brown hackle palmered over the thorax.
**Thorax:** Orange chenille (some prefer a larger size here than in the abdomen).
**Comments:** A proven old-timer from a pioneer.

## TERRIBLE TROTH — Al Troth

*Tied by Skip Morris*

**Hook:** Heavy wire, 4X to 6X long, sizes 4 to 2.
**Thread:** Dark brown 3/0.
**Tail:** Dark brown turkey or goose biots.
**Antennae:** Dark brown turkey or goose biots.
**Weight:** Lead wire under the thorax.
**Body:** Dark brown chenille—one layer over the abdomen area, two over the thorax area.
**Legs:** Dark brown neck hackle stems with fibers trimmed close (bent to shape, and the bends dotted with cement), or black rubber-strand.
**Rib:** Blend of black and brown seal's fur (or, now, a substitute) spun in a dubbing loop and spiraled over the abdomen and thorax. Trim the fur closely, top and bottom.
**Comments:** An intriguing design, the Terrible Troth has been around for years, which means that its effectiveness has been established. Besides, how can you disregard a fly pattern from the man who invented the Troth Pheasant Tail and the Elk Hair Caddis?

## TUNGSTEN YELLOW SALLIE — Shane Stalcup and Ray Chang

*Tied by Al Davis*

**Hook:** Heavy (or standard) wire, 2X long, sizes 18 to 10.
**Thread:** Tan 8/0 or 6/0.
**Antennae:** Tan goose biots, bound under the bead.
**Head:** Gold tungsten bead.
**Weight:** Lead wire, under the thorax.
**Tail:** Tan goose biots, outside one or two turns of tan ostrich herl (spin the ostrich around the thread).
**Abdomen:** One yellow turkey biot.
**Thorax:** Tan ostrich herl (spun around the thread).

**Wing case:** Tan Medallion sheeting, bound in three sections.
**Legs:** Tan Super Floss with black markings (made with a permanent marking pen). Bind one section of Super Floss along each side of the rear of the thorax, and up to the bead. Trim each set to length.
**Comments:** Yellow sallie, yellow sally — it's all the same.

## WHITLOCK'S GOLDEN STONE NYMPH — Dave Whitlock

*Top view*

*Tied by Dave Whitlock*

**Hook:** Heavy wire, 3X or 4X long, sizes 8 and 6.
**Thread:** Gold 6/0 or 3/0.
**Weight:** Lead wire.
**Tail:** Gold goose or turkey biots (darken the top edges with a brown permanent marking pen if you like).
**Rib:** Fine brass (or gold or copper) wire.
**Back:** Dark gold Swiss straw, marked with a dark brown permanent marking pen.
**Abdomen:** Dave Whitlock Plus SLF in golden stone nymph (#13), or some other shiny dubbing such as Antron or Arizona Sparkle Nymph Dubbing.
**Thorax:** Dave Whitlock Plus SLF in stonefly nymph gills (#23), or some other shiny synthetic dubbing.
**Legs:** Cock ring-necked pheasant neck feather fibers, in three bunches up each side of the thorax.
**Wing cases:** Dark gold Swiss straw, marked with a dark brown permanent marking pen. The two rear cases are notched and extend back; the forward case is bound on, folded forward, and bound in front.
**Antennae:** Same biots as used for the tail.
**Comments:** Though not as demanding at the vise as some patterns, the handsome Whitlock's Golden Stone Nymph is more demanding than most. It's hard to imagine a trout passing it up.

# Stonefly Adults

## BIRD'S STONEFLY DRY — *Cal Bird*

*Tied by Skip Morris*

**Hook:** Light wire, long shank, sizes 8 to 4.
**Thread:** Orange 8/0, 6/0, or 3/0.
**Tail:** Two moose body hairs, split.
**Antennae:** Same as the tail.
**Body:** Alternate bands of orange floss and trimmed brown hackle.
**Wing:** Natural brown buck tail or dyed brown squirrel tail.
**Hackle:** Brown, heavy.
**Comments:** I've never understood how the body of this fly is supposed to suggest the body of the natural, but the Bird's Stonefly Dry has been a standard for the salmonfly hatch for four decades.

## CDC BLACK PARA STONE — *Jay Buchner*

*Tied by Al Davis*

**Hook:** Light wire, standard length or 1X long, sizes 18 to 14.
**Thread:** Black 8/0.
**Abdomen:** Black synthetic dubbing.
**Wing:** Two or three gray CDC feathers.
**Parachute wing:** Butts of the CDC wing feather, trimmed short (instructions are on page 63).
**Parachute hackle:** Black or dark dun (grayish-brown). (Instructions are on page 63.)
**Thorax:** Black dubbing.
**Comments:** Imitates the little black stonefly of winter.

## CHUCK'S GOLDEN STONE — *Chuck Stranahan*

*Tied by Al Davis*

**Hook:** Light to heavy wire, 2X long, sizes 10 to 6.
**Thread:** Tan or golden-olive 6/0 or 3/0.
**Tail:** Elk hair.
**Body:** Fuzzy gold Antron or other synthetic yarn (Chuck uses Red Heart brand 100 percent acrylic four-ply yarn in old gold.). Color the top and sides of the body with a brown permanent marking pen.
**Wing:** Elk hair.
**Hackle:** Dyed gold ginger-grizzly hackle (or substitute ginger).
**Comments:** You can flatten the body with smooth-jawed flat-nose pliers before coloring it, if you like. Chuck believes that because his fly drops rear-end first to the water, it's a good match for the landing of a real golden stonefly and thus especially convincing to trout.

## CHUCK'S SALMONFLY — *Chuck Stranahan*

*Tied by Al Davis*

**Hook:** Light to heavy wire, 2X long, sizes 8 and 4.
**Thread:** Fluorescent red 6/0 or 3/0.
**Tail:** Dyed orange elk hair.
**Body:** Soft orange fuzzy Antron or other synthetic yarn (Chuck uses Red Heart brand 100 percent acrylic four-ply yarn in pumpkin). Color the top and sides of the body with a brown permanent marking pen.
**Wing:** Moose body hair topped with white calf tail.
**Hackle:** Two brown-dyed grizzly hackles and one golden ginger-dyed grizzly hackle, mixed.
**Comments:** See the comments for Chuck's Golden Stone above.

## CLARK'S LITTLE YELLOW STONE — Lee Clark

*Tied by Al Davis*

| | |
|---|---|
| **Hook:** | Light or standard wire, 3X long, sizes 16 and 14. |
| **Thread:** | Yellow 8/0 or 6/0. |
| **Body:** | Flat gold Mylar tinsel covering the shank, and combed-out gold macramé yarn (or poly yarn) on top, bound just behind the hook's eye. Trim the yarn just a little short of the end of the wing. |
| **Wing:** | Natural pale deer hair. (Lee prefers to use the hair straight off the hide and doesn't even the tips in a hair-stacking tool.) |
| **Hackle:** | Grizzly dyed yellow, trimmed in a shallow "V" underneath. |

**Comments:** Another hook-dangling, hank-of-yarn-bodied Lee Clark design, in this case, imitating the yellow sallies.

## CLARK'S STONEFLY, GOLDEN STONE — Lee Clark

*Tied by Al Davis*

| | |
|---|---|
| **Hook:** | Light or standard wire, long shank, size 10. |
| **Thread:** | Yellow 8/0, 6/0, or 3/0. |
| **Body:** | Flat gold tinsel wrapped up the shank, and combed-out gold (or gold and rust mixed) macramé yarn (or poly yarn) on top, bound just behind the hook's eye. Trim the yarn a little short of the end of the wing. |
| **Wing:** | Deer hair. (Lee prefers the hair straight off the hide and doesn't even it in a hair-stacking tool.) |
| **Hackle:** | Brown, fairly heavy. Trim a "V" from the underside of the fibers. |

**Comments:** This peculiar pattern (the salmonfly version follows) has become a standard among fly fishers in the Pacific Northwest. The gold-wrapped shank hanging beneath the winglike body of yarn seems to be the key to its effectiveness. (If the hook size seems small, remember that the hank of yarn that forms the body extends well past the bend of the hook.) Lee makes a big thread head on this fly.

## CLARK'S STONEFLY, SALMONFLY — Lee Clark

*Tied by Skip Morris*

| | |
|---|---|
| **Hook:** | Light or standard wire, long shank, size 8. |
| **Thread:** | Orange 8/0, 6/0, or 3/0. |
| **Body:** | Flat gold tinsel wrapped up the shank, and a blunt-cut bunch of orange or rust macramé or poly yarn over the shank and bound under the hackle, like a wing, and extending about a shank's length beyond the end of the tinsel body. |
| **Wing:** | Deer hair. (Lee prefers the hair straight off the hide and doesn't even it in a hair-stacking tool.) |
| **Hackle:** | Brown, fairly heavy. Cut a "V" in the fibers underneath. |

**Comments:** This peculiar pattern has become a standard among fly fishers in the Pacific Northwest. The gold-wrapped shank hanging beneath the winglike body of yarn seems to be the key to its effectiveness. (If the hook size seems small, remember that the hank of yarn that forms the body extends well past the bend of the hook.) Lee makes a big thread head on this fly.

## DARK STONE — Polly Rosborough

*Tied by Skip Morris*

| | |
|---|---|
| **Hook:** | Light or standard wire, 3X long, size 8. |
| **Thread:** | Black 6/0 or 3/0. |
| **Rib:** | Dark furnace hackle spiraled up the body. |

**Body:** Tangerine orange (or orange or darkish orange) synthetic yarn, such as poly yarn or Antron.

**Wing:** Dyed coffee brown (or natural dark brown) buck tail.

**Hackle:** Dark furnace.

**Comments:** In *Popular Fly Patterns,* author Terry Hellekson says that Polly preferred a size 8 hook for his Dark Stone, even though this makes the fly considerably smaller than the salmonfly adult it imitates, and that the fly is more effective for it.

## EGG-LAYING SNAKE RIVER STONEFLY

*Tied by Al Davis*

**Hook:** Light to heavy wire, 4X long, sizes 8 and 10.

**Thread:** Rusty dun (or rust) 8/0 or 6/0.

**Egg sac (tail):** Strip of black closed-cell foam sheeting or black poly yarn, twisted and doubled.

**Rib:** Badger hackle trimmed short.

**Abdomen:** Dark honey (dark amber) synthetic dubbing.

**Wing:** Six strands of root beer Krystal Flash under natural gray elk hair.

**Thorax:** Dark honey synthetic dubbing.

**Parachute wing:** White Saap Float-Viz (or poly yarn). Instructions for making a parachute wing are on page 63.

**Parachute hackle:** Cree (an uncommon hackle with black, cream, and brown barring). Furnace or badger or plain brown makes an effective substitute (instructions are on page 63).

**Comments:** An imitation of the substantial early-season *Skwala* stonefly, specifically, the female with her egg sac. You can skate this fly across the surface to suggest the female's lively egg laying.

## FLUTTERING SALMONFLY — Todd Smith

*Tied by Todd Smith*

**Hook:** Standard or light wire, 2X or 3X long, sizes 6 and 4.

**Thread:** Orange 8/0 or 6/0.

**Tail:** Natural black moose body hair, short.

**Rib:** One brown saddle hackle.

**Body:** Burnt orange Antron yarn (or synthetic dubbing).

**Wing:** Untrimmed natural elk hair under about 20 strands of root beer Krystal Flash, under moose body hair bound by its tip ends. The butts of the moose should be cut straight across over the tips of the tail.

**Bullet head and collar:** Moose body hair (instructions are on page 146).

**Legs:** Black rubber-strand, one section bound on each side of the thread collar securing the bullet head. The strands should angle out.

**Comments:** Todd's Fluttering Salmonfly (also called the F-150) suggests an adult female salmonfly stuck atop the water and trying to fly off. The black tail represents the egg sac, and the splayed wing seems to shiver and wave on the current. When the females get caught on the water, their dance of escape is something of a dinner bell for trout.

## GOLDEN STONE — Polly Rosborough

*Tied by Al Davis*

**Hook:** Light or standard wire, 3X long, size 8.

**Thread:** Antique gold (or gold or yellow) 6/0 or 3/0.

**Rib:** One dyed gold (or ginger) hackle spiraled up the body.

**Body:** Antique gold (or gold) synthetic yarn, such as poly or Antron.

**Wing:** Natural light brown buck tail dyed gold (or undyed).

**Hackle:** Dyed gold (or ginger).

**Comments:** One of the many older big dry flies that are similar to the contemporary Stimulator.

**Henry's Fork Stonefly.** These unusual stonefly adult imitations are especially buoyant due to their extended elk-hair bodies and elk-hair wings, heads, and collars. Their creator, Mike Lawson, knows western hatches and western rivers. He's a longtime guide who started the Henry's Fork Anglers fly shop and is now its general manager. He's also a sharp fly tier and fly designer who has developed some fine patterns.

## Making the Body of the Henry's Fork Stonefly (Henry's Fork Golden Stone)

**1.** Cut a bunch of elk hair from the hide. Hold the bunch by its tips and comb out the fuzz and short hairs. Trim off the tips of the hair. Start the thread on the shank and bind the hair by its cut tips, near the bend.

**2.** For this step, reverse the hook in the vise if you prefer. Wind the thread down the hair and off the bend, a distance equal to the width of the gape. Wind on three tight thread turns, then wind the thread back to the bend.

**3.** Work all the hair butts forward so that they surround the bound hair core. Bind the hair at the bend with a couple of tight thread turns. (You may find it easier to pull half the hair forward on one side and bind it; then do the same to the other half on the other side.)

**4.** Pull the hair butts forward around the shank. Spiral the thread forward up the hair about three-quarters up the shank. Bind the butts there and trim them closely.

### HENRY'S FORK GOLDEN STONE    *Mike Lawson*

*Tied by Skip Morris*

| | |
|---|---|
| **Hook:** | Light to heavy wire, 2X or 3X long, sizes 10 to 6. |
| **Thread:** | Tan 3/0. |
| **Body:** | Dyed gold elk hair (instructions above). |
| **Wing:** | Natural brown elk hair. |

**Bullet head and collar:** Dyed gold (or yellow) elk hair (instructions are on page 146).

## HENRY'S FORK SALMONFLY — *Mike Lawson*

*Tied by Al Davis*

**Hook:** Light to heavy wire, 2X or 3X long, sizes 8 to 4.
**Thread:** Orange 3/0.
**Body:** Burnt orange (brownish orange) elk hair (instructions are on page 138).
**Wing:** Natural gray elk hair.
**Bullet head and collar:** Dyed black elk hair (instructions are on page 146).

## IMPROVED GOLDEN STONE

*Tied by Skip Morris*

**Hook:** Light to heavy wire, 3X or 4X long, sizes 10 to 6.
**Thread:** Pale yellow 6/0 or 3/0.
**Tail:** Natural pale or bleached deer or elk hair.
**Rib:** One light ginger hackle spiraled up the body.
**Body:** Cream yarn or dubbing.
**Wing:** Natural pale or bleached deer or elk hair.
**Hackle:** Light ginger, heavy.
**Comments:** This fly is based on the Improved Sofa Pillow (see next), which is based on the original Sofa Pillow. It is bushy and high-riding.

## IMPROVED SOFA PILLOW — *Pat and Sig Barnes*

*Tied by Skip Morris*

**Hook:** Light to heavy wire, 2X long, sizes 10 to 4.
**Thread:** Black 6/0 or 3/0.
**Tail:** Elk hair.
**Body:** Orange synthetic yarn or dubbing.
**Rib:** One brown hackle (saddle hackle preferred), spiraled up the body. This hackle's fibers should be no longer than those of the hackle collar; they can be a bit shorter.
**Wing:** Elk hair.
**Hackle:** Brown; use plenty of hackle.
**Comments:** A more buoyant version of the popular Sofa Pillow, both of which imitate the salmonfly.

**Jacklin's Adult Stonefly.** If a fly designer's experience and credentials reflect on his or her original fly designs, Bob Jacklin's dry-fly stonefly patterns are a sure bet. He started tying professionally at age 16, began guiding in the late 1960s, opened Jacklin's fly shop in the early 1970s, and in 2000 won the prestigious Buz Buszek Memorial Fly-Tying Award. The bottom line is this: these patterns float long and catch fish. And tying them is certainly manageable for most tiers.

### JACKLIN'S EARLY BLACK STONE — Bob Jacklin

*Tied by Bob Jacklin*

| | |
|---|---|
| **Hook:** | Standard or heavy wire, 3X or 4X long (a slow-curve shank is optional), sizes 14 to 10. |
| **Thread:** | Black 8/0 or 6/0. |
| **Tail (egg sac):** | Black deer hair, trimmed short. |
| **Rib:** | Natural black (or dyed black) hackle spiraled up the body. Trim the fibers short underneath. |
| **Body:** | Light brown opossum dubbing. |
| **Wing:** | Natural gray deer hair. |
| **Bullet head and collar:** | Dyed black coastal deer hair (instructions are on page 146). |
| **Legs:** | Fine black rubber-strand, one length tightly bound against each side of the thread collar holding the bullet head. |
| **Comments:** | Imitates *Capnia*, the blackish little winter stonefly. |

### JACKLIN'S GIANT SALMONFLY — Bob Jacklin

*Tied by Bob Jacklin*

| | |
|---|---|
| **Hook:** | Standard or heavy wire, 3X or 4X long (a slow-curve shank is optional), sizes 6 and 4. |
| **Thread:** | Fluorescent orange 3/0. |
| **Tail (egg sac):** | Dyed black elk or deer hair, trimmed short. |
| **Rib:** | Two brown saddle hackles spiraled up the body. Trim the fibers short along the underside. |
| **Body:** | Soft orange synthetic dubbing or poly yarn. |
| **Wing:** | Long, natural light elk hair. |
| **Bullet head and collar:** | Dyed brown deer (or elk) hair (instructions are on page 146). |
| **Legs:** | Black medium-diameter rubber-strand, a short section bound tightly along each side of the thread collar. |

### JACKLIN'S GOLDEN STONE — Bob Jacklin

*Tied by Bob Jacklin*

| | |
|---|---|
| **Hook:** | Standard to heavy wire, 3X or 4X long (a slow-curve shank is optional), sizes 8 and 6. |
| **Thread:** | Rusty brown 6/0. |
| **Tail (egg sac):** | Dyed brown deer hair, trimmed short. |
| **Rib:** | Ginger hackle spiraled up the body. Trim the fibers short underneath. |
| **Body:** | Antique gold synthetic dubbing. |
| **Wing:** | Natural light elk hair. |
| **Bullet head and collar:** | Dyed tan elk hair (instructions are on page 146). |
| **Legs:** | Medium-diameter brown rubber-strand. Bind a short section tightly along each side of the thread collar holding the bullet head. |

## JACKLIN'S LITTLE BRIGHT GREEN STONEFLY
*Bob Jacklin*

*Tied by Bob Jacklin*

**Hook:** Standard to heavy wire, 3X or 4X long (a slow-curve shank is optional), sizes 16 and 14.
**Thread:** Yellow 8/0 or 6/0.
**Tail (egg sac):** Natural light gray deer hair, trimmed short.
**Rib:** White or cream hackle, trimmed short underneath.
**Body:** Bright green synthetic dubbing.
**Wing:** Natural light elk hair.
**Bullet head and collar:** Natural light deer hair (instructions are on page 146).
**Legs:** Fine cream rubber-strand. Bind a short section along each side of the body under the thread collar holding the bullet head.
**Comments:** Imitates similarly colored adults of the little green stonefly complex.

## JACKLIN'S LITTLE OLIVE STONE
*Bob Jacklin*

*Tied by Bob Jacklin*

**Hook:** Standard to heavy wire, 3X or 4X long (a slow-curve shank is optional), sizes 12 and 10.
**Thread:** Yellow 8/0 or 6/0.
**Tail (egg sac):** Light olive deer hair, trimmed short.
**Rib:** Natural light ginger hackle spiraled up the body. Trim the fibers short underneath.
**Body:** Pale olive synthetic dubbing.
**Wing:** Natural light elk hair.
**Bullet head and collar:** Natural gray deer hair dyed yellow or grayish yellow (instructions are on page 146).
**Legs:** Fine, light olive rubber strand, a short section bound along each side under the thread collar holding the bullet head.
**Comments:** Imitates similarly colored adults of the little green stonefly complex.

## JACKLIN'S WESTERN YELLOW STONEFLY
*Bob Jacklin*

*Tied by Bob Jacklin*

**Hook:** Standard to heavy wire, 3X or 4X long (a slow-curve shank is optional), sizes 12 to 8.
**Thread:** Yellow 6/0 or 3/0.
**Tail (egg sac):** Natural gray deer hair, trimmed short.
**Rib:** Natural pale ginger hackle spiraled up the body, the fibers trimmed short underneath.
**Body:** Pale yellow synthetic dubbing.
**Wing:** Natural light elk hair.
**Bullet head and collar:** Dyed pale yellow (or natural pale) elk hair (instructions are on page 146).
**Legs:** Fine, pale yellow rubber-strand, a short section bound under each side of the thread collar holding the bullet head.
**Comments:** Imitates *Isoperla*, one of the small summer yellow sally stoneflies.

## JUGHEAD
*Betty Hoyt*

*Tied by Skip Morris*

**Hook:** Light to heavy wire, 2X long, sizes 10 to 4.
**Thread:** Black 6/0 or 3/0. (I use size A rod-winding thread to make the head and collar.)
**Tail:** Elk hair.
**Rib:** One brown hackle with its fibers trimmed.
**Body:** Orange poly yarn (or orange synthetic dubbing).
**Underwing (optional):** Elk hair.
**Wing:** Red fox-squirrel tail.
**Head:** Undyed deer hair spun and shaped (instructions are on page 268).
**Collar (optional):** Tips of the hair used to make the head.
**Comments:** The strangely oversized head seems to be fine with the trout and helps the fly float for a long time. It's a standard for the salmonfly hatch.

## LANGTRY SPECIAL

*Tied by Skip Morris*

**Hook:** Light to heavy wire, 2X long, sizes 10 to 6.
**Thread:** Orange 6/0 or 3/0.
**Tail:** Natural tan elk hair.
**Rib:** One, brown, spiraled up the abdomen.
**Abdomen:** Cream synthetic dubbing.
**Wing:** Natural tan elk hair.
**Hackle:** One brown hackle spiraled up the thorax.
**Thorax:** Synthetic orange dubbing.
**Comments:** In his *Western Streamside Guide* (1987), author Dave Hughes presents the Langtry Special as his choice for an imitation of the adult salmonfly. I know Dave, and I know he's fished this hatch for decades, so his word's good enough for me.

## LITTLE BROWN STONE                 Polly Rosborough

*Tied by Al Davis*

**Hook:** Light (to standard) wire, 2X long, sizes 16 to 12.
**Thread:** Brown 8/0 or 6/0.
**Tail:** Originally, dark brown pheasant body feather fibers; pheasant tail fibers are the standard now.
**Rib (optional):** Brown 3/0 thread.
**Body:** Dark brown synthetic dubbing.

**Wing:** One natural dark grizzly hackle tip flat over the body and extending to the bend of the hook.
**Hackle:** Natural dark grizzly.
**Comments:** A straightforward imitation of the little brown stonefly (and possibly *Skwala,* if tied larger) with an unusual wing.

## LITTLE YELLOW STONE                 Polly Rosborough

*Tied by Al Davis*

**Hook:** Light (to standard) wire, 2X long, sizes 16 to 12.
**Thread:** Yellow 8/0 or 6/0.
**Tail:** Dyed pale yellow grizzly hackle fibers.
**Rear hackle:** Dyed pale yellow grizzly.
**Rib:** Heavy yellow thread.
**Body:** Chartreuse synthetic yarn.
**Front hackle:** Dyed pale yellow grizzly.
**Comments:** The rear hackle should be noticeably shorter than the front hackle. Although this represents a different approach to stonefly design, any fly pattern good enough for Polly deserves a second look.

## LITTLE YELLOW STONE ADULT

*Tied by Al Davis*

**Hook:** Light or standard wire, 1X or 2X long, sizes 18 to 12.
**Thread:** Red 8/0 or 6/0.
**Tag:** The red working thread.
**Body:** Bright yellow synthetic dubbing.
**Wing:** Dyed yellow deer or elk hair.
**Hackle:** Grizzly or ginger.
**Comments:** An imitation for the yellow sally complex of small stoneflies. Craig Mathews and John Juracek offer this one in their *Fishing Yellowstone Hatches.*

## MACSALMON
*Al Troth*

*Tied by Al Troth*

**Hook:** Light to heavy wire, 2X long, sizes 8 to 2.

**Thread:** Brown 3/0 (consider size A rod-winding thread for the head and collar).

**Body:** Section of orange polypropylene macramé yarn melted at the end.

**Wing:** Dark gray synthetic wing material cut to shape (Al prefers Fly Sheet), topped with natural pale elk hair.

**Head and collar:** Dyed dark brown deer hair, flared and trimmed in front (instructions are on page 268). Al likes to cut the front of the head flat, with the top angling forward. I assume the goal is to make the fly skate, rather than dive, on a twitch—twitching a big stonefly imitation can be a killing tactic.

**Comments:** To make the abdomen of the MacSalmon, carefully melt the end of some woven macramé yarn with a lighter, candle, or match. Stop when the cut ends of the fibers have all melted together. Trim the yarn to length. Push the hook eye into the yarn just ahead of the melted end, up the yarn's center, and out the end of the yarn. Mount the hook in the vise, push the yarn back a little, start the thread, and then bind the front of the yarn around the shank. Leave enough of the shank clear in front for the hair head. Continue tying the fly. A MacImitation of the MacSalmonfly.

## MATT'S ADULT STONE

*Tied by Skip Morris*

**Hook:** Light to heavy wire, 1X long, sizes 8 to 4.

**Thread:** Orange 3/0 (consider size A rod thread for flaring the hair).

**Body:** Orange woven macramé yarn, melted on the end.

**Wing:** Natural brown elk mane.

**Head and collar:** Natural dark deer hair, flared and trimmed; the evened tips make the collar (instructions are on page 268).

**Comments:** See the MacSalmon on this page for instructions on preparing the yarn body, except that the body for the Matt's Adult Stone is mounted not around the hook's shank but atop it. Craig Mathews and John Juracek, in their *Fly Patterns of Yellowstone,* say that they like to skitter and twitch the Matt's Adult Stone across the current "when fish are taking naturals behaving similarly."

## MORRIS FOAM GOLDEN STONE
*Skip Morris*

*Tied by Skip Morris*

**Hook:** Light or standard wire, 2X long (a slow-curve shank is optional), size 8.

**Thread:** Gold or yellow 6/0 or 3/0.

**Tail:** Tan (or brown) turkey flat (or other body feather).

**Body:** Strip of buoyant yellow closed-cell foam sheeting colored with an antique gold or ocher (dark-yellow) permanent marking pen.

**Eyes:** Premade plastic barbell eyes.

**Antennae:** Fine tan or yellow rubber-strand (instructions are on page 246).

**Wing:** Ethafoam colored on the underside with a brown permanent marking pen. (The color must be set with a coating of thinned Dave's Flexament or a spray of artist's fixative such as Tuffilm.) Atop the foam, you can use pearl Krystal Flash (optional) beneath natural pale or bleached elk hair. And you can put pearl Krystal Flash under the Ethafoam wing as well, if you like.

**Head and back:** Same foam strip used for the body.

**Legs:** Tan (or brown, yellow, or gold) medium- or fine-diameter round rubber-strands, one strand bound tightly along each side so that the ends angle out. (You can add two more legs by knotting a length of rubber-strand and pulling the strand through the body with a large needle; the knot secures the strand.)

**Comments:** Tying instructions are on page 144. This imitation of the golden stonefly is a stubborn floater with a convincing outline. If a tumble of current pulls it down, it pops back up!

## Tying the Morris Foam Stone (Morris Foam Salmonfly)

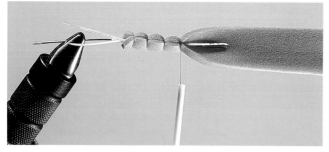

**1.** Strip the fibers from the sides of a turkey flat feather. Trim out the center of the feather, leaving a few tail fibers on each side (as with the tail on the Morristone Stonefly Nymph, described earlier; but leave the stem long this time). Mount a beading needle in your vise. Bind the feather lightly atop the needle, smear a tiny amount of low-odor epoxy glue along the needle, and then build the abdomen with a strip of foam sheeting (trim the end of the sheeting to a slight taper), as described for the Bunse Dun on page 58. Half-hitch the thread, cut it, and slide the abdomen off the needle. (Use proper ventilation for the epoxy, and don't get any on your hands.)

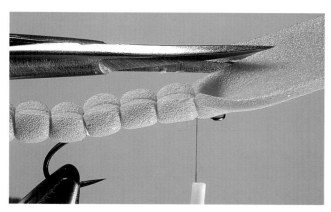

**2.** Wind a tight layer or two of thread over the entire shank. Bind the abdomen atop the bend. Bind the foam strip up the shank in sections, atop the shank. Build a thread collar just behind the eye. Trim back the sides of the remaining foam strip to make it narrower.

**3.** Bind a set of plastic barbell eyes atop the thread collar. Make the rubber-strand antennae now, if you want to include them, as described on page 246. Color a sheet of Ethafoam, and cut a wing from it. Bind the wing atop

the thread collar. (Bind Krystal Flash atop the foam wing next, if you want.) Cut, comb, and stack a bunch of elk hair and bind that atop the Ethafoam wing. (If your elk hair isn't long enough to nearly reach the tips of the foam wing, you can bind the hair atop the wing one body segment back. Just cross the thread back over the top of the segment, bind on the hair, and cross the thread forward to the thread collar.)

**4.** Hold all the wing materials down, centered over the body, with the strip of foam pulled back atop them. With the thread at the rear of the thread collar, add a few thread turns to make the top of the head. Wind the thread back over the top of the foam to the end of the next foam section, wind on a couple of turns of thread, and then do the same back to the end of the next section. Bind a length of rubber-strand tightly against each side of the depression between the segments.

**5.** Hold back the front ends of the rubber-strands, wind the thread forward over the top of the next section, and then bind both the rubber-strands tightly in the depression there, on the sides. Cross the thread forward over the segment to the thread collar behind the foam head; then whip-finish and trim off the thread. The rubber-strand legs should flare out from the body. Trim the legs to length. Trim the end of the foam strip short. If you want a third set of legs, knot some rubber-strand and use a needle to pull it through the body. Add head cement or low-odor epoxy glue to the thread collar, the shank of the hook, and the tip of the abdomen to secure the tails.

| MORRIS FOAM SALMONFLY | *Skip Morris* |

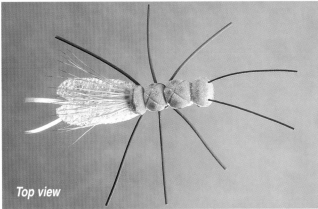

*Top view*

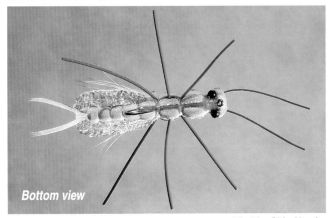

*Bottom view*

*Tied by Skip Morris*

**Legs:** Brown (or black) medium- or fine-diameter round rubber-strands, one strand bound tightly along each side so that the ends angle out. (You can add two more legs by knotting a length of rubber-strand and pulling the strand through the body with a large needle; the knot secures the strand.)

**Comments:** Tying instructions are on page 144. This fly floats as long as the foam survives and the elk hair doesn't become too sodden—which can be quite a while and amount to quite a few trout.

**Rod's Stonefly.** Rod Robinson of Portland, Oregon, developed his buoyant foam-core Goldenrod for the golden stonefly hatch on Oregon's Metolius River. According to Roger White (owner of the Camp Sherman store and fly shop, located only a stroll from the river), the Metolius golden stone hatch can be well under way as early as mid-June and last clear through Labor Day! That's not bad for what is normally a two- to three-week hatch. The Goldenrod worked so well that Rod altered it for the salmonfly hatch on the Deschutes River—thus, the Salmonrod.

| GOLDENROD | *Rod Robinson* |

*Tied by Skip Morris*

**Hook:** Light or standard wire, 2X long (a slow-curve shank is optional), sizes 8 and 6.

**Thread:** Orange 6/0 or 3/0.

**Tail:** Brown (or black) turkey flat.

**Body:** Strip of buoyant orange closed-cell foam marked with a dark brown permanent marking pen until the orange is subdued.

**Eyes:** Black premade plastic barbell eyes.

**Antennae:** Fine black or brown rubber-strand (instructions are on page 246).

**Wing:** Ethafoam colored brown, topped with undyed tan-brown or pale elk hair. (The color must be set on the Ethafoam with a coating of thinned Dave's Flexament or a spray of artist's fixative such as Tuffilm.) Atop the foam, you can use pearl Krystal Flash (optional) beneath the undyed tan-brown or pale elk hair. And you can put pearl Krystal Flash under the Ethafoam wing as well, if you like.

**Head and back:** Same foam strip used for the body.

**Hook:** Light or standard wire, 2X long, size 8.

**Thread:** Gold or yellow 8/0, 6/0, or 3/0.

**Tail:** Pheasant tail fibers, divided around a ball of the same dubbing used for the body.

**Body:** Rectangle cut from a foam cup, folded around the shank and bound. The foam should extend from the tail to about two-thirds up the shank. You can taper the ends with tight thread turns, but use only firm turns over most of the foam. Cover the foam with gold synthetic dubbing.

**Hackle:** Brown, palmered over the front half of the body and trimmed beneath.

**Wing:** Tan calf tail.

**Bullet head and collar:** Dyed gold elk hair. Trim off the hair tips underneath to expose the body (instructions are on page 146).

**Legs (optional):** Brown or tan rubber-strand, a section bound along each side of the thread collar securing the bullet head. Omit the hackle if you add these rubber-strand legs.

**Comments:** Imitates the golden stonefly.

**SALMONROD**                                    *Rod Robinson*

*Tied by Skip Morris*

Hook:       Light or standard wire, 2X long, sizes 6 and 4.
Tail:       Pheasant tail fibers split around some of the same dubbing used for the body.
Body:       Rectangle cut from a foam cup and folded around the shank, then bound. The foam should stretch from the tail about two-thirds up the shank. Taper the ends of the foam with tight thread turns, but use only firm turns over the rest of the foam. Cover the foam with dark orange-brown dubbing.
Hackle:     One, dark brown or brown, spiraled up the front half of the body.
Wing:       Dyed brown calf tail.
**Bullet head and hair collar:** Dyed dark brown elk hair. Trim off the collar hairs underneath, to expose the body (instructions are on this page).
**Legs (optional):** Brown or black rubber-strand, a section bound along each side of the thread collar securing the bullet head. Omit the hackle if you add these rubber-strand legs.
Comments:   Imitates the salmonfly.

**ROGUE GIANT FOAM STONE**              *Jack Schlotter*

*Tied by Al Davis*

Hook:       Light or standard wire, 2X long, (slow-curve shank is optional), size 4.
Thread:     Orange 3/0.
Body:       Buoyant orange closed-cell foam sheeting, bound in segments (see the instructions for the Bunse Dun on page 58). Or start the thread on a needle, push the center of a foam strip over the needle, and bind the sides of the foam up the needle in segments; then slide the foam body off the needle.

Wing:       A few strands of orange Krystal Flash under a long wing shape cut from Ethafoam sheeting, with natural brown moose mane atop the wing.
**Bullet head and hair collar:** Natural dark or dyed gray-brown or dark brown elk hair (instructions follow).
Legs:       Black round rubber-strand, medium; one strand bound tightly on each side of the thread collar.
Thread collar: Fluorescent fire-orange 6/0, started over the 3/0 and built as a band around the rear of the bullet head and securing the legs.
Comments:   Imitates the salmonfly.

## Making a Bullet Head (Rogue Foam Stone)

*(See video instructions on DVD.)*

**1.** With the body and wing completed, wind the thread to the eye.

**2.** Cut, comb out, and stack a bunch of elk hair (elk is much tougher than deer and therefore makes a better bullet head). Trim the butts of the hair even. Hold the cut butts of the hair over the eye and back far enough to bind. Work the hair butts down around the shank, make a couple of light thread turns around the hair butts, and then hold the butts firmly as you pull the thread tight.

**3.** Bind the butts of the hair thoroughly.

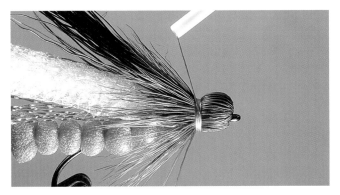

**4.** Wind the thread back to the front of the body or slightly short of it. Stroke all the hair back along the sides, top, and bottom of the shank. Wind on two tight thread turns and pull them tight. Continue holding the hair back as you build a thread collar. The hair tips will form a collar. Some tiers prefer to trim off the hairs on the underside of this collar to expose the fly's body to the trout.

### ROGUE GOLDEN FOAM STONE — Jack Schlotter

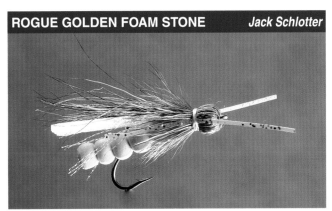

*Tied by Al Davis*

| | |
|---|---|
| **Hook:** | Light or standard wire, 2X long (slow-curve shank is optional), sizes 8 and 6. |
| **Thread:** | Yellow 3/0. |
| **Body:** | Buoyant yellow closed-cell foam sheeting, segmented (see the instructions for the Bunse Dun on page 58). Or start the thread on a needle, push the center of a foam strip over the needle, and bind the sides of the foam up the needle in segments. Then slide the foam body off the needle. |
| **Wing:** | Ethafoam over yellow Krystal Flash, topped with natural light moose mane. |
| **Bullet head and hair collar:** | Dyed golden brown deer or elk (instructions are on page 146). |

| | |
|---|---|
| **Legs:** | Pumpkin Sili-Legs with black speckles (or tan or pale rubber-strand). |
| **Thread collar:** | Tan 6/0, started over the 3/0 and built as a band around the rear of the bullet head, securing the legs. |
| **Comments:** | For more tying details, see the Rogue Giant Foam Stone above. |

### SALLY STONE DRY FLY — Scott Sanchez

*Top view*

*Tied by Scott Sanchez*

| | |
|---|---|
| **Hook:** | Standard wire, 3X long, slow-curve shank, sizes 16 to 10. |
| **Thread:** | Light cahill (pale yellow) 8/0. |
| **Butt:** | Strip cut from red closed-cell foam sheeting. |
| **Rib:** | Fine copper wire. |
| **Abdomen:** | Pale yellow synthetic dubbing (Super Fine Dry Fly, Antron, poly). |
| **Tail:** | Dyed light olive goose biots. The butts of the biots should lie outside the body and be secured with the rib. |
| **Wing:** | Pearl lure tape on clear plastic sheeting (or any pale, translucent synthetic wing sheeting) cut to shape. |
| **Antennae:** | Dyed light olive goose biots. |
| **Hackle:** | Golden badger or light ginger, spiraled over the thorax, trimmed to a shallow "V" underneath. |
| **Thorax:** | Same as the abdomen. |
| **Strike indicator:** | Short square of lime green buoyant closed-cell foam sheeting, bound atop the thorax and hackle. I'm not sure how Scott secures the foam, but I assume he completes the thorax and hackle, spirals the thread back through it, binds on the foam, raises the front of the foam as he spirals the thread forward again, and trims the ends of the foam strip to length. |
| **Comments:** | An especially colorful imitation of the adult yellow sally stonefly complex. |

## SOFA PILLOW — *Pat and Sig Barnes*

*Tied by Skip Morris*

**Hook:** Light to heavy wire, 2X long, sizes 10 to 4.
**Thread:** Black 6/0 or 3/0.
**Tail:** Section of dyed red duck quill.
**Body:** Red floss.
**Wing:** Red fox squirrel tail.
**Hackle:** Brown—use lots of hackle.
**Comments:** A proven old-time salmonfly imitation of historical value. It provides a real look into the principles of fly design of the 1940s and 1950s, if nothing else. But don't be so quick to write off a fly that's fooled far too many salmonfly-seeking trout to tally.

## SPORT UTILITY STONE, GOLDEN — *Damien Nurre*

*Top view*

*Tied by Damien Nurre*

**Hook:** Standard or light wire, 2X or 3X long (slow-curve shank preferred), sizes 10 to 6.
**Thread:** Brown or rust 3/0.
**Tail (egg sac):** Black Krystal Flash in a short loop.
**Abdomen:** Gold Antron yarn over a strip of tan buoyant closed-cell foam sheeting.
**First wing:** Yellow Krystal Flash over Etha-Wing (or any pale synthetic wing sheeting with dark vein markings), cut to an elongated wing shape.
**Top of thorax:** Strip of tan buoyant closed-cell foam sheeting bound at the rear and front of the thorax.
**Second wing:** Elk hair dyed gold.
**Legs:** Brown-barred tan rubber-strand, medium-fine. Bind one pair at the rear of the thorax to form two legs, and a second pair at the front of the thorax.
**Strike indicator:** Small rectangle of yellow buoyant closed-cell foam sheeting.
**Thorax:** Gold Antron dubbing.
**Comments:** To build the abdomen, start the floss at the hook's bend, build a short segment of the abdomen, bind on the end of the foam strip with a slim collar of floss, pull the long end of the foam back, and build another floss segment, bind the foam again with the floss, continue in this manner. To make the thorax, bind the rear of the thorax foam on top, the hair wing atop the foam, the rubber-strand legs on the sides, and the indicator atop that. Dub the thorax. Bind the foam at the front of the thorax, stroke the hair butts together and forward and bind them, and then bind on the second set of legs. This is quite an inventive pattern for imitating the golden stonefly.

## SPORT UTILITY STONE, SALMON — *Damien Nurre*

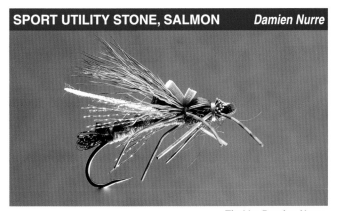

*Tied by Damien Nurre*

**Hook:** Standard or light wire, 2X or 3X long (slow-curve shank preferred), sizes 8 to 4.

**Thread:** Black 3/0.

**Tail (egg sac):** Black Krystal Flash in a short loop.

**Abdomen:** Rust or burnt orange Antron yarn over a strip of black buoyant closed-cell foam sheeting.

**First wing:** Orange Krystal Flash over Etha-Wing (or some other pale synthetic wing sheeting with dark vein markings) cut into an elongated wing shape.

**Top of thorax:** Strip of black buoyant closed-cell foam sheeting bound at the rear and front of the thorax.

**Second wing:** Elk hair dyed dark brown.

**Legs:** Black-barred brown rubber-strand, medium-fine. Bind one pair at the rear of the thorax to form two legs, and a second pair at the front of the thorax.

**Strike indicator:** Small rectangle of orange buoyant closed-cell foam sheeting.

**Thorax:** Black Antron dubbing.

**Comments:** For more tying information, see the Sport Utility Stone, Golden on page 148. The Sport Utility Stone, Salmon, imitates the salmonfly stonefly.

## SUNKEN STONEFLY, SALMONFLY — *Blue Ribbon Flies*

*Tied by Craig Mathews*

**Hook:** Light to heavy wire (depends on whether you fish it mostly dry or sunken), 2X long, sizes 6 and 4.

**Thread:** Orange 6/0.

**Tail (egg cluster):** Black Z-lon or Antron yarn, trimmed short.

**Body and wing:** Four to six sections consisting of dark orange Z-lon or Antron dubbing and a bunch of natural tan-gray deer hair (instructions are on page 111).

**Head:** Cut butts of the forwardmost bunch of deer hair.

**Comments:** For a golden stone version, use yellow thread, antique gold dubbing, and hooks one size smaller than for the salmonfly. You can fish the Sunken Stonefly as a dry fly or a dead-drifted wet fly. Craig says that he's seen a lot of big stoneflies pulled under by currents, and he believes trout like to smack the insects just as they go under, so he intentionally pulls his Sunken Stonefly underwater in likely spots. You could do this with a little lead putty on the leader and a sink-tip line.

## TERRANASTY — *Kim Keely*

*Tied by Al Davis*

**Hook:** Light to standard wire, 2X long, slow-curve shank, sizes 6 and 4.

**Thread:** Orange 3/0.

**Tail and antennae:** Dyed orange turkey biots.

**Body:** Strip of tan buoyant closed-cell foam sheeting, wound up the shank.

**Rib:** Fairly short-fibered brown saddle hackle.

**Legs:** Brown rubber-strand.

**Wing:** Elk hair over a loop of light dun (grayish-brown) Z-lon.

**Hackle:** Two brown saddle hackles spiraled up the thorax.

**Thorax:** Orange synthetic dubbing.

**Comments:** Intended to imitate the salmonfly (although it seems like a plausible choice for the golden stone as well). It's high floating with lots of hackle—a good design to skate across the surface like a lively or egg-laying natural.

# Midges

TINY AS THEY ARE—and they can match the smallest of fly hooks—midges are important to fly fishers for three reasons: (1) midges hatch year-round; (2) midges are going strong when most hatching insects are quiet in the fall, winter, and early spring; and (3) midges can hatch in real abundance, so their sheer mass is enough to encourage lots of trout, including some large ones, to sip quietly at the surface. Midges belong to the family Chironomidae and are often called chironomids. Many of the larvae inhabit the silt of slow currents, so lazy, silty rivers are often full of them. However, most quick rivers also hold plenty of midges in the pools and calmer water, and quite a few midge species actually prefer swift currents.

# Fishing the Stages of the Midge

## LARVA

*Midge larva*

The midge larva is a slender, featureless worm that tries to stay hidden in silt, among water plants, and around the stones in a riverbed. When the time for hatching nears, the larva constructs a crude shelter and then transforms into a pupa within it.

Typically, trout see large numbers of chironomid larvae only when the larvae "drift," just letting the current carry them downstream, around sunrise and sunset. Despite the minuteness of the larvae, this activity can really get the trout moving—chironomids are big on drifting, so there can be lots of them. Consequently, an imitation can be productive when fished dead drift at these times. Get the fly down either by attaching weight to the leader or by using a larger, heavier nymph to draw the lightweight midge fly down with a dropper rig.

## PUPA

*Midge pupa*

The fully developed midge pupa is stouter than the larva, though still slim, and has a rounded thorax and stubby wing pads. It leaves its shelter and half squirms, half swims laboriously to the surface. The pupa escapes its shuck at the surface as an emerger.

The wriggling, inefficient chironomid pupa rising to hatch presents an opportunity for the trout, and they know it. Early in a hatch, a pupa imitation fished deep can be effective. When the real pupae reach the surface, they can hang there for a full minute or longer—for the trout, an excellent shot at a full stomach. So a pupa imitation drifted in the surface or just under it is a fine choice during a chironomid hatch, as is an emerger fly fished dead drift.

## EMERGER

Like mayflies and caddisflies, midges are particularly vulnerable as they struggle from their shucks at or just below the river's surface, and trout welcome the opportunity this presents. Emerger midge patterns are normally fished dead drift to working trout.

## ADULT

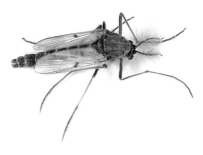

*Midge adult*

The adult midge looks like a mosquito, its close cousin. Eventually, the adult female midge buzzes out to swim down and deposit her fertilized eggs or drops to the water to release them. When female midges are active, which is usually early in the morning and again in the evening, trout move to them. That's when an imitation of a full adult midge, fished dead drift or with occasional twitches among the rising fish, is the right choice. At one time, the adult midge was the main target of the fly fisher's imitations, but the pupa and emerger have taken over that position.

# Specific Hatches

There are so many midge species that virtually no fly fisher tries to sort them out. When a hatch comes, we just try to catch a sample and match it with a fly. Typical midge colors for all stages are black, brown, green, light to dark olive, gray, tan, cream, and even red. Hook sizes to match larvae, pupae, and adults run from 26 to 14. I probably use 22s and 24s most often in my midge fishing.

# Midge Larvae and Pupae

Question: How do you tell a midge larva fly from a midge pupa fly? Answer: You don't. The point is, a real midge larva is basically a tiny segmented worm, and a real midge pupa is basically a tiny segmented worm that's swollen a bit at the head end. So fly fishers treat most midge-imitating nymphs as imitations of both the larval and pupal stages, and they do very well, thank you. We're talking about flies that are rarely tied larger than size 18, and often size 24, so who cares whether the thorax of such a tiny fly is swollen? Trout don't, and you shouldn't either.

### DALE'S MIDGE LARVA — *Dale Darling*

*Tied by Peter Morrison*

| | |
|---|---|
| **Hook:** | Light (or standard or heavy) wire, short to 1X long (humped shank is optional), sizes 24 to 16. |
| **Thread:** | Black 8/0 or 6/0. |
| **Rib:** | Fine copper wire, counterwrapped. |
| **Abdomen:** | Several strands of undyed mallard flank wound up the shank. |
| **Head:** | Prominent black thread head. |

**Comments:** Darling says his Dale's Midge Larva can be fished dead drift or on a slow swing. He says the pattern has proven itself on many of the famous trout rivers of the West and Southwest, the South Platte, San Juan, and Bighorn among them.

### DESERT STORM — *Johnny Gomez*

*Tied by Peter Morrison*

| | |
|---|---|
| **Hook:** | Heavy wire, humped shank (scud-pupa hook), sizes 22 to 16. |
| **Thread:** | Fire orange 8/0 or finer. |
| **Rib:** | Fire orange tying thread. |
| **Abdomen:** | Pearl Flashabou over the red working thread. |
| **Thorax:** | Black dubbing. |

**Disco Midge.** Developed on Colorado's challenging Frying Pan River, the Disco Midge in its array of colors has firmly established itself as a reliable imitation of a midge larva and pupa. An alternative to winding the Flashabou up a thread base is to start the thread well up the shank, bind the Flashabou there, and wind the Flashabou down the bare shank and then back up it.

### DISCO MIDGE, BLUE

*Tied by Peter Morrison*

| | |
|---|---|
| **Hook:** | Standard or light wire, humped shank, sizes 22 to 18. |
| **Thread:** | Blue 8/0 or finer. |
| **Abdomen:** | Blue Krystal Flash or Accent Flash over a layer of the blue working thread. |
| **Thorax:** | Peacock herl (or hare's mask dubbing or black thread). |

**Comments:** Ed Engle, author of *Tying Small Flies,* wrote in an article in *Fly Tyer* magazine that the blue version of the Disco Midge is especially good in winter.

## DISCO MIDGE, OLIVE

*Tied by Peter Morrison*

| | |
|---|---|
| **Hook:** | Standard or light wire, humped shank, sizes 22 to 18. |
| **Thread:** | Olive 8/0. |
| **Abdomen:** | Olive Krystal Flash or Accent Flash over a layer of the olive working thread. |
| **Thorax:** | Peacock herl (or hare's mask dubbing or black thread). |

## DISCO MIDGE, RED

*Tied by Peter Morrison*

| | |
|---|---|
| **Hook:** | Standard or light wire, humped shank, sizes 22 to 18. |
| **Thread:** | Red 8/0. |
| **Abdomen:** | Red Krystal Flash or Accent Flash over a layer of the red working thread. |
| **Thorax:** | Peacock herl (or hare's mask dubbing or black thread). |

## DISCO MIDGE, PEARL

*Tied by Skip Morris*

| | |
|---|---|
| **Hook:** | Standard or light wire, humped shank, sizes 22 to 18. |
| **Thread:** | Cream 8/0 or finer. |
| **Abdomen:** | Pearl Krystal Flash or Accent Flash over a layer of the cream working thread. |
| **Thorax:** | Peacock herl (or hare's mask dubbing or black thread). |

## MARABOU LARVA, OLIVE

*Tied by Wade Malwitz*

| | |
|---|---|
| **Hook:** | Standard (or light to heavy) wire, 2X long (or 1X or short, slow-curve shank preferred), sizes 20 and 18. |
| **Thread:** | Olive 8/0 or finer. |
| **Rib:** | Pearl Krystal Flash. |
| **Body:** | Dyed olive marabou. |
| **Comments:** | A simple and logical imitation of a midge larva, with supple marabou fibers to wave in the current and suggest life. |

## MARABOU LARVA, RED

*Tied by Wade Malwitz*

**Hook:** Standard (or light or heavy) wire, 2X long (or 1X or short, slow-curve shank preferred), sizes 20 and 18.
**Thread:** Red 8/0 or finer.
**Rib:** Pearl Krystal Flash.
**Body:** Dyed red marabou.
**Comments:** A simple and logical imitation of a midge larva, with supple marabou fibers to wave in the current and suggest life.

## MERCURY BLACK BEAUTY — Pat Dorsey

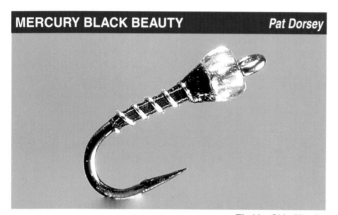

*Tied by Skip Morris*

**Hook:** Heavy wire (or standard to light wire), short shank to standard length, sizes 24 to 18.
**Head:** One tiny crystal (clear) bead.
**Thread:** Black 8/0 or finer.
**Rib:** Fine silver (or gold or fine copper) wire.
**Abdomen:** The black working thread.
**Thorax (optional):** Fine black synthetic (or natural) dubbing, as a slim collar.
**Comments:** The Mercury Black Beauty has gained a substantial following among those who fish the Colorado rivers of its birth. I can tell you from personal experience that the trout in those rivers tend to be tough, sometimes infuriating. Any fly that can move those trout must be a good fly.

## MERCURY MIDGE — Pat Dorsey

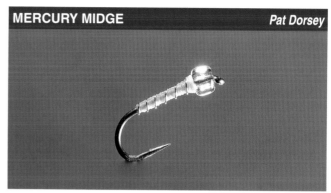

*Tied by Wade Malwitz*

**Hook:** Heavy wire (or standard to light wire), short shank to standard length, sizes 24 to 18.
**Head:** One small crystal (clear) bead.
**Thread:** White 8/0 or finer.
**Rib:** Fine silver (or gold or fine copper) wire.
**Abdomen:** The white working thread.
**Comments:** Essentially, the white version of the Mercury Black Beauty, on this page. Same story.

## MIDGLING, ROOT BEER — Mike Mercer

*Tied by Mike Mercer*

**Hook:** Heavy to light wire, humped shank, sizes 20 to 16.
**Head:** One root beer (a sort of honey brown) glass bead.
**Thread:** Camel 8/0.
**Tail:** Pearl Angel Hair, short.
**Body:** Brown Midge Tubing (or some other fleshy tubing or line) over pearl Krystal Flash.
**Wing case:** A few strands of pearl Krystal Flash, in a short loop.
**Collar:** Brown ostrich herl.
**Comments:** Mike says he was inspired to develop his Midgling after a meeting with trout-lake guru Brian Chan. The fly first proved itself in trout lakes, then in rivers. You can tie the Midgling in any midge color.

## MIRACLE BIOT

*Tied by Wade Malwitz*

**Hook:** Heavy wire, 1X long or standard length, sizes 20 to 16.
**Thread:** Black 8/0.
**Rib:** Fine gold or copper wire.
**Abdomen:** White goose biot.
**Thorax:** Dyed black opossum or other coarse dubbing.
**Comments:** Clean little imitation of a midge larva or pupa with a neat biot body.

## MIRACLE MIDGE, BLACK

*Tied by Wade Malwitz*

**Hook:** Heavy wire (or standard or even light wire), short shank to standard length, sizes 24 to 18.
**Thread:** Black 8/0 or finer.
**Rib:** Fine gold (or silver or copper) wire.
**Abdomen:** The black working thread.
**Thorax:** Black dubbing or thread.
**Comments:** The Miracle Midge, in both black and white, was originally a hot fly for the difficult trout of Colorado rivers, but now it's a hot pattern all over North America. Coat a thread thorax with head cement or low-odor epoxy glue if you like.

## MIRACLE MIDGE, WHITE

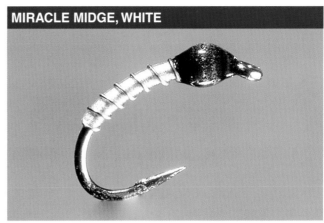

*Tied by Skip Morris*

**Hook:** Heavy wire (or standard or even light wire), short shank to standard length, sizes 24 to 18.
**Thread:** White 8/0 or finer for the body; black or dark gray 8/0 or finer for the thorax.
**Rib:** Fine gold (or silver or copper) wire.
**Abdomen:** The white working thread.
**Thorax:** Black or dark gray dubbing or thread.
**Comments:** The Miracle Midge, in both black and white, was originally a hot fly for the difficult trout of Colorado rivers, but now it's a hot pattern all over North America. Coat a thread thorax with head cement or low-odor epoxy glue if you like.

## PRINCESS *Johnny Gomez*

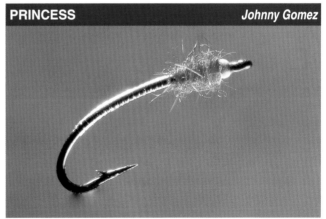

*Tied by Peter Morrison*

**Hook:** Heavy (or standard) wire, 2X or 3X long, sizes 22 to 16.
**Thread:** Yellow 8/0 or finer.
**Abdomen:** Pearl Flashabou.
**Thorax:** Red dubbing.
**Comments:** This one is dazzling even for a contemporary midge larva. But sometimes, bright works better than anything else.

## RED HOT                                          *Johnny Gomez*

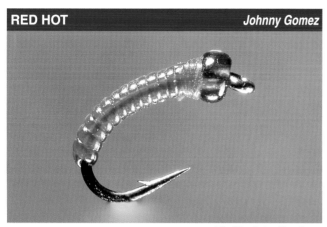

*Tied by Peter Morrison*

**Hook:**      Heavy wire, humped shank, sizes 22 to 16.
**Head:**      Tiny red glass bead.
**Thread:**    Red 8/0 or finer.
**Body:**      Fine red Larva Lace (or some other shiny, fleshy tubing or line).

## WILLY'S PIP                                          *Jim Jones*

*Tied by Carol Ann Morris*

**Hook:**      Heavy (or standard or light wire), standard length or short, sizes 24 to 16.
**Thread:**    Black 8/0.
**Abdomen:**   One or more strands of red, gray, green, or black floss, doubled, twisted, and bound atop the thorax area.
**Thorax:**    Peacock herl.
**Comments:**  Jim Jones designed his tiny nymph to sway or wiggle its extended body (unusual in midge larva and pupa imitations) in river currents. Jones fishes it deep and dead drift in Colorado's South Platte River, among others.

# Midge Emergers

**Brooks's Sprout Midge.** It's a simple design, buoyant, and easy to spot on the water, and it catches trout—what more could you want?

## BROOKS'S SPROUT MIDGE, BLACK          *Bob Brooks*

*Tied by Al Davis*

**Hook:**      Light wire, humped shank (pupa-emerger hook), sizes 26 to 18.
**Thread:**    Black 8/0 or finer.
**Body:**      The black working thread.
**Parachute wing:** Section of white, round, buoyant closed-cell foam, trimmed short (instructions are on page 44).
**Parachute hackle:** Black (instructions are on page 44).

## BROOKS'S SPROUT MIDGE, CREAM          *Bob Brooks*

*Tied by Al Davis*

**Hook:**      Light wire, humped shank (pupa-emerger hook), sizes 26 to 18.
**Thread:**    Cream 8/0 or finer.
**Body:**      The cream working thread.
**Parachute wing:** Section of white, round, buoyant closed-cell foam, trimmed short (instructions are on page 44).
**Parachute hackle:** Cream (instructions are on page 44).

## BROOKS'S SPROUT MIDGE, GRAY — *Bob Brooks*

*Tied by Al Davis*

**Hook:** Light wire, humped shank (pupa-emerger hook), sizes 26 to 18.
**Thread:** Gray 8/0 or finer.
**Body:** The gray working thread.
**Parachute wing:** Section of white, round, buoyant closed-cell foam, trimmed short (instructions are on page 44).
**Parachute hackle:** Dyed gray or natural blue dun (instructions are on page 44).

## BROOKS'S SPROUT MIDGE, OLIVE — *Bob Brooks*

*Tied by Al Davis*

**Hook:** Light wire, humped shank (pupa-emerger hook), sizes 26 to 18.
**Thread:** Olive 8/0 or finer.
**Body:** The olive working thread.
**Parachute wing:** Section of white, round, buoyant closed-cell foam, trimmed short (instructions are on page 44).
**Parachute hackle:** Dyed olive (instructions are on page 44).

## CDC EMERGING MIDGE — *René Harrop*

*Tied by Skip Morris*

**Hook:** Light wire, standard length, sizes 20 to 14.
**Thread:** Olive 8/0 or 6/0.
**Tail:** Teal flank fibers.
**Legs:** Gray CDC.
**Back:** Strip of gray buoyant closed-cell foam sheeting.
**Body:** Olive poly dubbing (or another synthetic dubbing, such as Super Fine Dry Fly or Antron).
**Head:** End of the back foam, trimmed short.
**Comments:** Lies low on the water like a hatching midge but stays afloat, buoyed by the foam and CDC.

## GRIFFITH'S GNAT — *George Griffith*

*Tied by Skip Morris*

**Hook:** Light wire, short to standard length, sizes 26 to 18.
**Thread:** Olive, gray, or black 8/0 or finer.
**Hackle:** One grizzly, spiraled up the body.
**Body:** Peacock herl.
**Comments:** A true standard for midge hatches because it's so easy to tie and because it works. I've caught scads of midge-eating trout on Griffith's Gnats. The rough body and the splay of hackle fibers suggest the unkempt shuck and body of a hatching midge.

## HERL MIDGE, BLACK

*Tied by Wade Malwitz*

**Hook:** Light wire, short to 1X long, sizes 28 to 20.
**Thread:** Black 8/0 or finer.
**Tail:** Black hackle fibers.
**Body:** Black ostrich herl.
**Comments:** Suggests a midge struggling from its shuck, awash in the water's surface.

## HERL MIDGE, GRAY

*Tied by Wade Malwitz*

**Hook:** Light wire, short to 1X long, sizes 28 to 20.
**Thread:** Gray 8/0 or finer.
**Tail:** Blue dun hackle fibers.
**Body:** Gray ostrich herl.
**Comments:** Suggests a midge struggling from its shuck, awash in the water's surface.

## HI-VIS GRIFFITH'S GNAT

*Tied by Al Davis*

**Hook:** Light wire, standard length to 1X long, sizes 22 to 14.
**Thread:** Black 8/0 or finer.

**Body:** Peacock herl.
**Wing:** Single short bunch of yellow poly yarn in the center of the body.
**Hackle:** Grizzly, spiraled up the body.
**Comments:** The yellow wing is for the angler, to make the fly easier to see.

## KF FLASHER, BLACK                    *Bear Goode*

*Tied by Skip Morris*

**Hook:** Light wire, humped shank (pupa-emerger hook), sizes 24 to 16.
**Thread:** Black 8/0.
**Rib:** Fine copper wire.
**Abdomen:** The working thread.
**Wing:** Four of five stands of pearl Krystal Flash.
**Thorax:** Black rabbit.
**Comments:** The rationale for putting a wing on a subsurface midge emerger is difficult to explain, but it works. Perhaps the wing suggests a bursting wing case. It really doesn't matter, as long as the trout take the fly.

## KF FLASHER, CHOCOLATE               *Bear Goode*

*Tied by Wade Malwitz*

**Hook:** Light wire, humped shank (pupa-emerger hook), sizes 24 to 16.
**Thread:** Dark brown 8/0 or finer.
**Rib:** Fine copper wire.
**Abdomen:** The dark brown working thread.
**Wing:** Four or five strands of pearl Krystal Flash.
**Thorax:** Dark brown natural or synthetic dubbing (some tiers prefer black dubbing).
**Comments:** The rationale for putting a wing on a subsurface midge emerger is difficult to explain, but it works. Perhaps the wing suggests a bursting wing case. It really doesn't matter, as long as the trout take the fly.

## KF FLASHER, OLIVE — *Bear Goode*

*Tied by Skip Morris*

**Hook:** Light wire, humped shank (pupa-emerger hook), sizes 24 to 16.
**Thread:** Olive 8/0.
**Rib:** Fine copper wire.
**Abdomen:** The working thread.
**Wing:** Four or five strands of pearl Krystal Flash.
**Thorax:** Light olive Hareline Dubbin (or olive dyed rabbit).
**Comments:** The rationale for putting a wing on a subsurface midge emerger is difficult to explain, but it works. Perhaps the wing suggests a bursting wing case. It really doesn't matter, as long as the trout take the fly.

## LACE MIDGE EMERGER — *Bruce Salzburg*

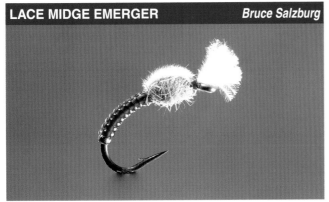

*Tied by Wade Malwitz*

**Hook:** Fine wire, humped shank (pupa-emerger hook), sizes 22 to 16.
**Thread:** Red 8/0 or finer.
**Abdomen:** Slender clear vinyl tubing over a layer of the working thread.
**Thorax:** Dyed golden brown rabbit fur.
**Wing case and tuft:** White CDC pulled over the thorax and bound at the hook's eye, the ends trimmed long.
**Comments:** The clear vinyl suggests a translucent abdomen, or one within a loosened and gas-filled shuck prior to the insect's hatching. The CDC holds the Lace Midge Emerger up to hang from the water's surface.

## MIDGE EMERGER, DUN — *John Betts*

*Top view*

*Tied by Wade Malwitz*

**Hook:** Light wire, short to standard length, sizes 28 to 20.
**Thread:** Black 8/0.
**Wing case, legs, and shuck:** White Z-lon or Antron fibers.
**Body:** The black working thread.
**Legs:** Dun (grayish-brown) Z-lon.
**Comments:** Cover the hook's shank with thread; bind on Z-lon fibers just behind the hook's eye; bind the fibers back partway down the shank. Divide the fibers and set them with thread turns so that they project out to the sides (as legs). Pull back the fibers projecting forward from the eye and bind them atop the bend. Whip-finish the thread at the bend. Trim the legs and shuck to length. This is a simple and sound imitation of a hatching midge pulling its wings from its shuck. Fish it dead drift atop the water.

**Palomino Midge.** This unusual but easy-to-tie pattern became possible when a fine, dense form of chenille called New Dub came out. New Dub melts cleanly on the end to make a neat taper—a critical element in the design of the Palomino Midge. Years ago this pattern caught on quickly, and it's still very popular. Usually it's fished awash in the water's surface, with floatant on the thorax and gills only. But it can also be fished slightly submerged, usually below a dry fly.

### PALOMINO MIDGE, BLACK — Brett Smith

*Tied by Wade Malwitz*

**Hook:** Light wire, humped shank (pupa-emerger hook), sizes 22 to 18.
**Thread:** Black 8/0 or finer.
**Abdomen:** Black New Dub, melted on the tip.
**Wing case and gills:** White Z-lon (or Antron yarn); trim the ends to gape length for the gills.
**Thorax:** Black rabbit.

### PALOMINO MIDGE, BROWN — Brett Smith

*Tied by Skip Morris*

**Hook:** Light wire, humped shank (pupa-emerger hook), sizes 22 to 18.
**Thread:** Brown 8/0 or finer.
**Abdomen:** Brown New Dub, melted on the tip.
**Wing case and gills:** White Z-lon (or Antron yarn); trim the ends to gape length for the gills.
**Thorax:** Brown rabbit.

### PALOMINO MIDGE, DARK OLIVE — Brett Smith

*Tied by Wade Malwitz*

**Hook:** Light wire, humped shank (pupa-emerger hook), sizes 22 to 18.
**Thread:** Olive 8/0 or finer.
**Abdomen:** Olive New Dub, melted on the tip.
**Wing case and gills:** Dun (grayish-brown) Z-lon (or Antron yarn); trim the ends to gape length for the gills.
**Thorax:** Olive rabbit.

### PALOMINO MIDGE, GRAY — Brett Smith

*Tied by Wade Malwitz*

**Hook:** Light wire, humped shank (pupa-emerger hook), sizes 22 to 18.
**Thread:** Gray 8/0 or finer.
**Abdomen:** Dun (grayish-brown) New Dub, melted on the tip.
**Wing case and gills:** Dun (grayish-brown) Z-lon (or Antron yarn); trim the ends to gape length for the gills.
**Thorax:** Gray rabbit.

## PARA MIDGE EMERGER

*Tied by Al Davis*

**Hook:** Light wire, short to 1X long, sizes 20 to 16.
**Thread:** Black or gray 8/0.
**Abdomen:** Stripped grizzly hackle stem.
**Parachute wing:** Black, white, yellow, or orange synthetic dubbing (whatever is most visible on the water).
**Parachute hackle:** Grizzly, black, or dun (grayish-brown). Instructions are on page 63.
**Thorax:** The working thread.
**Comments:** To make the parachute wing, dub moderately onto the unwaxed thread, hold the thread up as you slide the dubbing down in a bunch to the top of the shank, pull the thread tightly down the other side of the shank, and add a few tight turns to secure the thread. Build tight thread turns around the base of the dubbing ball, bind on the hackle, and make a parachute hackle. It can't hurt to smear a little low-vapor epoxy over the shank before winding the stem body, which will be much tougher once the epoxy sets.

## PARACHUTE MIDGE EMERGER
### Gary Willmott and Scott Sanchez

*Tied by Scott Sanchez*

**Hook:** Standard or light wire, short to regular length, sizes 22 to 16.
**Thread:** Black 8/0 or 10/0.
**Shuck:** One or two strands of pearl Krystal Flash, short.
**Wing:** White or orange Antron yarn or poly yarn.
**Rib:** Pearl Krystal Flash.
**Body:** Wapsi Peacock Super Bright Dubbing, or any shiny synthetic dubbing in emerald green.

**Hackle:** Grizzly, dry fly.
**Comments:** Scott has great faith in his Parachute Midge Emerger (which in fact lacks a parachute hackle) and calls it "an almost non-refusal fly when trout are rising to emerging midge pupae." He wants the body well down, almost vertical, and uses a loop knot in his tippet and floatant only on the wing and hackle to achieve this.

## PARASOL MIDGE EMERGER
### Jim Schollmeyer and Ted Leeson

*Tied by Ted Leeson*

**Hook:** Light wire, humped shank (pupa-emerger hook), sizes 20 to 14.
**Thread:** Black 8/0.
**Parasol:** Two 1-inch sections (one 1-inch section for hooks size 18 and smaller) of light gray poly yarn tied with a clinch knot to 4X tippet for hooks size 16 and 14; 5X for hooks size 20 and 18. The post should tip forward at about a 45-degree angle to the shank (instructions are on page 52).
**Shuck:** White Z-lon or Antron, trimmed short.
**Rib:** Fine copper wire.
**Abdomen:** Green Krystal Flash.
**Thorax:** Dark brown rabbit fur.
**Comments:** Quite a concept! Jim and Ted developed their Parasol series from similar emergers suspended from parachute hackles on posts.

**Serendipity.** The Serendipity came out of nowhere over a decade ago and moved rapidly to the top of the emerger fly list. It does work—I've caught difficult trout with it. Usually it's fished dead drift, hanging from its hair thorax made slick with floatant, cast into the line of current leading to a trout that is looking for another emerging midge.

### SERENDIPITY, BROWN

*Tied by Al Davis*

**Hook:** Light wire, humped shank (pupa-emerger hook), sizes 22 to 14.
**Thread:** Brown 8/0.
**Body:** Brown Z-lon or Antron yarn, twisted.
**Head and wing case:** Natural grayish deer hair flared either on top of or all around the hook. Then the head is trimmed smallish, and the wing case is trimmed back over the back of the body.

### SERENDIPITY, DARK GREEN

*Tied by Al Davis*

**Hook:** Light wire, humped shank (pupa-emerger hook), sizes 22 to 14.
**Thread:** Dark green 8/0.
**Body:** Dark green Z-lon or Antron yarn, twisted.
**Head and wing case:** Natural grayish deer hair. (See additional comments for the Serendipity, Brown, above.)

### SERENDIPITY, GRAY

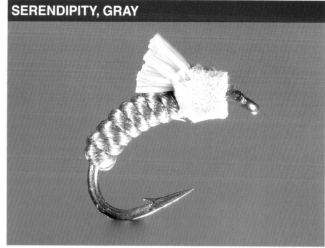

*Tied by Skip Morris*

**Hook:** Light wire, humped shank (pupa-emerger hook), sizes 22 to 14.
**Thread:** Gray 8/0.
**Body:** Gray Z-lon or Antron yarn, twisted.
**Head and wing case:** Natural grayish deer hair. (See additional comments for the Serendipity, Brown, on this page.)

### SERENDIPITY, RED

*Tied by Al Davis*

**Hook:** Light wire, humped shank (pupa-emerger hook), sizes 22 to 14.
**Thread:** Red 8/0.
**Body:** Red Z-lon or Antron yarn, twisted.
**Head and wing case:** Natural grayish deer hair. (See additional comments for the Serendipity, Brown, on this page.)

## SHELLBACK MIDGE PUPA

*Tied by Al Davis*

| | |
|---|---|
| **Hook:** | Light wire, standard length or 1X long, sizes 22 to 18. |
| **Thread:** | Black 8/0 or finer. |
| **Shuck:** | Gray poly yarn. |
| **Back:** | Gray poly yarn. The back-yarn should be bound atop the shuck-yarn, bound again at the eye, creating a hump that rises slightly above the abdomen and thorax. |
| **Abdomen:** | The black working thread. |
| **Thorax:** | Peacock herl. |

## SMITH'S BLACK CRIPPLE                    *Todd Smith*

*Tied by Todd Smith*

| | |
|---|---|
| **Hook:** | Light wire, humped shank (pupa-emerger hook), sizes 24 to 18. |
| **Thread:** | Black 8/0. |
| **Shuck:** | One strand of root beer (light brown) Krystal Flash. |
| **Abdomen:** | Black Krystal Flash. |
| **Wing:** | White CDC. Hold the tip of a feather, stroke the fibers down the sides of the stem, bind the trimmed and stroked feather atop the shank as a wing and trim off the feather's tip. (See the instructions on page 70.) Make and bind on a second wing (or bind the wings on together). |
| **Hackle:** | Grizzly, spiraled over the thorax and trimmed flat underneath. |
| **Thorax:** | Fine black natural (rabbit) or synthetic (Super Fine Dry Fly) dubbing. |

**Comments:** Although it's normally tied tiny to imitate an individual hatching midge, Smith's Black Cripple suggests a clump of tangled midges when tied on larger hooks. Todd finds his fly easier to spot than other emerger flies amid all the naturals of a heavy midge hatch, thanks to the pattern's reflective CDC wings. He wanted to capture the sparkle of a midge escaping its shuck without overdoing the pupa effect.

## STILLBORN MIDGE

*Tied by Al Davis*

| | |
|---|---|
| **Hook:** | Light wire, humped shank (pupa-emerger hook), sizes 20 to 16. |
| **Thread:** | Black 8/0 or finer. |
| **Shuck:** | Gray Antron. |
| **Abdomen:** | Stripped peacock herl quill. (A little low-vapor epoxy glue or other cement under or over the fragile quill abdomen will really toughen it.) |
| **Wing:** | Grizzly hackle tips. |
| **Thorax:** | Peacock herl. |
| **Comments:** | Imitates a midge that failed to fully hatch. Fish it dead drift. |

## Midge Adults

**DALE'S MIDGE ADULT** — *Dale Darling*

*Top view*

*Tied by Al Davis*

| | |
|---|---|
| **Hook:** | Light wire, 1X short to 1X long, sizes 24 to 18. |
| **Thread:** | Gray (or cream, black, or olive) 8/0 or finer. |
| **Abdomen:** | The working thread. |
| **Wing:** | Zing Wing or another clear synthetic wing material cut in a single longish wing, extending back over the abdomen to just past the far edge of the hook's bend. (Or you can substitute a bunch of light gray Antron yarn or CDC.) |
| **Wing case:** | Butts of the wings, doubled back and bound, and (after the thorax and hackle are completed) pulled forward over the thorax and hackle like a nymph wing case. |
| **Hackle:** | Grizzly, spiraled through the thorax, trimmed flat underneath. |
| **Thorax:** | Peacock herl (or fine dubbing in the body color). |

**Comments:** Dale Darling finds this fly particularly effective when a midge hatch is largely over, with just a few nearly hatched adults drifting through the rising trout.

**GRAY MIDGE** — *Darrel Martin*

*Tied by Al Davis*

| | |
|---|---|
| **Hook:** | Light wire, 1X short to 1X long, sizes 22 to 14. |
| **Thread:** | Gray 8/0 or finer. |
| **Body:** | Natural gray-cream goose biot. |
| **Wing:** | Cream or white hackle tips with their flats horizontal, lying in a shallow "V" back over the body. Cream CDC over the wings. |
| **Hackle:** | Light blue dun. |

**Midge.** The fly pattern long known as the Midge is as plain and traditional as it can be—just a hackle fiber tail, slim body, and spare hackle collar. There are no wings, no rib, no unnecessary parts to complicate this tiny, elemental design. Some may argue that the tail is unnecessary, since real midges have no tails. But the Midge comes from a time when a no-tail dry fly was close to heresy. What's important is that the Midge works, tail and all, on difficult trout, and it has for decades. The Midge can be tied in any midge color—black, brown, olive, gray, cream, tan, red, and probably others. The patterns presented here are among the most popular.

**MIDGE, ADAMS**

*Tied by Skip Morris*

| | |
|---|---|
| **Hook:** | Light wire, short to 1X long, sizes 24 to 16. |
| **Thread:** | Black or gray 8/0 or finer. |
| **Tail:** | Brown and grizzly hackle fibers, mixed. |

**Body:**      Muskrat underfur or fine gray synthetic dubbing.

**Hackle:**      One brown and one grizzly, one wound through the other.

**Comments:**      This is really just an Adams without wings—a midge fly with a great track record.

## MIDGE, BLACK

*Tied by Skip Morris*

**Hook:**      Light wire, short to 1X long, sizes 24 to 16.

**Thread:**      Black 8/0 or finer.

**Tail:**      Black hackle fibers.

**Body:**      The black working thread or fine black dubbing.

**Hackle:**      Black.

## MIDGE, BLUE DUN

*Tied by Skip Morris*

**Hook:**      Light wire, short to 1X long, sizes 24 to 16.

**Thread:**      Gray 8/0 or finer.

**Tail:**      Blue dun hackle fibers.

**Body:**      The gray working thread, muskrat fur, or fine natural or synthetic dubbing.

**Hackle:**      Blue dun.

## MIDGE, CREAM

*Tied by Skip Morris*

**Hook:**      Light wire, short to 1X long, sizes 24 to 16.

**Thread:**      Cream 8/0 or finer.

**Tail:**      Cream hackle fibers.

**Body:**      The cream working thread or cream natural or synthetic dubbing.

**Hackle:**      Cream.

## MIDGE, OLIVE

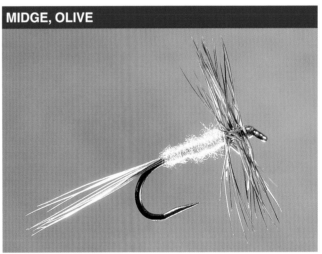

*Tied by Skip Morris*

**Hook:**      Light wire, short to 1X long, sizes 24 to 16.

**Thread:**      Olive 8/0 or finer.

**Tail:**      Dyed olive hackle fibers.

**Body:**      The olive working thread or olive natural or synthetic dubbing.

**Hackle:**      Dyed olive.

## SPENT MIDGE — *Mike Lawson*

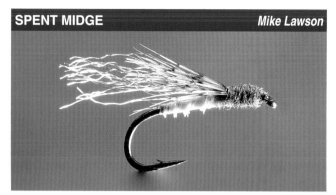

*Tied by Al Davis*

| | |
|---|---|
| **Hook:** | Light wire, standard length to 1X long, sizes 22 to 16. |
| **Thread:** | Olive 8/0. |
| **Abdomen:** | Natural gray-cream goose biot. |
| **Wing:** | Two light gray partridge feathers cupped together over a few strands of olive Z-lon or Antron yarn. Trim the Z-lon a gape length past the bend. The partridge feathers should reach back to the bend. |
| **Thorax:** | Olive Antron dubbing. |

## WD40 DRY — *Mark Engler*

*Top view*

*Tied by Al Davis*

| | |
|---|---|
| **Hook:** | Light wire, 1X long, sizes 24 to 16. |
| **Thread:** | Olive 8/0 or 6/0. |
| **Shuck:** | Natural light bronze mallard feather fibers (natural dark is an alternative). |
| **Abdomen:** | The olive working thread. |
| **Wing case:** | Butts of the bronze mallard feather fibers from the shuck. |
| **Hackle:** | Blue dun, spiraled through the herl thorax. |
| **Thorax:** | Peacock herl. |

**Comments:** This is a dry-fly version of the original WD40 and imitates an adult midge still partially trapped in the shuck. The WD40 Dry settles somewhere between a real emerger fly and a dry fly with a shuck. It ended up here, barely.

## WINGED GNAT

*Tied by Al Davis*

| | |
|---|---|
| **Hook:** | Light wire, standard or short shank, sizes 22 to 16. |
| **Thread:** | Black 8/0 or finer. |
| **Wing:** | White Antron, Z-lon, or hair, to form a single short, upright wing. |
| **Hackle:** | Grizzly (or black or blue dun) spiraled up the body. |
| **Body:** | Black or gray synthetic dubbing. |
| **Comments:** | Nearly a Griffith's Gnat, but designed to float a little higher, like a full adult midge. |

# 8

# Terrestrial Dry Flies

FLY FISHERS USE the term "terrestrials" to describe the creatures that trout eat that live not in the water but on land. The most common terrestrials are grasshoppers, ants, and beetles, but there are others. Under the right circumstances, a good imitation of any of the terrestrials can be critical for catching trout. Nearly all imitations of terrestrials are dry flies, so you'll find only dry flies in this chapter.

## Ants

*Flying ant*

There are winged ants, but it usually takes intensive mating or migrating activity to put enough of them on the water to interest trout. Common wingless ants scurry around the rocks and grasses along the river's edge and unintentionally tumble into the river. On most rivers, the winged ants are difficult to predict, but they are important at times. Wingless ants seem to be a staple for trout during the hot months; the fish get used to seeing and eating them, making these ants a natural for imitation. Fish flying-ant flies dead drift wherever trout are rising to them. Fish wingless-ant flies close to the banks, dead drift, and expect no more than a nose to quietly appear and the fly to vanish.

### BEETLES

*Beetle*

JIM SCHOLLMEYER

According to my friend Rick Hafele, who is both an entomologist and a fly-fishing author, trout see plenty of beetles from spring into fall on many western rivers, especially the ones that are bordered by forests. Add to that the heft of a beetle—which is considerably greater than that of a dainty mayfly or minuscule midge—and you have a pretty attractive food source from the trout's perspective. Fish beetle imitations dead drift, typically close to the banks.

## GRASSHOPPERS

*Grasshopper*

Any river with grassy banks—especially with grassy fields along its banks—is ripe with the opportunity to fish grasshopper imitations. Timing is important, though. Grasshoppers usually appear in midsummer and start to thin out steadily in the fall. Midday is typically best, when the insects are active and the air is hot. A windy day can really fuel the action, with the big insects startled and driven down onto the water by gusts. The appeal of grasshoppers to trout should be obvious—these insects are huge. You can fish a grasshopper imitation dead drift and catch fish. But sometimes smacking the fly down is the best approach—real grasshoppers go down hard. Twitching the fly, even a little, between pauses can help.

## CICADAS

*Cicada*

Cicadas are generally not an important food for western river trout. The exception is Utah's Green River, which is famous for its cicada fishing. Cicadas are big and stout, and when they're plentiful and active around a river, enough of them plop down on the water to get the trout's attention to the exclusion of all else.

## MOTHS

In some parts of the West there are big terrestrial hatches of moths. Bob Jacklin (many of whose flies appear in this book) told us that on his Yellowstone Park rivers he has seen a reliable and very good hatch of the spruce moth for the past several years.

## BEES AND WASPS

I've never seen bees so plentiful on rivers that trout would become selective to them, but I've heard of it happening. The wonderful Canadian fishing writer Roderick Haig-Brown wrote of a day when a thunderstorm had pounded bees to the water. He slit open a fish (this was way back when catch-and-release was a curiosity) and found a stomach full of honeybees. Wasps are probably just as uncommon, but under the right conditions, who knows? I'd tend to fish a bee or wasp fly dead drift, maybe with a twitch now and then, since bees on the water do kick around a bit.

## CRANEFLIES

*Cranefly*

Most craneflies live as larva in muddy shallows along the edges of rivers; others live in marshy wetlands far from any river or creek. So on the whole, this insect is more aquatic than terrestrial. Though craneflies aren't commonly a big item on trout rivers, I've seen enough of them flitting around pools and runs to make the fish respond to both the insects and my imitations. Gangly cranefly adults aren't hard to spot—many are big, and all are slow, laborious fliers. Fish a cranefly dry fly dead drift or with an occasional twitch. (Flies that imitate cranefly larvae are in chapter 9.)

# Ants and Flying Ants

**Ant Carol.** Originally designed to imitate the termite of the Pacific Northwest that is so fond of dropping onto trout lakes, the Ant Carol imitates all sorts of flying ants on both rivers and lakes. The buck tail wings are buoyant and suggest the venation of a real flying ant's wings.

**ANT CAROL, BROWN**                               *Skip Morris*

*Top view*

*Tied by Skip Morris*

**ANT CAROL, BLACK**                               *Skip Morris*

*Tied by Skip Morris*

| | |
|---|---|
| **Hook:** | Light wire, standard length or 1X long, sizes 20 to 10 (14 and 12 are the most common sizes). |
| **Thread:** | Black 8/0 or 6/0. |
| **Abdomen:** | Black synthetic dubbing (poly, Superfine Dry Fly, Antron). |
| **Wing:** | Brown (or black or dark gray) buck tail. |
| **Hackle:** | One black, wound in three to five open spirals up the thread-covered center of the hook's shank and bound behind the thorax. (Trim the fibers from the underside if you wish. This makes the fly slightly more convincing but slightly less buoyant.) |
| **Thorax:** | Same as the abdomen. |

| | |
|---|---|
| **Hook:** | Light wire, standard length or 1X long, sizes 20 to 10 (14 and 12 are the most common sizes). |
| **Thread:** | Brown 8/0 or 6/0. |
| **Abdomen:** | Orange-brown (or just brown) synthetic dubbing (poly, Superfine Dry Fly, Antron). |
| **Wing:** | Brown buck tail. |
| **Hackle:** | One brown (or just brown), wound in three to five open spirals up the thread-covered center of the hook's shank and bound behind the thorax. (Trim the fibers from the underside if you wish. This makes the fly slightly more convincing but slightly less buoyant.) |
| **Thorax:** | Same as the abdomen. |

## BETTS' RED FLYING ANT — *John Betts*

*Tied by Skip Morris*

**Hook:** Light wire, standard length or 1X long, sizes 18 to 12.
**Thread:** White 8/0 or 6/0.
**Abdomen and thorax:** Strip of white buoyant closed-cell foam sheeting, colored with a red permanent marking pen.
**Wing:** Zing Wing or another synthetic wing material sheeting, cut to shape.
**Hackle:** Brown, a few turns behind the thorax and in front of the wings.
**Comments:** Bind the foam slightly down the hook's bend, double it forward atop the shank, and bind it just behind the center of the shank. Bind and compress the foam up the center of the shank to the hook's eye. Wind the thread back down the shank, double the foam back, and bind it and trim it there. Then bind on the wings and make the hackle collar.

## BLACK ANT

*Tied by Skip Morris*

**Hook:** Light wire, standard length or 1X long, sizes 20 to 14.
**Thread:** Black 8/0 or 6/0.
**Abdomen:** Black synthetic dubbing (poly, Superfine Dry Fly, Antron . . .).
**Hackle:** One black, spiraled up the thread-covered center of the shank and bound behind the thorax.
**Thorax:** Same as the abdomen.

## BLACK FLYING ANT

*Tied by Skip Morris*

**Hook:** Light wire, standard length or 1X long, sizes 18 to 10.
**Thread:** Black 8/0 or 6/0.
**Abdomen:** Black synthetic dubbing (poly, Superfine Dry Fly, Antron . . .).
**Wing:** Two black hen neck hackle points.
**Hackle:** One brown or black, spiraled up the thread-covered shank and bound behind the thorax.
**Thorax:** Same as the abdomen.

## BRIGHT SPOT CARPENTER ANT — *Dave Whitlock*

*Tied by Skip Morris*

**Hook:** Light wire, standard length or 1X long, sizes 16 to 8.
**Thread:** Black 8/0 or 6/0.
**Abdomen:** Black moose body or elk hair.
**Thorax:** Black moose body or elk hair.
**Legs:** Black moose body or elk hair.
**Strike indicator:** Fluorescent pink or orange deer hair bound on over the legs and trimmed closely.
**Comments:** Bind the hair on at the bend, then pull it forward and trim it. Bind on the thorax hair behind the eye, then pull it back and trim it. Add the legs and the pink or orange hair for the strike indicator.

## CALCATERRA ANT — *Paul Calcaterra*

*Tied by Skip Morris*

**Hook:** Light wire, standard length or 1X long, sizes 22 to 12.
**Thread:** Black 8/0 or 6/0.
**Abdomen and thorax:** Dyed black deer hair (elk hair is tougher).
**Comments:** Bind the hair on at the bend, pull the hair forward, snip a few hairs free at the bend to form legs, advance the thread, pull the hair forward, and bind and trim it at the hook's eye. Optional: add a coating of lacquer over the body sections.

## FOAM ANT, BLACK

*Tied by Wade Malwitz*

**Hook:** Light wire, standard length or 1X long, sizes 20 to 14.
**Thread:** Black 8/0 or 6/0.
**Body:** Strip of black closed-cell foam sheeting, bound to make it slim over the center third of the shank.
**Strike indicator (optional):** Yellow (or orange, red, or white) poly or Antron yarn.
**Hackle:** One black, spiraled up the center of the shank. Trim off the fibers on the underside if you wish.

## FOAM ANT, CINNAMON

*Tied by Skip Morris*

**Hook:** Light wire, standard length or 1X long, sizes 20 to 14.
**Thread:** Brown or tan 8/0 or 6/0.
**Body:** Strip of cinnamon (light reddish brown) buoyant closed-cell foam sheeting, bound to make it slim over the center third of the shank.
**Strike indicator (optional):** Yellow (or orange, red, or white) poly or Antron yarn.
**Hackle:** One brown, spiraled up the center of the shank. Trim off the fibers on the underside if you wish.

## FOAM ANT, RED

*Tied by Wade Malwitz*

**Hook:** Light wire, standard length or 1X long, sizes 20 to 14.
**Thread:** Red (or brown) 8/0 or 6/0.
**Body:** Strip of red buoyant closed-cell foam sheeting (or white foam colored with a permanent marking pen), bound to make it slim over the center third of the shank.
**Strike indicator (optional):** Yellow (or orange, red, or white) poly or Antron yarn. Trim off the fibers on the underside if you wish.
**Hackle:** One brown, spiraled up the center of the shank. Trim off the fibers on the underside if you wish.

## TWO-TONE FLYING ANT — *Blue Ribbon Flies*

*Top view*

*Tied by Craig Mathews*

**Hook:** Light wire, standard length or 1X long, sizes 22 to 12.
**Thread:** Tan or black 8/0.
**Abdomen:** Strip of red buoyant closed-cell foam sheeting, bound down the shank, pulled over the top, and bound just ahead of the center of the shank.
**Thorax:** Strip of black buoyant closed-cell foam sheeting, bound up the shank to the eye, then pulled back over the top and bound.
**Wing:** White Z-lon or Antron.
**Legs:** Fine black rubber-strand, a section bound on each side of the shank.
**Comments:** The Two-Tone Ant can also be tied with a cinnamon (light reddish brown) abdomen or entirely in black, red, or cinnamon.

# Beetles

## BLACK CROWE BEETLE

*Tied by Skip Morris*

**Hook:** Light wire, standard length or 1X long, sizes 22 to 12.
**Thread:** Black 8/0 or 6/0.
**Back:** Dyed black deer or elk hair (elk is tougher).
**Legs:** A few of the hair butts.
**Comments:** Bind the hair (tips forward) on the center of the shank; then spiral the thread back over the hair and shank to the bend. Add a few tight thread turns at the bend; then spiral the thread forward to its starting point at midshank. Trim away all but a few of the hair tips. Divide the remaining hair tips to the sides, advance the thread to a little short of the eye, pull the butts of the hair down, and bind them with a thread collar behind the eye. Trim the butts to a short head. Trim the leg hairs to length. There's no reason you can't bind a tuft of bright yarn on the back as a strike indicator. Hair beetles have a long history of success, and they're easy to tie.

**GIDLOW BEETLE**                           *Arnie Gidlow*

*Top view*

*Tied by Arnie Gidlow*

**Hook:**      Light wire, standard length, sizes 16 to 8.
**Thread:**    Black 6/0.
**Body and head:** Olive Ice Dubbing under Bill's Hard Shell Foil Foam (buoyant closed-cell foam sheeting with a metallic veneer on one side). The head is the front of the foam strip.
**Legs:**      Olive Mini Centipede Legs (fine olive rubber-strand; brown or black would also be fine). The first pair of legs is a single strand bound crossways. The other four are two sections of rubber-strand bound tightly against the narrow thread collar behind the foam head, one strand per side.
**Strike indicator:** Narrow strip of red buoyant closed-cell foam sheeting.

**HAIR BEETLE**                             *Mike Lawson*

*Tied by Wade Malwitz*

**Hook:**      Light or standard wire, 1X long, sizes 16 to 10.
**Thread:**    Black 8/0 or 6/0.

**Back:**      Dyed black deer hair (elk hair is tougher), bound on at the bend, pulled forward and down after the body and legs are completed, and bound behind the eye.
**Rib:**       Two strands of pearl Krystal Flash.
**Body:**      Black buoyant synthetic dubbing.
**Legs:**      Root beer (medium brown) or black Krystal Flash, bound crossways just back from the eye, trimmed along the sides.
**Strike indicator:** Orange (or any bright color) egg-fly yarn (Glo-Bug, McFlyfoam).
**Head:**      Trimmed butts of the back hair.

# Grasshoppers

**BC DROPPER HOPPER**
                            *John Barr and Charlie Craven*

*Tied by Wade Malwitz*

**Hook:**      Heavy or standard wire, 2X long, size 6.
**Thread:**    Yellow 3/0.
**Body:**      Strip of yellow closed-cell foam sheeting, trimmed to a point, bound atop the bend, and then bound up the shank in three sections.
**Wing:**      Mottled yellow Web Wing (or another synthetic wing material), cut into a long rectangle with a rounded end. Atop the wing, root beer (medium brown) Krystal Flash under undyed elk hair.
**Hopping legs:** Three sections of yellow round rubber-strand, still attached to one another, knotted, and then stripped on the end and trimmed so that only one section remains. Make a bar on the single section with a red permanent marking pen.
**Bullet head and collar:** Dyed yellow or undyed gray-brown deer hair. (Elk hair is tougher. Instructions are on page 146.)
**Legs:**      Yellow round rubber-strand, a section bound along each side of the narrow thread band securing the bullet head.
**Strike indicator:** Fire orange (or any bright color) yarn (Antron, poly . . .).
**Comments:**  Designed for the "hopper-dropper" system in which a weighted nymph dangles a couple of feet below a big, buoyant dry fly, such as a grasshopper imitation.

**CHAOS HOPPER**                                            *Rowan Nyman*

*Top view*

*Bottom view*

*Tied by Craig Mathews*

**Hook:** Light (or standard) wire, 2X (or 3X) long (a slow-curve shank is optional), sizes 14 to 8.

**Thread:** Brown 6/0 or 3/0.

**Body:** Fairly wide strip of tan buoyant closed-cell foam sheeting, trimmed to rounded on the ends and bound with only a narrow thread collar about two-thirds up the shank.

**Legs:** Yellow square rubber-strands, knotted and bound under the thread collar, trimmed medium-short in front.

**Wing:** Pale yellow or gold Z-lon, poly yarn, or Antron.

**Hackle:** Brown, over the thread collar only.

**Comments:** Craig says that "the legs, body, and head are all prominent" on the Chaos Hopper, which "seems very important in hopper imitations."

**CLUB SANDWICH**                                        *Ken Burkholder*

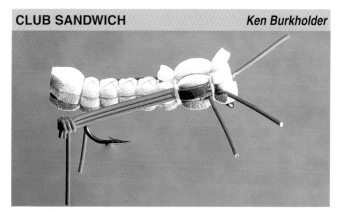

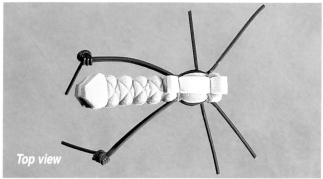

*Top view*

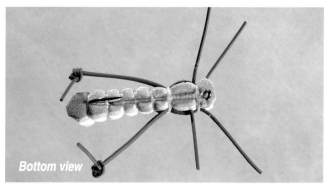

*Bottom view*

*Tied by Wade Malwitz*

**Hook:** Heavy (or standard) wire, 4X (or 3X) long, sizes 10 to 6.

**Thread:** Yellow 3/0 (or 6/0).

**Body:** Strip of foam, blunt in front and tapered at the rear. The foam is composed of three layers of buoyant closed-cell foam sheeting, laminated with glue: the top layer is gray, the middle layer is peach, and the bottom layer is tan. (Some tiers don't bother to laminate the foam layers.)

**Hopping legs:** Still-connected strands of brown rubber-strand, knotted, and two strands peeled off the tip.

**Legs:** Brown rubber-strand.

**Strike indicator:** Strip of white buoyant closed-cell foam sheeting over the thorax.

**Comments:** Tying instructions follow. This fly became wildly popular soon after it appeared. It's one toylike, buoyant hopper fly that keeps catching trout.

## Tying the Club Sandwich

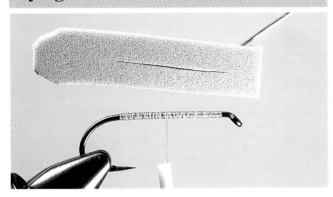

**1.** Cover the shank with tight thread turns. Normally, you would glue the three layers of foam together, but it's not required, and I won't here. Cut a strip twice the length of the shank and as wide as the gape from each color of foam sheeting. Trim what will be the rear end of each strip to rounded. Using a razor blade or sharp knife, cut a slit partway through the underside of the tan strip, down the center; the cut should be about shank long and should start near the front, squared end of the strip.

**2.** Stack the three strips of foam with their rounded ends together and evened. With the thread at the center of the shank, push the stacked foam down onto the shank—with the square-cut end of the foam projecting just slightly past the eye. Bind the foam there with a few firm thread turns.

**3.** Wind the thread back (towards the bend) over the top of the foam and then add a couple of turns around the foam and shank to create a segment. Wind the thread back over the top of the foam again to make another segment. Continue making segments along the shank—and then onto the *foam only*—until just the rounded end of the foam remains.

**4.** Work the thread forward the same way—over the top of the foam, twice around it, and on to the next segment. The thread should now cross itself over each segment, and the thread should be back at midshank.

**5.** Tie and tighten an overhand knot in two sections of three rubber-strands that are still connected to one another. Trim off two on the end to leave a single strand angling down. Bind the sections along the sides of the body at midshank with a few firm thread turns. Bind the rear end of a short, slim section of white foam sheeting atop the body there (at midshank).

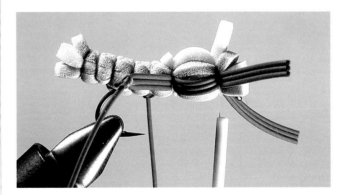

**6.** Raise the front of the foam layers and wind the thread to just short of the eye. Lower the foam and bind it with a narrow thread collar. Bind the front ends of the rubber-strand on the sides of the thread collar. Bind the front of the white foam atop the thread collar.

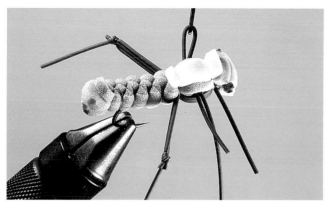

**7.** Whip-finish and trim the thread. Split the top two strands off the top of the front of the rubber-strand sections and trim them off, leaving a single leg on each side. Trim the front of the white foam fairly short. Make eyes on the sides of the foam head with a black permanent marking pen. Push the angle-cut end of some rubber-strand through the eye of a big sewing needle, push the needle into the side of the thorax area, and pull through the rubber-strand for a second set of legs; trim these legs to length. Add epoxy glue or head cement to the whip finish and the underside of the body, along the shank.

## DAVE'S HOPPER — *Dave Whitlock*

*Top view*

*Tied by Dave Whitlock*

**Hook:** Heavy or standard or wire, 2X or 3X long shank, sizes 14 to 6.
**Thread:** Yellow or tan 3/0; size A rod-winding thread for the head and collar.

**Tail (optional):** Dyed red deer hair.
**Body:** Yellow poly yarn as a loop for the butt, wound up the shank for the body.
**Rib:** Brown hackle, trimmed.
**Wing:** Mottled turkey quill, toughened with Dave's Flexament or an artist's fixative such as Tuffilm, over dyed yellow deer hair (optional). Trim the quill section to a point.
**Hopping legs:** Knotted golden pheasant tail fibers, standard (ring-necked) pheasant tail fibers, or grizzly-dyed-yellow trimmed hackles (instructions follow).
**Head and collar:** Natural gray deer hair. Alternatively, use natural deer hair on top and dyed yellow deer hair on the underside (instructions are on page 268).
**Comments:** This has been the standard grasshopper imitation in the West for decades.

## ENSOLITE HOPPER — *Richard Bunse*

*Tied by Skip Morris*

**Hook:** Light or standard wire, 2X long, sizes 12 to 8.
**Thread:** Yellow or tan size A rod-winding thread.
**Body:** Section cut from a block of white buoyant closed-cell foam (Richard originally used something called Ensolite), trimmed to rounded in cross section and on the butt end, and colored with a yellow permanent marking pen. The hook point is pushed through the foam and out again just up from the butt end, then bound in sections up the shank.
**Legs:** Knotted pheasant tail fibers, the tips trimmed to length (instructions are on page 177).
**Head and collar:** Undyed tan-gray deer hair, flared and shaped (instructions are on page 268).
**Comments:** This is a sort of pared-down foam version of the Dave's Hopper.

## Making Pheasant Tail Hopping Legs

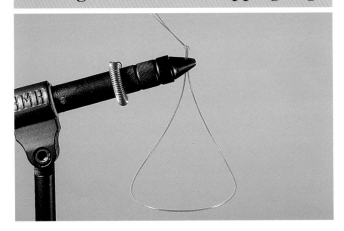

**1.** Double about one foot of heavy monofilament and knot its ends together. Mount the loop in the vise near the knotted ends. The looped end of the mono should hang down. (I used colored monofilament here to make the loop easily visible).

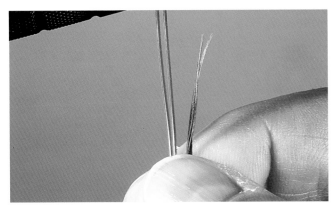

**2.** Stroke a section of fibers off to a right angle to the quill on a pheasant tail, to even the tips. Snip the fibers from the quill. Hold the fibers, with their tips pointing up, in your right hand. Hold the fibers, near their cut base, up against the right side of the mono loop. Pull the sides of the loop in between your right-hand thumb and finger, next to the pheasant fibers.

**3.** Move your right hand to bend the mono loop so that the tips of the pheasant go in front of the loop and to the left.

**4.** With your left hand, reach around behind and pull the pheasant fibers to the right behind the mono loop, then down in front of the loop. You can swing your hand over the top of the vise to accomplish this.

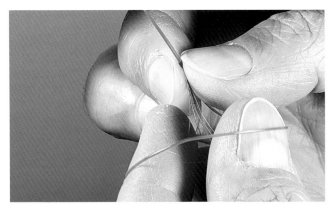

**5.** Pinch the fibers in the tips of your right-hand thumb and finger to hold them down in front of the loop. With your left-hand thumb and finger, reach up into the loop from behind and grasp the tips of the pheasant tail fibers.

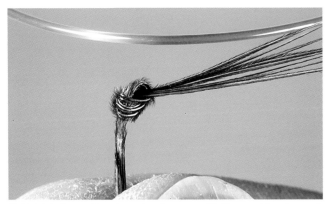

**6.** Maintain the position of your hands as you slide them and the pheasant fibers down off the loop. When you reach the end of the loop, the tips of the fibers will go up through themselves to make a knot. Carefully tighten the knot in the pheasant fibers. Add a drop of head cement or odorless epoxy glue to the knot now or after the pheasant hopping legs are mounted on a fly.

## FLAT CREEK HOPPER — *Ralph Headrick*

*Tied by Wade Malwitz*

**Hook:** Heavy or standard wire, 3X long, sizes 12 to 6.
**Thread:** Yellow 3/0 or size A rod thread.
**Body:** Dyed gold elk hair, bound with spiraling crisscrossed turns of thread.
**Hopping legs:** Knotted golden (or standard ring-necked) pheasant tail fibers (instructions are on page 177).
**Wing:** Turkey tail toughened with clear acrylic spray, Dave's Flexament, or Tuffilm.
**Bullet head:** Natural deer hair (instructions are on page 146).

## FOAM HOPPER — *Dick Talleur*

*Tied by Skip Morris*

**Hook:** Light wire, standard length or 1X long, size 10.
**Thread:** Green 8/0 or 6/0.
**Body:** Green buoyant closed-cell foam cylinder melted to rounded on the end. Push the hook into the cut end of the cylinder and out just before the melted end. Start the thread and bind the cut end of the cylinder about two-thirds up the shank.
**Wing:** Pheasant body feather (with yellow arches—tiers call it a church-window feather), toughened with Pliobond or Flexament.
**Hopping legs:** Red fox-squirrel hair, knotted and the knots secured with cement.
**Head:** Short section of the same foam cylinder used for the body, melted on the end to rounded, pierced with a needle, and then pushed back over a tight thread layer coated with cement—essentially glued into place.

## GIDLOW HOPPER — *Arnie Gidlow*

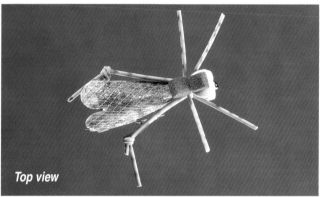

*Top view*

*Tied by Arnie Gidlow*

**Hook:** Standard wire, 3X (or 2X) long, slow-curve shank, sizes 12 to 8.
**Thread:** White 3/0.
**Body:** Strip of brown buoyant closed-cell foam sheeting over a strip of cream.
**Wing:** Foust Hopper Wing (or any gray-brown synthetic wing sheeting), trimmed to a long wing with a notch and rounded ends.
**Hopping legs:** Tan Rainey's oval rubber legs (or rubber-strand), barred with a brown permanent marking pen. To make each leg, tie an overhand knot in two still-attached sections; then trim off one on the end of each.
**Legs:** Tan Rainey's oval rubber legs (or rubber-strand), barred with a brown permanent marking pen. These are simply the front of the hopping leg sections, separated.
**Eyes:** Front of the brown foam strip, inside the doubled end of the cream foam strip.
**Head:** Front of the cream foam strip doubled back over the top of the brown foam strip and the hook's eye pushed through the cream foam.
**Strike indicator:** Slim strip of red buoyant closed-cell foam sheeting, short on the ends.
**Comments:** The point of the hook should be pushed down through the strip of cream foam; then the brown foam is added on top. The cream foam runs under the shank and the brown foam runs over. Both layers of foam are bound together in segments.

## HENRY'S FORK HOPPER — *Mike Lawson*

*Tied by Skip Morris*

**Hook:**       Light to heavy wire, 2X long, sizes 12 to 8.
**Thread:**    Yellow 3/0.
**Body:**       Natural light or dyed yellow elk hair, doubled forward and extending off the bend (instructions are on page 138).
**Wing:**       Pheasant rump feather with pale arches (called a church-window feather) or mottled brown hen back feather coated with Flexament. Under the wing, yellow elk hair.
**Hopping legs:** Knotted pheasant tail fibers. (Instructions are on page 177.) Alternatively, use a cream section of round rubber-strand barred with a brown permanent marking pen. Each section of rubber-strand is knotted for the rear hopping leg and bound under the narrow thread collar holding the bullet head; the forward end of the section is trimmed short to suggest a small front leg.
**Bullet head and collar:** Natural gray elk hair (instructions are on page 146).
**Comments:**  Based on the innovative Henry's Fork Stonefly.

## JOE'S HOPPER

*Tied by Skip Morris*

**Hook:**       Light to heavy wire, 2X or 3X long, sizes 12 to 6.
**Thread:**    Black 8/0, 6/0, or 3/0.

**Tail:**        Red hackle fibers.
**Rump:**      Loop of the body yarn over the tail.
**Rib:**         Brown hackle palmered up the body and trimmed.
**Body:**       Yellow synthetic yarn (poly or Antron).
**Wing:**       Turkey quill sections cupped back over the body with the tips up.
**Hackle:**    Brown and grizzly mixed.
**Comments:**  An old-time hopper imitation. I caught my first brown trout on one on Montana's Bitteroot River in the 1960s—it still works!

## LETORT HOPPER — *Ed Shenk*

*Tied by Skip Morris*

**Hook:**       Standard to heavy wire, 2X or 3X long (or standard length or 1X long), sizes 16 to 10.
**Thread:**    Gray, yellow, or white 8/0, 6/0, or 3/0 for the body and wing. Many tiers prefer size A rod-winding thread for flaring the deer hair.
**Body:**       Yellow buoyant synthetic dubbing (poly, Antron . . .).
**Wing:**       Mottled turkey quill section, trimmed to rounded on the end.
**Head and collar:** Natural tan-gray deer hair, flared and trimmed to shape (instructions are on page 268).
**Comments:**  The simple, buoyant, effective Letort Hopper has been around for decades. It's an excellent choice when a small grasshopper fly is appropriate.

## MACHOPPER · *Al Troth*

*Tied by Skip Morris*

| | |
|---|---|
| **Hook:** | Light or standard wire, 2X long, size 8. |
| **Thread:** | Yellow 3/0 (option: use size A rod-winding thread for flaring the hair). |
| **Body:** | Section of yellow polypropylene macramé yarn melted at the end. Push the hook's point partway down the yarn and out; bind the front of the yarn firmly to the shank. |
| **Wing:** | Yellow synthetic wing material cut to shape. Atop the wing, yellow elk or deer hair. |
| **Hopping legs:** | Yellow rubber-strand—each leg is made of three sections still attached, knotted, and then two sections stripped from the tip and trimmed off. |
| **Head and collar:** | Olive or olive-yellow deer hair, flared and shaped (instructions are on page 268). |

## MEADOW HOPPER · *Polly Rosborough*

*Tied by Wade Malwitz*

| | |
|---|---|
| **Hook:** | Standard to heavy wire, 3X long, sizes 14 to 8. |
| **Thread:** | Brown 8/0, 6/0, or 3/0. |
| **Rib:** | Light ginger hackle spiraled up the body. Trim the fibers off on the sides, and trim the remaining fibers so they taper down to very short at the front of the body. |
| **Body:** | Pale yellow synthetic yarn (poly or Antron). |
| **Wing:** | Mottled turkey quill sections dyed pale yellow, one tied on along each side. Atop the wing, a small bunch of dyed yellow buck tail. |
| **Hackle:** | Cream, dark ginger, and light grizzly mixed. |

## PARACHUTE HOPPER · *Ed Schroeder*

*Tied by Skip Morris*

| | |
|---|---|
| **Hook:** | Light or standard wire, 2X long, sizes 18 to 10. |
| **Thread:** | Cream 8/0, 6/0, or 3/0. |
| **Parachute wing:** | White calf tail (instructions are on page 63). |
| **Abdomen:** | Golden brown Antron dubbing (or another synthetic dubbing). |
| **Down-wing:** | Mottled turkey quill or tail, toughened with Dave's Flexament or Tuffilm. Trim the end of a section to rounded, and then mount the wing close to the parachute wing. |
| **Hopping legs:** | Knotted pheasant tail fibers (instructions are on page 177). |
| **Parachute hackle:** | Grizzly (instructions are on page 63). |
| **Thorax:** | Same as the abdomen. |
| **Comments:** | This is the companion to the Parachute Caddis. It's a good floater, the wing is easy to see, it has a convincing profile, and the body sits on the water with a real hopper's posture. |

## WHIT HOPPER · *Dave Whitlock*

*Top view*

*Tied by Dave Whitlock*

| | |
|---|---|
| **Hook:** | Heavy or standard wire, 3X long, sizes 12 to 6. |
| **Thread:** | Tan or yellow 3/0. |

**Body:** Dyed yellow elk or deer hair. Bind on the hair well up the shank; spiral the thread back tightly down the hair and shank, and then off the bend on the hair only for a distance about equal to the gape; add a few tight turns of thread; and then spiral the thread back up the hair. The result should be a series of thread "X"s along the hair. Trim the end of the hair straight across.

**Wing:** Section of mottled tan-brown turkey quill, toughened with Dave's Flexament, cut to rounded on the end; or synthetic wing material cut to a long rectangle with a rounded end, over dyed pale yellow deer hair.

**Hopping legs:** Knotted pheasant tail (instructions are on page 177) or knotted, trimmed dyed yellow grizzly hackles.

**Antennae:** Striped dry-fly hackle stems, colored brown with a permanent waterproof marking pen.

**Bullet head and collar:** Natural tan-brown deer hair on top, dyed pale yellow deer hair for the underside (or consider elk hair; instructions for making a bullet head and collar are on page 146.)

**Strike indicator:** Orange deer hair flared atop the thread collar on the bullet head, and trimmed short.

**Comments:** This is Dave's *other* famous grasshopper pattern.

---

# Cicadas

## CLARK'S CICADA — Clark Reid

*Tied by Wade Malwitz*

**Hook:** Standard (or light or heavy) wire, 2X or 3X long, sizes 10 and 8.

**Thread:** Olive 6/0 (I prefer size A rod thread for flaring deer hair—and this one's almost all deer hair).

**Body:** Olive deer hair, flared and trimmed (instructions are on page 268).

**Wing:** Shimazaki Fly Wing (or another cream or white synthetic wing sheeting with dark spotting), trimmed to a long wing notched and rounded at the end. Fold the wing lengthwise so it envelops the top of the body. Under the wing, pearl Krystal Flash.

**Head and collar:** Olive deer hair, flared and trimmed (instructions are on page 268).

**Eyes:** Black plastic barbell eyes.

**Comments:** Although Clark Reid is a New Zealand guide, his Clark's Cicada has become a trusted American imitation.

## MUTANT NINJA CICADA

*Tied by Skip Morris*

**Hook:** Light or standard wire, 2X long, sizes 10 to 6 (a slow-curve shank is optional).

**Thread:** Burnt orange 3/0.

**Body:** Strip of black buoyant closed-cell foam sheeting.

**Wing:** Natural tan-gray deer hair over gold Krystal Flash.

**Legs:** Black or brown rubber legs, medium diameter.

**Hackle:** One or two grizzly neck or saddle feathers.

**Comments:** An established pattern for the famous cicada action on Utah's Green River.

# Moths

### SPRUCE MOTH — *Bob Jacklin*

*Tied by Bob Jacklin*

**Hook:** Heavy to light wire, 1X long, sizes 14 and 12.
**Thread:** White or cream 8/0 or 6/0.
**Rib:** One short-fibered ginger saddle hackle, spiraled up the body and trimmed flat on the underside.
**Body:** Make a buoyant underbody of the butts of the wing and head. Dub over the underbody with creamy tan opossum.
**Head and wing:** Pale undyed or dyed ginger elk hair, doubled back and bound with a narrow thread collar to form both the head and wing; in essence, this is a bullet-head. (Instructions are on page 146.)
**Comments:** Bob has fished this fly for many years and first encountered trout feeding on spruce moths on the "Galatin River near Big Sky, Montana, back in the early 1970s." He adds, "We have had a very good hatch of spruce moths for the past few years and have come to count on it every year."

### SPRUCE MOTH

*Tied by Wade Malwitz*

**Hook:** Light wire, 1X long, sizes 14 and 12.
**Thread:** Orange 8/0 or 6/0.
**Body:** Cream buoyant synthetic dubbing.
**Wing and head:** Natural pale or bleached elk hair. The trimmed butts make the head.

# Bees and Yellow Jackets

### BUMBLE MCDOUGAL — *Jack Ellis*

*Tied by Skip Morris*

**Hook:** Heavy (or standard to light) wire, 2X long, sizes 12 to 8.
**Thread:** Black 8/0 or 6/0 (I use this for the tail, wings, and hackle, but I use size A rod thread for flaring the body hair).
**Tail:** Dyed yellow buck tail, the darker center hairs.
**Body:** Alternating bands of flared black and yellow deer hair, flared and trimmed to a plump body (instructions are on page 268).
**Wing:** Cree or grizzly hackle tips.
**Hackle:** Grizzly, cree, or one black and one dyed yellow hackle mixed.
**Comments:** Jack developed his Bumble McDougal for the bluegills in his east Texas ponds and lakes. However, it's a natural for imitating honeybees and bumblebees on trout rivers.

### YELLOW JACKET — *Andy Burk*

*Tied by Al Davis*

**Hook:** Standard to light wire, 2X or 3X long, sizes 12 and 10.
**Body:** Alternating bands of yellow and black Antron dubbing (or any synthetic dubbing, such as poly or Super Fine Dry Fly).
**Wing:** Furnace hackle tips.
**Eyes:** Black monofilament barbell eyes.
**Hackle:** Brown.

# Craneflies

## ADULT CRANEFLY — *Jay Buchner*

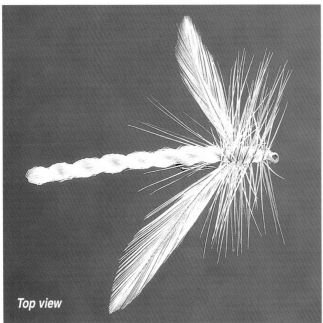

*Top view*

*Tied by Wade Malwitz*

**Hook:** Light wire, standard length or 1X long, sizes 14 to 8.
**Thread:** Tan 8/0, 6/0, or 3/0.
**Extended body:** Tan poly yarn, twisted and doubled.
**Wing:** Blue dun hackle tips.
**Hackle:** One large (suitable for a hook two sizes larger than the one you selected) blue dun saddle hackle, spiraled up the thorax.
**Thorax:** Butts of the poly yarn extended body, but not twisted.

## DEER HAIR DADDY — *Jeff Morgan*

*Tied by Wade Malwitz*

**Hook:** Standard wire, 2X long, slow-curve shank, sizes 12 to 8.
**Thread:** Black 8/0 or 6/0.
**Abdomen:** Dyed brown or natural brown-gray deer hair, spiral-wound with the working thread back and then forward again, making a pattern of "X"s. Make a few tight turns at the end of the abdomen. Trim the hair blunt at the rear end.
**Legs:** Six knotted pheasant tail fibers, four behind the hackle and two in front.
**Wing:** Shimazaki Fly Wing (or another synthetic wing material), trimmed to two long, narrow wings.
**Hackle:** Grizzly or dyed brown grizzly.
**Comments:** This is a fairly detailed cranefly, but if you can get the hang of making the leg-knots, it won't take long to tie. Guide David Child likes to vary the thread color on his similar cranefly pattern (which also has pheasant tail legs and an extended deer-hair body) from black to brown to olive to create different effects.

## RUDD'S CRIMINAL CRANE                            *Kelly Rudd*

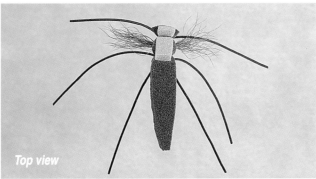

*Top view*

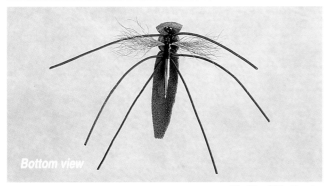

*Bottom view*

*Tied by Skip Morris*

**Hook:**     Fine wire, standard length or 1X long, sizes 10 to 6.
**Thread:**    Black 8/0 or 6/0.
**Wing:**     Brown calf tail.
**Legs:**     Fine round rubber-strand, black or brown—one section bound back along each side of the shank to make the two rear legs; two more sections, one bound along each side of the thread collar holding the foam body behind the wings, to make the remaining four legs.
**Body:**    Wrap gold floss up the shank. The tapered body is cut from brown buoyant closed-cell foam sheeting, bound behind the wings and in front with two narrow thread collars.
**Head:**     Front of the body foam.
**Strike indicator:** Small strip of orange buoyant closed-cell foam sheeting.

## WADE'S OVERHEAD CRANE                          *Wade Malwitz*

*Tied by Wade Malwitz*

**Hook:**     Light wire, standard length or 1X long, sizes 14 and 12.
**Thread:**    Brown 8/0 or 6/0.
**Abdomen:**  Brown round buoyant closed-cell foam dowel.
**Wing:**     White Antron yarn bound crossways, melted on the ends.
**Legs:**     Undyed pheasant tail fibers, set to radiate around the thorax with turns of thread.
**Thorax:**   Front of the foam dowel, pulled back over the thread holding the legs and wings, bound at the rear of the thorax area, and then trimmed close.
**Comments:**  The plausible appearance of the Wade's Overhead Crane makes me wonder whether we really need to spend our time knotting the legs on some adult cranefly patterns.

# Miscellaneous Imitative Nymphs

AQUATIC WORMS generally lie hidden in small numbers, and fish eggs usually aren't abundant in rivers, even when spawning fish are at their imprecise work. Nor will you see many rivers that contain scuds. Still, trout eat all these things and more, sometimes preferring them over all else.

## Fishing the Miscellaneous Nymphs

### AQUATIC WORMS

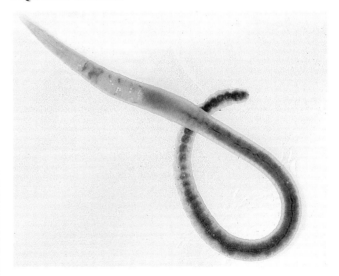

*Aquatic worm*

Turn over a few rocks in a western river and you'll be surprised to find what appear to be earthworms. They're not. They're what fly fishers commonly call aquatic worms, and trout seem to relish them as much as the earthworms you dangled below a bobber as a kid. Aquatic worms are fairly helpless when caught in the current, so fish imitations of them dead drift. You may need a heavy point fly with the worm fly as a dropper, or you may need to attach lead up the leader, because aquatic worm imitations are typically too slender to carry much weight.

## EGGS

The spawning process of fish in rivers is a difficult and somewhat inefficient business. The current carries away a significant number of eggs, often to the waiting mouths of trout. Trout eat trout eggs, salmon eggs, and probably the eggs of any other fish in the river. But sometimes egg flies that are far larger than anything in the river can be very effective—who knows why? And I've occasionally seen trout wildly aggressive for egg imitations when no fish were spawning. Fish egg flies dead drift, just like the natural.

## SCUDS AND SUCH

Rich, weedy, slow-moving rivers can be full of scuds. Scuds look like tiny shrimp—arched, translucent segments covering top and sides, antennae, and a flurry of legs. Scuds swim at a steady, unhurried pace, so dead drift is the standard way to fish imitations.

*Scud*

## SOWBUG

But in the laziest rivers, it may make sense to tease a scud fly along on a slow retrieve.

*Sowbug*

Like scuds, sowbugs prefer quiet currents and weedy riverbeds. They do best in really clean, clear water—spring creeks are ideal habitat. Sowbugs are poor swimmers, so an imitation should be fished dead drift or on a very slow retrieve.

According to Colorado fly-fishing guide Tim Heng, the mysis shrimp is a rarity in trout streams. It thrives in only the occasional reservoir where it is flushed through the dam into the river below. An imitation can be fished dead drift or with a slowish retrieve. Where you do find the mysis shrimp, it can fatten big trout and be important to the fly fisher.

## CRANEFLY LARVAE

Some cranefly larvae inhabit the shallow margins of rivers. These larva can be important during high water, when amplified currents may scour them out.

*Cranefly larva*

# Aquatic Worms

**ATOMIC WORM**                                  *Gord Kennedy*

*Tied by Peter Morrison*

**Hook:**            Heavy wire, 4X long (slow-curve shank preferred), sizes 10 to 6.
**Head (optional):** Gold metal bead.
**Thread:**          Red 3/0.
**Tail:**            Red four-strand floss, bound partway down the hook's bend, trimmed to gape length.
**Body:**            20- to 30-pound flat mono over red Flashabou.
**Comments:**  Gord Kennedy developed his Atomic Worm on and for Alberta's Bow River, but it has since proven its effectiveness on rivers across Canada and the United States and in Chile.

## SAN JUAN WORM

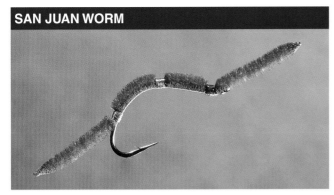

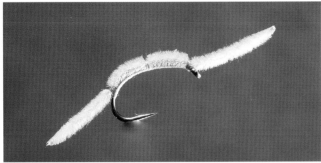

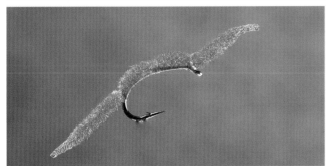

*Brown tied by Skip Morris, pink and red tied by Peter Morrison*

**Hook:** Heavy wire, humped shank (scud-pupa hook), sizes 12 to 8.

**Thread:** Brown, pink, or red (to match the body color) 8/0, 6/0, or 3/0.

**Body:** Brown, pink, or red Vernille or Ultra Chenille, both ends melted to tapers. Bind the body up the shank in three slim thread collars, a layer of thread up the shank between collars.

**Comments:** The San Juan Worm, like the Glo-Bug, was the seminal fly of its type, and it remains really popular to this day. Different fly tiers use all sorts of hook styles for San Juan Worms, and they all seem to hook and hold trout.

# Eggs

**Glo-Bug.** The Glo-Bug started the whole egg fly craze years ago and remains the standard for this sort of pattern.

## Tying the Glo-Bug

**1.** Start the thread at the center of the hook's shank. Cut two to four short sections of fluffy egg yarn (depending on the size of the hook). Hold the sections atop the hook and push them down until the shank is in their center. Bind the yarn with a narrow thread collar of tight thread turns.

**2.** Cut another yarn section of a contrasting color, strip a small amount of yarn off the side of the section, and bind it on the top or side of the other yarn with a couple of tight thread turns around the thread collar.

**3.** Pull the yarn back, make a few thread turns in front of the yarn, and then whip-finish and cut the thread.

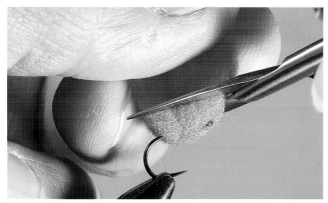

**4.** Firmly draw the ends of the yarn straight up and hold them there. Reach in with the scissors and make one snip (or two) to cut through all the yarn.

**5.** Draw back the front of the yarn and add head cement. Tease the cut ends of the yarn back into place. If there are irregularities in the globe shape of the yarn, trim them.

### GLO-BUG, PINK    *The Bug Shop, Anderson, California*

*Tied by Skip Morris*

| | |
|---|---|
| **Hook:** | Heavy wire, short shank, sizes 16 to 4. |
| **Thread:** | Pink 8/0 or 6/0. |
| **Body:** | Pink egg yarn (instructions begin on page 187). |
| **Spot:** | Egg yarn of any contrasting color. |

### GLO-BUG, ORANGE    *The Bug Shop, Anderson, California*

*Tied by Skip Morris*

| | |
|---|---|
| **Hook:** | Heavy wire, short shank, sizes 16 to 4. |
| **Thread:** | Orange 8/0 or 6/0. |
| **Body:** | Orange egg yarn (instructions begin on page 187). |
| **Spot:** | Egg yarn of any contrasting color. |

### GLO-BUG, RED    *The Bug Shop, Anderson, California*

*Tied by Carol Ann Morris*

| | |
|---|---|
| **Hook:** | Heavy wire, short shank, sizes 16 to 4. |
| **Thread:** | Red 8/0 or 6/0. |
| **Body:** | Red egg yarn (instructions begin on page 187). |
| **Spot:** | Egg yarn of any contrasting color. |

## PETTIS UNREAL EGG — *Jim Pettis*

*Tied by Peter Morrison*

**Hook:** Heavy wire, short shank, size 12.
**Thread:** Red 6/0.
**Body:** Glo-Bug-type yarn in orange, red, peach, or pink (any egg color), bound at the hook's eye. The yarn is bound around the eye, with short ends projecting back and long ends projecting forward. The bead is pushed forward against the butts of the yarn. The thread is passed or restarted behind the bead; the yarn is pulled back all around, bound, and trimmed closely.
**Bead:** One dark orange or red glass bead.
**Comments:** A smart twist on the egg fly. The bead adds some shine and weight.

# Scuds and Such

**Bead Head Scud.** This is a fast-sinking scud for those quick spots in otherwise slow-moving scud rivers.

## BEAD HEAD SCUD, OLIVE-GRAY — *Randall Kaufmann*

*Tied by Peter Morrison*

**Hook:** Heavy wire, humped shank (scud-pupa hook), sizes 16 to 10.
**Antennae:** Olive hackle fibers.
**Head:** Gold metal bead.
**Thread:** Olive 8/0 or 6/0.
**Tail:** Olive hackle fibers.
**Back:** Strip of clear plastic sheeting (Scud Back, Stretch Flex, freezer bag . . .) over a few strands of pearl Flashabou.
**Rib:** Heavy gray-olive thread or fine tippet.
**Abdomen:** Gray-olive Antron dubbing, teased out along the underside between the ribs.

## BEAD HEAD SCUD, ORANGE — *Randall Kaufmann*

*Tied by Peter Morrison*

**Hook:** Heavy wire, humped shank (scud-pupa hook), sizes 16 to 10.
**Antennae:** Orange hackle fibers.
**Head:** Gold metal bead.
**Thread:** Fluorescent orange 8/0 or 6/0.
**Tail:** Orange hackle fibers.
**Back:** Strip of clear plastic sheeting (Scud Back, Stretch Flex, freezer bag . . .) over a few strands of pearl Flashabou.
**Rib:** Heavy fluorescent orange thread.
**Abdomen:** Hot orange Antron dubbing, teased out along the underside between the ribs.

## BEAD HEAD SCUD, TAN — *Randall Kaufmann*

*Tied by Peter Morrison*

| | |
|---|---|
| Hook: | Heavy wire, humped shank (scud-pupa hook), sizes 16 to 10. |
| Antennae: | Tan hackle fibers. |
| Head: | Gold metal bead. |
| Thread: | Tan 8/0 or 6/0. |
| Tail: | Tan hackle fibers. |
| Back: | Strip of clear plastic sheeting (Scud Back, Stretch Flex, freezer bag...) over a few strands of pearl Flashabou. |
| Rib: | Fine tippet. |
| Abdomen: | Tan Hare-Tron mixed with ginger, amber, and cream goat hair (or tannish hare's mask mixed with tan Antron dubbing), teased out along the underside between the ribs. |

**Bighorn Shrimp.** Looking otherwise very much like its predecessor the Troth Scud, the Bighorn Shrimp stands out primarily for its gaudy colors. Despite those colors, it works. When natural-looking flies fail, always consider an unnatural pattern.

## BIGHORN SHRIMP, ORANGE

*Tied by Skip Morris*

| | |
|---|---|
| Hook: | Heavy wire, standard length or 1X long (a humped-shank scud-pupa hook is a popular alternative), sizes 16 to 10. |
| Thread: | Orange 8/0 or 6/0. |
| Weight (optional): | Lead wire. |
| Tail and antennae: | Orange hackle fibers. |
| Back: | Strip of clear plastic sheeting (Scud Back, Stretch Flex, freezer bag . . .). |
| Rib: | Heavy orange thread. |
| Body: | Orange Antron dubbing, or any shiny synthetic or natural dubbing, picked out between the ribs. |

## BIGHORN SHRIMP, PINK

*Tied by Peter Morrison*

| | |
|---|---|
| Hook: | Heavy wire, standard length or 1X long (a humped-shank scud-pupa hook is a popular alternative), sizes 16 to 10. |
| Thread: | Pink 8/0 or 6/0. |
| Weight (optional): | Lead or lead-substitute wire. |
| Tail and antennae: | Pink hackle fibers. |
| Back: | Strip of clear plastic sheeting (Scud Back, Stretch Flex, freezer bag . . .). |
| Rib: | Heavy pink thread. |
| Body: | Pink Antron dubbing, or any shiny synthetic or natural dubbing, picked out between the ribs. |

## EPOXY SCUD, AMBER — *Brad Befus*

*Tied by Skip Morris*

| | |
|---|---|
| Hook: | Heavy wire, 2X or 3X long, slow-curve shank, sizes 18 to 12. |
| Thread: | Orange 8/0 or 6/0. |
| Tail: | Mallard dyed wood-duck color. |
| Back: | Hot orange Krystal Flash, coated with epoxy glue. |
| Body: | Rough amber-colored dubbing (Antron, Ligas, Buggy Nymph . . .). |
| Eyes: | Two dots from a black marking pen, under the epoxy. |
| Comments: | A new approach to scud imitations from a fly fisher who knows flies. |

## EPOXY SCUD, OLIVE — *Brad Befus*

*Tied by Peter Morrison*

**Hook:** Heavy wire, 2X or 3X long, slow-curve shank, sizes 18 to 12.
**Thread:** Olive 8/0 or 6/0.
**Tail:** Mallard dyed wood-duck color.
**Back:** Pearl Krystal Flash, coated with epoxy glue.
**Body:** Rough olive dubbing (Antron, Ligas, Buggy Nymph . . .).
**Eyes:** Two dots from a black marking pen, under the epoxy.

## GIDLOW'S SOW BUG — *Arnie Gidlow*

*Tied by Arnie Gidlow*

**Hook:** Standard or heavy wire, standard length or 1X long, sizes 16 to 12.
**Body:** Bluish-gray opaque glass beads with gray SLF dubbing (or another coarse, shiny dubbing such as Arizona Simi Seal or Antron) wound forward and between the beads and picked out along the sides (instructions are on page 99).
**Thread:** Gray 8/0 or 6/0.
**Tail:** Dyed gray turkey (or goose) biots, curving apart.
**Antennae:** Dyed gray turkey (or goose) biots, curving apart.
**Head:** Same dubbing as used over the bead body.

## MYSIS SHRIMP — *Tim Heng*

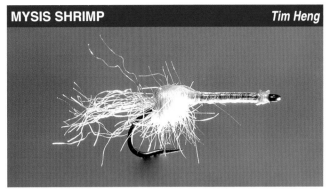

*Tied by Tim Heng*

**Hook:** Standard wire, 2X long, slow-curve shank, sizes 20 to 16.
**Thread:** White 14/0 (for the smallest hooks) or 8/0.
**Tail:** White Z-lon or Antron.
**Rib:** One strand of pearl Krystal Flash over white tying thread.
**Back and abdomen:** Strip cut from a plastic sandwich or freezer bag. Push the sides of the strip down around the shank and secure it there with the rib.
**Comments:** Tim usually fishes his Mysis Shrimp dead drift. But sometimes, near the dams from which the shrimp emerge from reservoirs, he swims it to imitate the still lively naturals before they die downstream in the moving water.

**Rainy's Bead Back Scud.** The prevalence of glass bead fly patterns has been rising steadily over the past decade, and they vary greatly. Some have bodies built entirely of beads; others have the bead attached outside the body or even dangling from it. The body of beads strung on the shank of Rainey's Bead Back Scud is the most common approach to making a glass bead fly. The method of adding the legs to her pattern is a variation on the standard approach to dubbing over bead bodies. Glass beads add color, shine, translucence, and weight.

## RAINY'S BEAD BACK SCUD, DARK AMBER
### Rainy Riding

*Tied by Peter Morrison*

Hook:  Heavy wire, humped shank (scud-pupa hook), sizes 16 to 12.

Body and legs: Five or six small, dark amber glass beads and amber Rainy's Sparkle Dub (or any shiny and fairly coarse synthetic or natural dubbing, such as Antron, Arizona Sparkle Nymph, Ice Dub . . .). Wind the bare thread forward under the rearmost bead, bind a hank of dubbing under the shank, advance the bare thread under the next bead, bind on another hank of dubbing, and continue up all the beads in this manner.

Thread:  Amber (or tan) 8/0 or 6/0.

## RAINY'S BEAD BACK SCUD, OLIVE
### Rainy Riding

*Tied by Peter Morrison*

Hook:  Heavy wire, humped shank (scud-pupa hook), sizes 16 to 12.

Body and legs: Five or six small, olive glass beads and olive Rainy's Sparkle Dub (or any shiny and fairly coarse synthetic or natural dubbing, such as Antron, Arizona Sparkle Nymph, Ice Dub . . .). Wind the bare thread forward under the rearmost bead, bind a hank of dubbing under the shank, advance the bare thread under the next bead, bind on another hank of dubbing, and continue up all the beads in this manner.

Thread:  Olive 8/0 or 6/0.

## RAINY'S BEAD BACK SCUD, SHRIMP PINK
### Rainy Riding

*Tied by Peter Morrison*

Hook:  Heavy wire, humped shank (scud-pupa hook), sizes 16 to 12.

Body and legs: Five or six small, shrimp pink glass beads and shrimp pink (pale pink) Rainy's Sparkle Dub (or any shiny and fairly coarse synthetic or natural dubbing, such as Antron, Arizona Sparkle Nymph, Ice Dub . . .). Wind the bare thread forward under the rearmost bead, bind a hank of dubbing under the shank, advance the bare thread under the next bead, bind on another hank of dubbing, and continue up all the beads in this manner.

Thread:  Pink 8/0 or 6/0.

## TROTH SCUD
*Al Troth*

*Tied by Skip Morris*

**Hook:** Heavy wire, humped shank (scud-pupa hook), sizes 16 to 10.

**Thread:** 8/0 or 6/0 similar to the body color.

**Weight (optional):** Lead wire.

**Tail and antennae (optional):** Hackle fibers roughly matching the body color.

**Back:** Strip of clear plastic sheeting (Scud Back, Stretch Flex, freezer bag . . .).

**Rib:** Fine tippet (or fine copper wire).

**Body:** Natural fur or coarse synthetic dubbing in olive, gray, orange, brown, or cream.

**Comments:** One of the earliest versions of the contemporary scud fly, and still an excellent choice.

# Cranefly Larvae

## D. B. CRANEFLY LARVA
*Dennis Brown*

*Tied by Peter Morrison*

**Hook:** Heavy wire, 3X long (slow- or "S"-curve shank preferred), sizes 8 and 6.

**Thread:** Black 3/0.

**Abdomen:** Medium-diameter bluish or bluish gray glass beads wound with gray or olive mohair yarn. (Option: add one large root beer, brown, bead toward the front of the abdomen.) Bind on the yarn slightly down the bend; whip-finish and cut the thread. Wind on a butt; pull back a bead and wind the yarn forward under it. Wind the yarn around the shank. Pull back the next bead and wind the yarn under it. Wind the yarn around the shank. Continue up the shank and beads in this manner. Restart the thread, bind and then trim the end of the yarn, and complete the tying of the fly.

**Thorax:** Gray spiky or shaggy natural dubbing (hare's mask, squirrel . . .) in a dubbing loop, picked out (instructions are on page 95).

**Comments:** Imitates a dark cranefly larva.

## HIGHWATER CRANEFLY LARVA

*Tied by Peter Morrison*

**Hook:** Heavy wire, 3X long, sizes 10 to 4.

**Thread:** Black 8/0, 6/0, or 3/0.

**Weight:** Lead wire.

**Tail:** Grizzly hackle fibers.

**Body:** White Sparkle Chenille or Krystal Flash.

**Head:** Peacock herl.

# 10

# Multipurpose Imitations

A PRECISE IMITATION can be a blessing—if you are an hour early for the green drake mayfly hatch that's been coming off reliably every afternoon, you may increase your odds of good fishing with a fly that really matches the nymph, such as an Anatomical Green Drake or Gold Bead Poxyback Green Drake Nymph. But much of the time, a general fly pattern will catch just as many trout as an intricate dressing modeled closely on a specific variety of insect. Consider this: if you don't look too closely, you could mistake a small stonefly nymph for a mayfly nymph, or a small caddis larva for a large midge pupa. Don't feel bad—trout do it all the time. The fact that trout do it means that a general sort of imitation can be deadly wherever the trout aren't sophisticated or aren't in a discriminating mood, or don't get much of a chance to inspect a fly, as in fast or colored water. And a loose imitation suggests a number of creatures the trout might be focused on. In other words, maybe they're not seeking those green drake nymphs at all but are instead darting after *Rhyacophila* caddis pupae, in which case an Olive Bird's Nest would have you covered. True, the green drake nymph is darker than the *Rhyacophila* pupa, and the pupa lacks tails. But both insects are stout, both can be of similar size, and both can be olive—so both can resemble Cal Bird's imprecise nymph enough to make for fast fishing.

The general-purpose imitation starts to make even more sense when you consider flies that trout get to inspect in only a limited way: emergers and dry flies. Trout give their real attention to what they see in the water; I don't think that there's any real debate about that. So to them, an adult salmonfly looks like an elongated pad of dirty orange and some feet, maybe a little bit of tail or antennae if these happen to touch down. But the salmonfly's wings lie up in a blurred and foreign world, the world of air. Perhaps the fish notices the insect's wings, perhaps not, but they're definitely not a main feature to the trout. So emerger flies that hang half submerged and half up in the air give the trout only half a real look at them. This makes a general purpose emerger like the Klinkhammer Special even more reliable, in theory, than a general-purpose nymph like the Bird's Nest that drifts down in full view. A general-purpose imitative dry fly takes the whole thing a step further: riding high on the water, neither fly nor insect makes much contact with the water, so there is little for trout to critique. Consequently, it's particularly difficult for the trout to be picky about such flies (though somehow, they sometimes are).

A final argument for broad-purpose imitative flies: if you carry an ample assortment of Klinkhamer Specials, Brassies, Woolly Wings, and other such versatile patterns in a good range of size and color, along with your realistic Anatomical Salmonflies and Foam Drake Mackeral Emergers, even if you don't have a perfect match, you'll probably have a viable fly for whatever hatch you meet.

In my opinion, multipurpose imitative fly patterns deserve serious acreage in every fisherman's fly box.

# Multipurpose Imitative Nymphs

**BEAVER**

*Tied by Peter Morrison*

**Hook:** Heavy wire, 2X long, sizes 14 to 10.

**Weight (optional):** Lead wire.

**Thread:** Gray 8/0 or 6/0.

**Tail:** Gray partridge flank fibers (or barred mallard or mallard dyed wood-duck color).

**Rib:** Fine gold wire.

**Body:** Beaver underfur.

**Legs:** Same fibers as the tail, bound in a bunch under the thread head.

**Comments:** The Beaver, which has been around for decades, is simple enough to suggest just about anything—a mayfly or stonefly nymph, even a caddis larva or pupa.

**Bird's Nest.** Cal Bird's stonefly nymph and adult patterns, the Bird's Stonefies, were well known among fly fishers and fly tiers long before his Bird's Nest caught on. But the Bird's Nest became a standard in Cal's native California seemingly overnight, and for one reason: trout were jumping all over it. I took it to be an attractor pattern at first, and it is useful in that role. But most fly fishers consider it a loose imitation of nearly anything in a trout stream with legs—stonefly nymphs, mayfly nymphs, caddisfly pupae, and so on.

**BIRD'S NEST (STANDARD)** *Cal Bird*

*Tied by Skip Morris*

**Hook:** Heavy wire, 1X or 2X long, sizes 16 to 8.

**Thread:** Tan 8/0 or 6/0.

**Weight:** Lead wire.

**Tail:** Mallard or teal flank feather fibers dyed bronze (or natural bronze mallard).

**Rib:** Fine copper wire.

**Abdomen:** Undyed grayish tan Australian opossum, Buggy Nymph Dubbing color #16, or any grayish tan dubbing.

**Legs:** Same fibers as the tail, bound as a sparse collar around the abdomen. One approach is to hold a flat section of the fibers over the hook in your right hand, push them down around the shank with your left-hand thumb and finger, and bind them. Or you can just bind the fibers a few at a time around the shank.

**Thorax:** Same as the abdomen.

**BIRD'S NEST, LIGHT CREAM** *Cal Bird*

*Tied by Skip Morris*

**Hook:** Heavy wire, 1X or 2X long, sizes 16 to 8.

**Thread:** Cream or tan 8/0 or 6/0.

**Weight:** Lead wire.

**Tail:** Natural light mallard flank.

**Rib:** Fine copper wire.

**Abdomen:** Cream Australian opossum.

**Legs:** Same fibers as the tail, bound as a sparse collar around the abdomen. One approach is to hold a flat section of the fibers over the hook in your right hand, push them down around the shank with your left-hand thumb and finger, and bind them. Or you can just bind the fibers a few at a time around the shank.

**Thorax:** Same as the abdomen.

## BIRD'S NEST, OLIVE — *Cal Bird*

*Tied by Peter Morrison*

| | |
|---|---|
| **Hook:** | Heavy wire, 1X or 2X long, sizes 16 to 8. |
| **Thread:** | Olive 8/0 or 6/0. |
| **Weight:** | Lead wire. |
| **Tail:** | Mallard or teal flank feather fibers dyed bronze (or natural bronze mallard). |
| **Rib:** | Fine copper wire. |
| **Abdomen:** | Dyed olive Australian opossum (or some other dyed dubbing, such as rabbit). |
| **Legs:** | Same fibers as the tail, bound as a sparse collar around the abdomen. One approach is to hold a flat section of the fibers over the hook in your right hand, push them down around shank with your left-hand thumb and finger, and bind them. Or you can just bind the fibers a few at a time around the shank. |
| **Thorax:** | Same as the abdomen. |

**Brassie.** The Brassie has long been popular for imitating caddis larvae and, on tiny hooks, midge larvae and pupae. Some even consider it an imitation of mayfly and small stonefly nymphs. The Brassie also serves as an attractor nymph. Like any good fly, the Brassie has inspired a load of variations; the most popular of these follow.

## BRASSIE (STANDARD) — *Gene Lynch*

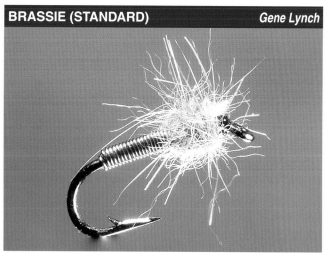

*Tied by Skip Morris*

| | |
|---|---|
| **Hook:** | Heavy wire, regular shank, 1X or 2X long, sizes 20 to 10. |
| **Thread:** | Black 8/0 or 6/0. |
| **Abdomen:** | Copper wire, diameter dependent on hook size. |
| **Thorax:** | Muskrat fur with guard hairs (an alternative is peacock herl). |
| **Comments:** | The dressing above is the original—and it's still a first-rate trout fly—but color variations are now established and in common use. The olive and red described below are probably the most popular of these. They differ from the original Brassie in abdomen color only (and, if you wish, thread color); hook and thorax are the same as in the dressing above. |

### *Gene Lynch*

*Tied by Peter Morrison*

*Brassie, Olive: black or olive thread, and olive copper wire or Ultra wire abdomen.*

### *Gene Lynch*

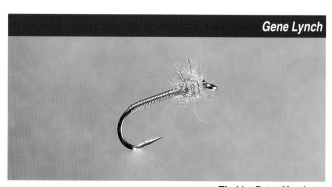

*Tied by Peter Morrison*

*Brassie, Red: black or red thread, and red copper wire or Ultra Wire abdomen.*

## BRASSIE BEAD HEAD (STANDARD)      *Gene Lynch*

*Tied by Peter Morrison*

**Hook:**      Heavy wire, humped shank (scud-pupa hook),
sizes 20 to 14.
**Head:**      Gold metal bead.
**Thread:**      Black 8/0 or 6/0.
**Abdomen:**      Copper wire, diameter dependent on hook size.
**Thorax:**      Peacock herl.
**Comments:**      This bead-head version of the original Brassie cuts right
down through swift currents—good idea. And like the original Brassie, it is
frequently tied and fished in olive and red. The hook and bead (and thread,
if you choose) are the same on the olive and red.

*Gene Lynch*

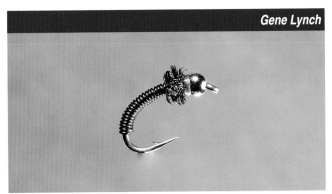

*Tied by Peter Morrison*

**Brassie, Bead Head, Olive:** *Black or olive thread, olive copper wire or
Ultra Wire abdomen.*

*Gene Lynch*

*Tied by Peter Morrison*

**Brassie Bead Head, Red:** *Black or red thread, red copper wire or Ultra
Wire abdomen.*

## CASUAL DRESS      *Polly Rosborough*

*Tied by Skip Morris*

**Hook:**      Heavy wire, 3X long, sizes 10 to 4.
**Thread:**      Black 8/0, 6/0, or 3/0.
**Weight (optional):** Lead wire.
**Tail:**      Bunch of muskrat fur, with the guard hairs retained.
**Body:**      Muskrat fur. Spin the fur tightly in a dubbing loop to give a
slightly segmented effect.
**Collar:**      Muskrat fur, bound in bunches around the shank.
**Head:**      Black ostrich.
**Comments:**      In my 1965 edition of his *Tying and Fishing the Fuzzy
Nymphs,* Polly says that his Casual Dress simply suggests "food." This
makes it a *real* multipurpose imitation, since everything an artificial nymph
might imitate in a trout stream *is* food. I have friends who swear by this
venerable old fly pattern.

## FEATHER DUSTER — *Wally Eagle*

*Tied by Skip Morris*

| | |
|---|---|
| **Hook:** | Heavy wire, 1X or 2X long, sizes 16 to 10. |
| **Thread:** | Brown or olive 8/0 or 6/0. |
| **Tail:** | For hooks size 12 and larger, pheasant tail; for size 14 and smaller, natural brown partridge flank. |
| **Rib:** | Fine copper wire. |
| **Body:** | Natural gray-brown ostrich herl. |

**Wing case and legs:** For hooks size 12 and larger, pheasant tail; for size 14 and smaller, natural brown partridge flank.

**Comments:** After binding on the tail, wire, ostrich, and wing-case fibers, draw the wing-case fibers forward and bind them lightly. Wind the ostrich up to the wing-case fibers, back off the thread turns holding the fibers, and then wind the ostrich the rest of the way to the eye. Bind the ostrich at the eye. Follow these same steps to wind the wire in ribs all the way up to the eye. Double back the tips of the wing-case fibers to make the legs. This popular pattern probably imitates mayfly nymphs more often than small stonefly nymphs, but it's good for both.

## GRAY NYMPH

*Tied by Skip Morris*

| | |
|---|---|
| **Hook:** | Heavy wire, standard length or 1X long, sizes 16 to 6. |
| **Thread:** | Gray 8/0 or 6/0. |
| **Weight:** | Lead wire. |
| **Tail:** | Same fibers as the hackle. |
| **Body:** | Muskrat. |
| **Hackle:** | Grizzly hen back or hen neck. |

**Comments:** An old-timer that imitates just about anything gray a trout might eat in a river.

**Hackled Skip Nymph.** The original Skip Nymph, with its guard-hair legs, imitates primarily mayfly nymphs, so it's normally tied on small- to medium-size hooks. The Hackled Skip Nymph, however, is tied larger—from size 12, 2X long and up—so it needs substantial legs to look convincing. The webby hackle spiraled up its thorax (and made tough with counter-windings of the rib wire) does the job. Mayfly and stonefly nymphs look much alike—elongated body, two or three tails, swollen thorax, six legs—so a Hackled Skip Nymph can suggest the nymph of the salmonfly stonefly, green drake mayfly, yellow sally stonefly, and the like. It's all a matter of coloring and size and how the fly is fished. You can use a black metal bead for a head—or a gold bead, if you think the trout won't be suspicious—and weight the fly a little or a lot. Tie it with a sparkling dubbing, if you like, and in any color scheme that matches what the trout are taking.

To make the thorax and legs, bind the copper wire used for the ribs at the front of the abdomen, but don't cut it off. Double back and bind the pheasant fiber butts. Strip one side of a hen back hackle with fibers of appropriate length. Bind the hackle, stripped side down, behind the eye—the hackle should project off the eye. Dub the thorax. Spiral the hackle gently back in three or four turns to the rear of the abdomen. Wind a turn of the copper wire over the tip of the hackle and then continue winding the wire forward in three or four spirals to the eye—now the hackle's fragile stem is reinforced and greatly toughened. Bind and cut the wire, trim out the hackle's tip, part the hackle fibers to the sides, and complete the pheasant fiber wing case and a thread (or dubbed) head. (The instructions for tying the Ultimate Skip Nymph on page 40 will help.)

This fly works—and not only as an imitation. Sometimes I just throw it out there when I think a big nymph with waving legs will move a trout. Often, it does.

## HACKLED SKIP NYMPH (STANDARD) — *Skip Morris*

*Tied by Skip Morris*

| | |
|---|---|
| **Hook:** | Heavy or standard wire, 2X or 3X long (a slow-curve shank is optional), sizes 12 to 6. |
| **Thread:** | Brown or tan 8/0, 6/0, or 3/0. |
| **Weight:** | Lead wire. |
| **Rib:** | Fine copper wire. |
| **Abdomen:** | Hare's mask fur or tan-brown rabbit fur. |

**Tail, back, and wing case:** One uncut section of pheasant tail fibers.

**Thorax:**   Same as the abdomen.

**Legs:**   One mottled brown hen back hackle, stripped on one side.

**Head (optional):** The same dubbing as in the abdomen.

**Comments:**   Imitates a number of large tannish brown mayfly and medium to fairly large stonefly nymphs.

## HACKLED SKIP NYMPH, DARK    *Skip Morris*

*Tied by Skip Morris*

**Hook:**   Heavy or standard wire, 2X or 3X long (a slow-curve shank is optional), sizes 12 to 6.

**Thread:**   Dark brown or brown 8/0, 6/0, or 3/0.

**Weight:**   Lead wire.

**Rib:**   Fine copper wire.

**Abdomen:**   Dyed brown hare's mask fur or dyed brown rabbit fur.

**Tail, back, and wing case:** One uncut section of dyed dark brown pheasant tail fibers.

**Thorax:**   Same as the abdomen.

**Legs:**   One dark brown hen back hackle, stripped on one side.

**Head (optional):** The same dubbing used for the abdomen.

**Comments:**   Imitates a number of large, dark mayfly and medium to fairly large stonefly nymphs.

## HACKLED SKIP NYMPH, ULTIMATE (STANDARD)    *Skip Morris*

*Tied by Carol Ann Morris*

**Hook:**   Heavy or standard wire, 2X or 3X long (a slow-curve shank is optional), sizes 12 to 6.

**Head:**   Black metal bead, smallish.

**Weight (optional):** Lead or lead-substitute wire.

**Thread:**   Brown or tan 8/0, 6/0, or 3/0.

**Rib:**   Fine copper wire.

**Abdomen:**   Arizona Sparkle Nymph Dubbing in Skip's tannish brown, or hare's mask or tan-brown rabbit fur blended with fine Mylar in brown, silver, and pearl.

**Tail, back, and wing case:** One uncut section of undyed pheasant tail fibers.

**Thorax:**   Same as the abdomen.

**Legs:**   One mottled brown hen back hackle, stripped on one side.

**Comments:**   The Ultimate versions of the Hackled Skip Nymph sink faster than the original, and sparkle. A little brilliance can suggest a nymph ripe to hatch or just catch a trout's attention. Imitates a number of large tannish-brown mayfly and medium to fairly large stonefly nymphs.

## HACKLED SKIP NYMPH, ULTIMATE, DARK    *Skip Morris*

*Tied by Al Davis*

**Hook:**   Heavy or standard wire, 2X or 3X long (a slow-curve shank is optional), sizes 12 to 6.

**Head:**   Black metal bead, smallish.

**Weight (optional):** Lead wire.

**Thread:**   Dark brown or tan 8/0, 6/0, or 3/0.

**Rib:**   Fine copper wire.

**Abdomen:**   Arizona Sparkle Nymph Dubbing in dark brown, or hare's mask or dyed dark brown rabbit fur blended with fine Mylar in brown, silver, and pearl.

**Tail, back, and wing case:** One uncut section of dyed dark brown pheasant tail fibers.

**Thorax:**   Same as the abdomen.

**Legs:**   One natural or dyed dark brown hen back hackle, stripped on one side.

**Comments:**   See the comments for the Hackled Skip Nymph, Ultimate, on this page. Imitates a number of large, dark mayfly and medium to fairly large stonefly nymphs.

## HACKLED SKIP NYMPH, ULTIMATE, OLIVE
### Skip Morris

*Tied by Al Davis*

| | |
|---|---|
| **Hook:** | Heavy or standard wire, 2X or 3X long (a slow-curve shank is optional), sizes 12 to 6. |
| **Head:** | Black metal bead, smallish. |

**Weight (optional):** Lead wire.

| | |
|---|---|
| **Thread:** | Olive 8/0, 6/0, or 3/0. |
| **Rib:** | Fine copper wire. |
| **Abdomen:** | Arizona Sparkle Nymph Dubbing in olive, or dyed olive hare's mask or rabbit fur blended with fine Mylar in olive, silver, and pearl. |

**Tail, back, and wing case:** One uncut section of dyed dark green or olive pheasant tail fibers.

| | |
|---|---|
| **Thorax:** | Same as the abdomen. |
| **Legs:** | One mottled brown hen back hackle (or dyed olive or green), stripped on one side. |
| **Comments:** | See the comments for the Hackled Skip Nymph, Ultimate (Standard) on page 199. Imitates a number of large, dark mayfly and medium to fairly large stonefly nymphs. |

## HALFBACK

*Tied by Skip Morris*

| | |
|---|---|
| **Hook:** | Heavy wire, 1X to 3X long, sizes 12 to 8. |
| **Thread:** | Black 8/0 or 6/0. |

**Weight (optional):** Lead or lead-substitute wire.

| | |
|---|---|
| **Tail:** | Pheasant rump or pheasant tail fibers. |
| **Abdomen:** | Peacock herl, spun around the working thread. |

**Wing case and legs:** Same fibers as the tail, pulled over the thorax for a wing case; the tips are pulled down (or divided to the sides) and bound for legs.

| | |
|---|---|
| **Thorax:** | Peacock herl, spun around the working thread. |
| **Comments:** | A Canadian pattern that's very popular on lakes but also a fine choice for imitating the mayfly and stonefly nymphs of rivers. |

## MATT'S FUR
### Matt Levell

*Tied by Skip Morris*

| | |
|---|---|
| **Hook:** | Heavy wire, 3X to 6X long, sizes 12 to 6. |
| **Thread:** | Brown 8/0, 6/0, or 3/0. |

**Weight (optional):** Lead wire.

| | |
|---|---|
| **Tail:** | Fibers from a mallard flank feather dyed wood-duck color. |
| **Rib:** | Oval gold tinsel. |
| **Abdomen:** | Half otter and half cream seal-like dubbing (SLF or Simi Seal), blended. |

**Wing case and legs:** Mallard feather dyed wood-duck color, pulled forward for the wing case; the tips are divided to the sides and bound for legs.

| | |
|---|---|
| **Thorax:** | Same as the abdomen. |
| **Comments:** | A golden stonefly nymph? A large yellow sally nymph? A green drake nymph just molted? The Matt's Fur can suggest all sorts of pale nymphs, and trout just seem to like it. |

## MUSKRAT
### Polly Rosborough

*Tied by Skip Morris*

| | |
|---|---|
| **Hook:** | Heavy wire, 2X or 3X long, sizes 14 to 8. |
| **Thread:** | Black 8/0, 6/0, or 3/0. |
| **Body:** | Muskrat fur, twisted tightly in a dubbing loop to suggest segmentation (instructions are on page 95), then scored to appear shaggy. |
| **Legs:** | Speckled fibers from a guinea flank feather (or dark teal) tied in as a beard. |
| **Head:** | Black ostrich herl. |
| **Comments:** | Can suggest just about any gray living thing in a river. |

## RED FOX-SQUIRREL HAIR NYMPH — *Dave Whitlock*

*Tied by Dave Whitlock*

**Hook:** Heavy wire, 2X or 3X long (a slow-curve shank is optional), sizes 18 to 2.
**Thread:** Black or orange 6/0.
**Weight:** Lead wire.
**Tail:** Guard hairs and under-fur from the back of a red fox-squirrel.
**Rib:** Fine oval gold tinsel.
**Abdomen:** Blend of one part natural light red fox-squirrel belly fur and one part Antron dubbing in a similar shade, or Dave Whitlock SLF Dubbing in color #1.
**Thorax:** Blend of one part natural dark red fox-squirrel back guard hairs and underfur and one part charcoal Antron dubbing, or Dave Whitlock SLF Dubbing in color #2.
**Hackle:** Natural tan-brown hen back or partridge, one turn only.
**Comments:** A popular nymph that can suggest a larva, pupa, or nymph—especially one that is pale or just molted.

## RED FOX-SQUIRREL HAIR NYMPH, BEAD HEAD, HACKLED — *Dave Whitlock*

*Tied by Peter Morrison*

**Hook:** Heavy wire, 2X or 3X long, sizes 18 to 2.
**Head:** Gold metal bead.
**Weight:** Lead or lead-substitute wire.
**Thread:** Black 6/0 or 8/0 or, for the largest hooks, 3/0.
**Tail:** Red fox-squirrel back guard hairs and underfur inside two strands of pumpkin seed Sili Legs (or any fine rubber-strand in pale orange or tan). Trim the strands to match the length of the squirrel hairs.
**Rib:** Fine oval gold tinsel.

**Abdomen:** Whitlock+SLF Dubbing #2, Red Fox-Squirrel Nymph—Abdomen. Or a blend of one part red fox-squirrel belly fur and one part Antron dubbing in a similar shade.
**Legs:** Sili Legs in pumpkin seed with orange metal flake (or any pale orange or tan fine rubber-strand). One strand bound under the thorax dubbing on either side, resulting in four legs, each just short of a full hook length.
**Thorax:** Whitlock+SLF Dubbing #1, Red Fox-Squirrel Nymph—Thorax. Or red fox-squirrel back guard hairs and underfur.
**Hackle:** One turn of natural dark ginger hen back. Wind the hackle at the front of the abdomen.
**Comments:** The hackled version, with its supple tentacle legs, suggests a mayfly or stonefly nymph more than a larva.

## TELLICO

*Tied by Peter Morrison*

**Hook:** Heavy wire, standard length or 1X long, sizes 16 to 10.
**Thread:** Black 8/0 or 6/0.
**Weight:** Lead wire.
**Tail:** Guinea.
**Rib:** Peacock herl spun with heavy olive or black thread.
**Back:** Peacock herl.
**Body:** Yellow floss.
**Hackle:** Brown hen back.
**Comments:** The original used just fragile bare peacock herl as a rib, which was always the first component to fail. But spun with thread, the rib is tough. This old-timer keeps coming back, so it must be good. It suggests caddis larvae and pupae and cranefly larvae. It's also a good attractor pattern.

202

**Multipurpose Imitations**

## WD40 (HEAVY WIRE HOOK) — *Mark Engler*

*Tied by Skip Morris*

**Hook:** Heavy wire, short to 1X long (straight or humped shank), sizes 28 to 16.
**Thread:** Olive-brown 8/0 or 6/0.
**Tail:** Natural dark bronze mallard.
**Abdomen:** The working thread, wound up the tail and wing-case fibers.
**Wing case:** Butts of the fibers used for the tail, uncut, doubled back, and then pulled forward after the thorax is dubbed.
**Thorax:** Muskrat.
**Comments:** The WD40 is generally seen as a midge emerger, but Mark often ties it as described above, on a heavy wire hook, and fishes it deep as an imitation of a *Baetis* mayfly nymph or midge larva or pupa.

## ZUG BUG — *Cliff Zug*

*Tied by Skip Morris*

**Hook:** Heavy wire, 1X or 2X long, sizes 14 to 10.
**Thread:** Black 8/0 or 6/0.
**Weight:** Lead or lead-substitute wire.
**Tail:** Peacock sword fibers.
**Rib:** Narrow oval gold tinsel.
**Body:** Peacock herl.
**Hackle:** Brown hen neck.
**Wing case:** Section of mallard dyed wood-duck color, trimmed short (or a triangular section left from stripping the lower stem and trimming off the tip end, bound on by the stripped stem, as shown in the photo).
**Comments:** Imitates all sorts of dark nymphs and larvae. Most fly fishers trust the quiet sparkle of peacock herl, and the Zug Bug is loaded with it.

# Multipurpose Imitative Emergers

In other chapters you'll see soft-hackled flies and flymphs, and many of these are treated as multipurpose emergers too (as are some wet flies).

## CDC PARACHUTE EMERGER — *Cliff Sullivan*

*Tied by Todd Smith*

**Hook:** Light wire, humped shank (pupa-emerger hook), sizes 22 to 14.
**Thread:** Black 8/0 or 6/0.
**Shuck:** Section of turkey tail (fibers without the white tip).
**Rib:** Fine copper wire.
**Abdomen:** The section of turkey tail used for the shuck.
**Parachute wing:** White Float-Vis or poly yarn (instructions are on page 63).
**Thorax:** Brown Super Fine Dry Fly dubbing (or any fine, buoyant synthetic dubbing).
**Parachute hackle:** White CDC (instructions are on page 70).
**Comments:** Buoyed by its CDC hackle, the CDC Parachute Emerger suggests hatching mayflies, caddisflies, and even midges.

## KLINKHAMER SPECIAL — Hans Van Klinken

*Tied by Skip Morris*

**Hook:** Light wire, curved shank (pupa-emerger hook or slow-curve shank), sizes 18 to 8. (Hans has developed his own line of hooks for the Klinkhamer with the Partridge company.)

**Thread:** Originally, gray or tan 8/0 or 6/0, but dark olive to match the thorax makes sense as an alternative.

**Parachute wing:** White poly yarn (instructions are on page 63).

**Abdomen:** Tan (or any imitative color) synthetic dubbing.

**Parachute hackle:** Natural light or dark or chestnut, but Hans says any hackle color is fair game (instructions are on page 63).

**Thorax:** Peacock herl.

**Comments:** Developed by Dutch gunnery-school commander Hans Van Klinken, the Klinkhamer Special flourished when it hit North America. Hans says that it imitates both emerging mayflies and caddisflies.

## NYMERGER — Darrel Martin

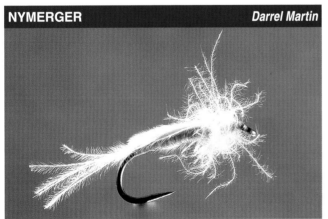

*Tied by Todd Smith*

**Hook:** Light wire, standard length or 1X long, sizes 24 to 18.

**Thread:** Tan 8/0.

**Tail-shuck and back:** Tan CDC. Pull most of the fibers forward over the top of the abdomen for the back and trim the remaining fibers for a tail-shuck.

**Abdomen:** The working thread.

**Thorax and legs:** Tan CDC fibers, dubbed back from the eye and then teased out the sides and trimmed to leg length.

**Wing case:** Tips of the back fibers doubled back and bound at the rear of the thorax.

**Comments:** Darrel Martin—a knowledgeable and creative fly tier and author of some fine tying books—says that "If trout are sipping small stuff from the water, the Nymerger is my first choice." His Nymerger, made with just thread and CDC, imitates tiny emerging midges, mayflies, and caddis. You can tie it in whatever color suits you or matches the insects you wish to imitate.

## PARA-EMERGER — Gerhard Laible

*Tied by Todd Smith*

**Hook:** Light wire, standard length or 1X long, sizes 18 to 12.

**Thread:** Black 8/0.

**Tail:** Brown hackle fibers.

**Body:** Brown mink dubbing (or buoyant synthetic dubbing such as Antron or Super Fine Dry Fly).

**Wing (wing case):** Strip of yellow closed-cell foam, doubled.

**Parachute hackle:** Dyed tan CDC (instructions are on page 70).

**Thorax:** Same as the abdomen.

**Comments:** Easy to see, thanks to the yellow foam wing, and buoyant, thanks to both the wing and the CDC. Imitates hatching mayflies in particular, but also caddisflies and midges.

## SNOWSHOE-HARE EMERGER — *Jim Cannon*

*Tied by Todd Smith*

| | |
|---|---|
| **Hook:** | Fine wire, humped shank (pupa-emerger hook), sizes 22 to 18. |
| **Thread:** | Olive 8/0. |
| **Abdomen:** | Dyed olive goose biot. |
| **Burst shuck:** | Butts of the wing. |
| **Wing:** | Snowshoe hare. |
| **Thorax:** | Dyed olive beaver underfur (or buoyant synthetic dubbing such as poly, Super Fine Dry Fly, Antron . . .). |

**Comments:** Dub the thorax. Trim off a bunch of fur from the middle to the heel of a snowshoe hare's foot. Mix the fur in your hands. Grasp the tips of the fur and pull them out—this will remove aligned fibers whose tips are not quite even. Bind these evened fibers atop the thorax area, trim off the butts over the rear of the thorax, pull the tips of hair back, build thread turns against the front of the hair to lock it upright, and then dub in front of the wing. The design is similar to my Morris Emerger (see chapter 4), but with snowshoe hare in place of deer. Snowshoe hare foot fur is naturally buoyant, making this a long-floating fly pattern. It imitates midges primarily but looks like an emerging mayfly to me. You can tie it in tan, brown, gray, or whatever.

## WD40 — *Mark Engler*

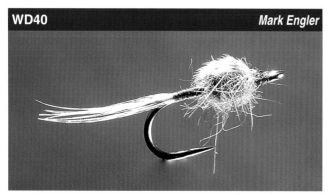

*Tied by Skip Morris*

| | |
|---|---|
| **Hook:** | Light wire, short shank or standard length (straight shank or scud-type curved shank), sizes 28 to 16. |
| **Thread:** | Olive-brown 8/0 or 6/0. (Olive-brown was the original color, but brown, olive, black, gray, and dark gray are now common. The thread color often echoes thorax color.) |
| **Tail-shuck:** | Bronze mallard. (Mark prefers mallard from the shoulder of the bird, which is tougher than mallard flank. Bronze mallard can be light or dark; light was used on the original, but Mark now uses both.) |
| **Abdomen:** | The working thread, wound up the tail and wing-case fibers. |
| **Wing case:** | Butts of the fibers used for the tail, uncut, doubled back, and then pulled forward after the thorax is dubbed. |
| **Thorax:** | Muskrat. (Rabbit in black, dark gray, and dark brown is also popular—black and gray for midges, dark gray and dark brown for *Baetis*.) |

**Comments:** The WD40 has really caught on as an imitation of both an emerging midge, in which case the tail suggests a shuck, and an emerging *Baetis* mayfly, in which case the tail suggests a tail. Fish the WD40 dead drift.

# Multipurpose Imitative Dry Flies

## BLUE DUN PARACHUTE (OR PARACHUTE BLUE DUN)

*Tied by Skip Morris*

| | |
|---|---|
| **Hook:** | Light wire, standard length or 1X long, sizes 18 to 10. |
| **Thread:** | Gray 6/0 or 8/0. |
| **Parachute wing:** | White calf-tail hair (or, for higher visibility, bright poly yarn in orange, yellow, red, or white; instructions for making a parachute hackle are on page 63). |
| **Tail:** | Blue dun hackle fibers. |
| **Parachute hackle:** | Blue dun (instructions are on page 63). |
| **Body:** | Muskrat fur or medium gray synthetic dubbing. |

**Comments:** A parachute version of the classic Blue Dun dry fly that can imitate all sorts of grayish-bodied mayfly duns and just about anything grayish if the trout are open-minded.

## CANOE FLY

*Tied by Carol Ann Morris*

**Hook:** Light (or standard) wire, standard length or 1X long, sizes 16 to 6.

**Thread:** 8/0, 6/0, or 3/0 in a color to blend with the body color.

**Body:** Synthetic dubbing (poly, Antron, Super Fine Dry Fly) in any caddis or stonefly color.

**Wing and head:** Natural dark or light deer hair.

**Comments:** An extremely simple and modestly buoyant dry fly that can be adjusted (by changing hook size and coloring) to loosely imitate most caddisflies and stoneflies.

## GENERAL PRACTITIONER                     *Ed Engle*

*Tied by Al Davis*

**Hook:** Light wire, short to 1X long, size 18 and smaller.

**Thread:** 8/0 in a color close to the wing color.

**Abdomen:** Very fine dubbing in any color that matches the natural.

**Wing:** Bleached elk or deer hair; Z-lon or Antron for the tiniest hooks. The tips make a down-wing, and the butts are tipped upright as the foundation for the parachute hackle.

**Parachute hackle:** Barred ginger, grizzly, or cree, wound parachute style around the trimmed butts of the wing (instructions are on page 63).

**Thorax:** Same as the abdomen.

**Comments:** Ed uses his General Practitioner for midge, microcaddis, and blue-winged olive hatches.

## LIGHT CAHILL PARACHUTE

*Tied by Skip Morris*

**Hook:** Light wire, standard length or 1X long, sizes 18 to 10.

**Thread:** Tan 8/0 or 6/0.

**Parachute wing:** White calf tail (instructions are on page 63).

**Tail:** Ginger hackle fibers.

**Parachute hackle:** Ginger (instructions are on page 63).

**Body:** Badger underfur (or cream-colored synthetic dubbing).

**Comments:** An all-around pale mayfly imitation, but also an all-around imitation of a caddis adult, midge adult, or even small adult stonefly, if the trout aren't picky.

## PARACHUTE ADAMS

*Tied by Skip Morris*

**Hook:** Light wire, standard length or 1X long, sizes 20 to 10.

**Thread:** Black 8/0 or 6/0.

**Parachute wing:** White calf tail (instructions are on page 63).

**Tail:** Grizzly and brown hackle fibers, mixed, or natural black moose body hair.

**Parachute hackle:** Brown and grizzly, mixed (instructions are on page 63).

**Body:** Dubbed muskrat fur or darkish gray synthetic dubbing.

**Comments:** Wind the hackle as you would a conventional hackle—wind one hackle in open spirals; then wind the second in the space between the previous hackle turns. This is the parachute version of the somber and venerable Adams. Lots of fly fishers use it for nearly everything—mayflies, caddisflies, midges, small stoneflies, craneflies, moths, flying ants—and as an attractor.

**Stimulator.** Randall Kaufmann's Stimulator has become a true standard fly pattern. A lot of fly fishers reach for it out of reflex whenever a big dry fly seems in order. It needn't always be tied large, though. Mainly it's an imitation of stonefly and caddis adults. But often it's just a bushy attractor dry fly that struck someone as appropriate for the moment.

## STIMULATOR, GREEN — Randall Kaufmann

*Tied by Skip Morris*

| | |
|---|---|
| **Hook:** | Standard (or light) wire, 3X (or 2X) long (slow-curve shank preferred), sizes 18 to 10. |
| **Thread:** | Fluorescent fire orange (or orange or green) 8/0, 6/0, or 3/0. |
| **Tail:** | Natural gray elk hair (the butts of the hair help build up the abdomen while adding buoyancy). |
| **Rib:** | Fine gold wire. |
| **Abdomen:** | Bright green or olive Hare-Tron dubbing (or other coarse synthetic dubbing). |

**Abdomen hackle:** Brown saddle hackle, two sizes smaller than normally suited to the hook size. Bind the hackle on at the front of the abdomen, then wind it back to the bend in spirals. Bind the tip of the hackle at the bend with a couple of turns of the rib wire, and then spiral the wire forward through the hackle to the front of the abdomen. Bind and trim the wire, and continue tying.

| | |
|---|---|
| **Wing:** | Natural gray elk hair. |

**Thorax hackle:** Grizzly, spiraled over the thorax.

| | |
|---|---|
| **Thorax:** | Dyed amber goat hair, dubbed (or any amber synthetic dubbing). |

**Comments:** In his *Tying Dry Flies,* Randall calls his Green Stimulator "an excellent searching pattern and particularly effective for greenish-colored stoneflies and caddis."

## STIMULATOR, BLACK — Randall Kaufmann

*Tied by Skip Morris*

| | |
|---|---|
| **Hook:** | Standard (or light) wire, 3X (or 2X) long (slow-curve shank preferred), sizes 8 and 6. |
| **Thread:** | Fluorescent fire orange (or orange or black) 8/0, 6/0, or 3/0. |
| **Tail:** | Dyed black elk hair (the butts of the hair help build up the abdomen while adding buoyancy). |
| **Rib:** | Fine gold wire. |
| **Abdomen:** | Blend of dyed goat hair—black, purple, claret, rust, and orange—dubbed (or just black synthetic dubbing). |

**Abdomen hackle:** Dark blue dun saddle, two sizes smaller than normally suited to the hook size. Bind the hackle on at the front of the abdomen, then wind it back to the bend in spirals. Bind the tip of the hackle at the bend with a couple of turns of the rib wire, and then spiral the wire forward through the hackle to the front of the abdomen. Bind and trim the wire, and continue tying.

| | |
|---|---|
| **Wing:** | Dyed black elk hair. |

**Thorax hackle:** Grizzly, spiraled over the thorax.

| | |
|---|---|
| **Thorax:** | Fluorescent fire orange Antron dubbing (or any orange synthetic dubbing). |

**Comments:** Designed to imitate the salmonfly, but the Black Stimulator also makes a good attractor pattern.

## STIMULATOR, ORANGE — *Randall Kaufmann*

*Tied by Skip Morris*

**Hook:** Standard (or light) wire, 3X (or 2X) long (slow-curve shank preferred), sizes 16 to 4.

**Thread:** Fluorescent fire orange (or orange) 8/0, 6/0, or 3/0.

**Tail:** Natural dark elk hair (the butts of the hair help build up the abdomen while adding buoyancy).

**Rib:** Fine gold wire.

**Abdomen:** Bright orange or rust-orange Hare-Tron or Antron dubbing.

**Abdomen hackle:** Furnace saddle, two sizes smaller than normally suited to the hook size. Bind the hackle on at the front of the abdomen, then wind it back to the bend in spirals. Bind the tip of the hackle at the bend with a couple of turns of the rib wire, and then spiral the wire forward through the hackle to the front of the abdomen. Bind and trim the wire, and continue tying.

**Wing:** Natural dark elk hair.

**Thorax hackle:** Grizzly, spiraled over the thorax.

**Thorax:** Dyed amber goat hair (or amber coarse synthetic dubbing, such as poly or Antron).

**Comments:** Mainly for imitating the salmonfly and October caddis, but all Stimulators make good attractor patterns.

## STIMULATOR, YELLOW — *Randall Kaufmann*

*Tied by Skip Morris*

**Hook:** Standard (or light) wire, 3X (or 2X) long (slow-curve shank preferred), sizes 16 to 6.

**Thread:** Fluorescent fire orange (or orange or yellow) 8/0, 6/0, or 3/0.

**Tail:** Natural light elk hair (the butts of the hair help build up the abdomen while adding buoyancy).

**Rib:** Fine gold wire.

**Abdomen:** Bright yellow Antron or Hare-Tron dubbing (or any coarse synthetic dubbing).

**Abdomen hackle:** Badger or ginger saddle hackle, two sizes smaller than normally suited to the hook size. Bind the hackle on at the front of the abdomen, and then wind it back to the bend in spirals. Bind the tip of the hackle at the bend with a couple of turns of the rib wire, then spiral the wire forward through the hackle to the front of the abdomen. Bind and trim the wire, and continue tying.

**Wing:** Natural light elk hair.

**Thorax hackle:** Grizzly, spiraled over the thorax.

**Thorax:** Dyed amber goat, dubbed (or any coarse synthetic dubbing in amber).

**Comments:** Designed mainly to imitate the yellow sally stoneflies but can probably pass for a grasshopper at times. All Stimulators make good attractor patterns.

**Woolly Wing.** The fact that wool floats has been almost entirely overlooked by fly tiers. It's possible they were fooled by the frequent use of wool for the heads of various sinking imitations of the sculpin, a broad-headed little fish that trout relish. But deer hair is also common in sculpin fly heads, and *everyone* knows that it's buoyant. In any case, it's time to spill the beans: wool indeed floats—high and long. I came to recognize this by chance, ignored it for a couple of decades, and finally ran with it. The result of my experiments is the Woolly Wing.

From underneath, where the trout see them, stoneflies and caddis look much alike, and both look a lot like the Woolly Wing. I'm convinced that a dry fly riding with its body down on the surface of the water, as the Woolly Wing rides, is the most convincing imitation of stoneflies and caddis, since both insects typically do the same with their bodies. And that stout bulk piercing the mirrored underside of the water offers a lot more to signal the trout than do the fine hackle points that hoist many bristly dry flies high atop the surface.

You can tie the Woolly Wing in the standard color and size variations I designed to imitate the most common western stoneflies and caddis, or you can tie it in whatever sizes and colors you prefer. Although I normally use it as an imitation, it also makes a fine attractor or just an all-purpose big dry fly.

Tying the Woolly Wing (which some call the Woolly Wonder) is much like tying the Mikulak Sedge (instructions are on page 111). The differences are (1) the Woolly Wing lacks the Mikulak's tail (which is actually part of the wing), (2) the wing of the Mikulak is uncut hair while the wing of the Woolly Wing is wool trimmed to shape, and (3) the Mikulak Sedge has a conventional hackle, while the Woolly Wing has a parachute hackle. (You can make a conventional hackle collar on the Woolly Wing if you prefer—it's easier and functions just fine. If you use the conventional hackle, add a short tuft of yellow wool atop the last section of the wing, as a strike indicator.)

To tie the Woolly Wing, bind on a butt of dubbing at the bend, then a hank of wool, a section of dubbing, another hank of wool, and so on, until you've covered about two-thirds of the shank with dubbing and wool. Hand-mix the wool for each wing section with fine Mylar strands, keeping the wool fibers and Mylar more or less aligned. Whip-finish the thread, but don't cut it. Remove the hook from the vise and trim the wing to the tapered shape of a real caddis wing. Return the hook to the vise. Bind a section of yellow wool (or another bright color) tightly against the front of the last wing section. Raise the ends of the yellow wool, bind up its base, and then complete a standard parachute hackle (instructions for making a parachute hackle are on page 63). Dub in front of the wing. Make a thread head.

## WOOLLY WING (OR WOOLLY WONDER), DARK BROWN
*Skip Morris*

*Tied by Skip Morris*

**Hook:** Light wire, standard length or 1X long, sizes 16 to 12.
**Thread:** Dark brown, olive or green 8/0 or 6/0.
**Wing:** Dyed dark brown wool mixed with fine black strands of Mylar (Lite Brite, Angel Hair . . .), bound at the bend and then in bunches up the body, trimmed to a low wing shape.
**Body:** Dark brown or black (blackish green is a good choice for the American grannom) Antron dubbing (or any buoyant synthetic dubbing) over the butts of each wing section.
**Parachute wing:** Yellow (or orange, red, or another highly visible color) wool or egg yarn, poly yarn, or Antron yarn (instructions are on page 63).
**Parachute hackle:** Brown (instructions are on page 63).
**Comments:** Imitates the American grannom caddis and the little black and little brown stoneflies.

## WOOLLY WING (OR WOOLLY WONDER), GOLD
*Skip Morris*

*Tied by Skip Morris*

**Hook:** Standard wire, 2X or 3X long, straight or slow-curve shank, sizes 10 to 6.
**Thread:** Gold or yellow 8/0, 6/0, or 3/0.
**Wing:** Dyed tan wool mixed with fine brown strands of Mylar (Lite Brite, Angel Hair . . .), bound at the bend and then in bunches up the body, trimmed to a low wing shape.
**Body:** Gold Antron dubbing (or any gold buoyant synthetic dubbing) over the butts of each wing section.
**Parachute wing:** Yellow (or orange, red, or another highly visible color) wool or egg yarn, poly yarn, or Antron yarn (instructions are on page 63).
**Parachute hackle:** Ginger (instructions are on page 63).
**Comments:** Imitates the golden stonefly.

## WOOLLY WING (OR WOOLLY WONDER), GREEN — *Skip Morris*

*Tied by Skip Morris*

**Hook:** Light wire, standard length or 1X long, sizes 14 to 8.
**Thread:** Green or olive 8/0 or 6/0.
**Wing:** Dyed gray wool mixed with strands of fine pearl Mylar (Lite Brite, Angel Hair . . .), bound at the bend and then in bunches up the body, trimmed to a low wing shape.
**Body:** Green Antron dubbing (or any green buoyant synthetic dubbing) over the butts of each wing section.
**Parachute wing:** Yellow (or orange, red, or another highly visible color) wool or egg yarn, poly yarn, or Antron yarn (instructions are on page 63).
**Parachute hackle:** Dyed green grizzly (instructions are on page 63).
**Comments:** Imitates the adult *Rhyacophila* or green rock worm. Can also suggest the greener specimens of the yellow sally stonefly complex.

## WOOLLY WING (OR WOOLLY WONDER), ORANGE — *Skip Morris*

*Tied by Skip Morris*

**Hook:** Light wire, 2X or 3X long, straight or slow-curve shank, sizes 8 to 4.
**Thread:** Orange 8/0, 6/0, or 3/0.
**Wing:** Dyed dark brown wool mixed with fine strands of brown Mylar (Lite Brite, Angel Hair . . .), bound at the bend and then in bunches up the body, trimmed to a low wing shape.
**Body:** Two-thirds orange Antron dubbing (or any buoyant synthetic dubbing) mixed with one-third brown, over the butts of each wing section.
**Parachute wing:** Yellow (or orange, red, or another highly visible color) wool or egg yarn, poly yarn, or Antron yarn (instructions are on page 63).
**Parachute hackle:** Brown (instructions are on page 63).
**Comments:** Imitates the two giants of western rivers: the salmonfly and the October caddis.

## WOOLLY WING (OR WOOLLY WONDER), TAN — *Skip Morris*

*Top view*

*Bottom view*

*Tied by Skip Morris*

**Hook:** Light wire, standard length or 1X long, sizes 16 to 8.
**Thread:** Tan 8/0 or 6/0.
**Wing:** Dyed medium brown wool mixed with fine brown strands of pearl Mylar (Lite Brite, Angel Hair . . .), bound at the bend and then in bunches up the body, trimmed to a low wing shape.
**Body:** Tan Antron dubbing (or any buoyant synthetic dubbing) over the butts of each wing section.
**Parachute wing:** Yellow (or orange, red, or another highly visible color) wool or egg yarn, poly yarn, or Antron yarn (instructions are on page 63).
**Parachute hackle:** Brown (instructions are on page 63).
**Comments:** Primarily for imitating the *Hydropsyche* or spotted sedge caddis, but also useful with the yellow sallies. The Woolly Wing, Tan is probably mistaken for a grasshopper now and then, if you tie it big enough.

# 11

# Wet Flies

SOMETHING RESEMBLING the traditional wet fly originated a few hundred years ago in England, where most authorities agree that fly fishing got its start. None of the patterns that follow is quite that old, but some go back well over a century and have endured for a good reason: they work. In addition, there are some new wet-fly patterns here that also work. Some of these newer patterns are fished differently from the traditional wet fly, and instructions for fishing them are provided in the "comments" sections of the dressings.

Traditional wet flies, such as the Alder and the Light Cahill, were long fished by dragging them slowly across the current—a wet-fly swing—and the fly fisher really added some action, made the flies jiggle and dart. Wet flies were often fished in groups of two or three strung up the leader on short lengths of tippet. But the dead-drift wet fly goes back at least five decades and makes a very natural and convincing presentation. Fished upstream and dead drift, the wet fly can suggest a mayfly dun that emerged from its shuck *underwater* to swim up to the water's surface (some do), a female caddis adult swimming down to lay her eggs (again, some do), or a drowned mayfly dun or alderfly adult. There are lots of possibilities for these elemental and versatile fly designs.

## ALDER — *Charles Kingsley*

*Tied by Skip Morris*

| | |
|---|---|
| **Hook:** | Heavy wire, standard length or 1X long, sizes 14 to 10. |
| **Thread:** | Black 8/0 or 6/0. |
| **Body:** | Peacock herl. |
| **Hackle:** | Black or brown hen neck. |
| **Wing:** | Mottled brown turkey quill sections. |

**Comments:** This one came from England long ago and remains, on both sides of the Atlantic, a popular imitation of the caddis-like alderfly that lives in the trees lining some rivers and lakes. Alderflies sink quickly after hitting the water, being erratic and clumsy fliers. Look for them on warm days in May, June, and into July. Fish the Alder dead drift or on a slow wet-fly swing.

## BLACK GNAT WET

*Tied by Peter Morrison*

| | |
|---|---|
| **Hook:** | Heavy wire, standard length or 1X long, sizes 16 to 10. |
| **Thread:** | Black 8/0 or 6/0. |
| **Tag:** | Red floss. |
| **Tail:** | Red hackle fibers. |
| **Body:** | Fine black chenille or black rabbit fur. |
| **Hackle:** | Black hen neck. |
| **Wing:** | Natural dark gray mallard wing quill sections. |

**Comments:** An old-timer that can suggest a drowned flying ant or even a beetle.

## COWDUNG

*Tied by Skip Morris*

| | |
|---|---|
| **Hook:** | Heavy wire, standard length to 1X long, sizes 16 to 10. |
| **Thread:** | Black 8/0 or 6/0. |
| **Tag:** | Flat gold tinsel. |
| **Body:** | Olive floss or wool yarn. |
| **Hackle:** | Brown hen neck. |
| **Wing:** | Mottled tan-brown turkey quill. |

## DARK CAHILL WET

*Tied by Skip Morris*

| | |
|---|---|
| **Hook:** | Heavy wire, standard length to 1X long, sizes 16 to 12. |
| **Thread:** | Black 8/0 or 6/0. |
| **Tail:** | Lemon wood duck (or mallard flank dyed wood-duck color). |
| **Body:** | Muskrat back fur. |
| **Hackle:** | Brown (or furnace) hen neck. |
| **Wing:** | Wood-duck (or mallard dyed wood-duck color) flank fibers. |

## DARK STONE — *Polly Rosborough*

*Tied by Peter Morrison*

| | |
|---|---|
| **Hook:** | Heavy wire, 3X long, sizes 6 and 4. |
| **Thread:** | Black 6/0 or 3/0. |
| **Tail:** | Dark brown turkey tail fibers, short. |
| **Rib:** | Heavy gray thread (such as size A rod thread). |
| **Body:** | Tangerine-orange synthetic yarn. |
| **Hackle:** | Dark furnace hen neck; try to find a relatively soft-fibered hackle. |
| **Wing:** | Natural dark brown buck tail, sparse. Painting a fluorescent orange band over the top half of the thread head, in front of the wing, is optional. |

**Comments:** Hardly a traditional representative of the wet fly, this underwater version of Polly's Dark Stone imitates a salmonfly adult that has drowned. It's a perfectly plausible concept, guides have assured me. Fish it dead drift, unweighted, so it tumbles along freely. A strike indicator may help.

## DIVING CADDIS, BRIGHT GREEN — *Gary LaFontaine*

*Tied by Peter Morrison*

| | |
|---|---|
| **Hook:** | Heavy wire, standard length or 1X long, sizes 16 to 12. |
| **Thread:** | Black 6/0. |
| **Body:** | Bright olive green Antron dubbing. |
| **Wing:** | Clear Antron yarn over grouse fibers. |
| **Hackle:** | Brown dry-fly hackle (or hen neck), sparse. |

**Comments:** Gary was something of a caddisfly authority and designed his Diving Caddis to imitate those species that swim underwater to deposit their eggs, which makes them pretty easy prey. The standard approach is to fish a Diving Caddis dead drift, perhaps below a larger dry fly as an indicator.

## DIVING CADDIS, GRAY — *Gary LaFontaine*

*Tied by Todd Smith*

| | |
|---|---|
| **Hook:** | Heavy wire, standard length or 1X long, sizes 16 to 12. |
| **Thread:** | Black 6/0. |
| **Body:** | Medium gray Antron dubbing. |
| **Wing:** | Clear Antron yarn over grouse fibers. |
| **Hackle:** | Bronze-dun (gray with a touch of brown) dry-fly hackle (or hen neck), sparse. |

**Comments:** See the comments for the Diving Caddis, Bright Green, on this page.

## DIVING CADDIS, TAN — *Gary LaFontaine*

*Tied by Skip Morris*

| | |
|---|---|
| **Hook:** | Heavy wire, standard length or 1X long, sizes 16 to 12. |
| **Thread:** | Black 6/0. |
| **Body:** | Tan-brown Antron dubbing. |
| **Wing:** | Clear Antron yarn over grouse fibers. |
| **Hackle:** | Brown dry-fly hackle (or hen neck), sparse. |

**Comments:** See the comments for the Diving Caddis, Bright Green, on this page.

## GOLDEN STONE — *Polly Rosborough*

*Tied by Skip Morris*

**Hook:** Heavy wire, 3X long, sizes 6 to 4.
**Thread:** Gold (or yellow) 6/0 or 3/0.
**Rib:** Heavy antique gold thread (such as size A rod thread).
**Body:** Antique gold synthetic yarn (such as Antron).
**Hackle:** Dyed gold barred teal fibers as a beard.
**Wing:** Natural light brown buck tail, dyed gold (or undyed).
**Comments:** Polly's Golden Stone, in this wet fly version, imitates a golden stonefly adult that has drowned. Fish it dead drift, unweighted, so it tumbles along freely. A strike indicator may help.

## HARE'S EAR WET

*Tied by Skip Morris*

**Hook:** Heavy wire, standard length or 1X long, sizes 16 to 12.
**Thread:** Orange or black 6/0 or 8/0.
**Tail:** Brown hackle fibers.
**Rib:** Gold oval or narrow flat tinsel.
**Body:** Hare's mask, heavier and picked out around the thorax area.
**Wing:** Natural gray duck quill sections (or hen pheasant wing quill sections).
**Comments:** Also known as the Gold-Ribbed Hare's Ear Wet—the companion to the ever-popular Gold-Ribbed Hare's Ear nymph. This somber wet fly can imitate mayfly or caddisfly adults that have drowned or are swimming down to lay their eggs.

## LEADWING COACHMAN

*Tied by Skip Morris*

**Hook:** Heavy wire, standard length or 1X long, sizes 16 to 10.
**Thread:** Black 8/0 or 6/0.
**Tag (optional):** Gold tinsel.
**Body:** Peacock herl.
**Hackle:** Brown hen back.
**Wing:** Natural gray duck quill sections.

## LIGHT CAHILL WET

*Tied by Skip Morris*

**Hook:** Heavy wire, standard length or 1X long, sizes 16 to 12.
**Thread:** Cream or tan 8/0 or 6/0.
**Hackle:** Light ginger hen neck.
**Tail:** Light ginger hen neck fibers.
**Body:** Cream fox fur or dyed fur substitute.
**Wing:** Wood-duck (or mallard dyed wood-duck color) flank fibers.

## MCGINTY

*Tied by Skip Morris*

**Hook:**      Heavy wire, standard length or 1X long, sizes 14 to 10.
**Thread:**    Black 8/0 or 6/0.
**Tail:**      Barred teal over red hackle fibers.
**Body:**      One strand each of black and yellow chenille wound
               together for a banded effect.
**Hackle:**    Brown hen neck.
**Wing:**      White-tipped mallard secondary quill sections.
**Comments:**  Obviously based on some kind of bee. Trout do eat bees (or
so I've been told by reliable sources), but it's probably fairly rare. Still, the
McGinty offers trout something distinctive and familiar. This is a popular fly
among warm-water fly fishers targeting bluegills and panfish.

## ROYAL COACHMAN WET

*Tied by Todd Smith*

**Hook:**      Heavy wire, standard length or 1X long, sizes 14 to 10.
**Thread:**    Black 8/0 or 6/0.
**Tail:**      Golden pheasant tippets.
**Body:**      Front and rear thirds are peacock herl; center third is red
               floss.
**Hackle:**    Brown hen neck.
**Wing:**      White mallard wing quill.
**Comments:**  The century-long popularity of the Royal Coachman dry fly
led to this wet-fly version. Though fanciful, it works—a sort of attractor wet
fly.

## SUNKEN STONEFLY, SALMONFLY

See chapter 6, Stoneflies.

# Soft-Hackled Flies and Flymphs

A WINGLESS, ELEMENTAL fly design with long, supple fibers waving around the bend of its hook made a comeback in 1975 when Sylvester Nemes's book *The Soft-Hackled Fly* came out. The soft-hackled fly had originally debuted close to a century before, in 1886, in a book titled *North-Country Flies*. But it had largely been forgotten by the time Nemes pulled it out of obscurity and held it up to the fly-fishing world. It was well worth a second look. The characteristics that distinguish a soft-hackled fly, or soft-hackle, are its long-fibered hackle collar and its uncluttered form—only the fancy ones have a rib or a tail. Soft-hackles are meant to be fished very quietly—they seem to struggle weakly against the current and lose to it—with a slow cross-stream swing and plenty of mends of the line. But they can also be fished with floatant, half awash and dead drift, like a drowned mayfly or emerging caddis.

The flymph is the creation of Pete Hidy, who revealed the design in the 1971 edition of his book *The Art of Tying the Wet Fly*. In it, Hidy tells us to cast a flymph upstream of a working trout, tug the fly under, and then swing it gently across the trout's nose. Similar to the soft-hackle in appearance, the flymph has a shorter, slightly more rigid hackle, so the fibers can best catch and hold bubbles of air; under water the thread's color is supposed to shade the spiky, translucent dubbing of the body; and flymphs have tails.

## *BAETIS* SOFT-HACKLE

*Tied by Skip Morris*

**Hook:** Heavy wire, 1X long, sizes 20 to 14.
**Thread:** Gray 8/0 or 6/0.
**Tail:** Blue dun hen neck fibers.
**Body:** Gray dubbing (rabbit or, if you want some sparkle, Antron or Arizona Sparkle Nymph dubbing).
**Hackle:** Blue dun hen neck.
**Comments:** Imitates, specifically, the emerging *Baetis* mayfly. Fish it as you would any soft-hackled fly.

## ENGLE'S MICRO SOFT-HACKLE   *Ed Engle*

*Tied by Wade Malwitz*

**Hook:** Light wire, 1X long (or standard length or short), sizes 22 to 18.
**Thread:** Black 8/0.
**Abdomen:** Dyed olive rabbit underfur (or any midge body color).
**Hackle:** Partridge after-shaft feather (the fine, small, elongated, fluffy feather that lies along each big, broad feather). Wind the after-shaft feather with care—its stem is fragile.
**Comments:** The fibers of the after-shaft feather are so soft that too much imparted motion will flatten them back, but tiny movements will make them billow. Ed fishes his Engle's Micro Soft-Hackle to trout bulging the surface after emerging midges or deep along the streambed, dead drift, early in the hatch, when the trout are taking the ripe pupae as they begin their ascent.

## GRAY HACKLE PEACOCK

*Tied by Deken Loveless*

**Hook:** Heavy wire, standard wire or 1X long, sizes 16 to 10.
**Thread:** Black 8/0 or 6/0.
**Tag:** Oval or narrow flat gold tinsel.
**Tail:** Dyed scarlet red hackle fibers (any kind).
**Body:** Peacock herl.
**Hackle:** Grizzly hen neck.

## GRIZZLY AND GREY (FLYMPH)

*Tied by Dave Hughes*

**Hook:** Heavy wire, standard length (standard wet-fly hook), sizes 16 to 12.
**Thread:** Black 6/0 or 8/0 (silk preferred).
**Tail:** Grizzly hen neck.
**Rib:** Silver Mylar oval or flat tinsel.
**Body:** Muskrat.
**Hackle:** Grizzly hen neck.
**Comments:** Fly-fishing author Dave Hughes calls the Grizzly and Grey flymph "sort of an underwater version of the ubiquitous and fatal Adams, and works for the same reasons: it looks a little bit like a lot of living things." He fishes the Grizzly and Grey during mayfly spinner falls, egg-laying flights of caddis, and, especially, hatches of black midges (tied very small, I assume). Dave likes to fish flymph patterns, including the Grizzly and Grey, in various ways—floating, dead drift, swung. Flymphs were originally tied with a short collar of close turns of hackle, but Dave likes to wind the hackle back in open spiraled turns and then spiral the working thread forward through the turns of hackle. This spreads the hackle and toughens its stem.

## HARE'S EAR FLYMPH

*Tied by Dave Hughes*

**Hook:** Heavy wire, standard length, sizes 16 to 12.
**Thread:** Orange 8/0 or 6/0 (silk preferred).
**Tail:** Three pheasant tail fibers.
**Rib:** Oval gold tinsel.
**Body:** Hare's mask fur.
**Hackle:** Brown hen neck.
**Comments:** For tying instructions, see the Grizzly and Grey (Flymph) on page 216. An old and proven flymph dressing that Dave considers an excellent imitation of the *Hydropsyche* caddis adult as it swims down to deposit its eggs. When adults swarm, he casts the Hare's Ear Flymph above a working fish and swings the fly slowly in front of the fish's nose. If lots of fish are working together, he just swings the fly through the action.

## LITTLE OLIVE FLYMPH                *Dave Hughes*

*Tied by Dave Hughes*

**Hook:** Heavy wire, standard length, sizes 20 to 14.
**Thread:** Green 8/0 or 6/0 (silk preferred).
**Tail:** Light blue dun hen neck fibers.
**Rib:** Oval gold tinsel.
**Body:** Dyed olive rabbit (or Hare-Tron, a mix of rabbit and Antron fibers).
**Hackle:** Light blue dun hen neck.
**Comments:** Designed for hatches of *Baetis* mayflies. Dave often treats it as an emerger by snapping the moisture out of the fly on a sharp casting stroke and fishing it dead drift to trout rising during the hatch. If the fly makes it halfway through its drift without a take, he tugs it under and works it on a very slow swing "as the wingless wet fly it is tied to be." See the Grizzly and Grey flymph on page 216 for tying instructions.

## MARCH BROWN FLYMPH

*Tied by Rick Hafele*

**Hook:** Light wire, 1X long, sizes 20 to 10.
**Thread:** Maroon (or tan) silk (or 8/0).
**Tail:** Light brown hen neck hackle fibers.
**Rib:** Fine oval or flat gold tinsel.
**Body:** Dark to light brown natural dubbing (dyed rabbit is good).
**Hackle:** Light brown hen neck hackle.
**Comments:** Rick Hafele, professional entomologist and fly-fishing author, is a fan of flymphs. According to him, in addition to imitating the March brown mayfly, this fly tied in other sizes and colors can imitate the pale morning dun and western green drake, which also emerge from their shucks underwater. He fishes it both dead drift, just an inch or two down, and on a slow wet-fly swing, sometimes allowing it to sink a bit before it rises on the drag of the leader.

## MARCH BROWN SPIDER

*Tied by Skip Morris*

**Hook:** Heavy wire, standard length or 1X long, sizes 18 to 10.
**Thread:** Orange 8/0 or 6/0.
**Rib:** Fine oval or narrow flat gold tinsel.
**Body:** Hare's mask fur.
**Hackle:** Brown partridge flank (or substitute hen back).
**Comments:** This particularly versatile soft-hackled fly is my favorite. It can suggest just about anything that hatches at the water's surface, and I've caught a lot of trout on it.

## PARTRIDGE AND GREEN

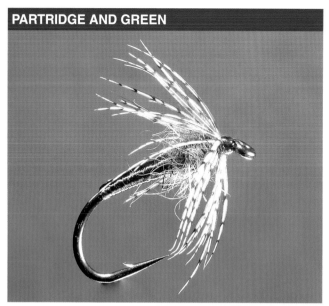

*Tied by Skip Morris*

**Hook:** Heavy wire, standard length or 1X long, sizes 18 to 10.
**Thread:** Olive 8/0 or 6/0.
**Abdomen:** Green floss.
**Thorax:** Hare's mask fur, dubbed.
**Hackle:** Natural gray partridge flank (or substitute hen back).

## PARTRIDGE AND ORANGE

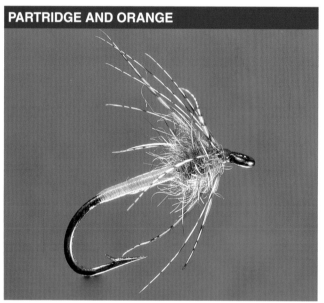

*Tied by Skip Morris*

**Hook:** Heavy wire, standard length or 1X long, sizes 18 to 10.
**Thread:** Orange 8/0 or 6/0.
**Abdomen:** Orange floss.
**Thorax:** Hare's mask fur, dubbed short and thick.
**Hackle:** Natural brown partridge flank (or substitute hen back).

## PARTRIDGE AND YELLOW

*Tied by Skip Morris*

**Hook:** Heavy wire, standard length or 1X long, sizes 18 to 10.
**Thread:** Yellow 6/0 or 8/0.
**Abdomen:** Yellow floss.
**Thorax:** Hare's mask fur.
**Hackle:** Gray partridge (or substitute hen back).

## PHEASANT TAIL SOFT-HACKLE

*Tied by Skip Morris*

**Hook:** Heavy wire, standard wire or 1X long, sizes 18 to 10.
**Thread:** Brown 8/0 or 6/0.
**Tail:** Pheasant tail.
**Rib:** Fine gold wire.
**Body:** Pheasant tail.
**Hackle:** Natural gray or brown partridge (or hen back).

## STARLING AND HERL

*Tied by Dave Hughes*

**Hook:** Heavy wire, standard length or 1X long, sizes 18 and 16.

**Thread:** Black 8/0.

**Body:** Peacock herl.

**Hackle:** Starling body feather with iridescent sheen.

**Comments:** Prolific fly-fishing author Dave Hughes is a great fan of the Starling and Herl. Here is a quote from the letter he sent along with the sample he tied for this book: "This ancient soft-hackled wet, or spider, works as well today as it did when it was originated, in all likelihood because there are as many or more of the small black caddis around that it imitates. These are generally called Grannoms or Mother's Day caddis (Brachycentridae), the latter emerging in abundance in spring, the former in late August and September. It's often difficult to hook trout on dry flies during these prolific hatches, though trout do appear to be lofting their snouts out of the water to take floating adults. If your drys aren't as effective as you'd like, try casting the Starling and Herl just upstream from the rises; give it a tug to get it under; then fish it across the rising trout on a very slow swing, or even a dead drift. It's especially effective on tailwater flats, and in large eddies. Trout in such waters are difficult on top but can be surprisingly easy on an imitation fished just subsurface."

# 13

# Traditional Dry Flies

TO BE *TRADITIONAL,* some would say, a dry fly must have the standard bunched hackle fiber tail, split upright wings, and dense hackle collar configuration of the Adams or Royal Coachman, and the fly must be at least a few decades old. That's a reasonable view, but we took a more open-minded one. After all, the hair-bodied Rat-Faced McDougal and thistle-down Bivisible have been nestled next to the classic Royal Coachman in many fly boxes for quite a long time. These are all elegant old dry flies (if you're open-minded about the definition of "elegant").

It's reasonable to say that most traditional dry flies were designed to imitate mayfly duns. I've even seen the bodyless and absurd spiders and variants listed as imitations of big mayflies in the old texts. But a few, such as the Royal Coachman and Bivisible, seem to have been designed as attractors. Therefore, some of the traditional dry flies, as I define them, can be a solid choice during a mayfly hatch; others are appropriate when something a bit outlandish and unnatural is required or, in the case of the hairy Wulff dressings, when a buoyant high-floater is needed. Traditional dry flies work—that's how they got to be traditional.

## ADAMS
*Leonard Halladay*

**Front view**

*Tied by Skip Morris*

**Hook:** Light wire, standard length or 1X long, sizes 20 to 10.
**Thread:** Black 8/0 or 6/0.
**Wing:** Grizzly hackle tips (hen neck is best).
**Tail:** Grizzly and brown hackle fibers, mixed.
**Body:** Dubbed muskrat fur or darkish gray synthetic dubbing.
**Hackle:** Brown and grizzly, mixed.
**Comments:** A couple of decades ago, the Adams was *the* dry fly, and it was fished with or without hatches in all sorts of water and under all sorts of conditions. It's still popular and widely trusted. Writers have always described the Adams as "buggy," and when you contemplate its somber grays, creams, and browns and its insect-like barring, you can see why.

## ADAMS IRRESISTIBLE

*Tied by Skip Morris*

**Hook:** Light wire, standard length or 1X long, sizes 16 to 10.
**Thread:** Gray 8/0 or 6/0 (I prefer size A rod thread to make the flared hair body).
**Tail:** Grizzly and brown hackle fibers, mixed.
**Body:** Deer hair, flared and trimmed to shape (instructions are on page 268).
**Wing:** Grizzly hen neck hackles.
**Hackle:** Brown and grizzly, mixed.
**Comments:** A plump and extra-buoyant version of the Adams.

## BLACK GNAT

*Tied by Skip Morris*

**Hook:** Light wire, standard length or 1X long, sizes 18 to 12.
**Thread:** Black 8/0 or 6/0.
**Wing:** Natural gray duck quill sections.
**Tail:** Black hackle fibers.
**Body:** Black synthetic dubbing (chenille used to be the norm).
**Hackle:** Black.
**Comments:** A very dark all-purpose dry fly with a long history. I fished it all the time as a kid, and it's still good.

## BLUE DUN

*Tied by Skip Morris*

| | |
|---|---|
| **Hook:** | Light wire, standard length or 1X long, sizes 18 to 12. |
| **Thread:** | Gray 8/0 or 6/0. |
| **Wing:** | Duck quill sections. |
| **Tail:** | Blue dun hackle fibers. |
| **Body:** | Muskrat fur (or gray synthetic dubbing). |
| **Hackle:** | Blue dun. |

**Bivisible.** Odd as it is, the Bivisible was once on every trout fisher's short list of all-purpose dry flies. It's easy to understand why—it floats long and high and is easy to see on the water. The standard white face of hackle fibers makes this fly especially visible to anglers, while the dark body against the light sky makes it visible to trout—hence Bivisible. Some believe that all those hackle fibers below can interfere with hooking trout, particularly small trout. Still, Bivisibles work, and there is certainly a reason for their large following.

## BIVISIBLE, BLACK

*Tied by Todd Smith*

| | |
|---|---|
| **Hook:** | Light wire, standard length or 1X long, sizes 16 to 10. |
| **Thread:** | Black 8/0 or 6/0. |
| **Tail:** | Black hackle fibers. |
| **Hackle:** | Black hackle up most of the shank, with a single white hackle in front. |

## BIVISIBLE, BROWN

*Tied by Skip Morris*

| | |
|---|---|
| **Hook:** | Light wire, standard length or 1X long, sizes 16 to 10. |
| **Thread:** | Black or brown 8/0 or 6/0. |
| **Tail:** | Brown hackle fibers. |
| **Hackle:** | Brown hackle up most of the shank, with a single white hackle in front. |
| **Comments:** | Probably the most common version of the Bivisible. |

## BIVISIBLE, GINGER

*Tied by Todd Smith*

| | |
|---|---|
| **Hook:** | Light wire, standard length or 1X long, sizes 16 to 10. |
| **Thread:** | Black, brown, or tan 8/0 or 6/0. |
| **Tail:** | Ginger hackle fibers. |
| **Hackle:** | Ginger hackle up most of the shank, with a single white hackle in front. |

## BIVISIBLE, GRIZZLY

*Tied by Todd Smith*

| | |
|---|---|
| **Hook:** | Light wire, standard length or 1X long, sizes 16 to 10. |
| **Thread:** | Black 8/0 or 6/0. |
| **Tail:** | Grizzly hackle fibers. |
| **Hackle:** | Grizzly hackle up most of the shank, with a single white hackle in front. |

## DARK CAHILL

*Tied by Skip Morris*

| | |
|---|---|
| **Hook:** | Light wire, standard length or 1X long, sizes 18 to 12. |
| **Thread:** | Brown or black 8/0 or 6/0. |
| **Wing:** | Lemon wood duck (or mallard dyed wood-duck color). |
| **Tail:** | Brown hackle fibers. |
| **Body:** | Muskrat fur (or gray synthetic dubbing). |
| **Hackle:** | Brown. |

**Comments:** Less popular than the Light Cahill, but still an excellent all-around mayfly-like dry.

## GINGER QUILL

*Tied by Skip Morris*

| | |
|---|---|
| **Hook:** | Light wire, standard length or 1X long, sizes 18 to 10. |
| **Thread:** | Tan or yellow 8/0 or 6/0. |
| **Wing:** | Duck quill sections. |
| **Tail:** | Ginger hackle fibers. |
| **Body:** | Stripped peacock herl quills. |
| **Hackle:** | Ginger. |

**Comments:** The peacock quill body tends to be fragile, but you can toughen it with a thin coating of head cement after the fly is completed or with a thin coating of two-part epoxy glue on the thread before wrapping the quill. The Ginger Quill is a handsome eastern pattern adopted in the West.

## IRRESISTIBLE

*Tied by Skip Morris*

| | |
|---|---|
| **Hook:** | Light wire, standard length or 1X long, sizes 16 to 8. |
| **Thread:** | Gray or black 8/0, 6/0, or 3/0 (heavy thread, such as size A rod-winding thread, for spinning the hair). |
| **Tail:** | Brown buck tail. |
| **Body:** | Deer or caribou hair flared and shaped (instructions are on page 268). |
| **Wing:** | Brown buck tail. |
| **Hackle:** | Blue dun, heavy. |

## LIGHT CAHILL

*Tied by Skip Morris*

**Hook:**      Light wire, standard length or 1X long, sizes 18 to 10.
**Thread:**    Tan or cream 8/0 or 6/0.
**Wing:**      Lemon wood duck.
**Tail:**      Ginger hackle fibers.
**Body:**      Badger underfur (or cream synthetic dubbing).
**Hackle:**    Ginger.
**Comments:**  A particularly elegant standard dry fly. I've used it successfully to imitate pale morning duns.

## PALE EVENING DUN

*Tied by Skip Morris*

**Hook:**      Light wire, standard length or 1X long, size 18 to 10.
**Thread:**    Yellow 8/0 or 6/0.
**Wing:**      Blue dun hackle tips (I prefer hen neck hackles).
**Tail:**      Blue dun hackle fibers.
**Body:**      Pale yellow synthetic dubbing (traditionally, a dyed natural fur such as rabbit).
**Hackle:**    Blue dun.
**Comments:**  Another old-time transplant from the East that's proved itself in the West.

## QUILL GORDON                          *Theodore Gordon*

*Tied by Skip Morris*

**Hook:**      Light wire, standard length or 1X long, sizes 18 to 12.
**Thread:**    Gray 8/0 to 6/0.
**Wing:**      Lemon wood duck.
**Tail:**      Blue dun hackle fibers.
**Body:**      Stripped peacock herl quills.
**Hackle:**    Blue dun.
**Comments:**  See the Ginger Quill earlier in this chapter for information on toughening the body. The great popularity of the eastern Quill Gordon spread west long ago.

## RAT-FACED MCDOUGAL                    *Percy Jennings*

*Tied by Skip Morris*

**Hook:**      Light wire, standard length or 1X long, sizes 16 to 10.
**Thread:**    White 8/0, 6/0, or 3/0. (I prefer size A rod thread for flaring the body hair.)
**Tail:**      Ginger hackle fibers.
**Body:**      Flared and shaped natural tan-gray deer hair (instructions are on page 268).
**Wing:**      White calf tail, split.
**Hackle:**    Ginger, full.
**Comments:**  A buoyant eastern pattern that really fits the wilder western rivers. Easy to spot on the water, too.

## ROYAL COACHMAN

*Tied by Skip Morris*

**Hook:** Light wire, standard length or 1X long, sizes 18 to 10.
**Thread:** Black 8/0 or 6/0.
**Wing:** White duck quill sections.
**Tail:** Golden pheasant tippet.
**Body:** Front and rear thirds are peacock herl; center third is red single-strand floss. (Toughen the herl by spinning it around the thread if you like.)
**Hackle:** Brown.
**Comments:** The Royal Coachman is a venerable dry fly created over a century ago. It has inspired all sorts of variations, including hair-wing dry flies, a streamer, and even a nymph (my own pattern, the Royal Flush). It is the granddaddy of attractor dry flies and remains a reliable standard.

**Spider and Variant.** Variants and spiders are the same— long tails, long hackles, and little else. These are peculiar flies, and they go way back. Sometimes their high dancing moves fish when nothing else will. Getting the hook past those long, stiff hackles and into the fish can be a challenge, however.

## SPIDER, BADGER

*Tied by Skip Morris*

**Hook:** Light wire, short shank, sizes 16 and 14.
**Thread:** Black 8/0 or 6/0.
**Tail:** Badger hackle fibers, long.
**Body (optional):** Flat silver tinsel.
**Hackle:** Badger, very long.

## VARIANT, CREAM

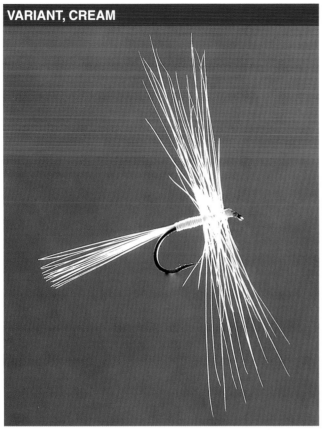

*Tied by Skip Morris*

| | |
|---|---|
| **Hook:** | Light wire, short shank, sizes 16 and 14. |
| **Thread:** | Yellow 8/0 or 6/0. |
| **Tail:** | Cream hackle fibers, long. |
| **Body:** | Cream hackle stem. |
| **Hackle:** | Cream, very long. |

## VARIANT, GRAY FOX

*Tied by Todd Smith*

| | |
|---|---|
| **Hook:** | Light wire, short shank, sizes 16 to 12. |
| **Thread:** | Light yellow 8/0 or 6/0. |
| **Tail:** | Ginger hackle fibers, long. |
| **Body:** | Ginger or cream hackle stem. |
| **Hackle:** | Three hackles—one dark ginger, one light ginger, and one grizzly—wound through one another. |

**Wulff.** Lee Wulff's series of dry flies consists of high-floating designs bristling with hair and hackle. I've always found the exact dressings elusive—one book lists yarn for the body of a particular pattern, while another lists dubbing; the wings might call for deer or calf tail or buck tail. According to my research, however, the dressings listed here are the most established versions. This isn't a big deal, though, because the Wulff patterns have been around since the 1930s and have proven themselves reliable in all their minor variations. Besides, Lee always considered these to be flexible dressings. Some would argue that the Wulffs are not true traditional dry flies, but I believe that 70 years of popularity and an overall traditional dry-fly shape settle the issue.

## WULFF, BLOND                          *Lee Wulff*

*Tied by Skip Morris*

| | |
|---|---|
| **Hook:** | Light wire, standard length or 1X long, sizes 16 to 8. |
| **Thread:** | Tan 8/0 or 6/0. |
| **Wing:** | Light tan deer or elk hair. |
| **Tail:** | Light tan deer or elk hair. |
| **Body:** | Light tan dubbing (synthetics tend to float best). |
| **Hackle:** | Ginger. |

## WULFF, GRAY — *Lee Wulff*

*Tied by Skip Morris*

| | |
|---|---|
| **Hook:** | Light wire, standard length or 1X long, sizes 16 to 8. |
| **Thread:** | Black 8/0 or 6/0. |
| **Wing:** | Brown buck tail. |
| **Tail:** | Brown buck tail. |
| **Body:** | Gray dubbing (synthetics tend to float best). |
| **Hackle:** | Blue dun. |

## WULFF, GRIZZLY — *Lee Wulff*

*Tied by Skip Morris*

| | |
|---|---|
| **Hook:** | Light wire, standard length or 1X long, sizes 16 to 8. |
| **Thread:** | Black 8/0, 6/0, or 3/0. |
| **Wing:** | Brown buck tail. |
| **Tail:** | Brown buck tail. |
| **Body:** | Yellow floss (or substitute yellow dubbing). |
| **Hackle:** | Brown and grizzly mixed; use plenty of hackle. |

## WULFF, IRRESISTIBLE — *Lee Wulff*

*Tied by Skip Morris*

| | |
|---|---|
| **Hook:** | Light wire, standard length or 1X long, sizes 16 to 8. |
| **Thread:** | Black 8/0, 6/0, or 3/0. (I prefer size A rod-winding thread for flaring the hair.) |
| **Wing:** | White calf tail. |
| **Tail:** | Moose body hair. |
| **Body:** | Natural tan-gray deer hair, flared and shaped (instructions are on page 268). |
| **Hackle:** | Brown. |
| **Comments:** | A Wulff pattern based on the ever-popular Irresistible. |

## WULFF, ROYAL

See page 248 in chapter 14, Attractors.

## WULFF, WHITE — *Lee Wulff*

*Tied by Skip Morris*

| | |
|---|---|
| **Hook:** | Light wire, standard length or 1X long, sizes 16 to 8. |
| **Thread:** | Black 8/0, 6/0, or 3/0. |
| **Wing:** | White calf tail. |
| **Tail:** | White calf tail. |
| **Body:** | White yarn (or dubbing). |
| **Hackle:** | Pale badger. |

# 14

# Attractors

SOMETIMES IT'S DIFFICULT to say whether a particular artificial nymph is an "imitation," meant to mimic a real creature such as a mayfly nymph or midge pupa, or an "attractor," designed never to be mistaken for anything actually living in or near water. The Prince Nymph, with its tusklike wings, is clearly an attractor. But the Copper John? It's a little shiny and likes to wink that slender strand of brilliance lying between its shoulders—characteristics that push it toward the classification of attractor. But with its natural shape and two distinct tails, it's not that far from being a stonefly or mayfly nymph, and I've seen it described that way in print. Then again, standard color schemes for the Copper John include blue and chartreuse. Nothing natural there! So when I decided that each of the dressings in this chapter was indeed an attractor, I sometimes had to rely heavily on research, experience, and even intuition. Most, however, were actually pretty easy to call.

Attractor dry flies are even stranger than attractor nymphs. It seems all those garish speckled and barred and metal-flake rubber-strands and the odd construction possibilities of buoyant foam-sheeting have led the dry fly down a bizarre path. For example, look at the Chernobyl Ant variations—they're like children's toys from an alternate universe.

Attractor streamers and bucktails are like attractor nymphs—some might function occasionally as imitations, but really are attractors, while others are way to weird to ever imitate anything.

The thing about all attractor fly patterns—and I fought this for years until I could no longer deny the obvious—is that unnatural attractor flies can outfish imitations. It's common, and sometimes the leap in action when you switch from a plausible Parachute Caddis to a goofy looking Super Predator is so dramatic that it's a genuine shock—even a revelation.

# Attractor Nymphs

## ATTRACTABAETIS — *Wade Malwitz*

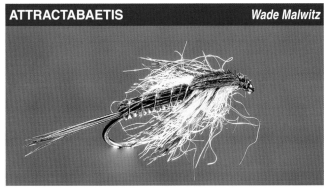

*Bottom view*

*Tied by Wade Malwitz*

**Hook:** Heavy wire, standard length or 1X long, sizes 14 to 10.
**Thread:** Black 6/0.
**Weight:** Lead wire.
**Tail:** Pheasant tail (dyed green with a chartreuse thorax).
**Rib:** Fine copper or gold wire.
**Back:** Pheasant tail pulled forward over the abdomen and the rib wound over it (dyed-green pheasant with a chartreuse thorax).
**Abdomen:** Brown D-Rib (or another slim, shiny, pliable body material).
**Wing case:** Pheasant tail (dyed green with a chartreuse thorax).
**Thorax:** Orange, pink, or chartreuse seal's fur or a seal substitute such as Simi Seal or SLF.
**Legs:** Section cut from a natural brown partridge feather (dyed green partridge with a chartreuse thorax), the section lying flat over the thorax.
**Comments:** In the Pacific Northwest, where Wade lives and often fishes, many trout rivers are home to runs of salmon. The heavy fish seem to spread through every pool and riffle. But it's not as bad for the trout as you might expect. Spawning in gravel among shifting currents is a precarious affair at best, so the salmon inadvertently send many of their protein-rich eggs downstream to the anxious mouths of trout. This opens the door for bright egg-colored flies such as the Attractabaetis. Wade says that one fall he caught "loads of rainbows" and six steelhead on this pattern in Oregon's Deschutes River.

## BLACK MARTINEZ — *Don Martinez*

*Tied by Skip Morris*

**Hook:** Heavy wire, standard length or 1X long, sizes 14 to 8.
**Weight:** Lead wire.
**Thread:** Black 8/0, 6/0, or 3/0.
**Tail:** Guinea feather fibers.
**Rib:** Oval gold tinsel.
**Abdomen:** Originally, black seal's fur; now, a coarse, shiny synthetic or blended natural-synthetic dubbing such as SLF, Arizona Sparkle Nymph Dubbing, or Arizona Simi Seal.
**Wing case:** Green raffia (or green Thin Skin or dyed green turkey quill).
**Thorax:** Black chenille.
**Legs:** Mallard flank feather fibers bound in a half circle under the thorax.
**Comments:** An old standby in the Yellowstone area.

**Burk's Bottom Rollers.** Andy Burk offers us these very heavy patterns, with no tails or legs to impede their descent, for the European Czech nymphing technique that is becoming increasingly popular in the United States. The heart of this technique is a rig with a very heavy fly (a Burk's Bottom Roller, perhaps?) either below another lighter nymph or between two such nymphs. It's a short-distance method, with no strike indicator, and the angler has to pull slightly downstream on the rig to keep tension on it. Strikes are felt rather than seen. And the whole thing depends on one very heavy nymph to draw the others down to the trout. Here are two of the most popular and established Czech nymphs in North America.

## BURK'S BOTTOM ROLLER, DEEP SHERBET ("SURE BET")
*Andy Burk*

*Tied by Andy Burk*

| | |
|---|---|
| **Hook:** | Heavy wire, humped shank, sizes 14 to 6. |
| **Head:** | Silver tungsten bead. |
| **Weight:** | Lead wire. |
| **Thread:** | Orange 6/0. |
| **Back:** | Strip of mother of pearl Sili Skin (or another pearl or clear sheeting such as Stretch Flex, Scud Back, or Medallion sheeting). The back goes over the top of the bead. Run a dark orange or red permanent marking pen up the back after the fly is completed. |
| **Rib:** | Tippet, 5X. The rib goes up the body, directly behind the bead, and then across the bead to be bound at the eye under a thread head. |
| **Body:** | Rear section: Wapsi Saltwater SLF dubbing in softshell (or any coarse, shiny, creamy orange dubbing, such as Arizona Synthetic Dubbing or Antron). Middle segment: orange Arizona Synthetic Dubbing. Front section: undyed tan-brown hare's mask. |

## BURK'S BOTTOM ROLLER, HARE'S EAR SPECIAL
*Andy Burk*

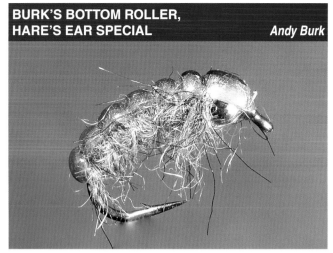

*Tied by Andy Burk*

| | |
|---|---|
| **Hook:** | Heavy wire, humped shank, sizes 14 to 6. |
| **Head:** | Gold tungsten bead. |
| **Weight:** | Lead wire. |
| **Thread:** | Beige (or tan) 6/0. |
| **Back:** | Strip of mother of pearl Sili Skin (or another pearl or clear sheeting such as Stretch Flex, Scud Back, or Medallion sheeting). The back goes over the top of the bead. Run a dark brown permanent marking pen up the back after the fly is completed. |
| **Rib:** | Tippet, 5X. The rib goes up the body, directly behind the bead, and then across the bead to be bound at the eye under a thread head. |
| **Body:** | Peacock Arizona Synthetic Dubbing in both light and dark hare's ear, blended (or any coarse, shiny, tan-brown dubbing, such as SLF or Antron). |

**Copper John.** This one caught on in a blink—and caught on big. Although it's sometimes used to imitate mayfly and stonefly nymphs, the Copper John is mainly an attractor pattern. John Barr wrote to me that it triggers a lot of "reflex or curiosity strikes." He designed it to dangle below a big dry fly—the hopper-dropper system. But it's also used right along the bottom below a strike indicator. There are all sorts of color variations, and those that follow are just examples. As John explained, selecting among them is "far from a scientific process, so feel free to try any color that looks good to you, and see how it works out." He prefers Ultra-Wire for all his Copper Johns because it doesn't tarnish. See John's book *Barr Flies* for more information on the Copper John and the rest of his inventive fly patterns.

**Comments:** The original version of the Copper John is probably the most versatile of the lot and the most likely to serve not only as an attractor but also as an imitation of mayfly and stonefly nymphs.

### COPPER JOHN, BLUE — *John Barr*

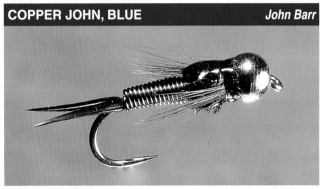

*Tied by Skip Morris*

| | |
|---|---|
| **Hook:** | Heavy wire, 2X long, sizes 20 to 12. |
| **Head:** | Gold metal bead, $5/64$ inch for size 20, $7/64$ inch for sizes 18 and 16, $1/8$ inch for size 14, $5/32$ inch for size 12. |
| **Weight:** | Lead wire. The lead should cover only the front half of the shank. Use the butts of the tails and copper wire (and a little dubbing, if required) to build the area behind the lead to taper up to the lead's diameter. |
| **Thread:** | Black 8/0 or 6/0. |
| **Tail:** | Dyed black goose biots (black hackle fibers for size 20). |
| **Abdomen:** | Blue copper wire, fine diameter for sizes 20 and 18, "brassie" (medium-fine) for sizes 16 and 14, medium for size 12. |
| **Wing case:** | One strand of pearl Krystal Flash over a strip of black Thin Skin, all topped with a drop of epoxy glue (instructions are on page 38). |
| **Thorax:** | Dyed blue (or undyed) peacock herl. |
| **Legs:** | Bunch of black hen back fibers bound along each side of the narrow thread collar holding the wing case. |

**Comments:** Probably mistaken only rarely as a mayfly or stonefly nymph—it is blue, after all. But it works.

### COPPER JOHN — *John Barr*

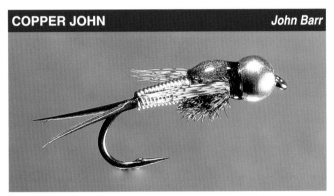

*Top view*

*Tied by Skip Morris*

| | |
|---|---|
| **Hook:** | Heavy wire, 2X long, sizes 20 to 12. |
| **Head:** | Gold metal bead, $5/64$ inch for size 20, $7/64$ inch for sizes 18 and 16, $1/8$ inch for size 14, $5/32$ inch for size 12. |
| **Weight:** | Lead wire. The lead should cover only the front half of the shank. Use the butts of the tails and copper wire (and a little dubbing, if required) to build the area behind the lead to taper up to the lead's diameter. |
| **Thread:** | Black 8/0 or 6/0. |
| **Tail:** | Dyed brown goose biots (or brown hen back fibers for size 20). |
| **Abdomen:** | Copper wire, fine diameter for sizes 20 and 18, "brassie" (medium-fine) for sizes 16 and 14, medium for size 12. |
| **Wing case:** | One strand of pearl Krystal Flash over a strip of brown Thin Skin, all topped with a drop of epoxy glue (instructions are on page 38). |
| **Thorax:** | Peacock herl. |
| **Legs:** | Bunch of natural brown partridge fibers bound along each side of the narrow thread collar holding the wing case. |

## COPPER JOHN, CHARTREUSE — *John Barr*

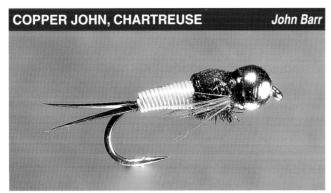

*Tied by Skip Morris*

| | |
|---|---|
| **Hook:** | Heavy wire, 2X long, sizes 20 to 12. |
| **Head:** | Gold metal bead, $5/64$ inch for size 20, $7/64$ inch for sizes 18 and 16, $1/8$ inch for size 14, $5/32$ inch for size 12. |
| **Weight:** | Lead wire. The lead should cover only the front half of the shank. Use the butts of the tails and copper wire (and a little dubbing, if required) to build the area behind the lead to taper up to the lead's diameter. |
| **Thread:** | Black 8/0 or 6/0. |
| **Tail:** | Dyed black goose biots (black hackle fibers for size 20). |
| **Abdomen:** | Chartreuse copper wire, fine diameter for sizes 20 and 18, "brassie" (medium-fine) for sizes 16 and 14, medium for size 12. |
| **Wing case:** | One strand of pearl Krystal Flash over a strip of black Thin Skin, all topped with a drop of epoxy glue (instructions are on page 38). |
| **Thorax:** | Peacock herl. |
| **Legs:** | Bunch of black hen back fibers bound along each side of the narrow thread collar holding the wing case. |
| **Comments:** | Imitative? Not likely. But such outlandish colors can really work when trout are in a mood. |

## FLEDERMAUS — *Jack Schneider*

*Tied by Rob McCormick*

| | |
|---|---|
| **Hook:** | Heavy wire, standard length or 1X long, sizes 10 to 4. |
| **Thread:** | Black 8/0, 6/0, or 3/0. |
| **Body:** | Muskrat fur, dubbed heavily (or in a dubbing loop) and picked out to look shaggy. |
| **Wing:** | Squirrel tail, extending to the rear of the body. |
| **Comments:** | Often confused with the similarly named Polly Rosborough pattern that follows. But like Rosborough's fly, this is a simple, effective pattern that looks a little odd and imitates nothing. |

## FLEDERMOUSE — *Polly Rosborough*

*Tied by Rob McCormick*

| | |
|---|---|
| **Hook:** | Heavy wire, 3X long, sizes 12 to 2. |
| **Thread:** | Tan 6/0 or 3/0. |
| **Body:** | Half muskrat and half dyed dark brown rabbit, blended and dubbed. |
| **Collar:** | Muskrat and dyed dark brown rabbit fur and guard hairs bound in bunches just behind the eye. |
| **Wing case:** | Dyed dark brown barred teal fibers bound on at the eye. |
| **Comments:** | In his *Tying and Fishing the Fuzzy Nymphs,* Polly says the Fledermouse "never really simulates anything but food," firmly establishing the pattern as an attractor. It's a reliable, "buggy-looking" old standard. |

**Gabriel's Trumpet.** I cooked this one up strictly as an attractor, and it's a killer when fished that way. However, the brown and black versions are probably mistaken for mayfly and small stonefly nymphs on occasion. One day, a Gabriel's Trumpet, Pink caught me cutthroat after cutthroat, including the biggest of the day, from a riffle on a Montana river. This happened right after a few dry-fly fishers had previously managed to raise only a modest fish or two in the same spot. Gold is the reliable standard, but when gold doesn't do the trick, try brown or pink or black, in that order.

## GABRIEL'S TRUMPET, BLACK — *Skip Morris*

*Tied by Skip Morris*

| | |
|---|---|
| **Hook:** | Heavy wire, humped shank (scud-pupa hook), sizes 16 to 10 (alternatively, use a straight-shank hook). |
| **Head:** | Black metal bead, $1/8$ inch for sizes 10 and 12, $7/64$ inch for size 14, $3/32$ inch for size 16. |

| | |
|---|---|
| **Weight:** | Lead wire, 0.015 inch. (You can use larger-diameter wire for the largest hook sizes.) |
| **Thread:** | Black 8/0 or 6/0. |
| **Tail:** | Dyed black goose biots. |
| **Rib:** | Natural copper wire (or, for more kick, hot yellow Ultra Wire). |
| **Abdomen:** | Black Flashabou (or Krystal Flash). |
| **Wing case:** | Mottled brown turkey primary (or Bug Skin or a durable synthetic such as Thin Skin). |
| **Thorax:** | Dyed black ostrich herl. Wind the herl back, bind its end with a few tight thread turns, and then spiral the thread forward through the herl to toughen it. |
| **Legs:** | Black hen neck hackle, wound as a short collar behind the bead, trimmed on top or parted down the sides before pulling the wing case over the top. |

## GABRIEL'S TRUMPET, GOLD — *Skip Morris*

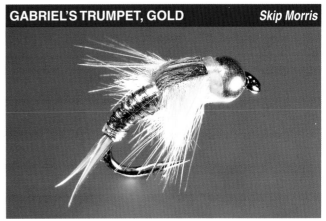

*Tied by Skip Morris*

## GABRIEL'S TRUMPET, BROWN — *Skip Morris*

*Tied by Skip Morris*

| | |
|---|---|
| **Hook:** | Heavy wire, humped shank (scud-pupa hook), sizes 16 to 10 (alternatively, use a straight-shank hook). |
| **Head:** | Gold metal bead, $^1/_8$ inch for sizes 10 and 12, $^7/_{64}$ inch for size 14, $^3/_{32}$ inch for size 16. |
| **Weight:** | Lead wire, 0.015 inch. (You can use larger-diameter wire for the largest hook sizes.) |
| **Thread:** | Brown 8/0 or 6/0. |
| **Tail:** | Dyed brown goose biots. |
| **Rib:** | Natural copper wire (or, for more kick, hot yellow Ultra Wire). |
| **Abdomen:** | Brown Flashabou (or Krystal Flash). |
| **Wing case:** | Mottled brown turkey primary (or Bug Skin or a durable synthetic such as Thin Skin). |
| **Thorax:** | Dyed brown ostrich herl. Wind the herl back, bind its end with a few tight thread turns, and then spiral the thread forward through the herl to toughen it. |
| **Legs:** | Brown hen neck hackle, wound as a short collar behind the bead, trimmed on top or parted down the sides before pulling the wing case over the top. |

| | |
|---|---|
| **Hook:** | Heavy wire, humped shank (scud-pupa style), sizes 16 to 10 (alternatively, use a straight-shank hook). |
| **Head:** | Gold metal bead, $^1/_8$ inch for sizes 10 and 12, $^7/_{64}$ inch for size 14, $^3/_{32}$ inch for size 16. |
| **Weight:** | Lead wire, 0.015 inch. (You can use larger-diameter wire for the largest hook sizes.) |
| **Thread:** | Gold or yellow 8/0 or 6/0. |
| **Tail:** | Gold, amber, or yellow goose biots. |
| **Rib:** | Fine red copper wire. |
| **Abdomen:** | Gold Flashabou (or Krystal Flash). |
| **Wing case:** | Mottled brown turkey primary (or Bug Skin or a durable synthetic such as Thin Skin). |
| **Thorax:** | Tan (or gold or amber) ostrich herl. Wind the herl back, bind its end with a few tight thread turns, and then spiral the thread forward through the herl to toughen it. |
| **Legs:** | One ginger (or gold or tan) hen neck hackle, wound as a short collar behind the bead, trimmed on top or parted down the sides before pulling the wing case over the top. |

## GABRIEL'S TRUMPET, PINK — *Skip Morris*

*Tied by Skip Morris*

| | |
|---|---|
| **Hook:** | Heavy wire, humped shank (scud-pupa style), sizes 16 to 10 (alternatively, use a straight-shank hook). |
| **Head:** | Gold metal bead, $1/8$ inch for sizes 10 and 12, $7/64$ inch for size 14, $3/32$ inch for size 16. |
| **Weight:** | Lead wire, 0.015 inch. (You can use larger-diameter wire for the largest hook sizes.) |
| **Thread:** | Pink 8/0 or 6/0. |
| **Tail:** | White or cream goose biots. |
| **Rib:** | Fine red copper wire. |
| **Abdomen:** | Pink Flashabou (or Krystal Flash). |
| **Wing case:** | Mottled brown turkey primary (or Bug Skin or a durable synthetic such as Thin Skin). |
| **Thorax:** | Pink ostrich herl. Wind the herl back, bind its end with a few tight thread turns, and then spiral the thread forward through the herl to toughen it. |
| **Legs:** | One white or cream hen neck hackle, wound as a short collar behind the bead, trimmed on top or parted down the sides before pulling the wing case over the top. |

## KEMP BUG — *Roy Donnelly*

*Top view*

*Tied by Skip Morris*

| | |
|---|---|
| **Hook:** | Heavy wire, 2X long, sizes 12 to 8. |
| **Thread:** | Black 8/0, 6/0, or 3/0. |
| **Tail:** | Peacock sword, or peacock herl trimmed short. |
| **Body:** | Peacock herl. |
| **Wing case:** | Two webby grizzly hackle tips, or short hackles, extending halfway down the top of the body. The tips should be set in a "V". (You'll probably do best with hen neck hackles.) |
| **Hackle:** | Brown hen neck or saddle, as a collar. |
| **Comments:** | Bears some resemblance to the ever-popular Prince Nymph. The Kemp Bug (or Kemp's Bug) is an older standard pattern of the West. |

## LIGHTNING BUG — *Larry Graham*

*Tied by Rob McCormick*

| | |
|---|---|
| **Hook:** | Heavy wire, standard length or 1X long, sizes 16 to 12. |
| **Head:** | Gold metal bead. |
| **Thread:** | Black or brown 8/0 or 6/0. |

**Tail:** Pheasant tail fibers.
**Rib:** Fine copper wire.
**Abdomen:** Pearl tinsel, Flashabou, or Krystal Flash.
**Legs:** Short section of barred tan-brown (or natural mottled brown) hen back hackle bound by the stem to lie flat over the thorax, covered in the center by the wing case.
**Wing case:** Strip cut from a sheet of pearl Mylar, or pearl tinsel, Flashabou, or Krystal Flash.
**Thorax:** Peacock herl.
**Comments:** Developed by guide Larry Graham on Washington's Yakima River. Arguably an ultrabright imitation of a mayfly nymph—like the BLM in chapter 4—but the Lightning Bug is considered primarily an attractor.

## NORTH FORK SPECIAL — *Tim Wade*

*Tied by Rob McCormick*

**Hook:** Heavy wire, humped shank (scud-pupa hook), sizes 12 and 10.
**Head:** Silver metal bead.
**Weight (optional):** Lead wire, 0.020-inch diameter.
**Thread:** Black 8/0 or 6/0.
**Tail:** Natural gray goose biots.
**Rib:** Fine red or copper wire.
**Abdomen:** Black Fine-as-Frog's Hair dubbing (or any fine black dubbing—rabbit, Super Fine Dry Fly . . .).
**Thorax:** Same as the abdomen.
**Wing cases:** Butts of three dyed black goose biots, trimmed short.
**Legs:** Two natural gray goose biots, one bound along each side and reaching to the rear of the abdomen, curving out from the body.
**Comments:** Mr. Wade developed his dark, spiny pattern on Wyoming's North Fork of the Shoshone River, and it's his favorite attractor nymph for spring.

## PEPPERONI YUK BUG — *Robbie Garrett*

*Tied by Carol Ann Morris*

**Hook:** Heavy wire, 3X or 4X long, sizes 10 to 4.
**Thread:** Black 6/0 or 3/0.
**Weight:** Lead wire.
**Tail:** Red fox-squirrel tail.
**Legs:** White rubber-strand. Bind it in two sections, each made of two strands still attached. Bind one two-strand section just ahead of the bend and the other at midshank. After the fly is completed, strip the attached strands apart to create eight legs.
**Abdomen:** Black medium to large chenille.
**Hackle:** Brown saddle hackle, spiraled up the thorax.
**Thorax:** Orange medium to large chenille.
**Comments:** Mr. Garrett likes to fish his fly dead drift, but working the rod tip occasionally gives the legs more action.

## PRINCE NYMPH — *Doug Prince*

*Tied by Skip Morris*

**Hook:** Heavy wire, 2X (or 1X) long, sizes 16 to 6.
**Thread:** Black 8/0, 6/0, or 3/0.
**Weight:** Lead wire.
**Tail:** Dyed brown goose biots.
**Rib:** Fine oval (or flat) gold tinsel.
**Body:** Peacock herl.
**Hackle:** Brown hen neck.
**Wings (wing case):** Two white goose biots, curving upward and slightly spread, lying back over the body.
**Comments:** There has been some confusion about the name of this fly over the decades. It has been known as the Brown Forked Tail and the Black Forked Tail, but it now seems to be well established as the Prince Nymph. It's still popular after all these years. There's just something about those long, white horn-wings that trout like.

## PRINCE NYMPH, GOLD BEAD

*Tied by Skip Morris*

Hook:       Heavy wire, 2X (or 1X) long, sizes 16 to 6.
Head:       Gold metal bead.
Weight:     Lead wire.
Thread:     Black 8/0, 6/0, or 3/0.
Tail:       Dyed brown goose biots.
Rib:        Fine oval (or flat) gold tinsel.
Body:       Peacock herl.
Hackle:     Brown hen neck.
**Wings (wing case):** Two white goose biots, curving upward and slightly
            spread, lying back over the body.
Comments:   Has become about as popular as the original.

## PSYCHO PRINCE NYMPH          *Mike Mercer*

*Tied by Mike Mercer*

Hook:       Heavy wire, standard length, sizes 18 to 12.
Head:       Gold metal bead.
Thread:     Camel (soft brown) 8/0.
Tail:       Dyed dark brown turkey biots.
Rib:        Fine copper wire.
Back:       Section of natural dark, mottled, golden brown turkey tail.
Abdomen:    Orange Ice Dub (or any sparkling dubbing, such as Antron
            or Arizona Sparkle Nymph Dubbing).
Wing case:  Bunch of electric banana (light yellow) Angel Hair (or Lite
            Brite or Flashabou dubbing) bound at the rear of the thorax
            and trimmed straight across, halfway down the abdomen.
Thorax:     Same as the abdomen.
Legs:       Dyed amber turkey biots, one per side, bound under the
            collar.
Collar:     Peacock Arizona Synthetic Dubbing (or another peacock or
            emerald shiny dubbing); keep the collar narrow.
Comments:   A sort of jazzed-up, rearranged Prince Nymph.

**Rainbow Warrior.** This pale, gleaming little nymph has become a hit, and it's easy enough to tie. The standard version is listed first, but like so many popular flies, this one has variations. The Rainbow Warrior apparently started with a glass bead, but faster-sinking tungsten bead versions have also caught on.

## RAINBOW WARRIOR              *Lance Egan*

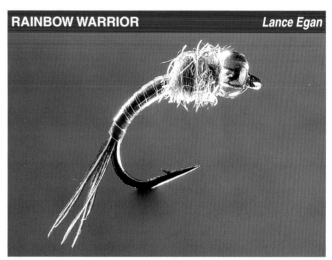

*Tied by Al Davis*

Hook:       Heavy wire, humped shank (scud-pupa hook),
            sizes 22 to 14.
Head:       Pearl glass bead.
Thread:     Red 8/0 or 6/0.
Tail:       Pheasant tail fibers.
Abdomen:    Flat pearl tinsel, Flashabou, or Krystal Flash.
Wing case:  Butts of the abdomen strands, doubled back, bound, and
            then pulled forward and down over the thorax.
Thorax:     Wapsi Sow-Scud dubbing in rainbow, or any coarse light tan
            dubbing with a touch of pink, such as a squirrel or hare's
            mask blend or Buggy Nymph Dubbing.

## RAINBOW WARRIOR, BLACK — *Lance Egan*

*Tied by Mike Thompson*

| | |
|---|---|
| **Hook:** | Heavy wire, humped shank (scud-pupa hook), sizes 22 to 14. |
| **Head:** | Pearl glass bead. |
| **Thread:** | Red 8/0 or 6/0. |
| **Tail:** | Pheasant tail fibers. |
| **Abdomen:** | Flat black tinsel, Flashabou, or Krystal Flash. |
| **Wing case:** | Pearl tinsel, Flashabou, or Krystal Flash. |
| **Thorax:** | Wapsi Sow-Scud dubbing in rainbow, or any coarse light tan dubbing with a touch of pink, such as a squirrel or hare's mask blend or Buggy Nymph Dubbing. |

## RAINBOW WARRIOR, RED — *Lance Egan*

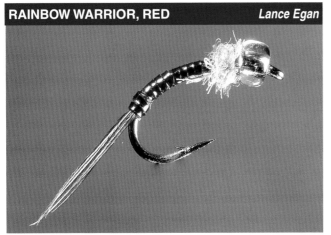

*Tied by Alejandro Cruz*

| | |
|---|---|
| **Hook:** | Heavy wire, humped shank (scud-pupa hook), sizes 22 to 14. |
| **Head:** | Pearl glass bead. |
| **Thread:** | Red 8/0 or 6/0. |
| **Tail:** | Pheasant tail fibers. |
| **Abdomen:** | Flat red tinsel, Flashabou, or Krystal Flash. |
| **Wing case:** | Pearl tinsel, Flashabou, or Krystal Flash. |
| **Thorax:** | Wapsi Sow-Scud dubbing in rainbow, or any coarse light tan dubbing with a touch of pink, such as a squirrel or hare's mask blend or Buggy Nymph Dubbing. |

## RAINBOW WARRIOR, TUNGSTEN — *Lance Egan*

*Tied by Al Davis*

| | |
|---|---|
| **Hook:** | Heavy wire, humped shank (scud-pupa hook), sizes 22 to 14. |
| **Head:** | Silver tungsten bead. |
| **Thread:** | Red 8/0 or 6/0. |
| **Tail:** | Pheasant tail fibers. |
| **Abdomen:** | Flat pearl tinsel, Flashabou, or Krystal Flash. |
| **Wing case:** | Butts of the abdomen strands, doubled back, bound, and then pulled forward and down over the thorax. |
| **Thorax:** | Wapsi Sow-Scud dubbing in rainbow, or any coarse light tan dubbing with a touch of pink, such as a squirrel or hare's mask blend or Buggy Nymph Dubbing. |
| **Comments:** | You can tie any of the color variations of the Rainbow Warrior with a tungsten bead. |

**ROYAL FLUSH** — *Skip Morris*

*Curved shank*

*Tied by Skip Morris*

**Hook:** Heavy wire, standard length to 1X long (or humped shank, scud-pupa hook), sizes 16 to 10.

**Head:** Gold metal bead, $^3/_{32}$ inch for size 16 hooks, $^7/_{64}$ inch for size 14, $^1/_8$ inch for sizes 12 and 10.

**Weight (optional):** Lead wire, 0.015 inch, covering the forward half of the shank, pushed up into the rear of the bead.

**Thread:** Red or black 8/0 or 6/0.

**Tail:** Golden pheasant tippets.

**Rib:** Fine red copper wire over a strand of red Flashabou. Make a few ribs up the abdomen, but only two or three through the thorax. Wind the rib opposite the normal direction to toughen the herl.

**Abdomen and thorax:** Peacock herl.

**Wing case:** Section of white duck or goose primary. (You can toughen the wing case by covering it with clear Stretch Flex, Scud Back, or Medallion sheeting.)

**Hackle:** Brown hen neck, two to four turns at the front of the thorax, with the top fibers parted to the sides beneath the wing case. Pinch the fibers down so they sweep back.

**Comments:** An attractor nymph inspired by the granddaddy of attractor dry flies, the Royal Coachman, the Royal Flush really works when trout are in the mood.

**Woolly Worm.** The Woolly Worm was once the number-one nymph in the West. Then it began to seem old-fashioned, so its tail changed to a marabou plume and it became the Woolly Bugger. But the Woolly Worm never lost its appeal to trout.

You'll need a long hackle—a soft-fibered saddle hackle is the standard. Some tiers toughen the hackle by winding it from the front of the body back to the bend, securing its tip with fine copper wire, and spiraling the wire forward up the body and through the hackle. Grizzly hackle is typical, but hackles of any color or markings are fair game for a Woolly Worm. Due to its popularity, it's been tied and fished in just about every conceivable variation.

**WOOLLY WORM, BLACK AND GRIZZLY**

*Tied by Skip Morris*

**Hook:** Heavy wire, 2X or 3X long, sizes 12 to 2.

**Thread:** Black 6/0 or 3/0.

**Weight (optional):** Lead wire.

**Tail:** Red hackle fibers (or red yarn, short).

**Body:** Black chenille.

**Hackle:** Grizzly, spiraled up the body.

**WOOLLY WORM, OLIVE AND GRIZZLY**

*Tied by Carol Ann Morris*

**Hook:** Heavy wire, 2X or 3X long, sizes 12 to 2.

**Thread:** Black 6/0 or 3/0.

**Weight (optional):** Lead wire.

**Tail:** Red hackle fibers (or red yarn, short).

**Body:** Dark olive chenille.

**Hackle:** Grizzly, spiraled up the body.

## WOOLLY WORM, PEACOCK AND GRIZZLY

*Tied by Stephen Carey*

**Hook:** Heavy wire, 2X or 3X long, sizes 12 to 2.
**Thread:** Black 6/0 or 3/0.
**Weight (optional):** Lead wire.
**Thread:** Black 6/0 or 3/0.
**Tail:** Red hackle fibers (or red yarn, short).
**Body:** Peacock herl.
**Hackle:** Grizzly, spiraled up the body.

## YUK BUG
*Al Troth*

*Tied by Skip Morris*

**Hook:** Heavy wire, 4X long, sizes 8 to 2.
**Thread:** Black 3/0.
**Weight (optional):** Lead wire.
**Legs:** Three lengths of white rubber-strand bound crossways and spaced evenly up the shank.
**Tail:** Gray squirrel tail hairs.
**Rib:** Long badger hackle (usually a soft-fibered rooster saddle), spiraled up the body.
**Body:** Black chenille.
**Comments:** Big, bristly, and waving its silly white legs, the Yuk Bug is one of those surreal western monstrosities that, for reasons understood only by trout, work.

# Attractor Dry Flies

## BLACK LEGGED WATER WALKER
*Bruce E. James*

*Tied by Skip Morris*

**Hook:** Light wire, 2X long, sizes 10 to 6.
**Thread:** Black 6/0 or 3/0.
**Underbody:** Black synthetic dubbing wound up a foam core. The foam core is made from a strip of black or gray $1/8$-inch-thick buoyant closed-cell foam sheeting, wound up the shank. Add a coating of vaporless cement over the foam core before adding the dubbing. Use light thread tension when you dub so as not to compress the buoyancy out of the foam.
**Legs:** Black rubber-strand, a section bound along each side of the narrow thread collar at the rear of the bullet head.
**Wing:** White calf tail.
**Bullet head and collar:** Natural tan-brown elk hair (instructions are on page 146).
**Comments:** Based on the Madam X. The Black Legged Water Walker floats for a long time with that foam center and lots of elk hair.

**Chernobyl Ant.** The Chernobyl Ant was originally developed to imitate the great Mormon cricket that periodically swarms over the western grasslands. But it's been fished as an attractor fly almost since it first appeared. Now there are Chernobyl Ants with multicolor bodies and legs, fuzzy or hackled undersides, and whatever other craziness can be wedged into the pattern. And all these variations seem to work when the trout are in the right mood. The ones that follow provide a good cross section of what's being used today.

A few years ago, when I wrote an article on the Chernobyl and its wild departures for a fly-fishing magazine, I used Weston McKay as a source. He can frequently be found tying flies right in the Flyfishing Center fly shop in Hamilton, Montana, and is something of a Chernobyl Ant specialist. Weston is serious about securing the bodies of all his Chernobyls, because the soft foam bodies are bound only with narrow bands of thread and tend to twist around the hook. He winds *seven* tight layers of 3/0 thread over the shank as a base, then binds the bodies in three spots rather than the standard two. Additionally, he adds cement along the thread-covered shank to bond it with the foam. Follow his lead if you like.

## CHERNOBYL ANT (ORIGINAL)
*Allan Woolley*

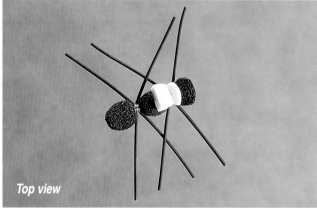

*Top view*

*Tied by Skip Morris*

**Hook:** Light or standard wire, 2X long (a slow-curve shank is optional), sizes 10 to 4.
**Thread:** Orange 3/0.
**Body:** Strip of fairly thick black buoyant closed-cell foam sheeting.
**Legs:** Black rubber-strand, a section bound along each side of the two thread collars—a total of four sections creating eight legs.
**Strike indicator:** Short strip of yellow buoyant closed-cell foam sheeting.

## CHERNOBYL ANT (VARIATION)

*Tied by Skip Morris*

**Hook:** Light or standard wire, 2X long (a slow-curve shank is optional), sizes 10 to 4.
**Thread:** Black 3/0.
**Body:** Strip of fairly thick black buoyant closed-cell foam sheeting.

**Legs:** Metallic brown flat rubber-strand with black "V" markings, a section bound along each side of the front and rear thread collars—a total of four sections creating eight legs.
**Wing:** Dyed yellow elk hair.

## CHERNOBYL ANT (VARIATION)

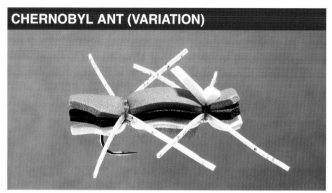

*Tied by Skip Morris*

**Hook:** Light or standard wire, 2X long (a slow-curve shank is optional), sizes 10 to 4.
**Thread:** Red 3/0.
**Body:** Strip of medium-thin yellow buoyant closed-cell foam sheeting, under a strip of black, under a strip of red. (The foam layers can be laminated with glue or simply bound on together, as here.) Dyed-red ostrich herl under the body, wound up the shank.
**Legs:** Amber or tan black- and gold-flaked rubber-strand, a section bound along each side of each of the two thread collars—a total of four sections creating eight legs.
**Strike indicator:** Short strip of yellow buoyant closed-cell foam sheeting.

## CHERNOBYL ANT (VARIATION)

*Tied by Skip Morris*

**Hook:** Light or standard wire, 2X long (a slow-curve shank is optional), sizes 10 to 4.
**Thread:** Tan 3/0.
**Body:** Strip of medium-thin tan buoyant closed-cell foam sheeting, under a strip of gray. (The foam layers can be laminated with glue or simply bound on together, as here.) Short-fibered ginger dry-fly saddle hackle under the body, wound up the shank. Bind the body in three spots.
**Legs:** Tan black-barred rubber-strand, a section bound along each side of the front and rear thread collars—a total of four sections creating eight legs.
**Strike indicator:** Short strip of yellow buoyant closed-cell foam sheeting.

## DOUBLE HUMPY, ORANGE — *Joe Allen*

*Tied by Todd Smith*

Hook:     Heavy (or standard) wire, 3X long, sizes 12 to 4.
Thread:   Orange flat waxed nylon (or 8/0, 6/0, or 3/0).
Tail:     Natural tan-brown deer hair.
Back and wing: Two bunches of natural tan-brown deer hair—one bunch for the rear hump and wings, and the second bunch for the forward hump and wings.
Body:     Orange poly yarn, orange floss, or the working thread.
Hackle:   Grizzly saddle or neck hackles—a hackle collar around the rear set of wings, and another around the forward set.
Comments:   What do you know? —mating Humpies...sort of. As odd as this pattern seems, it has been popular at the Jackson Hole One Fly Contest, which says a lot.

## DOUBLE HUMPY, YELLOW — *Joe Allen*

*Tied by Todd Smith*

Hook:     Heavy (or standard) wire, 3X long, sizes 12 to 4.
Thread:   Yellow flat waxed nylon (or 8/0, 6/0, or 3/0).
Tail:     Natural tan-brown deer hair.
Back and wing: Two bunches of natural tan-brown deer hair—one bunch for the rear hump and wings, and the second bunch for the forward hump and wings.
Body:     Yellow poly yarn, yellow floss, or the working thread.
Hackle:   Grizzly saddle or neck hackles—a hackle collar around the rear set of wings, and another around the forward set.
Comments:   See the comments for the Double Humpy, Orange, above.

## DOUBLE UGLY TICKLER — *Larry Tullis*

*Tied by Todd Smith*

Hook:     Light or standard wire, 2X (or 3X) long, sizes 16 to 6.
Thread:   Olive 6/0.
Tail:     Black, white, or yellow rubber legs.
Body:     Peacock herl.
Hackle:   Rear and front hackles are grizzly; center is brown.
Comments:   According to Larry Tullis, in *Fly Tying* magazine (later absorbed by *Fly Fishing & Tying Journal*), "this cross between the Double Renegade, Gray Ugly and French Tickler has proven to be an excellent all-around attractor dry fly." He goes on to say that it can also suggest an insect cluster, stonefly, cranefly, or grasshopper.

## H AND L VARIANT

*Tied by Skip Morris*

Hook:     Light wire, standard length or 1X long, sizes 16 to 10.
Thread:   Black 8/0 or 6/0.
Tail:     White calf tail.
Wing:     White calf tail, divided into two wings.
Body:     Rear half is stripped peacock herl stem; front half is peacock herl. Wind the stem over a thin layer of cement or odorless epoxy glue and spin the herl around the thread if you want to toughen the body.
Hackle:   Brown, heavy.
Comments:   Also known as the House and Lot, this unique and high-riding western pattern was almost placed in the traditional dry-fly chapter, but I decided it wasn't quite old enough and too strongly an attractor to escape its position here. It's buoyant, easy to spot, and still popular.

**Humpy.** The high-floating Humpy has been a western favorite for decades. The hump will be toughest if you make it with elk hair rather than deer. Try building the body and hump with flat waxed nylon and then switching to thread to set the wings and complete the fly.

To tie the standard Humpy with the tips of the hump hair making the wings, begin by measuring and binding on the tail, which must exactly equal the full length of the hook (not just the shank). Comb and stack a bunch of elk hair. Hold the elk hair over the hook so the tips are directly over the tips of the tail. Snip off the butts of the elk directly over the front edge of the eye. Set the cut edge of the bunch of elk hair on the center of the shank and then bind the hair back to the bend, atop the tail. Cover the tail and elk hair bindings with thread, pull the elk forward over the thread body for a hump, divide the tips of the elk for wings of just the right length, and make a conventional hackle to complete what should now be a neatly proportioned Humpy.

## HUMPY (STANDARD)

*Tied by Skip Morris*

| | |
|---|---|
| **Hook:** | Light wire, standard length or 1X long, sizes 16 to 8. |
| **Thread:** | Yellow 3/0, 6/0, 8/0, or flat waxed nylon. |
| **Tail:** | Natural blackish moose body or undyed elk or deer hair. |
| **Hump:** | Natural tan-brown elk. |
| **Body:** | Yellow thread or flat waxed nylon. |
| **Wing:** | Tips of the elk hair are used for the hump. |
| **Hackle:** | Brown and grizzly, one hackle wound through the other. |
| **Comments:** | Yellow is the standard color for the Humpy. |

## HUMPY, GREEN

*Tied by Todd Smith*

| | |
|---|---|
| **Hook:** | Light wire, standard length or 1X long, sizes 16 to 8. |
| **Thread:** | Green 3/0, 6/0, or 8/0, or flat waxed nylon. |
| **Tail:** | Natural blackish moose body or undyed elk or deer hair. |
| **Hump:** | Natural tan-brown elk. |
| **Body:** | Green thread or flat waxed nylon. |
| **Wing:** | Tips of the elk hair are used for the hump, or white calf tail. Calf tail wings are bound on after the hump is formed and trimmed. |
| **Hackle:** | Brown. |

## HUMPY, ROYAL

*Tied by Skip Morris*

| | |
|---|---|
| **Hook:** | Light wire, standard length or 1X long, sizes 16 to 8. |
| **Thread:** | Red 3/0, or 6/0, or 8/0, or flat waxed nylon. |
| **Tail:** | Natural blackish moose body or undyed elk or deer hair. |
| **Hump:** | Natural tan-brown elk. |
| **Body:** | Red thread or flat waxed nylon. |
| **Wing:** | White calf tail; the wings are bound on after the hump is formed and trimmed. |
| **Hackle:** | Brown. |
| **Comments:** | A blending of the eternally popular Royal Coachman and the Humpy—as flashy as the former and as buoyant as the latter. |

**Madam X.** Doug Swisher's Madam X—with its long, quivering, waving legs—has become a true standard among western attractor dry flies, although some use it as a stonefly imitation. Like most popular patterns, it has inspired a lot of variations—good to bad, clever to crude. (Only the good, clever ones are included here, of course.) I prefer tougher elk hair over deer for the wing, head, and body.

## MADAM X (ORIGINAL) — *Doug Swisher*

*Tied by Skip Morris*

**Hook:** Light (or standard) wire, 2X or 3X long, sizes 10 to 6.
**Thread:** Yellow 3/0.
**Body and tail:** Natural deer (or elk) hair bound on well up the shank; the working thread is spiraled down the body and back up, making a pattern of "X"s.
**Head and wing:** Natural deer (or elk) hair tied in behind the eye, pulled up and back, and then secured with a thread collar (the hair should stay on top, not radiate as collar as with a typical bullet head).
**Legs:** White (I prefer yellow) round rubber-strand, one section bound along each side, under the narrow thread collar.
**Comments:** The original, and still perfectly effective.

## MADAM X (VARIATION)

*Tied by Skip Morris*

**Hook:** Light or standard wire, 2X or 3X long, sizes 10 to 6.
**Thread:** Yellow 3/0 (or yellow flat waxed nylon).
**Tail:** Natural deer or elk hair.
**Body:** The yellow working thread, covering the hair completely.
**Head and wing:** Natural tan-gray deer or elk hair. Instructions are in the Madam X (original), on this page.
**Legs:** Yellow round rubber-strand, one section bound along each side, under the narrow thread collar.
**Comments:** Covering up the hair completely with thread, as here, is now popular. A really heavy thread covers quickly—flat waxed nylon does it in a snap.

## MADAM X (VARIATION)

*Tied by Skip Morris*

**Hook:** Light (or standard) wire, 2X or 3X long, sizes 10 to 6.
**Thread:** Orange 3/0 (or orange flat waxed nylon).
**Tail:** Natural deer or elk hair.
**Body:** The orange working thread, with a short-fibered dry-fly saddle hackle spiraled up its length.
**Head and wing:** Natural deer or elk hair. Instructions are in the Madam X (original), on this page.
**Legs:** White round rubber-strand, one section bound along each side, under the narrow thread collar.

## MADAM X, PARACHUTE, ORANGE (OFTEN CALLED THE PMX)
*Doug Swisher*

*Tied by Wade Malwitz*

**Hook:** Light (or standard) wire, 1X or 2X long, sizes 10 to 6.
**Thread:** Orange, green, or black 3/0 (or flat waxed nylon).
**Tail:** Undyed tan-gray elk hair.
**Body:** Orange 3/0 or flat waxed nylon.
**Down-wing:** Undyed tan-gray elk hair.
**Parachute wing:** White Antron (or poly) yarn (instructions are on page 63).
**Parachute hackle:** Grizzly or brown (instructions are on page 63) .
**Legs:** White, brown, or black rubber-strand, a section bound tightly on each side of the thorax to create a total of four legs.
**Thorax:** Peacock herl.
**Comments:** When I researched the Parachute Madam X, I found it with various colors of legs and hackle and body—no doubt, they all work. This pattern is frequently tied in yellow, red, and red with a peacock herl butt (the Royal Parachute Madam X).

## MUDDLER, DRY

*Tied by Skip Morris*

**Hook:** Light to heavy wire, long shank, size 14 to 8.
**Thread:** Yellow 6/0 or 3/0 (option: use size A rod-winding thread for the head).
**Tail:** Brown mottled turkey quill section.
**Body:** Yellow poly yarn.
**Underwing:** White calf tail.
**Wing:** Brown mottled turkey quill sections.
**Head and collar:** Natural tan-gray deer hair, flared and shaped (instructions are on page 268).

**Comments:** The Muddler Minnow was originally a popular imitation of a sculpin, but before it soaked up enough water to sink, trout would take it on top—thus this dry version.

## PETER'S ANT
*Peter Morrison*

*Tied by Peter Morrison*

**Hook:** Light wire, standard length or 1X long, sizes 16 to 12 (Peter nearly always uses size 14).
**Thread:** Black 8/0 or 6/0.
**Parachute wing:** White poly yarn (or Antron), in a loop (instructions are on page 63).
**Parachute hackle:** Black (instructions are on page 63).
**Body:** Black Super Fine Dry Fly Dubbing (or any buoyant synthetic dubbing, such as Antron or poly dubbing).
**Comments:** Peter's Ant gradually evolved from the standard Parachute Ant, until it became its own unique pattern. The distinctive features of the Peter's Ant—the looped wing, the mayfly-like body—are absent on the Parachute Ant. I've watched Peter take lots of trout, mainly cutthroats, on his Ant, with no evidence of real ants being on the water. Besides, it doesn't look like a real ant, so it must be an attractor—and a particularly understated one in comparison to such gaudy dry-fly attractors as the Lime Trude and the Double Ugly Tickler.

**Predator.** The Predator began life as an imitation of a dragonfly nymph, intended to dart just above a full-sinking line—and snags—in trout lakes. Once the fly was commercially available, fly fishers started using it as a dry fly—and catching trout. So I put a lighter wire hook in it, added a strike indicator, and caught some fish of my own. I've found it deadly on cutthroats—especially when switched off with a Chernobyl Ant, whenever one or the other starts failing—but I've taken browns and rainbows with it too. Both the simple original version and the fancier Super Predator tend to float low, which gives the trout plenty to see below the water's surface. Like most of the big, silly foam flies, it doesn't always land upright, but this may not matter a lick to the fish, especially if you omit the strike indicator.

## PREDATOR (ORIGINAL) — *Skip Morris*

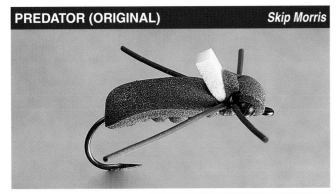

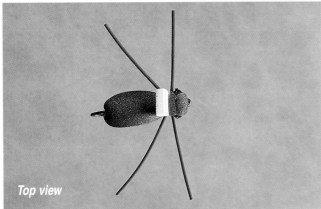

*Top view*

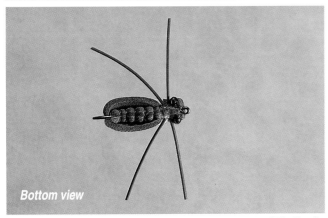

*Bottom view*

*Tied by Skip Morris*

**Hook:** Light or standard wire, 2X long (a straight eye and slow-curve shank are optional), sizes 10 to 6.

**Thread:** Brown 3/0.

**Body and head:** Strip of brown buoyant closed-cell foam sheeting, bound down and back up the rear two-thirds of the shank in a pattern of "X"s, pulled forward and down, and bound two-thirds up the shank. The front of the strip should be trimmed back along the sides before it's bound forward to the hook's eye, then doubled back atop the barbell eyes for a head.

**Eyes:** Black premade plastic barbell eyes.

**Legs:** Length of brown round rubber-strand, bound along each side of the thread collar holding the rear of the head strip, to make four legs.

**Strike indicator (optional):** Short strip of yellow buoyant closed-cell foam sheeting.

## PREDATOR, SUPER, BROWN — *Skip Morris*

*Tied by Skip Morris*

**Hook:** Light or standard wire, 2X long (a straight eye and slow-curve shank are optional), sizes 10 to 6.

**Thread:** Brown 6/0 or 3/0.

**Tail:** Small bunch of pearl Krystal Flash trimmed short, flanked by tails of fine black or brown rubber-strand.

**Body and head:** Strip of brown buoyant closed-cell foam sheeting, bound down and back up the rear two-thirds of the shank in a pattern of "X"s, pulled forward and down, and bound two-thirds up the shank. The front of the strip should be trimmed back along the sides before it's bound forward to the hook's eye, then doubled back atop the barbell eyes for a head.

**Eyes:** Black premade plastic barbell eyes.

**Antennae:** Fine black or brown rubber-strand, either bound on the shank behind the eye or pushed into and out of the foam head with a needle and bound to the shank before the head is formed (instructions follow).

**Legs:** Length of yellow round rubber-strand (barred with black, if you like), bound along each side of the thread collar holding the rear of the head strip, to make four legs.

**Strike indicator:** Short strip of yellow buoyant closed-cell foam sheeting.

**Comments:** After the success of the original Predator, I jazzed it up and found the new version at least as effective as the original. The fine tails and antennae sway in even light currents, leaving the stiffer legs to do the dancing in faster water. If you leave off the strike indicator, the fly fishes just as well upside down as right side up.

## Making Rubber-Strand Antennae in a Foam Head (Super Predator)

**1.** It's possible that someone else figured this out before I did, but if so, I'm unaware of it, so I'll claim this as my original method for making rubber-strand antennae. Double back the front of the foam strip and bind it back from the hook's eye—temporarily—with a few firm turns of thread, creating a foam head.

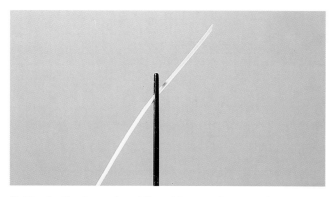

**2.** Trim the tip of a section of fine rubber-strand at an angle, to make it pointed. Push the pointed end through the eye of a big-eyed sewing needle. (If you can't get the strand all the way through, work the pointed tip partway through the needle's eye, and then catch the tip with tweezers or English hackle pliers and pull the strand through.)

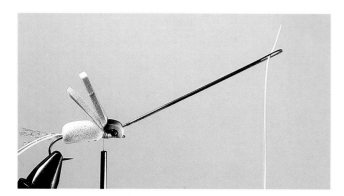

**3.** Push the needle into the head, at whatever angle you want the antenna to take.

**4.** Unwind the turns of thread holding the foam. Pull the needle and some of the rubber-strand through the foam. Push the needle back out of the foam where you want to make a second antenna. Bind the doubled end of the strand atop the shank.

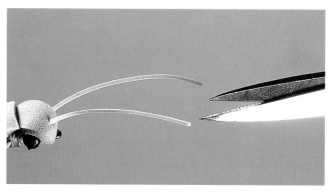

**5.** Pull the foam back again and bind it as you did before—but this time, the bindings are permanent. Trim the rubber-strand antennae to length.

**PREDATOR, SUPER, TAN**     *Skip Morris*

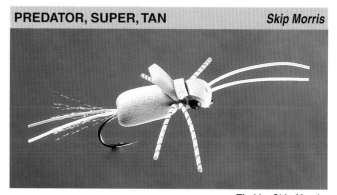

*Tied by Skip Morris*

| | |
|---|---|
| **Hook:** | Light or standard wire, 2X long (a straight eye and slow-curve shank are optional), sizes 10 to 6. |
| **Thread:** | Tan 6/0 or 3/0. |
| **Tail:** | Small bunch of pearl Krystal Flash trimmed short, flanked by tails of fine tan, white, or yellow rubber-strand. |
| **Body and head:** | Strip of tan buoyant closed-cell foam sheeting, bound down and back up the rear two-thirds of the shank in a pattern of "X"s, pulled forward and down, and bound two-thirds up the shank. The front of the strip should be trimmed back along the sides before it's bound forward to the hook's eye, then doubled back atop the barbell eyes for a head. |

**Eyes:** Black premade plastic barbell eyes.

**Antennae:** Fine tan, white, or yellow rubber-strand, either bound on the shank behind the eye or pushed into and out of the foam head with a needle and bound to the shank before the head is formed (instructions are on page 246).

**Legs:** Length of tan or yellow round rubber-strand (barred with black, if you like), bound along each side of the thread collar holding the rear of the head strip, to make four legs.

**Strike indicator:** Short strip of yellow buoyant closed-cell foam sheeting.

**Comments:** After the success of the original Predator, I jazzed it up and found the new version at least as effective as the original. The fine tails and antennae sway in even light currents, leaving the stiffer legs to do the dancing in faster water. If you leave off the strike indicator, the fly fishes just as well upside down as right side up.

## PURPLE HAZE (ALSO CALLED CARLSON'S PURPLE HAZE CHUTE) *Andre Carlson*

*Tied by Skip Morris*

**Hook:** Light wire, standard length or 1X long, sizes 18 to10.

**Thread:** Purple 8/0 or 6/0.

**Parachute wing:** Undyed white calf tail (instructions are on page 63).

**Tail:** Undyed tan-brown elk mane or buck tail.

**Parachute hackle:** One brown and one grizzly, the grizzly hackle wound through the brown hackle (instructions are on page 63).

**Body:** Purple MFC Wonder Wrap (or purple Span-Flex, Super Floss, or the like). Carlson stretches the Wonder Wrap tight at the tail and uses less stretch working forward, to create a tapered body.

**Comments:** Who knows why a purple dry fly will take trout when nothing else seems to work? Floating purple insects are rare indeed. But many western anglers swear by this fly. The Purple Haze has really caught on big; we've heard enthusiastic reports from Oregon, Montana, and British Columbia.

## RENEGADE

*Tied by Skip Morris*

**Hook:** Light wire, standard length or 1X long, sizes 16 to 8.

**Thread:** Black 8/0 or 6/0.

**Rear hackle:** Brown.

**Body:** Peacock herl.

**Front hackle:** White.

**Comments:** The Renegade, even though it emerged in the 1930s and has been around long enough to fall into the traditional category, seemed more like an attractor dry fly to me. Just look at it—do you see anything traditional there? The Renegade is often fished as a peculiar wet fly, dead drift, and there are plenty of fly fishers who'll testify that it works that way.

## ROYAL COACHMAN

See chapter 13, Traditional Dry Flies.

## ROYAL WULFF                                    *Lee Wulff*

*Tied by Todd Smith*

**Hook:**      Light wire, standard length or 1X long, sizes 16 to 8.
**Thread:**    Black 8/0, 6/0, or 3/0.
**Wing:**      White buck tail or calf tail.
**Tail:**      Natural brown buck tail or elk hair.
**Body:**      Collar of peacock herl, spun around the thread to toughen it, then a band of red floss and another collar of peacock herl.
**Hackle:**    Brown.
**Comments:**  Unlike the rest of the Wulff series of dry flies, which are a shade more imitators than attractors, this one is a blend of the Wulff style and the Royal Coachman (see chapter 13). The Royal Wulff is as popular today as at any time since Lee first cooked it up more than 70 years ago. The other, more plausible, Wulffs are in chapter 13.

**Trude.** The Trude flies came along decades ago, representing some of the earliest rough-water fly designs. They are stubborn floaters, especially when tied with lots of hackle.

## TRUDE, LIME COACHMAN                           *A. S. Trude*

*Tied by Skip Morris*

**Hook:**      Light wire, standard length or 1X long, sizes 16 to 8.
**Thread:**    Black 8/0, 6/0, or 3/0.
**Tail:**      Golden pheasant tippets.
**Body:**      Lime green synthetic dubbing.
**Wing:**      White calf tail tied down-wing style.
**Hackle:**    Brown; use plenty of hackle.

## TRUDE, RIO GRANDE KING                          *A. S. Trude*

*Tied by Carol Ann Morris*

**Hook:**      Light wire, standard length or 1X long, sizes 16 to 6.
**Thread:**    Black 8/0, 6/0, or 3/0.
**Tag:**       Flat gold tinsel.
**Tail:**      Golden pheasant tippet.
**Body:**      Black synthetic dubbing (some use chenille).
**Wing:**      White calf tail, back atop the body.
**Hackle:**    Brown; use plenty of hackle.

## TRUDE, ROYAL COACHMAN                           *A. S. Trude*

*Tied by Skip Morris*

**Hook:**      Light wire, standard length or 1X long, sizes 16 to 8.
**Thread:**    Black 8/0, 6/0, or 3/0.
**Tail:**      Golden pheasant tippets.
**Body:**      Front and rear thirds are peacock herl; center third is red floss.
**Wing:**      White calf tail, back atop the body.
**Hackle:**    Brown; use plenty of hackle.

## TURCK TARANTULA · *Guy Turck*

*Tied by Skip Morris*

| | |
|---|---|
| **Hook:** | Heavy (or standard) wire, 3X (or 2X) long, sizes 12 to 4. |
| **Thread:** | Tan 3/0. |
| **Tail:** | Golden pheasant tippet. |
| **Body:** | Hare's mask. |
| **Underwing:** | White calf tail. |
| **Wing:** | Pearl Krystal Flash over natural deer hair. |
| **Legs:** | White or brown rubber-strand, one section bound tightly along each side, resulting in four legs. Bind on the legs at the front of the abdomen, just behind the flared hair head. |

**Head and collar:** Natural tan-brown deer hair, flared and trimmed (instructions are on page 268).

**Comments:** Like a number of peculiar and effective attractor flies, the Turck Tarantula held its coming-out party at the Jackson Hole One Fly Contest, as the winner.

# Attractor Streamers and Bucktails

Streamers (flies with feather wings) and bucktails (flies with hair wings) have a long history both as imitations of tiny fishes and as nonimitative attractor flies. Fish attractor streamers or bucktails as described in chapter 15, Tiny Fish and Leeches. The one exception is that, occasionally, stripping an attractor wildly across a river can stir a trout into doing something stupid.

## AUTUMN SPLENDOR · *Tim Heng*

*Tied by Tim Heng*

| | |
|---|---|
| **Hook:** | Heavy wire, 3X long, sizes 12 to 4. |
| **Head:** | Copper bead for sizes 12 to 8: $7/64$ inch for size 12, $5/32$ inch for sizes 10 and 8. Copper cone for sizes 6 and 4: medium for size 6, large for size 4. |
| **Weight:** | Lead wire. |
| **Thread:** | Brown 3/0 or 210 denier. |
| **Tail:** | Dyed brown marabou, with four to six strands of copper Krystal Flash along each side. |
| **Rib:** | Fine copper wire, wound over the tip of the wound hackle and then spiraled forward through the hackle to the bead or cone. |
| **Body:** | Medium brown chenille. |
| **Legs:** | Yellow rubber-strand, the strands bound crossways so that each strand makes two legs. Use two sets of legs for a size 12 hook; three sets for sizes 10 and larger. |
| **Hackle:** | Dyed yellow grizzly and dyed orange grizzly, bound up close to the bead or cone, spiraled back over the body and around the legs, then secured with the wire and counterwound with it. |

**Comments:** Tim often fishes his Autumn Splendor from a drift boat as the lead fly in a two-streamer rig. His pattern is highly visible, making the fishing of both flies efficient and permitting the easy detection of strikes.

## BLACK GHOST

*Tied by Skip Morris*

**Hook:** Heavy wire, 4X to 6X long, sizes 10 to 6.
**Thread:** Black 8/0, 6/0, or 3/0.
**Tail:** Dyed yellow hackle fibers.
**Rib:** Flat silver tinsel, thin to medium.
**Body:** Black floss.
**Throat:** Yellow (usually a bunch of fibers bound underneath the shank, but sometimes a wound hackle with the fibers pulled down and bound at their base to stay there).
**Wing:** Four white saddle hackles in two sets, the sets cupped together.
**Cheek (optional):** Two jungle cock feathers (or "nails"), one per side.
**Comments:** An old-timer that's still in general use because it works.

## BOW RIVER BUGGER
*Peter Chenier*

*Tied by Wade Malwitz*

**Hook:** Heavy wire, 4X long, sizes 8 to 2.
**Weight:** Lead wire.
**Tail:** Black marabou mixed with a few strands of blue Flashabou.
**Hackle:** Black, spiraled up the body.
**Body:** Olive chenille.
**Head and collar:** Natural tan-gray deer hair, flared and trimmed (instructions are on page 268).
**Comments:** A hit streamer on Alberta's legendary Bow River.

## CONEHEAD THE BARBARIAN (MICKEY FINN VERSION)
*Scott Sanchez*

*Tied by Scott Sanchez*

**Hook:** Heavy wire, standard length, straight eye (Scott uses the Dai-Riki 930 or Mustad 3366), size 2. Bend the shank, about one-quarter of its length back from the eye, about 15 degrees. If you hold the hook inverted with its shank horizontal and its bend up, its straight eye (once the hook is bent) should angle slightly downward.
**Thread:** Red 3/0.
**Head:** Large silver metal cone head. Pearl prism tape wrapped over the cone and trimmed back beyond the cone head.
**Wing:** Polypropylene fibers (Scott uses EP Fibers) in blue over chartreuse over white (with the hook inverted). Between the blue and chartreuse fibers, place a few strands of pearl Krystal Flash.
**Eyes:** Adhesive-backed white eyes with red or black pupils. Once the eyes are on, coat the entire head with low-odor epoxy glue.
**Comments:** Build up thread behind the eye until the cone head slips over it snugly. Cut the thread. Push the cone head up to the eye. (Scott adds glue to the thread before pushing the cone forward.) Restart the thread behind the cone head. Add the wing close behind the cone head, and trim it to three full hook-lengths. From there, complete the head as described in the dressing. Scott developed this pattern for the fresh- and saltwater species around Austin, Texas, where he used to live: largemouth bass, stripers, white bass, and even flounder. When he moved to Montana, he found that his Conehead the Barbarian was effective on trout rivers when fished on shooting heads and sinking lines. Scott also fishes it on full-floating lines, since the fly is heavy enough to go down well on its own. He advises: "Vary the speed and tempo of your retrieve to figure out what is best on the particular day." Because the hook rides inverted, you can fish the fly low across the riverbed without much worry of hanging up.

## DOUBLE BUNNY — *Scott Sanchez*

*Tied by Scott Sanchez*

Hook: Heavy wire, 4X long, size 2.
Thread: White 3/0 or heavier.
Weight: Lead wire, 0.035-inch diameter.
Body and wing: Magnum (extra-wide) natural gray Zonker strip bound atop the shank at the eye, and a magnum white Zonker strip pushed over the hook's point and bound below the eye. Cement the strips together around the shank and lead and beyond the bend. (Scott uses Val-A-Tearmender cement. He also uses olive over white and olive over yellow for the wing.)
Sides: A few strands of pearl Krystal Flash and silver Holographic Flashabou.
Eyes: Red plastic molded eyes with black pupils, $^{7}/_{32}$-inch diameter. (Scott uses a glue called Goop for cementing on the eyes.)
Comments: Though it's quite minnow-like, my instincts tell me the Double Bunny is primarily an attractor. It doesn't really matter—big trout move for this fly, and it has become a standard all over the West.

## HALF AND HALF — *Lefty Kreh and Bob Clouser*

*Tied by Skip Morris*

Hook: Heavy wire, 3X or 4X long, sizes 10 to 4.
Thread: Dark gray (or dark brown or any dark color) 6/0 or 3/0.
Eyes: Lead barbell eyes, mounted on top of the shank so the fly inverts in the water.
Tail: Eight long grizzly saddle hackles in two sets, the sets cupped together. Use a few strands of pearl Flashabou outside the hackles and, beneath the hackles, a bunch of white buck tail.
Body: Butts of the buck tail bound up the shank, with the butts of the Flashabou bound down and then up the sides of the buck tail to form a pattern of "X"s.

Wing: Dark gray or brown buck tail. The butts of the wing are bound over the stem of the eyes, as with the Clouser Minnow.
Comments: A blend of the Clouser Minnow and Lefty's Deceiver. This version was my attempt to suggest a small trout. It took a 19-inch rainbow-cutthroat hybrid for me on a Canadian river soon after I tied it, among other fish. Lefty especially likes the Half and Half with either yellow or white tail-hackles and a chartreuse wing for all fish species—definitely attractor-fly colors.

## HARE'S EAR AGGRAVATOR — *Andy Burk*

*Tied by Andy Burk*

Hook: Standard or heavy wire, 3X long (slow-curve shank preferred), sizes 12 to 4.
Head: Gold metal bead.
Weight: Lead wire.
Thread: Beige 6/0.
Tag: Pearl Krystal Flash.
Tail: Dyed tan marabou.
Rib: Pearl Krystal Flash.
Abdomen: Undyed tan-brown hare's mask.
Legs: Pumpkin Sili Legs with black flakes. Four legs are made from two lengths of rubber-strand and bound to sweep back from the sides of the thorax. Trim the legs long.
Thorax: Undyed tan-brown hare's mask.
Wing case: Section of mottled turkey tail, coated on the underside with cement, notched in the end.
Collar: Natural dark hare's mask.
Comments: Andy describes this as his "favorite attractor/nymph/streamer/creature fly." Our friend Lynn Hescock, who guides for huge rainbows on Oregon's Williamson River, swears by the Hare's Ear Aggravator.

## MARABOU, BLACK

*Tied by Wade Malwitz*

**Hook:**      Heavy wire, 3X or 4X long, sizes 10 to 4.
**Thread:**    Black 8/0, 6/0, or 3/0.
**Tail:**      Dyed red hackle fibers.
**Body:**      Flat silver tinsel.
**Wing:**      Dyed black marabou, topped with a few peacock herls.
**Throat:**    Dyed red hackle fibers.
**Comments:**  The Marabou streamers are exceptionally lively, and
although they may suggest small fish, I tend to think of them as attractors.

## MARABOU, YELLOW

*Tied by Skip Morris*

**Hook:**      Heavy wire, 3X or 4X long, sizes 10 to 4.
**Thread:**    Black 8/0, 6/0, or 3/0.
**Tail:**      Dyed red hackle fibers.
**Body:**      Flat silver tinsel.
**Wing:**      Dyed yellow marabou, topped with a few peacock herls.
**Comments:**  The Marabou streamers are exceptionally lively, and
although they may suggest small fish, I tend to think of them as attractors.

## MICKEY FINN

*Tied by Skip Morris*

**Hook:**      Heavy wire, 4X to 6X long, sizes 12 to 2.
**Thread:**    Black 6/0 or 8/0.
**Rib:**       Oval silver tinsel.
**Body:**      Flat silver tinsel.
**Wing:**      Yellow buck tail over red buck tail over yellow buck tail; the
               top bunch of yellow buck tail should equal the bulk of the red
               and lower yellow combined.
**Comments:**  The Mickey Finn has been fooling trout for decades and is
still widely trusted.

## PLATTE RIVER SPECIAL                                    *Bud Miller*

*Tied by Bob Jacklin*

**Hook:**      Heavy wire, 4X long, sizes 6 to 2.
**Weight:**    Lead wire, 0.015-inch diameter.
**Thread:**    Black 3/0.
**Rib:**       Gold wire.
**Body:**      Earthworm brown (a light brown) Ultra Chenille.
**Wing:**      Two long ginger saddle or rooster hackles enclosing two
               yellow hackles. The hackles should cup together.
**Hackle:**    Large, soft yellow hackle wound on first, then a large, soft
               ginger hackle wound in front of it.
**Comments:**  According to Bob Jacklin, Bud Miller's Platte River Special
made its debut in 1951. This version is Bob's slight variation on the original.
But when I looked through my pattern books, I discovered that the standard dressing varies plenty from one text to the next. Way back, it was
often tied with no body at all. Bob describes it as his "go-to fly when fall
fishing for big brown trout."

## SPRUCE FLY

*Top view*

*Tied by Skip Morris*

**Hook:** Heavy wire, 3X or 4X long, sizes 10 to 4.
**Thread:** Black 8/0, 6/0, or 3/0.
**Tail:** Peacock sword.
**Body:** Rear one-third to two-thirds: red floss or red yarn. Front one-third to two-thirds: peacock herl.
**Wing:** Two badger neck or saddle hackles, curving apart. (Some tiers use two sets of two hackles per set, the sets curving apart.)
**Hackle:** Badger.
**Comments:** My limited research suggests that the Spruce Fly goes back several decades and was originally developed for sea-run cutthroat trout in Oregon. Nowadays, most fly fishers think of it as a streamer for trout rivers, largely associated with Montana. Anyway, the separated wing is unique, or at least rare, among streamer flies, and the Spruce takes a lot of trout.

**Woolly Bugger.** This is a simple fly pattern—a pushover at the tying vise—and it spends more time in the water than a rock-scarred old wading shoe. Many fly fishers just grab it out of reflex whenever there's no reason to do otherwise. Undoubtedly the Woolly Bugger can suggest a leech or maybe even a small fish. I'm convinced, however, that it's fished most often as an attractor.

## WOOLLY BUGGER, BLACK   *Russell Blessing*

*Tied by Skip Morris*

**Hook:** Heavy wire, 3X or 4X long, sizes 14 to 2.
**Thread:** Black 8/0, 6/0, or 3/0.
**Weight (optional):** Lead wire.
**Tail:** Dyed black marabou.
**Rib:** One dyed black saddle or neck hackle, spiraled up the body.
**Abdomen:** Black chenille.
**Comments:** Some tiers wind the hackle back down the body toward the tail and then spiral copper wire forward through the hackle to the front of the body, as with the Stimulator and Elk Hair Caddis dry flies. The repeated crossing of wire over hackle stem makes the hackle tough indeed.

## WOOLLY BUGGER, BROWN   *Russell Blessing*

*Tied by Carol Ann Morris*

**Hook:** Heavy wire, 3X or 4X long, sizes 14 to 2.
**Thread:** Brown 8/0, 6/0, or 3/0.
**Weight (optional):** Lead wire.
**Tail:** Dyed brown marabou.
**Rib:** One dyed brown saddle or neck hackle, spiraled up the body.
**Abdomen:** Brown chenille.
**Comments:** See Woolly Bugger, Black, above.

## WOOLLY BUGGER, GRIZZLY AND WHITE
*Russell Blessing*

*Tied by Skip Morris*

| | |
|---|---|
| **Hook:** | Heavy wire, 3X or 4X long, sizes 14 to 2. |
| **Thread:** | White 8/0, 6/0, or 3/0. |
| **Weight (optional):** | Lead wire. |
| **Tail:** | White marabou. |
| **Rib:** | One grizzly saddle or neck hackle, spiraled up the body. |
| **Abdomen:** | White chenille. |
| **Comments:** | See Woolly Bugger, Black, on page 253. |

## WOOLLY BUGGER, OLIVE
*Russell Blessing*

*Tied by Carol Ann Morris*

| | |
|---|---|
| **Hook:** | Heavy wire, 3X or 4X long, sizes 14 to 2. |
| **Thread:** | Olive 8/0, 6/0, or 3/0. |
| **Weight (optional):** | Lead wire. |
| **Tail:** | Dyed olive marabou. |
| **Rib:** | One dyed olive saddle or neck hackle, spiraled up the body. |
| **Abdomen:** | Olive chenille. |
| **Comments:** | See Woolly Bugger, Black, on page 253. |

# Tiny Fish and Leeches

**15**

TROUT EAT TROUT, and the questionable etiquette of feasting on your own species aside, it's easy to see why—compared with a spindly little midge larva or *Baetis* mayfly nymph, a plump, fleshy baby brown trout looks like a load of protein, a real stomach-full. In the West, another fish dinner for a trout might be a sculpin—a drab, bottom-hugging little fish with a big, broad, flat, and undisputedly ugly head. Some rivers are full of them. Leeches also inhabit slow and weedy rivers. They are big, sleek, and disgusting; and trout relish them.

Imitations of tiny fish and leeches are fished much the same way. Since both fish and leeches swim, fly fishers usually make their flies do the same, swinging them slowly across the current with twitches or teasing them along undercut banks. The trick, of course, is to make the fly do whatever the fish or leech it represents does.

The word on fish- and leech-imitating flies is that they move big trout, and in my experience, that's true. It's possible to catch a big trout on a dry fly, and you always have a good shot at one with an artificial nymph, but if you really want to see the heaviest trout in a river, your best chance is with a Zoo Cougar or Janssen's Minnow or some other tiny fish or leech imitation.

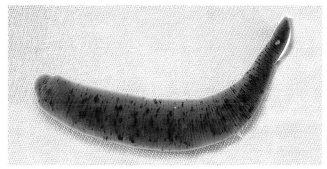

*Brown leech*

*Juvenile rainbow trout*

JIM SCHOLLMEYER PHOTO

*Sculpin*

JIM SCHOLLMEYER PHOTO

255

# Fish

## CHUCK'S MOSS SCULPIN — *Chuck Stranahan*

*Tied by Skip Morris*

| | |
|---|---|
| **Hook:** | Heavy wire, 3X long, sizes 8 to 4. |
| **Thread:** | Cream 3/0 for the body, olive size A rod thread for the head and collar. |
| **Weight:** | Lead wire, wound over the center of the hook but ending well short of the eye or bend. (Chuck uses 0.025-inch for a size 8 hook, 0.030-inch for a size 6, and 0.035-inch for a size 4.) |
| **Body:** | Cream yarn, such as fuzzy Antron or wool. |
| **Wing:** | Dyed olive Zonker rabbit strip over 12 to 16 strands of fine pearlescent Doug's Bugs Actionflash (or Krystal Flash or Flashabou). |
| **Gills:** | Doug's Bugs bright red TLC dubbing (or any natural or synthetic dubbing), shaggy and spun in a dubbing loop. |
| **Head and collar:** | Dyed olive or dark olive deer hair, flared and trimmed to a broad and flattened head, leaving hair tips as a collar (instructions are on page 268). |

**Comments:** Imitates a greenish sculpin. You can vary the colors, depending on your local sculpins.

**Clouser Minnow.** The Clouser Minnow is both popular and easy to tie. Although it's often used as an attractor, it's also a natural for imitating tiny fish. The Clouser takes trout, but it also takes smallmouth and largemouth bass, pike, bonefish, permit, and others.

Tying a Clouser Minnow is quick and easy once you understand the process. Bind the heavy barbell eyes firmly atop the shank—leave some room behind the hook's eye. Bind the belly hair behind the stem of the barbell eyes with a tight thread collar. Advance the thread to just ahead of the eye stem and bind and trim the butts of the hair there. Remove the hook from the vise, invert the hook, and mount it again in the vise. Bind the Flashabou on in front of the eye stem; then bind the buck tail for the wing atop the Flashabou, in front of the eye stem. Build and complete a tapered thread head.

## CLOUSER MINNOW, BLACK AND WHITE — *Bob Clouser and Lefty Kreh*

*Tied by Skip Morris*

| | |
|---|---|
| **Hook:** | Standard to heavy wire, standard length to 3X long, sizes 10 to 6. |
| **Thread:** | Black 8/0, 6/0, or 3/0. |
| **Eyes:** | Lead barbell eyes, yellow with black pupils. |
| **Belly (bottom wing):** | White buck tail. |
| **Top wing:** | Dyed black buck tail over pearl Krystal Flash. |

**Comments:** Jim McLennan presents this black-backed, yellow-eyed version of the Clouser Minnow in his book *Blue Ribbon Bow*. He says that "olive, brown, and black are the favored colors for Bow River trout" and provides a chart that lists the Clouser as an imitation of a minnow.

## CLOUSER MINNOW, BROWN AND YELLOW — *Bob Clouser and Lefty Kreh*

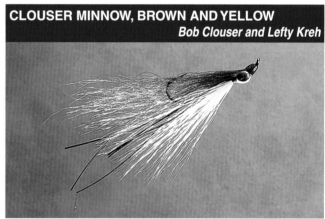

*Tied by Skip Morris*

| | |
|---|---|
| **Hook:** | Standard to heavy wire, standard length to 3X long, sizes 10 to 6. |
| **Thread:** | Brown 8/0, 6/0, or 3/0. |
| **Eyes:** | Lead barbell eyes, red with black pupils (or plain lead or silver color). |
| **Belly (bottom wing):** | Dyed yellow calf tail (or buck tail). |
| **Top wing:** | Dyed brown calf tail (or buck tail) over brown or pearl Flashabou. |

**Comments:** Lefty Kreh says of the Clouser Minnow in his book *Advanced Fly Fishing Techniques:* "The two most effective color combinations, at least for me, have been a yellow belly of calf tail with either a brown or olive wing of calf tail." He believes that in these colors, the fly suggests a sculpin or crayfish. However, these colors are also close to those of a tiny trout, so I suspect that the big fish sometimes take them as such.

## CLOUSER MINNOW, OLIVE AND YELLOW
### Bob Clouser and Lefty Kreh

*Tied by Skip Morris*

**Hook:** Standard to heavy wire, standard length to 3X long, sizes 10 to 6.

**Thread:** Olive 8/0, 6/0, or 3/0.

**Eyes:** Lead barbell eyes, red with black pupils (or plain lead or silver color).

**Belly (bottom wing):** Dyed yellow calf tail (or buck tail).

**Top wing:** Dyed olive calf tail (or buck tail) over olive or pearl Flashabou.

**Comments:** See the comments for the Clouser Minnow, Brown and Yellow, above.

## GANDER
### Mike Edgar

*Tied by Peter Morrison*

**Hook:** Heavy wire, 4X long (or any long-shank streamer hook), sizes 8 to 2.

**Thread:** White 6/0 or 3/0.

**Weight:** Lead wire.

**Tail:** White marabou.

**Body:** Gray or olive fuzzy yarn (wool, fuzzy Antron).

**Rib:** Gold oval tinsel.

**Wing:** Natural gray-brown rabbit strip.

**Collar:** Deer-hair tips.

**Head:** Wool, gray on top and white underneath, trimmed to a wide, tapered head. Bind the belly wool on the underside of the shank first; then bind the top wool over that with a few turns of thread around the previous turns. Pull the front of the wool firmly back as you pull the thread forward and then wind it around the shank a few times. Bind another bunch of white wool under the shank and gray on top, back against the previous bunches. Add a third section of gray-over-white wool in front of the last, and a fourth, if necessary. Whip finish the thread and trim all the wool with scissors.

**Comments:** A trusted standard on Alberta's famous Bow River. Usually used to imitate a sculpin.

**Janssen's Minnow.** Hal Janssen really stirred up fly tying with his original ideas—nymphs with glassy beads of epoxy on their tops; a dragonfly nymph with a fluffy, breathing abdomen; and, in his Minnow, a sleek and detailed body with a lively marabou tail. Janssen's Minnow has developed lots of fans.

## JANSSEN'S MINNOW, BROOK
### Hal Janssen

*Tied by Wade Malwitz*

**Hook:** Heavy wire, 3X long, sizes 10 to 4.

**Thread:** White 3/0.

**Weight (optional):** Lead wire.

**Tail:** Dyed olive marabou.

**Body:** Foundation of adhesive metal Zonker tape, folded around the shank and trimmed to shape. Bind woven gold Mylar tubing just behind the eye, push it back so it turns inside out over the shank, and then bind and trim it at the bend. Paint the body green on the back and yellow along the throat, with black specks over the back and partway down the flanks. Eyes are yellow with black pupils (instructions follow).

**Comments:** Imitates a baby brook trout.

# Tying the Janssen's Minnow (Janssen's Minnow, Rainbow)

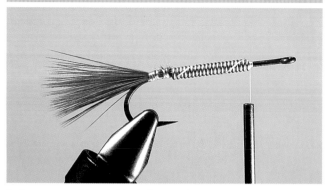

**1.** If you want weight, wind lead wire over the center part of the shank. Start the thread at the bend, and bind on a fairly short bunch of marabou for a tail. Bind the wire; whip-finish and cut the thread.

**2.** Press two rectangles of Zonker tape (shiny metal sheeting with adhesive backing) together around the shank (or fold a square of the tape over it). Make the tape short enough to leave some bare shank just behind the eye and ahead of the bend.

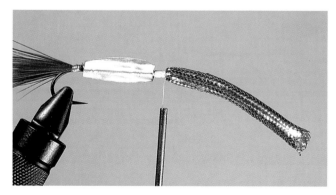

**3.** Trim the Zonker tape to the shape of a fish body, but trim it close enough so that it doesn't block the hook's point. Restart the thread behind the eye. Push the end of a short length of woven Mylar tubing (about one and a half times the full length of the hook) over the eye, bind the end of the Mylar, and whip-finish and cut off the thread.

**4.** Push the tubing back over the shank and Zonker tape—the tubing will turn inside out as you work it back. This may take a little practice and experimentation.

**5.** Restart the thread over the tubing and shank at the bend. Bind the end of the tubing with a tight thread collar. Whip-finish and cut off the thread. Unravel the rear of the tubing around the hook's bend and trim it closely.

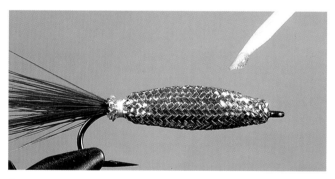

**6.** Coat the body with low-odor epoxy glue. Put the hook in a fly turning wheel or stick it in a board and turn the board over frequently as the epoxy sets.

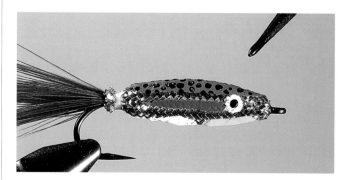

**7.** When the glue is almost fully cured, paint details on the body with any kind of paint. Epoxy contains no water, so you can even use poster paints, and the next coating won't make them run. Give the body a second coat of epoxy, and turn it frequently until the epoxy is fully cured.

## JANSSEN'S MINNOW, RAINBOW — *Hal Janssen*

*Tied by Skip Morris*

**Hook:** Heavy wire, 3X long, sizes 10 to 4.
**Thread:** White 3/0.
**Weight (optional):** Lead wire.
**Tail:** Olive marabou.
**Body:** Foundation of adhesive metal Zonker tape, folded around the shank and trimmed to shape. Bind woven silver Mylar tubing just behind the eye, push it back so it turns inside out over the shank, and then bind and trim it at the bend. Paint the back green, a red stripe down the center of each flank, and yellow along the throat, with black specks over the back and partway down the sides. Eyes are white with black pupils (instructions are on page 258).
**Comments:** Imitates a baby rainbow trout.

## JANSSEN'S MINNOW, BROWN — *Hal Janssen*

*Tied by Wade Malwitz*

**Hook:** Heavy wire, 3X long, sizes 10 to 4.
**Thread:** White 3/0.
**Weight (optional):** Lead wire.
**Tail:** Dyed gold marabou.
**Body:** Foundation of adhesive metal Zonker tape, folded around the shank and trimmed to shape. Bind woven gold Mylar tubing just behind the eye, push it back so it turns inside out over the shank, and then bind and trim it at the bend. Paint the body light brown on the back and yellow along the flanks and throat, with black specks over the back and partway down the flanks. Eyes are yellow with black pupils (instructions are on page 258).
**Comments:** Imitates a baby brown trout.

## JR'S CONEHEAD STREAMER — *John Rohmer*

*Tied by John Rohmer*

**Hook:** Heavy wire, 4X long, straight eye, size 4.
**Conehead:** Small, metal, silver.
**Collar:** Red glass bead, against the rear of the cone.
**Rib:** Medium-thin silver wire. Part the fur for each turn of the rib so that the rib binds the hide to the body.
**Tail and body:** White Arizona Simi Seal (or substitute another fine and sparkling dubbing, such as Ice Dub).
**Back:** Undyed tan-over-gray rabbit Zonker strip—a strip of rabbit hide with fur—the fur canting down the length of the strip.
**Hackle:** Dyed light gray hen back sweeping back over the body and Zonker strip.
**Eyes:** Pearl with black pupils, 3D molded 3.5 mm (or any similar artificial eyes), glued to the sides of the body (John uses 3M Superadhesive and then adds a little superglue between the eyes after the 3M glue is fully set).
**Comments:** You can tie this fly in any colors that suggest the tiny fishes you need to imitate. John tells me that JR's Conehead Streamer is catching on in Montana. He has had great days with this fly on Montana's Bighorn River and Utah's Green River by stripping it in fast. He finds it especially good on big brown trout.

## LITTLE BROOK TROUT — Sam Slaymaker

*Tied by Wade Malwitz*

| | |
|---|---|
| **Hook:** | Heavy wire, 3X to 6X, sizes 12 to 4. |
| **Thread:** | Black 8/0, 6/0, or 3/0. |
| **Tail:** | Dyed green calf tail or buck tail over red floss. |
| **Rib:** | Flat silver tinsel. |
| **Body:** | Cream natural dubbing (such as rabbit) or wool or Antron yarn. |
| **Wing:** | Badger guard hairs, or gray squirrel tail, over dyed orange buck tail or calf tail, over white (undyed) buck tail or calf tail. (Green buck tail between orange buck tail and badger is optional.) |
| **Throat:** | Orange calf tail or buck tail. |
| **Cheeks (optional):** | Jungle cock eyes. |
| **Comments:** | A reliable old standard for imitating baby brook trout. |

## LITTLE BROWN TROUT — Sam Slaymaker

*Tied by Wade Malwitz*

| | |
|---|---|
| **Hook:** | Heavy wire, 3X to 6X, sizes 12 to 4. |
| **Thread:** | Black 8/0, 6/0, or 3/0. |
| **Tail:** | Natural tan pheasant body feather fibers. |
| **Rib:** | Oval or flat gold tinsel. |
| **Body:** | White natural dubbing (such as rabbit) or wool or Antron yarn. |
| **Wing:** | Dyed brown squirrel tail over dyed red-orange calf tail or buck tail, over dyed yellow calf tail or buck tail. |
| **Throat (optional):** | Orange calf tail or buck tail. |
| **Cheeks (optional):** | Jungle cock eyes. |
| **Comments:** | A reliable old standard for imitating baby brown trout. |

## LITTLE RAINBOW TROUT — Sam Slaymaker

*Tied by Skip Morris*

| | |
|---|---|
| **Hook:** | Heavy wire, 3X to 6X, sizes 12 to 4. |
| **Thread:** | Black 8/0, 6/0, or 3/0. |
| **Tail:** | Dyed green calf tail or buck tail. |
| **Rib:** | Narrow flat silver tinsel. |
| **Body:** | Dyed pink natural dubbing (such as rabbit) or wool or Antron yarn. |
| **Wing:** | Badger guard hairs over dyed green calf tail or buck tail over dyed pink calf tail or buck tail over natural white calf tail or buck tail. |
| **Throat:** | Dyed orange or pink calf tail or buck tail. |
| **Cheeks (optional):** | Jungle cock eyes. |
| **Comments:** | A reliable old standard for imitating baby rainbow trout. |

**Marabou Muddler.** Obviously a close cousin of the original Muddler Minnow, the Marabou Muddler offers a soft and billowing wing that some fly fishers prefer.

## MARABOU MUDDLER, BROWN

*Tied by Skip Morris*

| | |
|---|---|
| **Hook:** | Heavy wire, 3X or 4X long, sizes 12 to 2. |
| **Thread:** | Brown 8/0, 6/0, or 3/0 (I switch to size A rod thread for flaring the hair). |

**Weight (optional):** Lead wire under the body.

**Tail (optional):** Red hackle fibers.

**Body:**          Flat gold tinsel. (Many tiers now wrap braided gold Mylar tinsel for the body, especially over lead wire.)

**Wing:**          One dyed brown marabou plume, topped with several peacock herls.

**Head and collar:** Natural tan-gray deer hair, flared and trimmed (instructions are on page 268).

**Comments:**      This brown version is as sculpin-like as any.

## MARABOU MUDDLER, OLIVE

*Tied by Peter Morrison*

**Hook:**          Heavy wire, 3X or 4X long, sizes 12 to 2.

**Thread:**        Olive 8/0, 6/0, or 3/0 (I switch to size A rod thread for flaring the hair).

**Weight (optional):** Lead wire under the body.

**Tail (optional):** Red hackle fibers.

**Body:**          Flat gold tinsel. (Many tiers now wrap braided gold Mylar tinsel for the body, especially over lead wire.)

**Wing:**          One olive marabou plume, topped with several peacock herls.

**Head and collar:** Dyed olive deer hair, flared and trimmed (instructions are on page 268).

**Comments:**      Some sculpin are olive, so this is definitely another imitative version.

## MARABOU MUDDLER, WHITE

*Tied by Peter Morrison*

**Hook:**          Heavy wire, 3X or 4X long, sizes 12 to 2.

**Thread:**        White 8/0, 6/0, or 3/0 (I switch to size A rod thread for flaring the hair).

**Weight (optional):** Lead wire under the body.

**Tail (optional):** Red hackle fibers.

**Body:**          Flat gold tinsel. (Many tiers now wrap braided gold Mylar tinsel for the body, especially over lead wire.)

**Wing:**          One white marabou plume, topped with several peacock herls.

**Head and collar:** Natural gray-brown deer hair, flared and trimmed (instructions are on page 268).

**Comments:**      This white version, though pale compared to any sculpin I've ever seen, probably loosely imitates that flat-headed little trout entree.

**Matuka.** Developed in New Zealand, the Matuka has proven itself on American waters as a first-class streamer. Many believe that this fly's big advantage over conventional streamers is its wing, which is bound all down the body and therefore doesn't separate from the body when the fly is fished and won't catch around the hook's bend. Although fish-like and normally tied in fishy colors, Matukas inhabit that gray area between attractors and imitators, leaning one way or the other as needed.

To tie the Matuka, bind the rib material down the top of the shank and then build the body. Strip the undersides of the wing feathers back only to the end of the body. Bind the feathers atop the hook at the front of the body. Wind the rib one-half turn forward, and hold it there. Hold the feathers down against the body, part the fibers over the rear of the body, and wind the rib between the fibers and over the stem. Continue parting the fibers as you spiral the rib up the body, securing the stem of the wing hackles with each turn of the rib.

## MATUKA, BLACK

*Tied by Wade Malwitz*

**Hook:**          Heavy wire, 3X to 6X long, sizes 10 to 2.

**Thread:**        Black 8/0, 6/0, or 3/0.

**Rib:**           Oval gold tinsel (or copper wire).

**Body:**          Black chenille (or dubbing).

**Wing and tail:** Four dyed black hen neck or back hackles, or what is now called soft hackle; or just big rooster saddle hackles.

**Hackle:**        Dyed black hen neck or back hackle (soft hackle) or, really, any hackle.

## MATUKA, BROWN

*Tied by Wade Malwitz*

| | |
|---|---|
| **Hook:** | Heavy wire, 3X to 6X long, sizes 10 to 2. |
| **Thread:** | Brown 8/0, 6/0, or 3/0. |
| **Rib:** | Oval gold tinsel (or copper wire). |
| **Body:** | Brown chenille (or dubbing). |
| **Wing and tail:** | Four dyed brown grizzly hen neck or back hackles, or what is now called soft hackle; or just big rooster saddle hackles. |
| **Hackle:** | Dyed brown grizzly hen neck or back hackle (soft hackle) or, really, any hackle. |

## MATUKA, OLIVE

*Tied by Skip Morris*

| | |
|---|---|
| **Hook:** | Heavy wire, 3X to 6X long, sizes 10 to 2. |
| **Thread:** | Olive or black 8/0, 6/0, or 3/0. |
| **Rib:** | Oval gold tinsel (or copper wire). |
| **Body:** | Olive chenille (or dubbing). |
| **Wing and tail:** | Four dyed olive grizzly hen neck or back hackles, or what is now called soft hackle; or just big rooster saddle hackles. |
| **Hackle:** | Dyed olive grizzly hen neck or back hackle (soft hackle) or, really, any hackle. |

## MATUKA SCULPIN, GOLD          *Dave Whitlock*

*Top view*

*Bottom view*

*Tied by Dave Whitlock*

| | |
|---|---|
| **Hook:** | Heavy wire, 4X to 6X long (or a low-water Atlantic salmon hook with an upturned eye), sizes 8 to 5/0 (imagine the trout that would eat a 5/0 fly!). |
| **Thread:** | Cream or yellow flat waxed nylon (or 3/0; perhaps size A rod thread for flaring the hair). |
| **Weight:** | Lead wire approximately the diameter of the hook's shank. |
| **Rib:** | Medium brass (or copper) wire. |
| **Body:** | Coarse natural or synthetic cream dubbing. |
| **Matuka wing and tail:** | Four natural cree neck hackles outside four dyed olive cree neck hackles—two sets of four, the two sets cupped together. (See the instructions for making a Matuka wing on page 261.) |
| **Pectoral fins:** | Pheasant rump feathers, one per side. |
| **Gills:** | Red Crystal Seal (or any long, coarse, shiny dubbing) picked out. |
| **Head and collar:** | Cream deer hair under; each top bunch is dyed gold deer hair topped with dyed black and then a small bunch of dyed gold (instructions are on page 268). |
| **Eyes:** | Brown plastic eyes with black pupils, one glued on each side of the head. (I use low-odor epoxy glue, but any tough, waterproof glue will do.) |

**Comments:** Dave has been making sculpin-imitating flies for decades, and his Matuka Sculpin may be his most plausible yet. It's hard to imagine a sculpin eater turning it down. The Matuka Sculpin can also be tied in black, with a hair collar and head entirely black on top (cream beneath) and an all-black wing; or it can be tied in olive, with a hair collar and head entirely olive on top (cream underneath) and dyed olive grizzly hackles for the wing.

**Morris Minnow.** As shiny as some of the tiny fishes trout eat may be, none is quite so stunning as a chromelike Morris Minnow. Yet this fly can be deadly when trout are in the right mood, and those trout tend to be big: a wild 12-pound rainbow is my best on a Morris Minnow so far. Part of the Morris Minnow's effectiveness must be due to it's pliant Mylar body—the slightest twitch of the fly or shift of the current sends a soft wave of life down its sparkling flanks. Another reason for its success is all that flash. Real juvenile trout are covered in shining metal-like scales, and the Morris Minnow captures that brilliance (that it exceeds that brilliance by a degree is apparently a plus, too, judging by all the big trout that grab the fly). The details on the head—eyes, gills, spots, and the rest—surely add realism.

I've had the most experience with the rainbow and cutthroat versions of my Morris Minnow, but you can alter the colors to make it suggest baby brown and brook trout, too. Tied mostly in silver with a dark blue back, the fly also works in saltwater for salmon and sea-run cutthroat trout, probably suggesting the young of both fish, along with needlefish and herring.

If you *really* want to see a Morris Minnow shimmy, tie it to your tippet with a loop knot.

## MORRIS MINNOW, CUTTHROAT     *Skip Morris*

*Tied by Skip Morris*

| | |
|---|---|
| **Hook:** | Heavy wire, standard length to 3X long, straight or ring eye (helps the fly ride upright), sizes 6 to 2. |
| **Thread:** | Gold or tan 6/0 or 3/0. |
| **Weight:** | A doubled length of lead wire bound from behind the eye to about halfway down the shank (a second single length bound under that, with big hooks). The lead is bound beneath the shank to turn the fly upright. |
| **Body:** | Fine gold (or copper or yellow or chartreuse) Mylar (Angel Hair, Lite Brite) bound along the sides, with fine dark green Mylar on top, and fine pearl Mylar on the underside, bound up the shank in sections. All trimmed to fish-shape, top, bottom, and sides. |
| **Head:** | Woven gold Mylar tubing, a short section bound at the eye, and then pushed back and turned inside out over the shank. Paint the head dark green dotted black on top, gill slashes red, eyes white with black pupils, underside white, and add two cutthroat slashes of red or orange under the throat. The paint is secured with low-odor epoxy glue. (The instructions for tying the Janssen's Minnow on page 258 will help you complete the head.) |

## Tying the Morris Minnow

**1.** To tie the Morris Minnow, bind a doubled length of lead wire under the shank, just behind the eye. Trim the ends of the lead at about the center of the shank.

**2.** Bind a section of Mylar along the far side of the hook just ahead of the bend; then double back the forward end of the strands and bind it to project back on the near side.

**3.** Advance the thread and make another such section of three colors of Mylar a little ahead of the first. Continue making such sections, five or more, with the last atop the lead. Make the last section quite full on top.

**4.** Whip finish the thread, trim it, and remove the hook from your vise. Trim the Mylar body to fish-shape: top, bottom, and sides.

**5.** Return the hook to your vise and start the thread behind the eye.

**6.** Cut a short length of woven Mylar tubing and bind it behind the eye. Whip finish and then cut the thread.

**7.** Push and stroke the Mylar tubing back down the shank; the tubing should turn inside out.

**8.** Coat the tubing with low-odor epoxy glue, back to about midshank. When the glue is almost cured, trim the end of the Mylar at about midshank.

**9.** Paint the head. (Nontoxic water-based paints such as poster paints do a fine job, and won't run under the epoxy.) Give the head a second and final coating of epoxy.

**Critical note:** Don't let the head block much of the hook's gape. You can achieve this in several ways: by using a hook with a wide gape, using lead wire that's not over-thick, really building up the fine Mylar over the lead, using Mylar tubing that isn't oversized, keeping the epoxy coatings thin, or all of the above.

## MORRIS MINNOW, RAINBOW — *Skip Morris*

*Tied by Skip Morris*

| | |
|---|---|
| **Hook:** | Heavy wire, standard length to 3X long, straight or ring eye (helps the fly ride upright), sizes 6 to 2. |
| **Thread:** | White or gray 6/0 or 3/0. |
| **Weight:** | A doubled length of lead wire bound from behind the eye to about halfway down the shank (a second single length bound under that, with big hooks). The lead is bound beneath the shank to turn the fly upright. |
| **Body:** | Fine silver Mylar (Angel Hair, Lite Brite) bound along the sides, with fine dark blue Mylar on top, fine pearl Mylar on the underside, bound up the shank in sections. All trimmed to fish shape, top, bottom, and sides. After the Mylar is all trimmed, bind on some fine red Mylar to lie back along the sides of the body, and then trim this to blend with the trimmed body. |
| **Head:** | Woven silver Mylar tubing, a short section bound at the eye, and then pushed back and turned inside out over the shank. Paint the head dark blue dotted black on top, gill slashes red, eyes white with black pupils, underside white, and add a red stripe along each side (a green back with pink sides is another option). The paint is secured with low-odor epoxy glue. (Instructions for tying the Janssen's Minnow on page 258 will help you complete the head.) |

**Muddler Minnow.** Don Gapen developed the Muddler Minnow decades ago, and it remains a popular imitation of the sculpin to this day. Like all popular flies, the Muddler has inspired lots of variations; some are merely different colorings for the original, while others, such as the Marabou Muddler, represent significant innovations in essential construction. Some variations—such as the Bow River Bugger (page 250)—are clearly (though barely) connected with Gapen's design.

## MUDDLER MINNOW — *Don Gapen*

*Tied by Skip Morris*

| | |
|---|---|
| **Hook:** | Heavy wire, 3X or 4X long, sizes 12 to 2. |
| **Thread:** | White or gray 8/0, 6/0, or 3/0 (I switch to size A rod thread for flaring the hair). |
| **Weight (optional):** | Windings of lead wire under the body. |
| **Tail:** | Single section of mottled tan-brown turkey quill. |
| **Body:** | Flat gold tinsel. (Many tiers now wrap braided gold Mylar tinsel for the body, especially over lead wire.) |
| **Wing:** | Dyed brown calf tail (or gray squirrel tail) enclosed within two sections of mottled tan-brown turkey quill. |
| **Head and collar:** | Natural gray deer hair, flared and trimmed (instructions are on page 268). |
| **Comments:** | This is the original Muddler Minnow pattern. |

## MUDDLER MINNOW, BLACK

*Tied by Skip Morris*

| | |
|---|---|
| **Hook:** | Heavy wire, 3X or 4X long, sizes 12 to 2. |
| **Thread:** | Black 8/0, 6/0, or 3/0 (I switch to size A rod thread for flaring the hair). |
| **Weight (optional):** | Windings of lead wire under the body. |

**Tail:** Single section of natural dark or dyed bronze or brown mottled tan-brown turkey quill.

**Body:** Flat gold tinsel. (Many tiers now wrap braided gold Mylar tinsel for the body, especially over lead wire.)

**Wing:** Dyed black squirrel tail enclosed within two sections of natural dark or dyed brown or bronze mottled tan-brown turkey quill.

**Head and collar:** Dyed black deer hair, flared and trimmed (instructions are on page 268).

## RAG SCULPIN — *Mike Mercer*

*Top view*

*Bottom view*

*Tied by Mike Mercer*

**Hook:** Heavy wire, 2X or 3X long, sizes 6 to 2.

**Thread:** Olive 3/0. Olive 8/0 for binding the end of the tail.

**Tail:** Tan EZE Bug Yarn. Bind the tip of the yarn tail (which is really part of the body) with the 8/0 thread before binding the tail onto the shank. Add head cement later. Color the top of the tail with an olive permanent marking pen after the fly is completed.

**Eyes:** Lead barbell eyes, painted green with black pupils. (Mike uses black 3/16-inch I-Balz nontoxic prepainted eyes.)

**Body and head:** Tan EZE Bug Yarn. Wind the yarn up the shank to just short of the barbell eyes, bind on the pectoral fins, and then wind the yarn up to the hook's eye and trim it off there. You can use the butt of the tail yarn, without cutting it, to build the body if you like. Color the top of the body and head with an olive permanent marking pen when the fly is completed; then color them with a dark brown permanent marking pen.

**Pectoral fins:** Tan Medallion sheeting, trimmed to shape. Color the pectorals with an olive permanent marking pen after the fly is completed; then color them with a dark brown permanent marking pen.

**Comments:** Mike Mercer's Rag Sculpin can be tied fairly quickly, and it has a tail that waves convincingly. It does require a specific material—EZE Bug Yarn—but this is a popular material that should be readily available. Mike fishes his pattern on a sinking-tip line with twitches through deep runs.

## SOUTH BRANCH CHUB — *Bob Jacklin*

*Tied by Bob Jacklin*

**Hook:** Heavy wire, 4X long, sizes 10 to 6.

**Thread:** Black 6/0.

**Rib:** Gold wire.

**Body:** Flat gold Mylar tinsel.

**Wing:** Barred teal sections enclosing, and partly above, a mix of black and white Monga Ringtail hair (or buck tail or the like). (Bob likes to stroke dubbing wax down the wing to gather it).

**Cheeks:** Jungle cock eyes, one per side.

**Comments:** On small water, Bob works his South Branch Chub upstream, so it appears to be making slow headway against the current. On substantial rivers, he fishes it across and downstream on a sinking line with occasional quick strips of the line. The fly is named for the South Branch of the Raritan River in New Jersey, where Bob developed it when he was still a teenager. He brought the fly with him when he headed west and at first used it primarily in creeks and small rivers—much like the South Branch—for modest-sized fish. He eventually tried it on the Madison River inside Yellowstone Park and discovered that big trout like it too. Although Bob developed the South Branch Chub to imitate an eastern chub, it can easily pass for a tiny trout.

## SPUDDLER                                   *Dan Bailey and Red Monical*

*Tied by Wade Malwitz*

**Hook:** Heavy wire, 3X or 4X long, sizes 10 to 2.

**Thread:** Brown 3/0. (I use brown size A rod thread for the head and collar.)

**Weight:** Lead wire over the center of the shank.

**Tail:** Dyed brown calf tail.

**Body:** Cream wool yarn or dubbing.

**Gills:** Short band of red wool yarn or red natural or synthetic dubbing.

**Wing:** Four dyed brown grizzly hackles, cupped together in two sets of two. Red fox squirrel tail over and down the sides of the wing.

**Head and collar:** Dyed brown antelope (or deer) hair, flared and trimmed to a broad, flattened head (instructions are on page 268).

**Comments:** Some fly pattern books describe the Spuddler as having a wing laid flat over the body, but most do not. The Spuddler is probably in a tie with the Marabou Muddler as the most popular of the Muddler Minnow spin-offs. It has a long and distinguished track record. In his *Western Trout Fly Tying Manual,* Jack Dennis advises us to throw a Spuddler "under the grassy and willow stream banks, then jerk it backward with a quick retrieve." Or you can swing the fly out of these spots with the drift of the line in the current. The Spuddler is, Dennis says, "one of the hottest flies in the many rivers of Montana."

## THUNDER CREEK RAINBOW TROUT                *Keith Fulsher*

*Tied by Wade Malwitz*

**Hook:** Heavy wire, 3X to 6X long, sizes 10 to 2.

**Thread:** White 8/0, 6/0, or 3/0.

**Body:** Embossed silver tinsel, wound up the shank.

**Lateral stripe:** Dyed pink buck tail, bound back over the body.

**Wing and head:** Bunch of dyed olive-brown buck tail, bound with the tips forward just behind the eye, atop the shank; another bunch of natural white buck tail, bound with the tips forward just behind the eye but underneath the shank. Draw both the top and bottom bunches of hair firmly back, and bind them with a narrow thread collar about one-third down the shank. Paint on cream eyes with black pupils, paint the thread collar red, and then coat the head and thread collar with clear lacquer or low-odor epoxy glue.

**Comments:** Mr. Fulsher's streamlined and plausible Thunder Creek fly patterns, which imitate several tiny fishes, were revealed in his book *Tying and Fishing the Thunder Creek Series,* back in the early 1970s. They were hot flies then, and remain popular today. Among the specific patterns, only one imitates a baby trout—the Thunder Creek Rainbow Trout. The rest, which imitate smelts and shiners, seem more suited for eastern fishing, but you could surely vary the colors to imitate any small trout.

**Zonker.** Dan Byford's Zonker, in both its original upright and current inverted designs, is a real staple among tiny fish imitations for river trout. Dan's fly really stands apart from traditional streamer designs. And, of course, it has proven its effectiveness countless times.

## ZONKER (ORIGINAL)                              *Dan Byford*

*Tied by Skip Morris*

**Hook:** Heavy wire, long shank, sizes 8 to 2.

**Thread:** Black 3/0 for both ends.

**Weight (optional):** Lead wire.

**Body:** Silver Mylar piping over Zonker tape—a silvery metal sheeting with adhesive backing. Press a rectangle of the tape down around the shank (or lead-wrapped shank) and trim the sheeting to a fish shape. Slide a short length of the piping over the shank and bind the ends with two different bobbins. Trim the front end of the piping, leaving the unraveled rear end a little long. Leave a bobbin hanging from the rear of the body, for binding the Zonker rabbit strip. If you want, coat the body with low-odor epoxy glue and let it fully cure before tying the rest of the fly. (Instructions for making the Janssen's Minnow body, on page 258, will offer some help in making the Zonker body.)

**Collar:** One webby grizzly hackle.

**Wing and tail:** Natural gray Zonker rabbit strip, bound with a narrow thread collar at the rear of the body (add head cement to the collar) and under the thread head in front. Trim the hide about a gape's length back from the bend.

**Comments:** This original version of the Zonker—the upright-hook version that took streamer fishing by storm in the early 1980s—remains a reliable standard. Just be sure that you don't make the body so deep that it impairs hooking. The original Zonker design can be tied in any of the color variations listed here for the newer, inverted Zonker.

## ZONKER, BLACK — *Dan Byford*

*Tied by Peter Morrison*

**Hook:** Heavy wire 4X to 6X long, sizes 8 to 2.
**Thread:** Black 6/0 or 3/0.
**Body:** Black woven Mylar tubing, bound at both ends over a foundation of thick lead wire bound to the shank, bent back over the top of the shank, and bound just ahead of the bend to create a fish body shape. The body is coated with low-odor epoxy glue. (The fly rides inverted owing to the weight of the lead.)
**Wing and tail:** Dyed black Zonker rabbit strip, the point of the hook pushed through the hide, and the hide pulled down to the hook and bound behind the eye.
**Throat:** Dyed red rabbit fur (cut from a Zonker strip).
**Eyes:** Yellow with black pupils, painted on and then coated with the epoxy glue.
**Comments:** Suggests dark little fish on which trout feed.

## ZONKER, NATURAL AND PEARL — *Dan Byford*

*Tied by Skip Morris*

**Thread:** White 6/0 or 3/0.
**Hook:** Heavy wire 4X to 6X long, sizes 8 to 2.
**Body:** Pearl woven Mylar tubing, bound at both ends over a foundation of thick lead wire bound to the shank, bent back over the top of the shank and bound ahead of the bend to create a fish body shape. The body is coated with low-odor epoxy glue. (The fly rides inverted owing to the weight of the lead.)
**Wing and tail:** Dyed black Zonker rabbit strip, the point of the hook pushed through the hide, and the hide pulled down to the hook and bound behind the eye.
**Throat:** Natural gray-tan rabbit fur (cut from a Zonker strip).
**Eyes:** Yellow with black pupils, painted on and then coated with the epoxy glue.
**Comments:** Imitates tiny light-colored fish on which trout feed.

## ZONKER, OLIVE — *Dan Byford*

*Tied by Peter Morrison*

**Thread:** White 6/0 or 3/0.
**Hook:** Heavy wire 4X to 6X long, sizes 8 to 2.
**Body:** Olive-pearl (or olive or gold) woven Mylar tubing, bound at both ends over a foundation of thick lead wire bound to the shank, bent back over the top of the shank and bound ahead of the bend to create a fish body shape. The body is coated with low-odor epoxy glue. (The fly rides inverted owing to the weight of the lead.)
**Wing and tail:** Dyed yellow-olive (or olive) Zonker rabbit strip, the point of the hook pushed through the hide, and the hide pulled down to the hook and bound behind the eye.
**Throat:** Dyed olive-yellow (or olive) rabbit fur (cut from a Zonker strip).
**Eyes:** Yellow with black pupils, painted on and then coated with the epoxy glue.
**Comments:** Imitates tiny olive-colored fish on which trout feed.

## Flaring and Shaping Deer Hair (Zoo Cougar)

*(See video instructions on DVD.)*

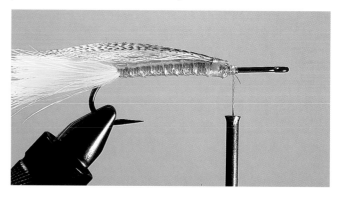

**1.** Build the body and wing of the fly, but leave plenty of bare shank in front. Whip-finish the working thread. (Note that I put some low-odor epoxy on the bindings that hold the wing—always an option with flies that have a wing behind a flared hair head.) Start some heavy thread securely in front of the body (size A rod thread is the standard, even for quite small flies). Be sure you start the heavy thread over the whip finish in the previous thread.

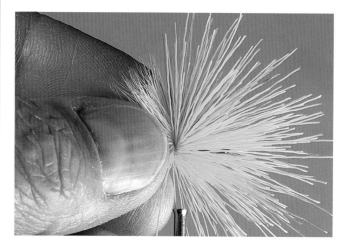

**2.** Cut a bunch of spongy deer hair from the hide. Hold the hair at its tip ends and comb out the short hairs and fuzz (any kind of comb will do). Even the tips of the hairs in a hair-stacking tool (to make the hair collar). Hold the hair down atop the shank. The tips of the hair should extend partway down the body. Work the hair down until the shank is about in the center of the hair. Wind two light-tension turns of thread around the hair. Hold the hair firmly by its tips as you pull the thread tight—the hair butts should flare widely. Pull from one side of the hook and then the other, alternating, as the thread tightens.

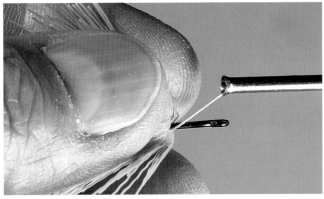

**3.** Continue holding the bobbin and thread tightly down as you stroke back the hair butts. Pull the thread forward. Wind a few tight thread turns around the shank.

**4.** Push the hair back hard, using your thumb and finger or a hair-packing tool such as this Brassie.

**5.** Cut and comb another bunch of hair (no need to stack this bunch). Work the hair down around the shank. Wind two turns of thread around center of the hair, about halfway between the hair tips and butts. Pull the thread tight, and then complete this bunch as you did the first one. Compress the hair back, as before. Continue flaring and compressing hair bunches up the shank to the eye. Make several half hitches in the thread, and then cut it.

**6.** Trim the hair to shape with either scissors or a razor blade. Trim only as far back as the stacked hair tips at the rear of the head, so they remain as a collar.

**ZOO COUGAR, YELLOW** *Kelly Galloup*

*Top view*

*Tied by Peter Morrison*

**Hook:** Heavy wire, 4X to 6X long, sizes 6 to 2.
**Thread:** Yellow 3/0 (I use yellow or white size A rod thread for flaring the hair head and collar).
**Tail:** Dyed yellow marabou.
**Body:** Pearl sparkle braid (or any shiny clear or pearl-colored body material).
**Wing:** Two mallard flank feathers dyed wood-duck color, lying flat atop white calf tail. The feathers should extend to the tip of the tail.
**Head and collar:** Dyed yellow deer hair, flared and then trimmed to a broad and flattened head (instructions begin on page 268).
**Comments:** Kelly Galloup has made a mark in streamer fishing, and this may be his signature fly; it suggests an injured sculpin. Kelly designed the fly to sink only slightly (like, I assume, a sculpin in trouble). Retrieve it in sharp strips of the line. You can vary the colors, but yellow is the original.

# Leeches

**Articulated Leech.** Hinged fly patterns were nothing new and fur leech patterns were commonplace when the Articulated Leech caught on among trout and steelhead fly fishers only a few years ago. But this fly was different. First, its hook was in the rear section rather than the front as with most hinged flies, and second, the tough, flexible connector between the two sections was genuinely new (to the best of my knowledge). That connection really lets the two body sections flex so that the fly moves with more sway than even the long, soft rabbit fur can provide. Because the Articulated Leech tends to move big fish, my friend Ray Chang, who among his many duties manages the tying of this pattern for the Solitude Fly Company, prefers to make the hinge of 30-pound Dacron backing.

The Articulated Leech is a genuine hit fly, and it's already busy producing offspring with its DNA but distinctive personalities. There is now an Articulated Flesh Fly, and I caught some big rainbow trout on it last fall with guide Patricia Edel in Alaska, where the trout were gorging on shreds of salmon carcasses drifting in the river. Anything that swims and that fish eat may soon have an articulated imitation.

Real leeches are common only in particularly slow, weedy rivers and are generally smaller than most Articulated Leeches, and the fly is sometimes tied in weird colors, all of which suggest an attractor fly. On the other hand, the Articulated Leech moves like a real leech, is often natural in color, and *can* be tied smaller. So attractor, imitation—it all depends on where and how and in what size and color you fish it. But you won't care about any of this when your five-inch Black Articulated Leech has you tethered to a leaping six-pound rainbow.

Articulated Leeches can be tied in all the standard leech-fly colors, both imitative (black, brown, tan, olive) and gaudy (red, burgundy, purple, chartreuse). Some tiers use long, supple marabou fibers for the tail, and twist them in a dubbing loop for the body sections.

### ARTICULATED LEECH, BLACK

*Tied by Peter Morrison*

**Rear hook:** Heavy wire, no longer than 1X long (the hook needs a substantial gape), up- or down-eye (straight eyes won't do), sizes 8 to 2. (Traditional loop-eye, heavy-wire Atlantic salmon-steelhead hooks are popular.)
**Thread:** Black 6/0 or 3/0.
**Tail:** Short section of black Zonker strip.
**Rear section:** Black cross-cut rabbit strip, wound up the shank.

**Front hook:** Any hook with a large-diameter eye. Because you'll score the hook and break off the critical part, the bend, this hook can be inexpensive and of only mediocre quality.
**Connection:** Fly-line backing through the eye of the rear-section hook, around the shank, and back out the eye. The ends of the backing are bound along the shank of the front-section hook.
**Front section:** Black cross-cut rabbit strip, wound up the shank.
**Weight (optional):** Lead barbell eyes. Dub around the eyes with fur cut from one of the hide strips.
**Comments:** Many real leeches are black. Tying instructions on page 271.

### ARTICULATED LEECH, DOUBLE

*Tied by Skip Morris*

**Rear hook:** Heavy wire, no longer than 1X long (the hook needs a substantial gape), up- or down-eye (straight eyes won't do), hook sizes 8 to 2. (Traditional loop-eye, heavy-wire Atlantic salmon-steelhead hooks are popular.)
**Thread:** 6/0 or 3/0 in a color similar to the Zonker strip color.
**Tail:** Short section of a dyed or undyed Zonker strip.
**Rear section:** Dyed or undyed cross-cut rabbit strip, wound up the shank.
**Connection:** Fly-line backing through the eye of the rear-section hook, around the shank, and back out the eye. The ends of the backing are bound along the shank of the center-section hook.
**Center hook:** Heavy wire, up- or down-eye (straight eyes won't do), sizes 8 to 2. (Cut most of the bend off the hook.)
**Center section:** Dyed or undyed cross-cut rabbit strip, wound up the shank.
**Connection:** Fly-line backing through the eye of the center-section hook, around the shank, and back out the eye. The ends of the backing are bound along the shank of the front-section hook.
**Front hook:** Any hook with a large-diameter eye, sizes 8 to 2. Because you score the hook and break off the critical part, the bend, this hook can be inexpensive and of only mediocre quality.
**Front section:** Dyed or undyed cross-cut rabbit strip, wound up the shank.
**Weight (optional):** Lead barbell eyes. Dub around the eyes with fur cut from one of the hide strips.
**Comments:** The Double Articulated Leech is basically the same as the Articulated Leech, but with one more section, which means that you can use up two cheap hooks you have lying around. You can tie the Double Articulated Leech in any of the colors used for the standard Articulated Leech or even in a combination of colors. Tying instructions are on page 271.

# Tying the Articulated Leech (Articulated Leech, Olive)

*(See video instructions on DVD.)*

**1.** Begin with a hook whose eye is tipped up or down, not a straight eye. Bind the end of a Zonker strip on the shank for a tail—the fur should cant straight back off the hide. Bind the end of a strip of cross-cut rabbit (a strip with fur canting to one side) atop the bend. Spiral the thread up to just behind the hook's eye. Wind the strip in close turns to just behind the eye. The fur on the strip should sweep back toward the fur tail. Bind the strip just behind the eye. Build a small thread head, whip-finish and trim off the thread, and add head cement to the head. Set the fly aside to allow the cement to dry as you tie up a few more Articulated Leech rear sections like this one.

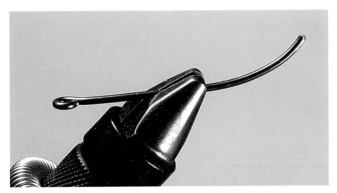

**2.** Cut or grind (with a bench grinder) through the bend of the front hook so that only a little bend remains curving down (see the photo). With a grinding wheel, a file, or sandpaper, smooth off the cut end of the hook to prevent wear on the backing used to make the joint.

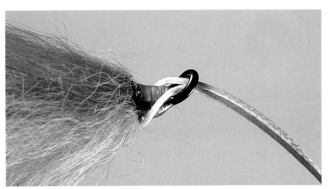

**3.** Mount the hook you just cut in the vise by the remaining bend. Start the thread just back from the eye. Spiral the thread to the bend. Loop some fly-line backing through the eye of the rear hook (the one that still has a bend), under the shank (with an up-eye) or over it (with a down-eye), and then back out the eye alongside the other end of the backing.

**4.** Bind the backing atop the front hook up its shank to its eye. Slip the ends of the backing down through the eye of the hook, draw the ends back under the shank, and bind the ends of the backing down to the bend and back up to the eye.

**5.** Trim off the ends of the backing. Add cement to all the bindings if you wish. Bind on another cross-cut rabbit strip as before. Spiral the thread up to the eye, wind the strip forward (as before), and bind and trim its end. Build and complete a thread head. If you want the fly to really dive, add metal bar-bell eyes for weight. The standard approach is to mount the eyes on top of the hook, but if you want to ensure that the fly will ride upright, mount them beneath the hook. Dub around the eyes, whip-finish and cut the thread, and add head cement to the whip finish.

## ARTICULATED LEECH, OLIVE

*Tied by Skip Morris*

**Rear hook:**     Heavy wire, no longer than 1X long (the hook needs a substantial gape), up- or down-eye (straight eyes won't do). (Traditional loop-eye, heavy-wire Atlantic salmon-steelhead hooks are popular.)

**Thread:**        Olive or green 6/0 or 3/0.

**Tail:**          Short section of dyed olive Zonker strip.

**Rear section:**  Dyed olive cross-cut rabbit strip, wound up the shank.

**Front hook:**    Any hook with a large-diameter eye, sizes 8 to 2. Because you score the hook and break off the critical part, the bend, this hook can be inexpensive and of only mediocre quality.

**Connection:**    Fly-line backing through the eye of the rear-section hook, around the shank, and back out the eye. The ends of the backing are bound along the shank of the front-section hook.

**Front section:** Dyed olive cross-cut rabbit strip, wound up the shank.

**Weight (optional):** Lead barbell eyes. Dub around the eyes with fur cut from one of the hide strips.

**Comments:**      Some real leeches are olive. (Tying instructions are on page 271.)

## ARTICULATED LEECH, PURPLE

*Tied by Peter Morrison*

**Rear hook:**     Heavy wire, no longer than 1X long (the hook needs a substantial gape), up- or down-eye (straight eyes won't do), sizes 8 to 2. (Traditional loop-eye, heavy-wire Atlantic salmon-steelhead hooks are popular.)

**Thread:**        Purple 6/0 or 3/0.

**Tail:**          Short section of dyed purple Zonker strip.

**Rear section:**  Dyed purple cross-cut rabbit strip, wound up the shank.

**Front hook:**    Any hook with a large-diameter eye, sizes 8 to 2. Because you score the hook and break off the critical part, the bend, this hook can be inexpensive and of only mediocre quality.

**Connection:**    Fly-line backing through the eye of the rear-section hook, around the shank, and back out the eye. The ends of the backing are bound along the shank of the front-section hook.

**Front section:** Dyed purple cross-cut rabbit strip, wound up the shank.

**Weight (optional):** Lead barbell eyes. Dub around the eyes with fur cut from one of the hide strips.

**Comments:**      A lot of leech imitations are purple—an exaggeration of a quality in the coloring of some of the naturals. (Tying instructions are on page 271.)

## BUNNY LEECH

*Tied by Skip Morris*

**Hook:**          Heavy wire, 3X to 6X long, sizes 8 to 2.

**Thread:**        6/0 or 3/0 in a color to blend with the body color.

**Tail:**          Zonker rabbit strip with the fur up, the hide cut to a point. Color choices include black, tan, olive, purple, brown, and blood or burgundy. Some tiers bind on red Krystal Flash and trim it short under the tail.

**Body:**          Cross-cut rabbit strip, bound by the hide and then wound up the shank. The fibers should cant back toward the hook's bend. The body color should match the tail color.

**Comments:**      Such a simple fly, but many trout fall to it. The Bunny Leech really does look like a leech, but it's often used simply because it's big and corpulent and looks alive, and big trout like to eat such things.

## BUNNY LEECH, CONE HEAD

*Tied by Peter Morrison*

| | |
|---|---|
| **Hook:** | Heavy wire, 3X to 6X long, sizes 8 to 2. |
| **Cone head:** | Gold, silver, or black metal. |
| **Thread:** | 6/0 or 3/0 in a color to blend with the body color. |
| **Tail:** | Zonker rabbit strip with the fur up, the hide cut to a point. Color choices include black, tan, olive, purple, brown, and blood or burgundy. Some tiers bind on red Krystal Flash and trim it short under the tail. |
| **Body:** | Cross-cut rabbit-strip, bound by the hide and then wound up the shank. The fibers should cant back toward the hook's bend. The body color should match the tail color. |

**Comments:** Use any of the colors mentioned for the Bunny Leech, on page 272. You can weight the Bunny Leech with a cone head, as here, or with lead wire or metal barbell eyes. Sometimes the weighted fly is best because it sinks quickly. The rising and dipping of the weighted head adds some good action, too.

## MARABOU LEECH, BLACK                    *Hal Janssen*

*Tied by Peter Morrison*

| | |
|---|---|
| **Hook:** | Heavy wire, 4X to 6X long, sizes 10 to 4. |
| **Thread:** | Black 8/0, 6/0, or 3/0. |
| **Tail:** | Dyed black marabou side fibers. |
| **Wing and body:** | Three or four bunches of dyed black marabou side fibers, separated by sections of thread. |
| **Head:** | Butts of the last bunch of wing fibers, spun around the thread and wound behind the eye. |

**Comments:** Simple and effective. A few years ago, I pulled one big trout after another out of a deep hole on a lazy tailwater river by fishing a black Marabou Leech on a full-sinking line at sunset.

## MARABOU LEECH, BROWN                    *Hal Janssen*

*Tied by Skip Morris*

| | |
|---|---|
| **Hook:** | Heavy wire, 4X to 6X long, sizes 10 to 4. |
| **Thread:** | Brown 8/0, 6/0, or 3/0. |
| **Tail:** | Dyed brown marabou side fibers. |
| **Wing and body:** | Three or four bunches of dyed brown marabou side fibers, separated by sections of thread. |
| **Head:** | Butts of the last bunch of wing fibers, spun around the thread and wound behind the eye. |

## MARABOU LEECH, OLIVE                    *Hal Janssen*

*Tied by Peter Morrison*

| | |
|---|---|
| **Hook:** | Heavy wire, 4X to X long, sizes 10 to 4. |
| **Thread:** | Olive 8/0, 6/0, or 3/0. |
| **Tail:** | Dyed olive marabou side fibers. |
| **Wing and body:** | Three or four bunches of dyed olive marabou side fibers, separated by sections of thread. |
| **Head:** | Butts of the last bunch of wing fibers, spun around the thread and wound behind the eye. |

**SIMI SEAL LEECH, BLOOD** — *John Rohmer*

*Tied by John Rohmer*

**Hook:** Heavy wire, 2X or 3X long, sizes 12 to 6.
**Head (optional):** Black metal bead (although any color—silver, gold, copper—is fine).
**Thread:** Maroon or red 8/0, 6/0, or 3/0.
**Tail:** Arizona Blood Leech Simi Seal.
**Body:** Arizona Blood Leech Simi Seal. Dub heavily and then tease out a shaggy body.
**Comments:** A popular leech imitation, particularly on Arizona trout streams. (Yes, Arizona has some fine trout streams. It's not all cactus and scorpions.) Also proven on Montana's Bighorn River and New Mexico's San Juan River.

**SIMI SEAL LEECH, CANADIAN BLACK** — *John Rohmer*

*Tied by John Rohmer*

**Hook:** Heavy wire, 2X or 3X long, sizes 12 to 6.
**Head (optional):** Black metal bead (although any color—silver, gold, copper—is fine).
**Thread:** Black 8/0, 6/0, or 3/0.
**Tail:** Arizona Canadian Black Simi Seal.
**Body:** Arizona Canadian Black Simi Seal. Dub heavily and then tease out a shaggy body.
**Comments:** A popular leech imitation, particularly on Arizona trout streams. (Yes, Arizona has some fine trout streams. It's not all cactus and scorpions.) Also proven on Montana's Bighorn River and New Mexico's San Juan River.

## WOOLLY BUGGER

Although the Woolly Bugger can be used to imitate leeches, it's used far more often as an attractor fly. You'll find it in chapter 14.

# The Tiers

I TIED MORE THAN 200 FLIES for this book, but we needed hundreds more. So we got help. Whenever we could pull it off (by wheedling, pleading, pestering . . . whatever was required) we got originators to tie their flies. In fact, we pulled it off frequently. All the tiers listed here either tied at least a dozen of the flies photographed for this book or sent dressings and information about their own original fly patterns, or both. Expect to see some top names in the world of fly tying.

**Andy Burk:** Andy has been tying since the age of 10 and now works at the Reno Fly Shop in Reno, Nevada, and Truckee River Outfitters in Truckee, California. Many of Andy's fly patterns have become standards in the West and are tied by the Umpqua Feather Merchants Company.

**Al Davis:** Al knows fish. He studied fisheries at Oregon State University and the University of Washington and then went to work for the Alaska Department of Fish and Game. He also knows fly fishing and flies. Al is now retired and lives on Washington's Olympic Peninsula.

**Arnie Gidlow:** Arnie is a recognized authority on trout fishing and speaks at a lot of events and clubs. He also owns the Missouri Riverside Outfitters & Lodge, a hub and source for fishing the legendary upper Missouri River in Montana.

**Rick Hafele:** Rick is a great guy, a top-drawer fly fisher, and a bona fide aquatic entomologist who just retired from his bug job in Oregon. Rick knows things about insects that perhaps no one *should* know: intimate things, none of our business. He is the author of *Nymph-Fishing Rivers & Streams* (which includes a DVD) and, with Dave Hughes, *Western Mayfly Hatches.*

**Tim Heng:** Known to his fellow Colorado guides as "Curly," Tim manages the Taylor Creek Fly Shops. His fly patterns are now gaining serious recognition around the West and are tied by the Umpqua Feather Merchants Company. Tim is the author of *The South Platte River (Colorado) Fishing Map and Guide.*

**Dave Hughes:** Author of far too many fly-fishing and fly-tying books to name here (including *Complete Book of Western Hatches, Trout Flies: The Tier's Reference, Essential Trout Flies,* and *Trout Rigs & Methods*), Dave is a dear, old friend, a skilled fly fisher, a fine writer, and a generally lovable grump.

**Bob Jacklin:** Bob opened Jacklin's fly shop in West Yellowstone more than 30 years ago. He's a creative tier and a pioneer of western trout fly designs. Bob is a recipient of the Buz Buszek fly-tying award and is the host on the DVD *Introduction to Fly-Tying with Bob Jacklin.*

**Ted Leeson:** Ted's prose makes many of us fly-fishing writers feel our technique could use some work. Ted has published several fly-tying books with photographer Jim Schollmeyer, including *The Fly Tier's Benchside Reference* and *Tying Emergers,* and, on his own, *The Habit of Rivers* and *Jerusalem Creek: Fly Fishing through Driftless Country.* Ted and Jim's fly patterns are tied by the Umpqua Feather Merchants Company.

**Wade Malwitz:** When our fishing buddy Wade isn't working or hunting, he's often fishing the nearby waters of

Washington and Oregon or somewhere much more exotic. And when he's not doing that, he might be tying some excellent flies, among them his original designs.

**Craig Mathews:** Craig and John Juracek own Blue Ribbon Flies in West Yellowstone, Montana. Together they wrote *Fly Patterns of Yellowstone,* among other titles, and Craig wrote *Western Fly-Fishing Strategies* on his own. Because the original fly patterns he provided were tested and developed by many of his friends and staff at the shop, he credits them all as the originators. Several of those patterns are tied by the Umpqua Feather Merchants Company.

**Mike Mercer:** For nearly 30 years, Mike has been with The Fly Shop in Redding, California, a big shop with a big catalog shipped across the United States. Mike's patterns are tied by the Umpqua Feather Merchants Company. His first book, *Creative Fly Tying,* came out in 2005.

**Carol Ann Morris:** That would by my wife. Carol has been a serious photographer for 15 years and took most of the photos in this book. Her photography and illustrations have appeared in many fly-fishing books and magazines (*Fly Fisherman, Yale Angler's Journal, American Angler,* and *Gray's Sporting Journal*, among others). Even though I was the decision-maker, she put more time into this book than I did. She also tied a lot of the flies—her surgical skills as a veterinarian prepared her well for handling a pair of tying scissors.

**Skip Morris:** That would be me. I'll give you my resume, but only because it is appropriate here. I wrote this book—my eleventh fly-fishing book and my eighth specifically on the subject of flies. I've been tying flies and fly fishing since before I understood why God made girls. I do a lot of speaking at fly clubs, fly shops, fly-fishing shows, sportsmen's shows, and such, and I've played host on a bunch of fly-tying and fly-fishing videos. My original fly patterns are tied by the Solitude Fly Company. I'm on the pro teams of Scientific Anglers, Daiichi hooks, and Temple Fork Rods, and helped develop Sparkle Nymph Dubbing with John Rohmer of Arizona Flyfishing, Inc. (Well . . . that felt awkward.)

**Peter Morrison:** Our fishing buddy, Peter, is an avid fly fisher, a part-time guide in British Columbia, and a skilled fly tier. Peter really came through for us, tying many of the flies pictured in this book.

**Damien Nurre:** The head guide at the Fly & Field fly shop in Bend, Oregon, Damien is a tying and fishing fanatic in his free time. Hs original fly patterns are tied by the Montana Fly Company.

**John Rohmer:** John is a dubbing guru. He makes and markets all sorts of excellent fly-tying products (his company is called Arizona Flyfishing, Inc.) and owns the Arizona Flyfishing fly shop in Tempe, Arizona. His original fly patterns are tied by Riverborn Flies.

**Scott Sanchez:** Many fly fishers know Scott through his magazine articles, his books *Introduction to Salt Water Fly Tying* and *A New Generation of Trout Flies,* and his video *Understanding Fly Tying Materials.* Scott's original fly patterns are tied by Dan Bailey. Variations on Scott's Double Bunny fly won the Jackson Hole One Fly Event three times—an impressive accomplishment. He works at the Jack Dennis Outdoor Shop in Jackson, Wyoming.

**John Smeraglio:** John owns the Deschutes Canyon Fly Shop in Maupin, Oregon, on the banks of the magnificent Deschutes River. He and Rick Hafele have appeared on several videos, including *Nymph Fishing Basics* and the *Fly Fishing Large Western Rivers* series.

**Todd Smith:** I know from a few days on the water with him that Todd can fish! He is also a remarkable production tier and recently came out with the video *Tying CDC with Todd Smith.* His original fly patterns are tied by Rainy's Flies & Supplies, Inc.

**Al Troth:** Al was a production fly tier and a guide on Montana's Beaverhead River for decades, but he is much more than that. His Troth Pheasant Tail nymph and Elk Hair Caddis are true standards wherever there are trout. He has been a real force in the world of fly tying and has justly earned a place in its history.

**Dave Whitlock:** Dave has had a big hand in making fly tying what it is today—a real innovator and pioneer. He also developed a lot of the concepts we still use in fishing nymphs. He lives with his wife, Emily, in Oklahoma, surrounded by trout, smallmouth bass, striped bass, and all kinds of fly-fishing opportunities. Dave has written a number of books over the years, including *Dave Whitlock's Guide to Aquatic Trout Foods, L. L. Bean Fly Fishing Handbook,* and the wonderful but out-of-print *The Fly-Tyer's Almanac* (with Robert Boyle) that so influenced my own tying. Dave has also made a bunch of videos on tying his fly patterns, many of which are tied by Rainy's Flies & Supplies, Inc. Regarding Dave, I'm both a friend and a fan.

# Bibliography

Boyle, Robert H. and Dave Whitlock. *The Fly-Tyer's Almanac.* New York: Crown Publishers, Inc., 1975.

Caucci, Al and Bob Nastasi. *Hatches II.* New York: Winchester Press, 1986.

Dennis Jack. *Tying Flies with Jack Dennis and Friends.* Jackson, WY: Snake River Books, 1993.

Dennis, Jack H., Jr. *Jack Dennis' Western Trout Fly Tying Manual.* Jackson Hole, WY: Snake River Books, 1974.

Flick, Art. *Art Flick's Master Fly-Tying Guide.* New York: Crown Publisher, Inc., 1972.

———. *Art Flick's New Streamside Guide.* New York: Crown Publisher, Inc., 1969.

Hafele, Rick and Dave Hughes. *Western Hatches.* Portland, OR: Frank Amato Publications, 1981.

Hellekson, Terry. *Popular Fly Patterns.* Salt Lake City, UT: Gibbs M. Smith, Inc., 1984.

Hughes, Dave. *American Fly Tying Manual.* Portland, OR: Frank Amato Publications, 1986.

———. *Wet Flies: Tying and Fishing Soft-Hackles, Winged and Wingless Wets, and Fuzzy Nymphs.* Mechanicsburg, PA: Stackpole Books, 1995.

———. *Essential Trout Flies.* Mechanicsburg, PA: Stackpole Books, 2000.

———. *Western Streamside Guide.* Portland, OR: Frank Amato Publications, 1998.

Jorgenson, Poul. *Modern Fly Dressings for the Practical Angler.* New York: Winchester Press, 1976.

Kaufmann, Randall. *American Fly-Tying Manual.* Portland, OR: Frank Amato Publications, 1975.

———. *Fly Patterns of Umpqua Feather Merchants.* 2nd ed. Glide, OR: Umpqua Feather Merchants, 1998.

———. *Tying Dry Flies.* Portland, OR: Western Fisherman's Press, 1991.

———. *Tying Nymphs.* Portland, OR: Western Fisherman's Press, 1994.

LaFontaine, Gary. *Caddisflies.* New York: The Lyons Press, 1981.

Lawson, Mike. *Spring Creeks.* Mechanicsburg, PA: Stackpole Books, 2003.

Leiser, Eric. *The Book of Fly Patterns.* New York: Alfred A. Knopf, Inc., 1987.

Martin, Darrel. *Fly-Tying Methods.* New York: Lyons and Burford, 1987.

Mathews, Craig and John Juracek. *Fly Patterns of Yellowstone.* West Yellowstone, MT: Blue Ribbon Flies, 1987.

McLennan, Jim. *Blue Ribbon Bow.* Alberta, Canada: Johnson Gorman Publishers, 1998.

Mercer, Mike. *Creative Fly Tying.* Mill Creek, WA: Wild River Press, 2005.

Morris, Skip. *Concise Handbook of Fly Tying.* Portland, OR: Frank Amato Publications, 1995.

———. *Fly Fisher's Guide to Western River Hatches.* Portland, OR: Frank Amato Publications, 2002.

———. *Fly Tying Made Clear and Simple.* Portland, OR: Frank Amato Publications, 1992.

———. *Morris on Tying Flies.* Portland, OR: Frank Amato Publications, 2006.

———. *The Art of Tying the Dry Fly.* Portland, OR: Frank Amato Publications, 1993.

———. *The Art of Tying the Nymph.* Portland, OR: Frank Amato Publications, 1993.

———. *Tying Foam Flies.* Portland, OR: Frank Amato Publications, 1994.

Rosborough, E. H. "Polly". *Tying and Fishing the Fuzzy Nymph.* Chiloquin, OR: self-published, 1965.

Schollmeyer, Jim. *Hatch Guide for Western Streams.* Portland, OR: Frank Amato Publications, 1997.

Schollmeyer, Jim and Ted Leeson. *Trout Flies of the West.* Portland, OR: Frank Amato Publications, 1998.

———. *Tying Emergers.* Portland, OR: Frank Amato Publications, 2004.

Schwiebert, Ernest G. *Matching the Hatch.* New York: The Macmillan Company, 1955.

Solomon, Larry and Eric Leiser. *The Caddis and the Angler.* New York: Lyons and Burford, 1990.

Stalcup, Shane. *Mayflies "Top to Bottom".* Portland, OR: Frank Amato Publications, 2002.

Stetzer, Randle Scott. *Flies: The Best One Thousand.* Portland, OR: Frank Amato Publications, 1992.

Stewart, Dick. *The Hook Book.* Intervale, NH: Northland Press, Inc. 1986.

Stewart, Dick, and Farrow Allen. *Flies for Trout.* North Conway, NH: Mountain Pond Publishing, 1993.

Warren, Joe. *Tying Glass Bead Flies.* Portland, OR: Frank Amato Publications, 1997.

# Index of
# Fly Patterns

# Index of Tying Sequences

*Listed in the order in which they appear*

# Index of Fly Designers

**Headrick, Ralph**
Flat Creek Hopper
Minimal Mayfly

**Heng, Tim**
Autumn Splendor
BLM Black
BLM Olive
BLM Peacock
Mysis Shrimp

**Hill, Roger**
Micro Devil Bug

**Hoffman, Henry**
Chickabou Stone Nymph, Brown

**Hughes, Dave**
Little Olive Flymph
Little Olive Parachute

**Hoyt, Betty**
Jughead

**Jacklin, Bob**
Jacklin's Bright Green Stonefly Nymph
Jacklin's Early Black Stone
Jacklin's Early Black Stonefly Nymph
Jacklin's Giant Salmonfly
Jacklin's Giant Salmonfly Nymph
Jacklin's Golden Stone
Jacklin's Golden Stonefly Nymph
Jacklin's Little Bright Green Stonefly
Jacklin's Little Olive Stone
Jacklin's Little Olive Stonefly Nymph
Jacklin's Western Yellow Stonefly
Jacklin's Western Yellow Stone Nymph
Little Green Rock Worm
March Brown Nymph
Para-Spin, Rusty Spinner
Para-Spin, Trico
South Branch Chub
Spruce Moth

**James, Bruce E.**
Black Legged Water Walker

**Janssen, Hal**
Janssen's Minnow, Brook
Janssen's Minnow, Brown
Janssen's Minnow, Rainbow
Marabou Leech, Black
Marabou Leech, Brown
Marabou Leech, Olive

**Jennings, Percy**
Rat-Faced McDougal

**Jones, Jim**
Willy's Pip

**Kaufmann, Randall**
Bead Head Scud, Olive-Gray
Bead Head Scud, Orange
Bead Head Scud, Tan
Kaufmann Black Stone
Kaufmann Black Stone, Bead Head
     Rubber Legs
Kaufmann Golden Stone
Kaufmann Golden Stone, Bead Head
     Rubber Legs
Stimulator, Black
Stimulator, Green
Stimulator, Orange
Stimulator, Yellow

**Keely, Kim**
Terranasty

**Kennedy, Gord**
Atomic Worm

**Kingsley, Charles**
Alder

**Kreh, Lefty and Bob Clouser**
Clouser Minnow, Black and White
Clouser Minnow, Brown and Yellow
Clouser Minnow, Olive and Yellow
Half and Half

**LaFontaine, Gary**
Deep Sparkle Pupa, Brown and Bright
     Green
Deep Sparkle Pupa, Brown and Yellow
Deep Sparkle Pupa, Dark Gray
Deep Sparkle Pupa, Ginger
Diving Caddis, Bright Green
Diving Caddis, Gray
Diving Caddis, Tan
Emergent Sparkle Pupa, Brown and Bright
     Green
Emergent Sparkle Pupa, Brown and Yellow
Emergent Sparkle Pupa, Dark Gray
Emergent Sparkle Pupa, Ginger
Halo Emerger

**Laible, Gerhard**
Para-Emerger

**Larimer, Tom**
Copper Back Yellow Sallie

**Lawson, Mike**
Hair Beetle
Henry's Fork Golden Stone
Henry's Fork Hopper
Henry's Fork Salmonfly
Paradrake, Brown Drake
Paradrake, Green Drake
Partridge Caddis Emerger, Olive
Partridge Caddis Emerger, Tan
P. T. Emerger, Pale Morning Dun
Spent Midge

**Leeson, Ted and Jim Schollmeyer**
Parasol Midge Emerger
Parasol Pheasant Tail
Parasol PMD/BWO

**Levell, Matt**
Matt's Fur

**Lynch, Gene**
Brassie (standard)
Brassie, Olive
Brassie, Red

**Malwitz, Wade**
Attractabaetis
Wade's Overhead Crane

**Marinaro, Vince**
Thorax Dun

**Martin, Darrel**
Gray Midge
Nymerger

**Martinez, Don**
Black Martinez

**Mercer, Mike**
Copper Bead Z-Wing Caddis, Amber
Copper Bead Z-Wing Caddis, Chartreuse
Glasstail Caddis Pupa, Emerald
Micro Mayfly Nymph, Brown
Micro Mayfly Nymph, Chartreuse Wire
Micro Mayfly Nymph, Electric Yellow
Micro Mayfly Nymph, Pheasant Tail
Micro Mayfly Nymph, Red Wire
Midgling, Root Beer
Poxyback Biot Golden Stone
Poxyback Green Drake Nymph, Gold
     Bead
Poxyback *Isonychia*
Poxyback PMD
Profile Spinner, Green Drake
Profile Spinner, Green Drake Foam Body
Profile Spinner, PMD
Profile Spinner, Trico
Psycho Prince Nymph
Rag Sculpin
Tungsten October Caddis Pupa

**Mikulak, Art**
Mikulak Sedge

**Miller, Bud**
Platte River Special

**Morgan, Jeff**
Deer Hair Daddy